BECOMING AN ILLUSTRATOR

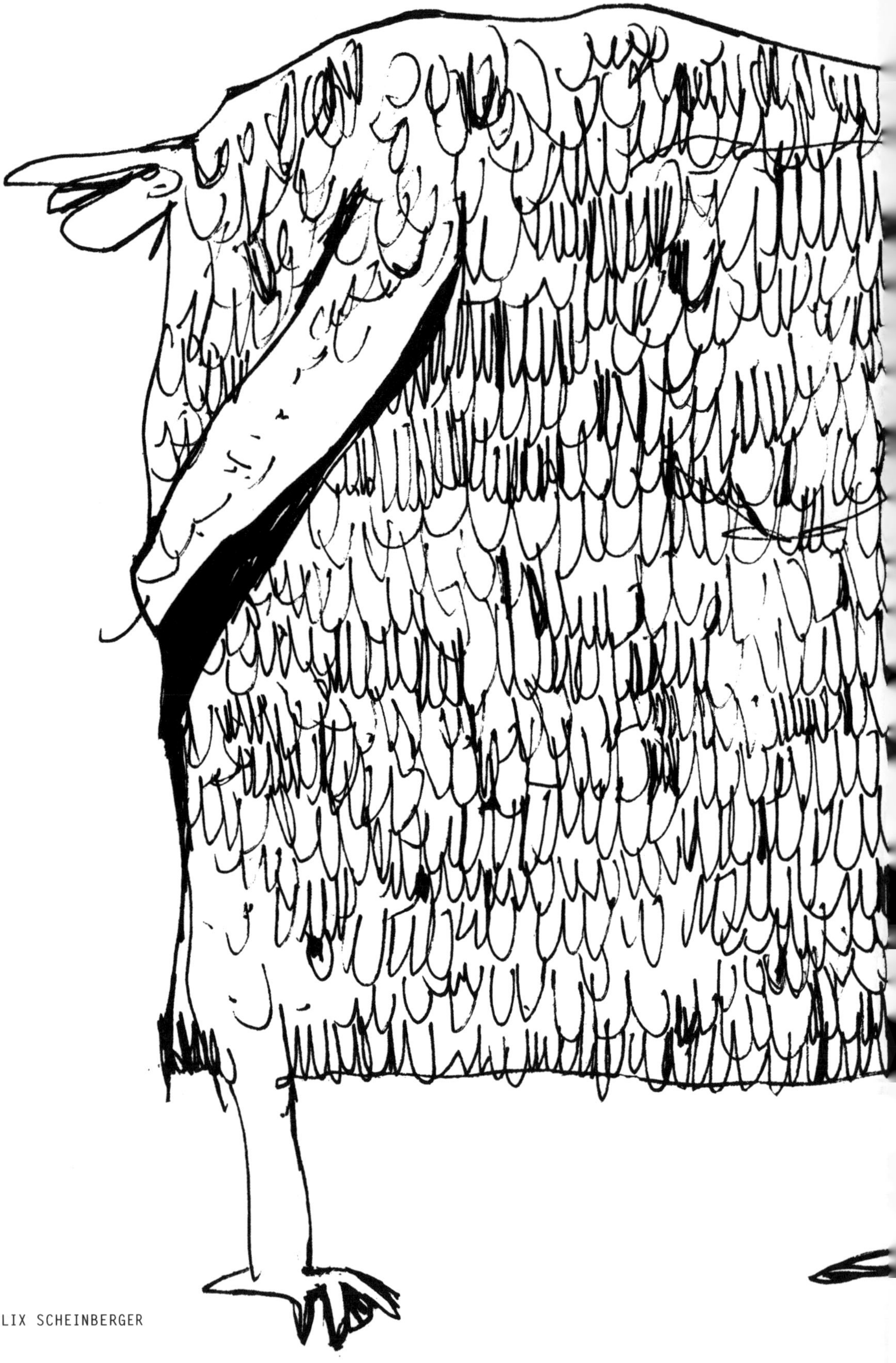

FELIX SCHEINBERGER

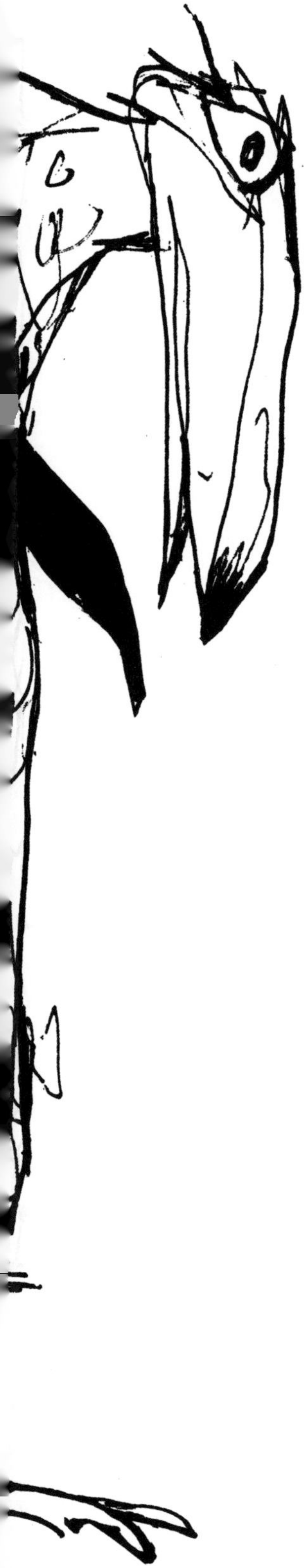

BECOMING AN ILLUSTRATOR

100 Ways to Draw a Bird and Turn Art into a Living

Felix
Scheinberger

HOAKI

... a Bird?

Foreword

Have you ever wished you were someone else? Ever wanted to slip into the skin of your better-looking classmate, that big pop star or some other random person? How about a historical figure? Or an animal? A bird?

The question touches on the subject of identity, making it one of humanity's great questions. We only have *one* life to live. We can't, as someone once said, "change skins." But our imagination can!
This is perhaps one explanation for our creative spirit: imagination is a solution to the dilemma of having billions of possibilities but only one life to live.

This book is about applied imagination: illustration.

Illustro is Latin for "enlighten" or "illuminate." During the act of illustrating, we reflect not only reality, but create something new, giving the world a new, personal point of view. Illustration is able to explain or to demonstrate, it can add, convey and immerse. It can develop aspects of the content or art or just look good. Illustrations are as different as the people who make them.

This book is not only about illustration; it contains illustrations – lots of them. They are works by very different illustrators in a wide variety of techniques and styles, images that, in spite of their diversity, remain comparable because they all show the same thing: a bird. Over 120 wonderful colleagues of mine provided me with images to illuminate the universe of illustration.

Thank you so very much - this is what this book is all about.

I chose birds because we all are familiar with them. Say the word "bird" and countless images come to mind, whether colorful, clever parrots, lame ducks or mighty eagles, a lightning-swift falcon or a dark raven cawing and clawing misfortune into our lives, a wise owl or a silly hen, a tiny sparrow as well as the phoenix rising from the ashes.
You see, the bird is an incredibly diverse symbol and that's what makes it suitable to accompany us through this book about illustration.

In recent years, illustration has grown to become one of the most important sectors in design. Illustration is hip.

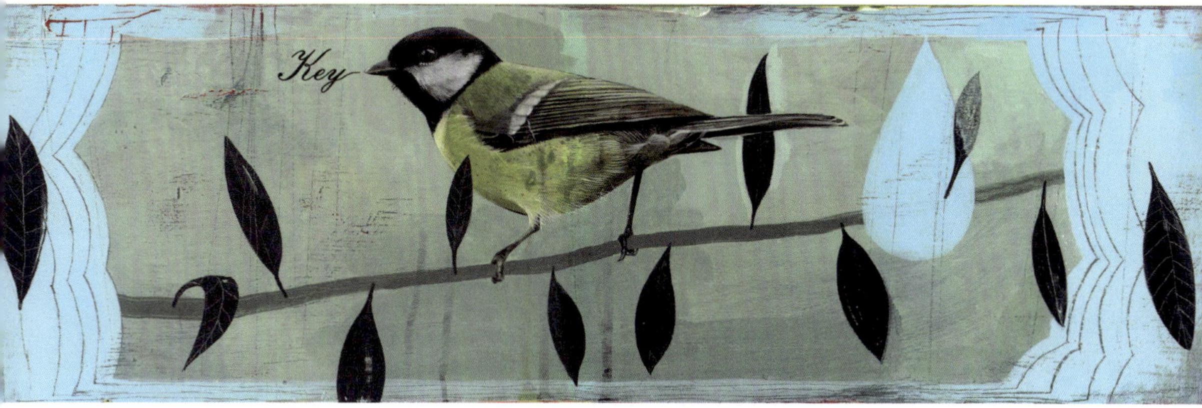

It is still one of the arts though, albeit a rather modest seeming art. That is partly due to the medium itself – comics, books and pictures are by nature rather quiet media – and also due to the natures of those who produce them: illustrators.

We illustrators are an odd bunch. Most of us putter around in our own highly personal visual worlds to create something magical. We love illustration and we have loved it for a long time. Actually many illustrators always knew that they wanted to make pictures or comics: illustrations. At a young age, while our classmates were still tongue-tied when asked what they wanted to be when they grew up, most of us already knew that we wanted to tell stories with pictures. Nonetheless many, especially younger illustrators are somewhat in the dark when it comes to the question, "How can I become an illustrator and how can I manage to make a living at it?"

This book, an "illustration primer," makes an effort to shed light on the darkness, to be useful and to answer as many of your questions as possible.

It examines the circumstances surrounding the profession of illustrator, from the vexing subject of money to the question of the right workplace. How do you get commissions? How do you negotiate successfully? What's the adequate price, how do you handle the everyday routine of work in illustration? It *also* presents a wide variety of illustration techniques.

I'm aware that an illustration primer about "the work and life of an illustrator" cannot provide *definitive* answers concerning such a complex subject, nor is there enough space between these covers to address all the questions. But just because I don't have all the answers doesn't mean I can't take a first step.

On this note, I hope that this book will help to make your everyday life as an illustrator a little simpler. The thing is, we're all different and just as some things are difficult for some of us, other things are easy. Let's start with the easy stuff.

Yours truly,

FELIX SCHEINBERGER

Contents

Introduction

So You Want To Be an Illustrator

Illustration Techniques

How to survive as a illustrator

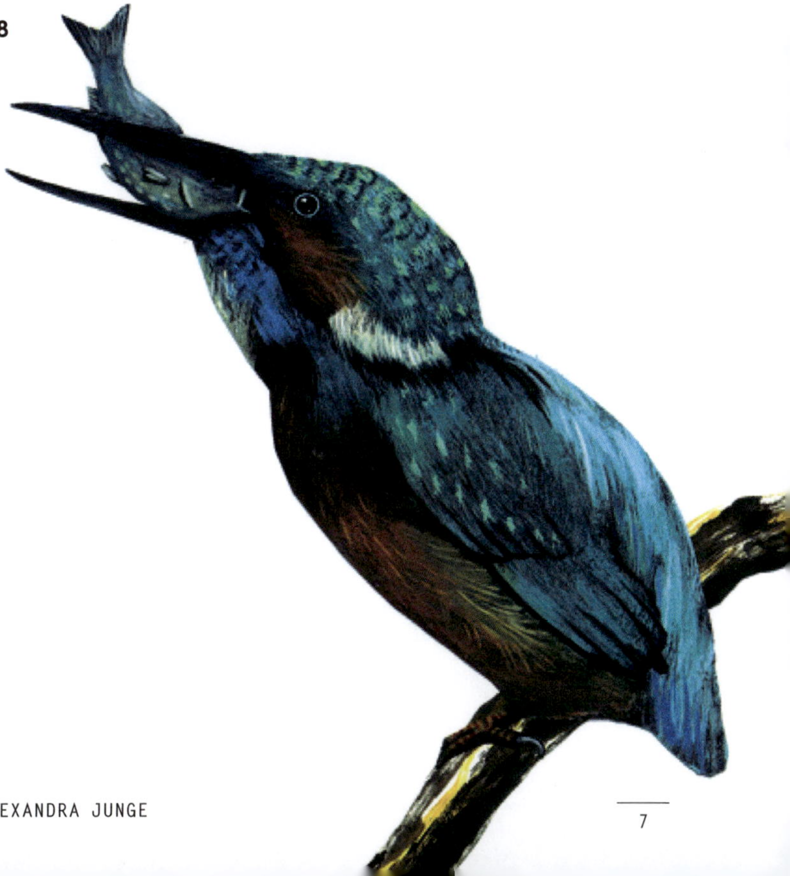

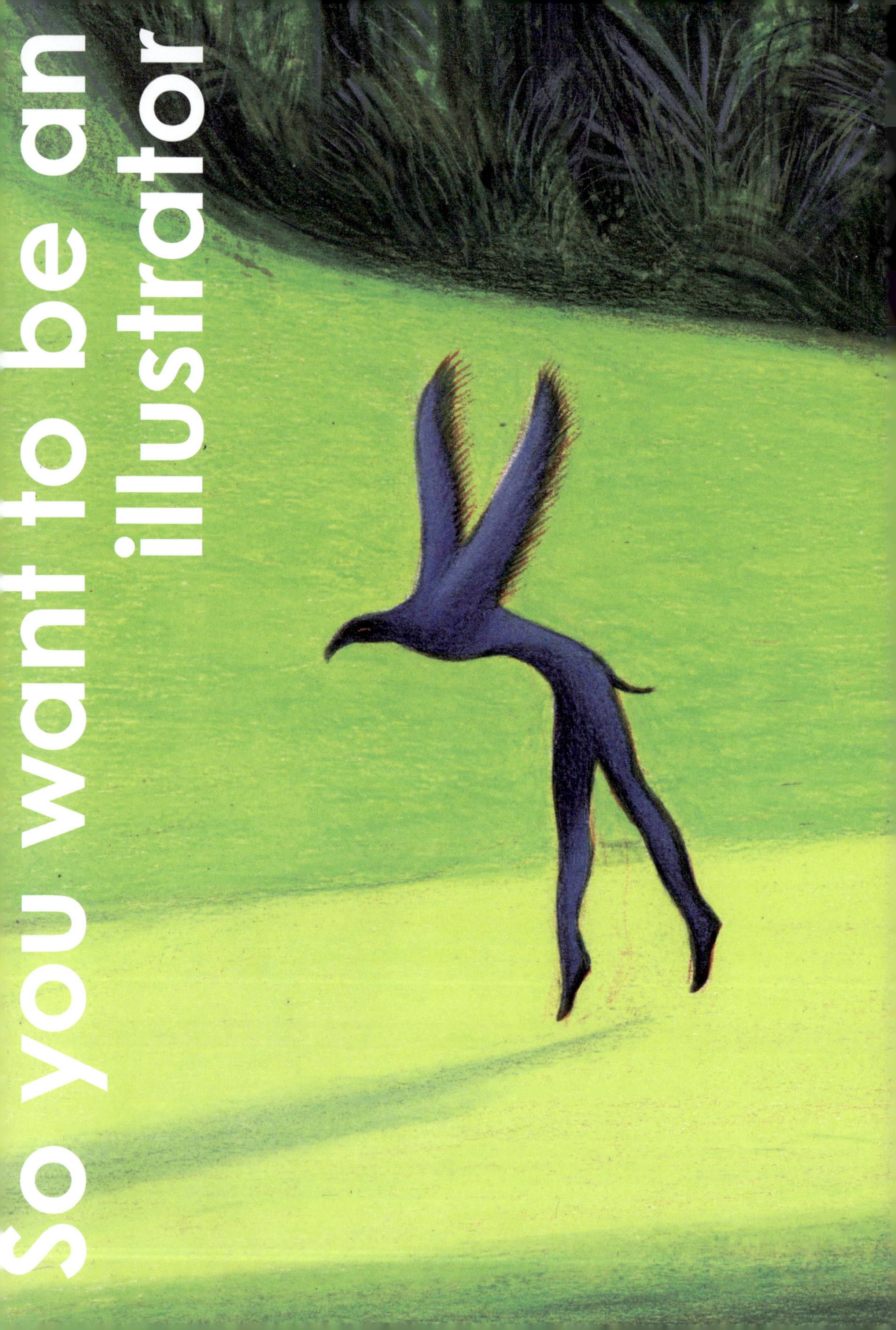
so you want to be an
illustrator

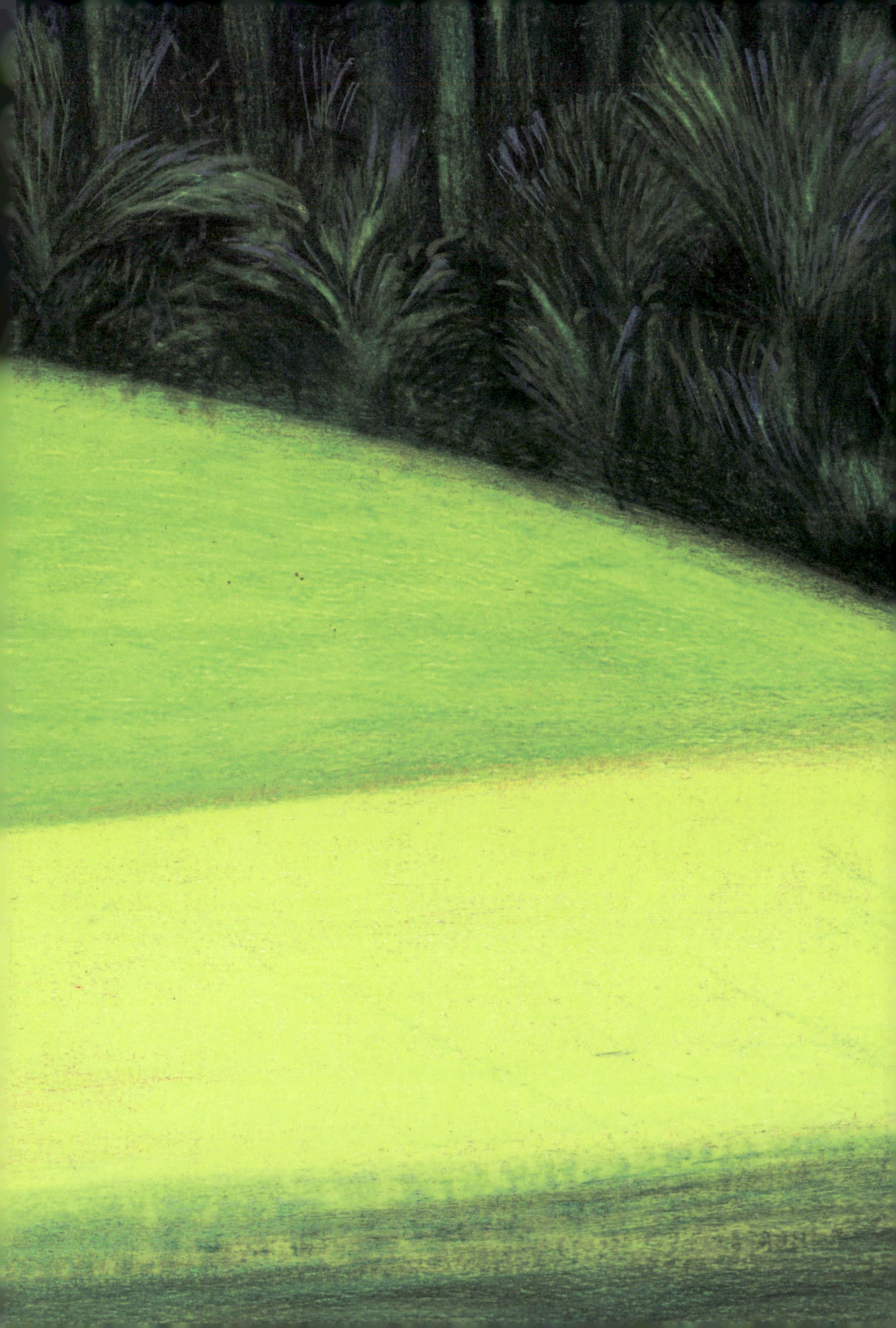

Fear of the Blank Page

Well anyway I'm not lost,
I know I'm still somewhere in Alaska.
DONALD DUCK, *FROZEN GOLD* 1944

Sound familiar? You're sitting at your desk with a pad of paper, a pencil sharpener and a couple of colored pencils ... any moment now you'll create a fabulous illustration! Sharpen all the pencils and go. Everything is ready. The pencils are sharp, take a deep breath and then ... wouldn't a cup of tea make it nicer? You go and make some tea ... now ... no, wait, maybe I'd better wash the dishes ... call my girlfriend ... check my email ... Facebook ... take a nap. On and on and on ... That sounds familiar?

This phenomenon is called "the fear of the blank page," and it has always been around. Artists, graphic designers, writers and thousands of other creative professionals have been battling it for generations. I bet that 17,000 years ago in Lascaux, France they called it the fear of the blank cave wall.

It's a mystery. Why do we make things so difficult for ourselves sometimes? Why not just grasp the artistic moment and get to work?

The famed fear of the blank page is nothing more than the fear of making mistakes.

It's the fear of not living up to our own or someone else's expectations; the fear that it might not "turn out well." Let's take a closer look at the phenomenon of "mistakes" then. At the computer, we deal with mistakes with Apple Z. It may be simple, but it doesn't help in the real world because it only works for pixels, not for pencils. In the real world, mistakes don't just go away.

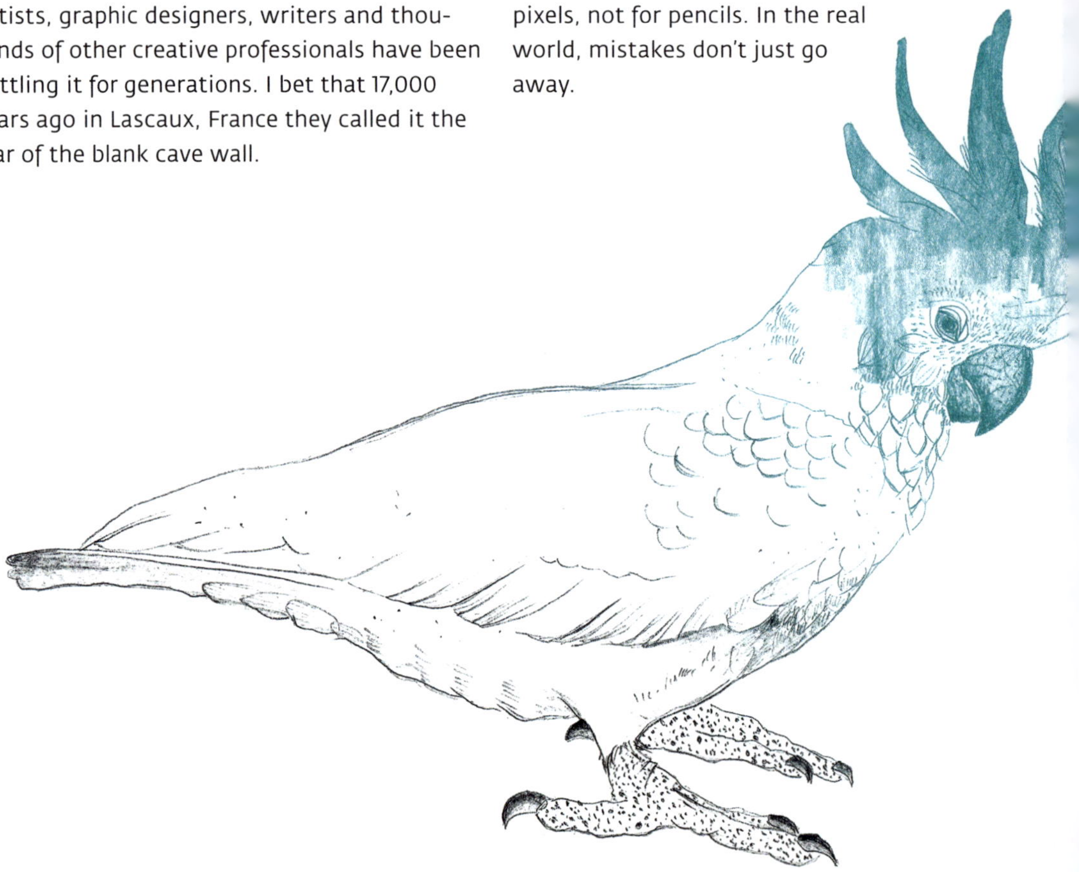

Also, using *undo* means we are losing an important benefit of mistakes: *learning* from them. When we are irritated by a mistake and can't make it go away with a snap of our fingers, it remains in our memory. Not being irritated means forgetting it, means repeating it. If we don't get irritated by a mistake, we'll make it again.

But there's another interesting thing about mistakes: they are full of creative potential. If all we produce is whatever we can produce without mistakes, we are robbing ourselves of the opportunity of discovering uncharted waters. Creative processes thrive on the unexpected, the uncontrollable, yes, on mistakes. Sometimes that stupid drop of coffee or the false stroke is exactly the thing that will give us new ideas and better drawings.

So, the fear of the blank page is unnecessary for two reasons, first because mistakes are normal and everyone – beginners and pros – make them, secondly because mistakes sometimes move us forward.

So my advice is to allow yourself to feel the fear of the blank page like actors allow themselves to have stage fright. It exists and even old hands battle it now and then.

Get out on the stage and begin. If you make mistakes, you make mistakes.

It's a bigger mistake to let it hold you back. You'll see: Your illustrations will surprise and reward you and someday you'll be proud of some of those successful "mistakes."

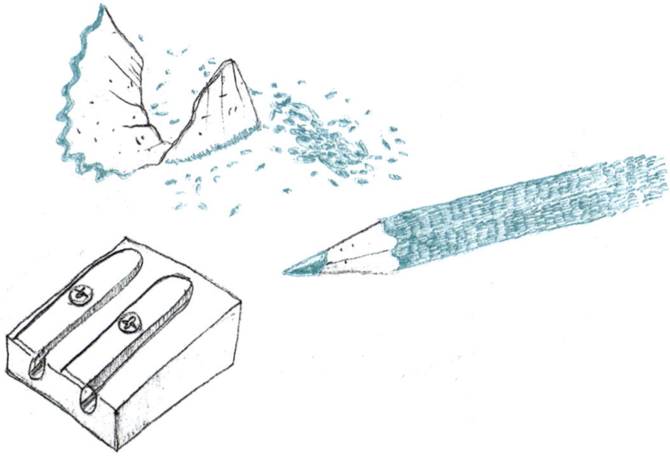

Talent

Talent means energy and perseverance and nothing more.
HEINRICH SCHLIEMANN

Remember gym class? It was a strange, weekly ritual devised to prove to some that they would never be able to climb that rope, while to others it was their easy compensation for bad grades in English. Only those who were already good at it did well, while most young couch potatoes banned sports from their lives as soon as they were able.

In illustration we encounter people with exactly the same experience as in gym class. In this case, though, it's not about physical abilities or inabilities, but about that thing called "talent." Because like with sports, the belief seems to be that people who can draw and illustrate were given that talent at birth. Of course, the reverse argument would be that if a person shows they cannot draw, they won't be able to learn it. And since you cannot possibly have a chance against the competition's God-given talent many people just put their pencil aside for good.

I have a few things to say about talent:
Drawing is one of the first art techniques that we learn as children. Long before we learn reading, writing and arithmetic we are already experienced in using wax crayons and paper. Not only that, but we all had fun doing it. When we look at our childhood drawings today, we are often surprised at how freely and exuberantly we used the medium to draw a sun, a chicken, a house, daddy, mommy, and child. We were – according to conventional thought – talented. So why didn't we all turn out to be master drafters? Why isn't the planet populated with legions of illustrators?

Most illustrator careers fail due to the way illustrator careers are perceived and the ostensible lack of talent.

One part of the answer lies in our expectations. Behind the drawing child there is often an adult saying, "What a pretty picture!" This praise, along with the later destructive words, "Don't make such a mess," produces a strange life of its own with regard to our careers. It is self-fulfilling. The pleasure of being praised becomes an end in itself and gradually replaces the pleasure of drawing a

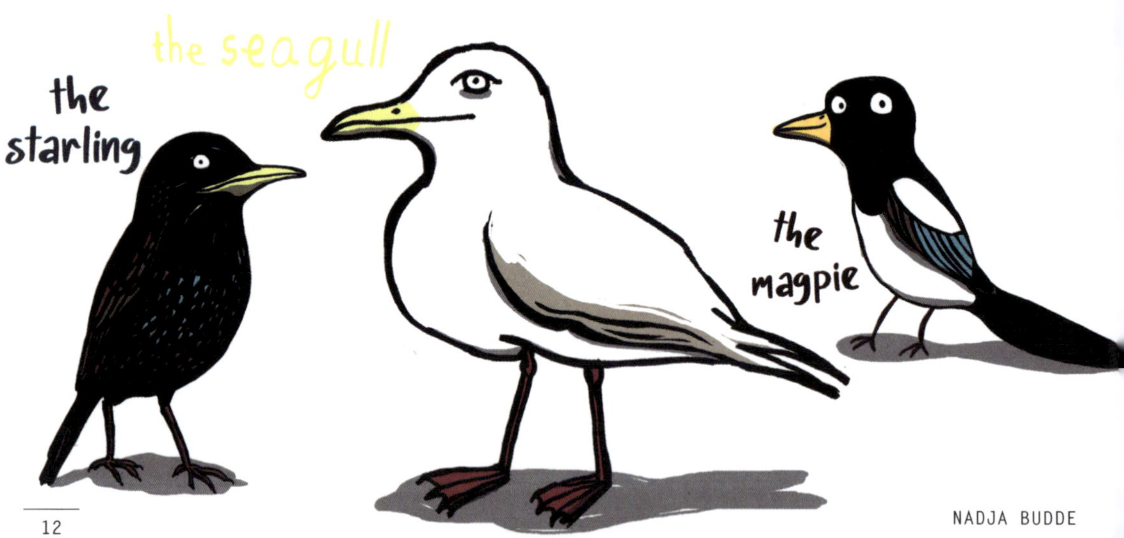

NADJA BUDDE

picture "just for fun." Thus almost all children enter a phase when they begin tracing and wanting their pictures to look "like the real thing." Drawing – a moment ago communication and creativity – becomes a vehicle for gaining approval.

On the other hand, the fear of no longer being able to do justice to other people's expectations blocks creativity. Very early on we stop drawing pictures for their own sake and instead draw for assumed critics or admirers. As we get older our demands on our own artistic skills increase and reach their limits, and we don't hear such ready praise from the lips of our elders. And later, when we enter the art academies as freshmen, we quickly learn that the competition hasn't been sleeping.

Yet we humans are learning creatures. When we enter the world we can't do anything but eat, sleep and digest. Everything else – playing the piano, cooking preserves, judo – has to be learned.
I suspect that the thing that we commonly call "talent" mainly means "early encouragement." Naturally, music lessons are easier for the children of musicians, but mainly because they were familiar with music at a younger age. Whether they will really become outstanding and successful musicians, though, also depends on the factors of effort, work, commitment, pleasure and inventiveness.

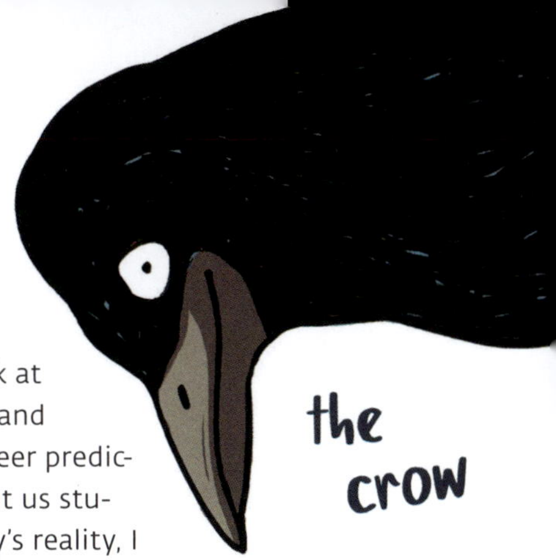

When I look back at my own studies and compare the career predictions made about us students with today's reality, I can say that the "winners" were by no means recognizable at the start. Many of the "talents" of whom great futures were predicted later took very different pathways. Conversely, many a purported "weaker" student later made their way. In my experience, personal commitment plays the biggest role. If you're lazy, your "talent" won't get you anywhere.

What you can't learn is to be interested. But when we sustain pleasure in drawing it puts a positive automatism in motion.

`If we enjoy doing it, we do it often and if we do it often, we do it well.`

So in my opinion the word "talent" is more than overrated. A passion for illustration is far more important than talent.

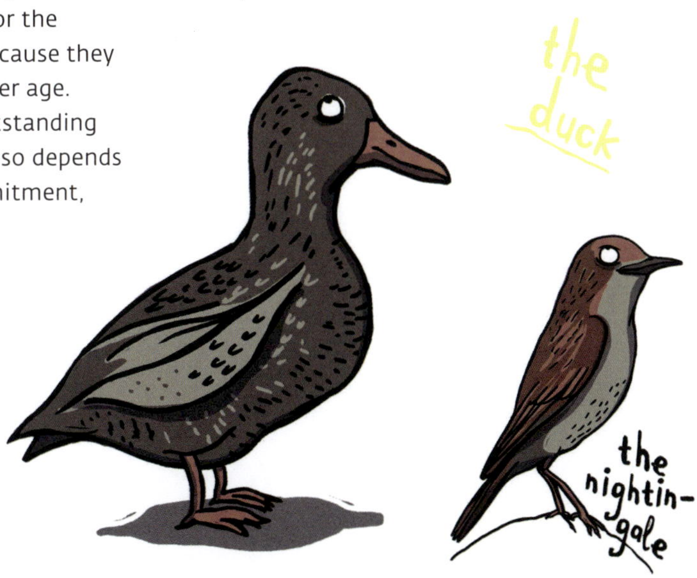

Illustrating is Decision-Making

If it looks like a duck,
swims like a duck,
and quacks like a duck,
then it probably is a duck.
THE DUCK TEST OR 'INDUCTIVE REASONING'

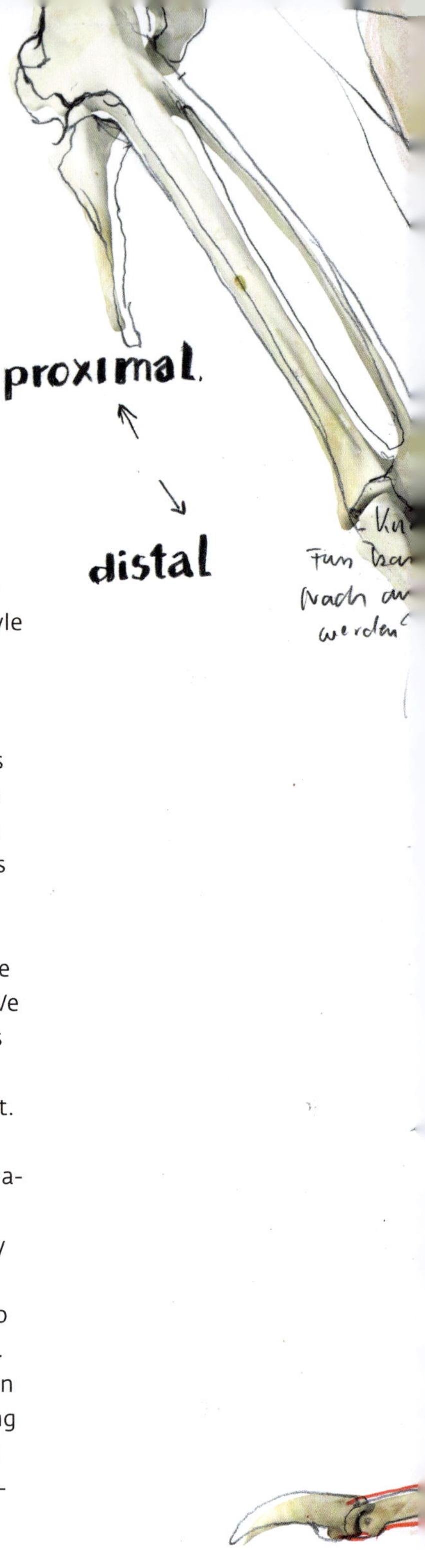

basically that's the whole truth, but sadly also the whole difficulty. Illustrating means you have to make decisions.
You make a decision with every stroke on the page, with every pixel you add to a computer graphic. What are your hands going to create?

What do you want to say?

Should the boy in the foreground wear a red shirt or a yellow one? Should he look like an infographic, will he be wearing armor, does he have a beak? It sounds simple, but between the first moment of the empty screen or the blank page to the finished illustration you make hundreds, maybe thousands of minor and major decisions. Depending on *how* you decide, you conclusively determine the result of your picture. Your minor and major decisions constitute illustration. It influences the question of your personal style as much as the question of what you want – and don't want – to depict.
So it's important that you, as the "image maker," recognize that the creative process is a series of decisions. And that's exactly the problem. You'll notice how difficult decision-making processes can be just buying a pair of shoes. We often stand there like the ass between two bales of hay, unable to decide which to eat. I would therefore encourage you to practice a little pragmatism and have more trust in your own abilities. It's usually not a matter of life or death, but merely of prioritizing two practically equal alternatives. The ass standing still between the bales of hay is also making an unconscious decision, but in his case it's the worst decision, because he doesn't decide on *either*.

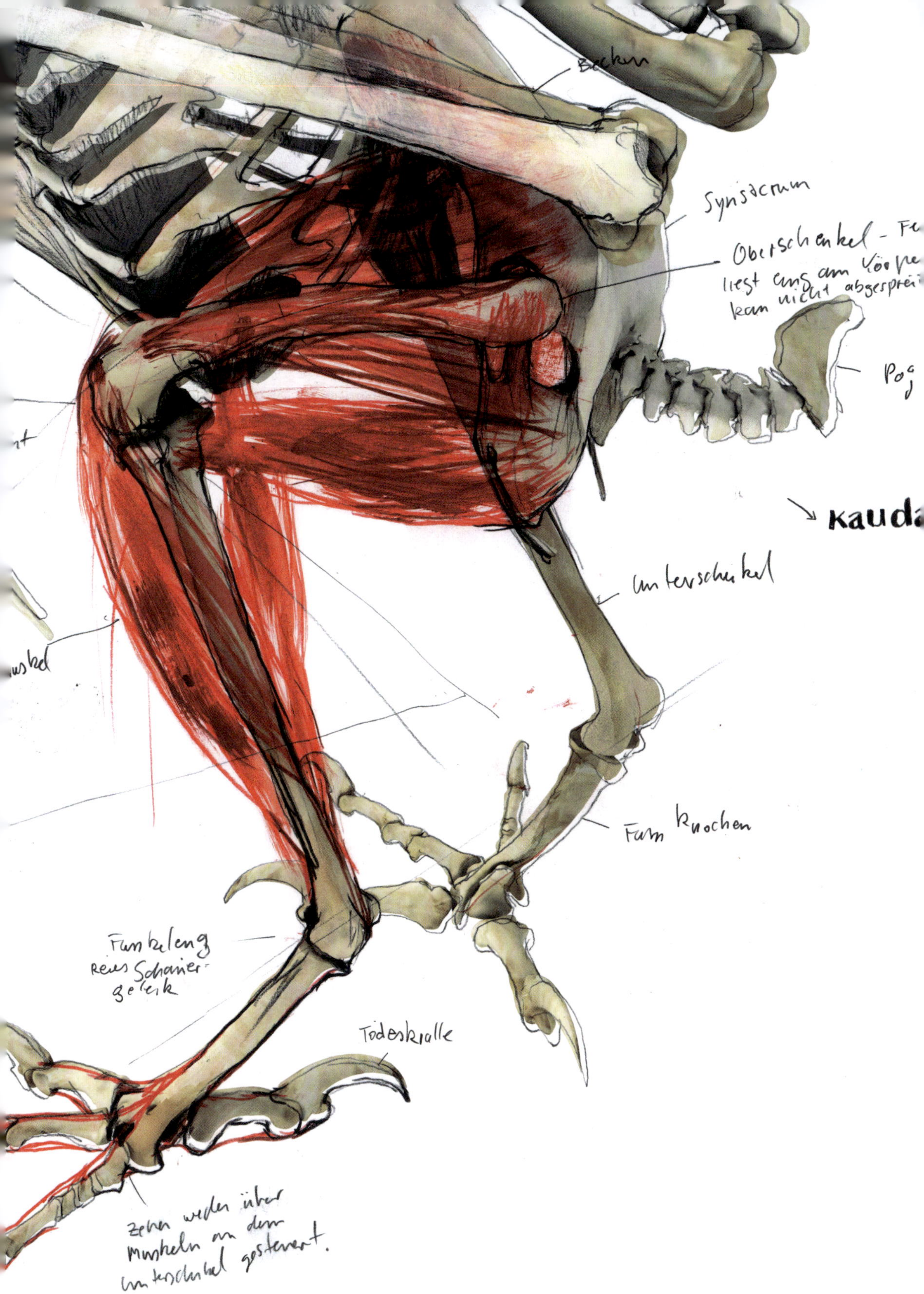
Becken
Synsacrum
Unterschenkel
Fußknochen
Fußgelenk
reines Scharnier-
gelenk
Todeskralle
Zehen werden über
Muskeln an dem
Unterschenkel gesteuert.

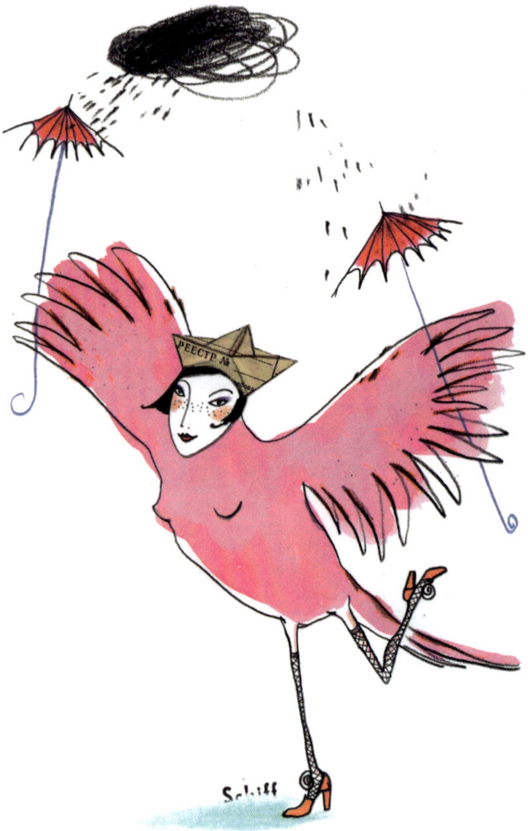

So my advice to you is to just valiantly keep moving ahead when it comes to illustrating. When you look back at your workday, you don't want to say you spent most of it doing nothing. Ruminating and hesitating usually won't make you a better illustrator. Be willing to take some risks in your work. In the time you spend wallowing in your decision-making neuroses you can paint two bold pictures rather than one fretful one.

Decisions have something to do with your personal viewpoint. Learn to trust yourself. As trite as it may sound, even that can be practiced.

Practice your "decision sense."

Don't spend hours mulling over the restaurant menu. Try to do it in one minute. Once you learn to accept that you are the sole decision-maker and to trust your feel for the right choice, you'll have taken the most important step. If you have to secretly practice at restaurants, it's no big deal.

Designing means deciding and illustrating means making one bold decision after the next until you reach the final result. Once you've internalized that you soon won't even notice how many decision hurdles you've taken before completing your picture.

Whether it's a stroll or a mountain hike is sometimes less a matter of the pathway than of the wanderer.

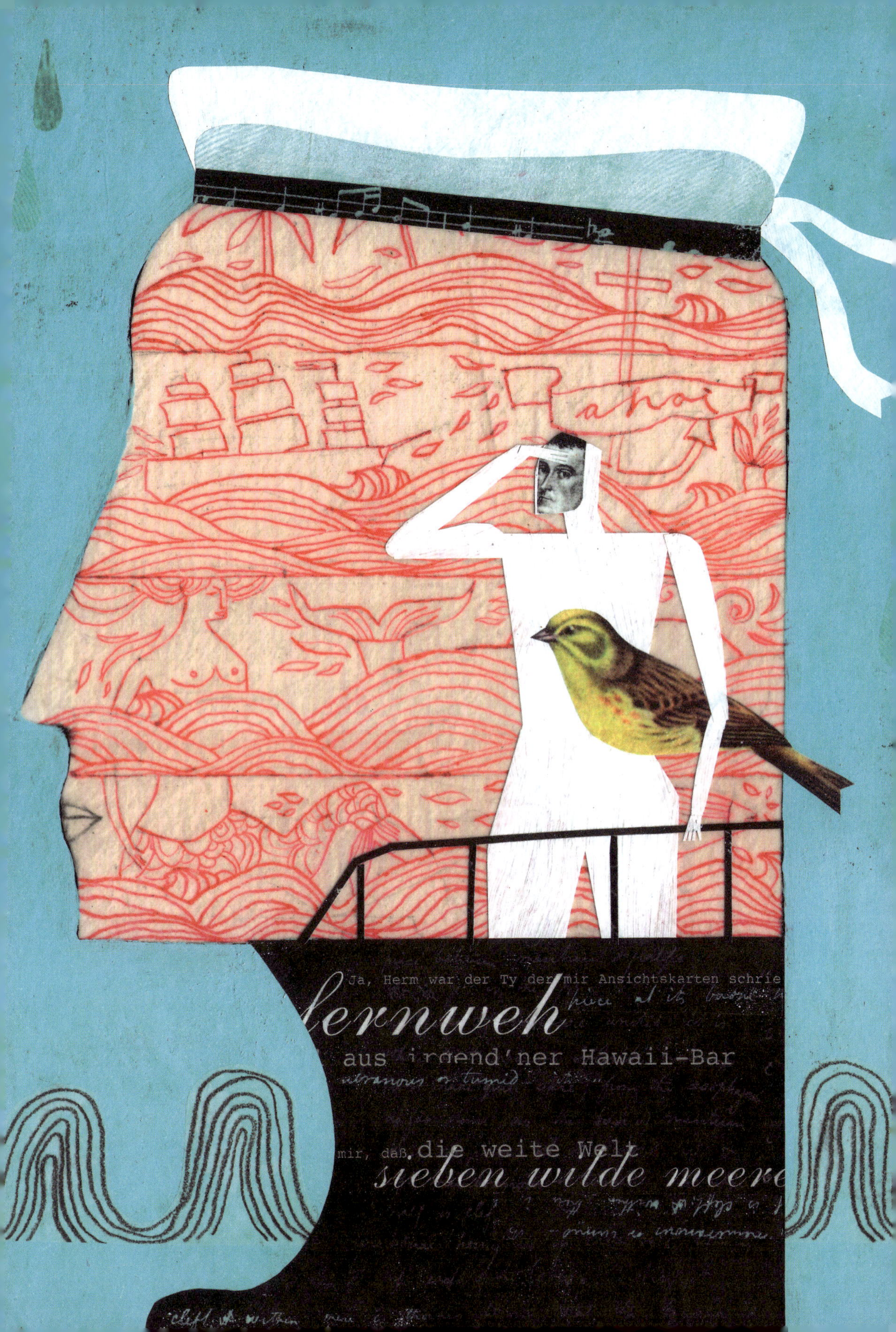
ahoi
Ja, Herm war der Ty der mir Ansichtskarten schrie
ernweh
aus irgend'ner Hawaii-Bar
mir, daß die weite Welt
sieben wilde meere

How We See What We See

Information is not knowledge.
FRANK ZAPPA

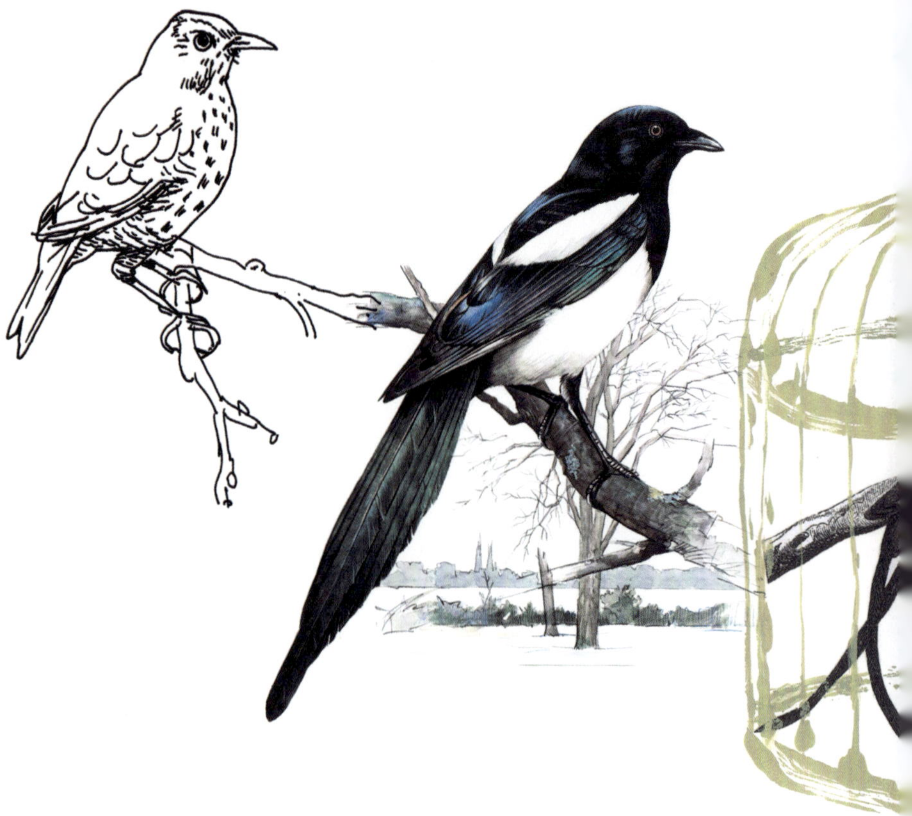

Illustration is not only characterized by the technique used. You are far more important than your choice of tools and materials. *Who* creates the illustration is decisive. Your way of illustrating represents your way of seeing the world. Because:

How we see what we see makes the difference.

How the world appears and we navigate in it depends on how we view the world. It's true that two individuals see a situation or circumstance two very different ways. If we were to see the world through someone else's eyes, it is doubtful whether it would be familiar to us. This is the key to the different styles we have when illustrating:

Illustration explains *our* view of the world to others.

Of course, it already begins with our "choice of weapons," our technique, but it goes much farther than that. Every decision that affects your illustration – from the idea to the direction your content takes to your composition and picture design – is the result of your own assessment. Your point of view determines the picture. So, if your view of the world is, say, more romantic, your illustrations will reveal a more romantic perspective. You may use more playful colors, seek out themes and subjects that tell stories or similar. This might also be the reason you are better at certain techniques. Likewise, a more objective, rational point of view will result in explanatory or

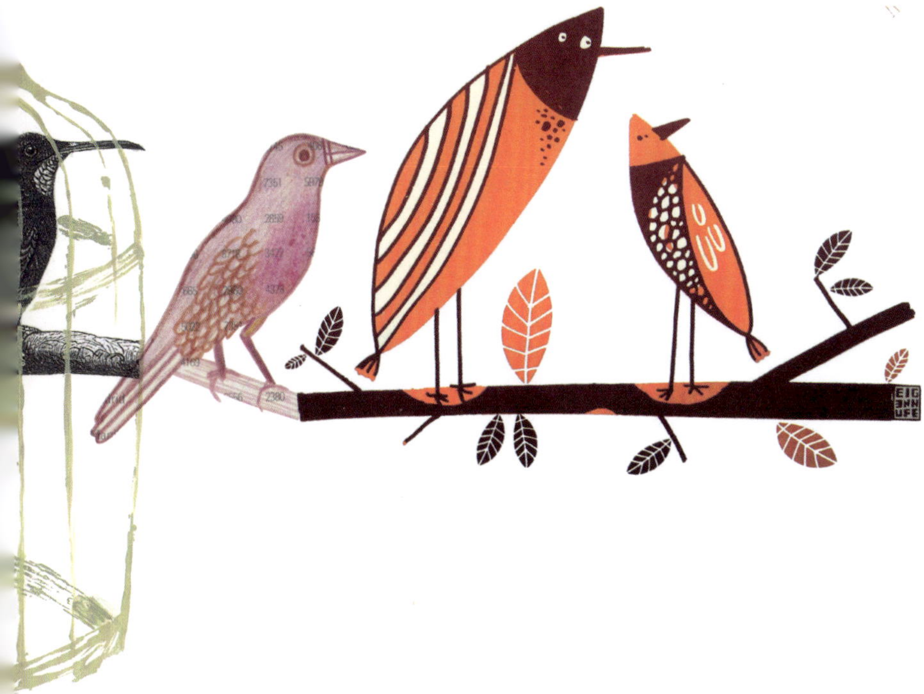

informative illustrations. You might then choose techniques that are better suited to describing textures and your manner or portrayal may be more subordinate to realism than purely atmospheric images.

Your sense of humor may be just as visible as aspects of fantasy, melancholy or playfulness. Everything that defines and moves you finds its way almost magically into your pictures. The thing that we casually call "taste" is therefore an unconscious expression of your mental state. By implication, the things that we like betray quite a lot about us. That's not meant judgmentally – we simply should be aware that this is the case.

Maybe this is why we react so strongly when our pictures are criticized. It may also explain why the question of an artist's "personal style" often seems so strangely significant: the search for our own personal artistic expression is a search for our own self.

Illustration is far from formalism. In reality, your soul is also drawing the picture.

LARISSA BERTONASCO

TOM EIGENHUFE

Concrete and Abstract

Without creativity, there is no life.
MR. SPOCK, STAR TREK, 1967

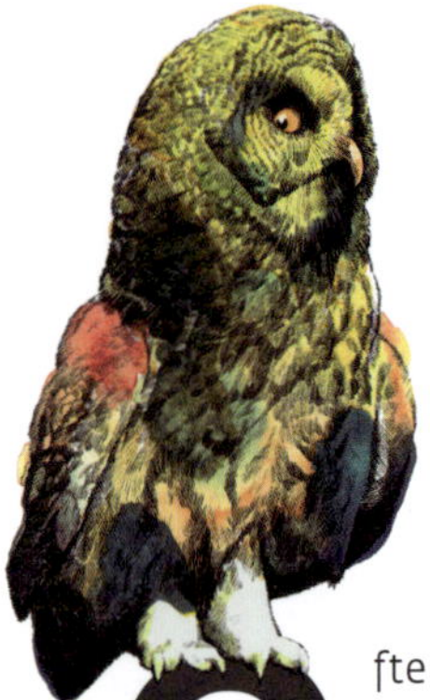

Often it sounds paradoxical, but at times excessively distinct realism generates a peculiar distance. When we look at something "real," say an object standing in front of us (like a chair in the kitchen), we naturally have a very clear and concrete image of it. We can look at our chair from all sides, turn it around and, if we want, upside down. The chair is present; its shape, color, size and proportions are obvious and verifiable.
But if the chair is not in our kitchen, but just in our mind – if it's an imagined chair – it looks less in focus.
For fun, examine the image with your imagination and compare it with something you can actually see: the imagined chair is vaguer and its color and shape may vary as it grows in our imagination.
Hence, the seen chair and the imagined chair differ considerably in quality. The chair that we imagine is far less clear, it visually *weighs* less than the chair seen in reality.
Considering these seeing and thinking habits may explain why we sometimes develop a peculiar distance to overly realistic pictorial worlds. The reverse is just as simple as it is paradoxical:
Unconsciously, when we see a blurry subject we assume that is must take place *inside* of us, while we locate what we actually see *outside* of us. The chair that we observed precisely cannot be inside of us, we must have *seen* it.
This effect leads overly concrete portrayals creating an inner distance to what we see. Actually, we can identify so easily with more abstract images, with vagueness, with blurred outlines and sketchiness because this type of portrayal is similar to the world inside of us when we shut our eyes. Anything concrete, detailed, becomes the outer world surrounding us, the foreign, while the abstract dwells inside of us.

This realization is crucial for us as the makers of visual worlds in as much as we can take advantage of the different effects to create new picture. Carried over to illustration, this paradox means that emotional closeness can be created better with un-concrete viewpoints because their impression is more like inner images. By the same token, realistic pictures, clear textures and concrete surfaces appeal to more objectivistic and therefore emotionally distanced viewpoints.

Thus an overly concrete view of the world is also a distanced view.

It is preferable to employ this knowledge just as deliberately as you ought to occasionally try to close your eyes when kissing.

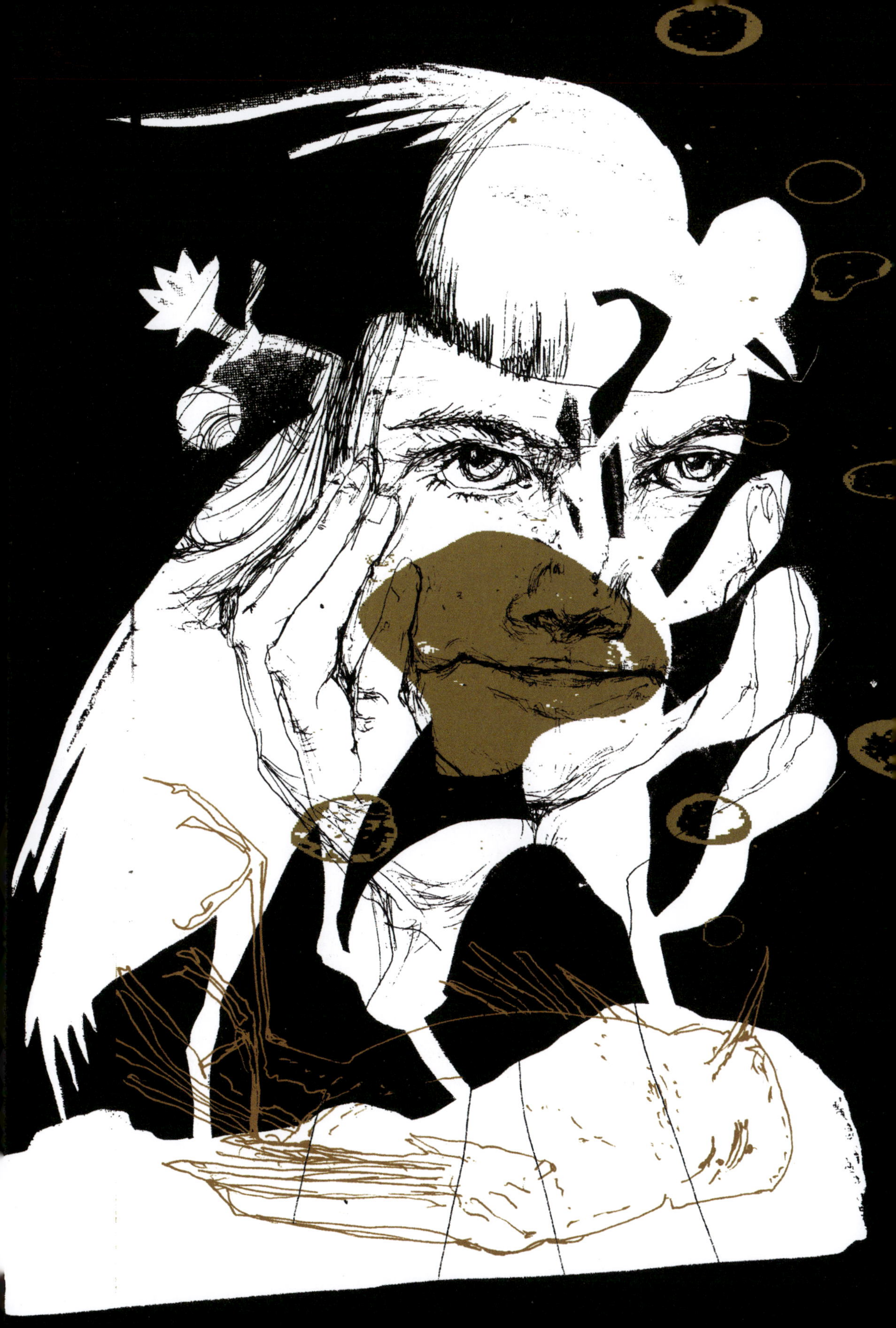

Everyone's an Artist

People become artists out of despair.
ERNST LUDWIG KIRCHNER

the statement that everyone's an artist is attributed to Joseph Beuys. Take a look around you at your friends and you'll see that it's basically true – even if Beuys probably meant something completely different. For example, if you were to walk around my Prenzlauer Berg neighborhood in Berlin, you'll see that most of the young people today are doing "something creative" or at east aspiring for such a career. Those who aren't graphic designers want to be actors, pop stars, game designers, models or illustrators. So, like all creative professions, illustration is "in." This is a good thing, but also bad in some ways. The fact that we want to develop our talents and earn money doing so is certainly good and proper.

Illustration is a wonderful profession that makes the world a more colorful place, explains the world a bit and brings a little beauty and light into our lives.

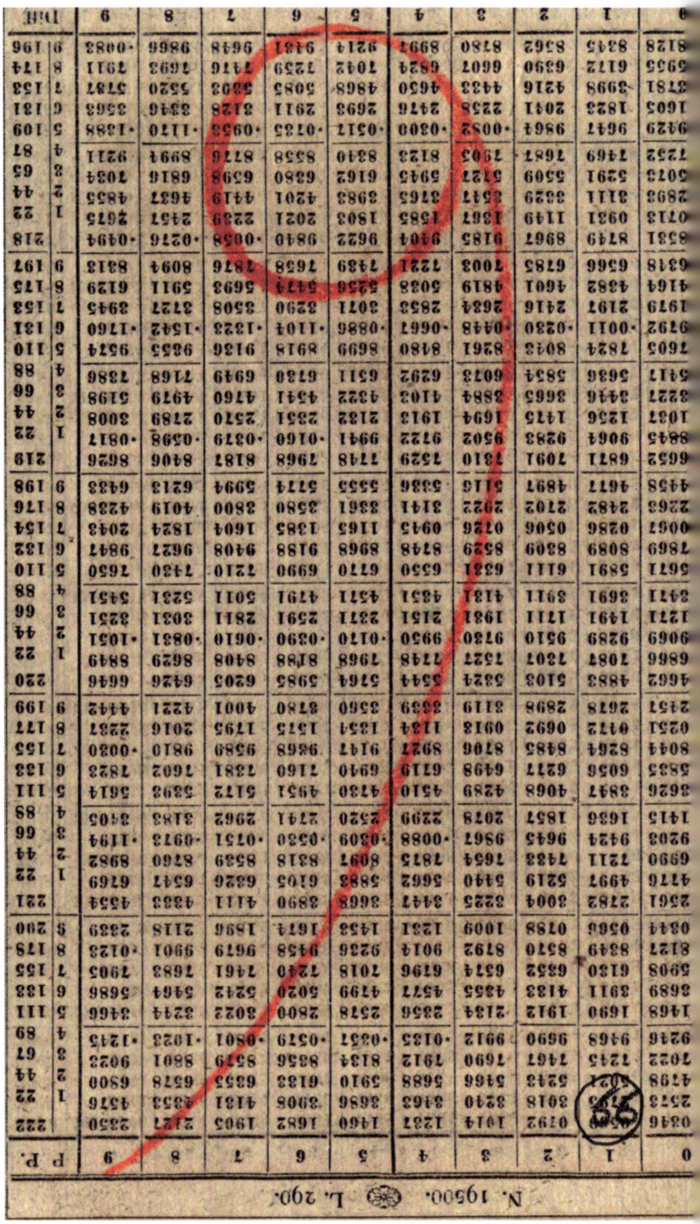

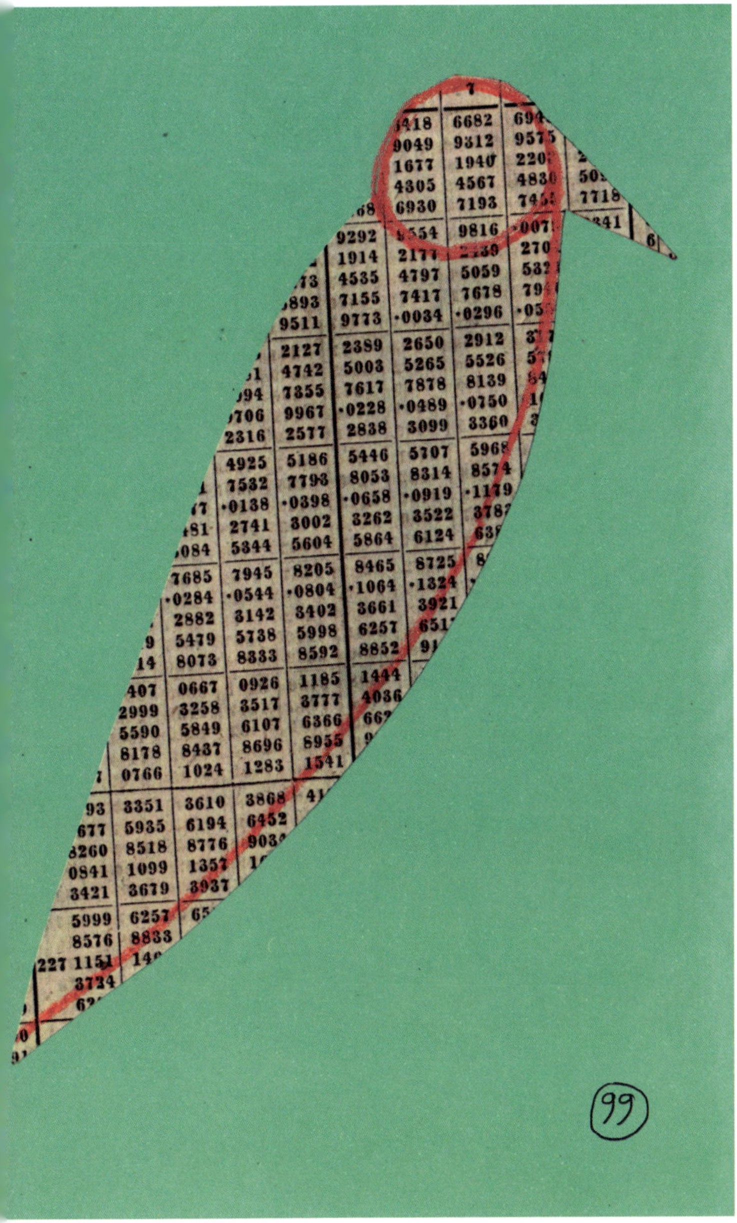

But on the negative side, the overabundance of illustrators creates a competitive climate in which many young illustrators in particular are at risk of failure. When a profession experiences inflationary growth, many rookies tend to undersell their work. Sadly, the belief that this will help you gain a foothold in the market is a fallacy. On the contrary, it often leads to an inescapable vicious circle of poor pay, the resulting under-estimation of one's own performance and renewed poor pay.
You'll soon find yourself going from one unpaid internship to the next and getting out of that grind can prove very difficult. The kind of clients who primarily go for "bargain prices" will rarely agree on raising your price later on. Instead they repeatedly refer to the price range they've become accustomed to.
In addition, low wages will lead to time management problems. If you do poorly paid work, it will take you much longer to earn your rent money.

Setting the restart button is made all the more difficult by one's own need for security, a lack of self-confidence, ignorance of the actual price structure and a simple lack of time. Does this mean you should throw up your hands in despair and throw in the "illustration towel"? Hardly. Markets are subject to the law of supply and demand. To get out of the mass dilemma it is wise – especially for younger illustrators – to take a closer look at their market. The market for illustrations is by no means one-dimensional. You can specialize in hundreds of different applications. There are book and magazine illustrators, caricaturists, game illustrators and cartoonists. You can earn a living with children's books, non-fiction or science illustration or animate films or computer games. You can be an all-rounder or scribble storyboards, create advertising illustrations or packaging or work for the educational sector.

Illustration offers us a huge, ever-growing market of countless applications in which the right place can certainly be found for the right product.

However, it doesn't make any sense to focus exclusively on the mainstream. On the contrary, you'll increase your market chances if you are not constantly chasing after the latest trend, but take advantage of the gaps that the market creates through its own mechanisms. A famous equation from the financial world, the so-called pork cycle, explains this using an example from farming. If, for example, lots of pork was produced one year, logically the price for pork is going to be low. Likewise, at the same time, the price of chicken may be high, as it may only be available in limited numbers. So far logical.
Now, in such times, the pork-producing farmers think it might be smarter if they had started raising chickens instead, and they switch markets. Usually, though, all of the farmers have that idea at once simply because the chicken price is high during the "pork years." Unfortunately, the consequence is that there is an over-supply of chicken the following year. Now chicken is cheap and all of the farmers are kicking themselves for not sticking with pork. And once again, they all decide simultaneously to produce more pork the following year and so on and so on.
The conclusion you can draw from this as a provider of creative services is to take a closer look. If, for example,

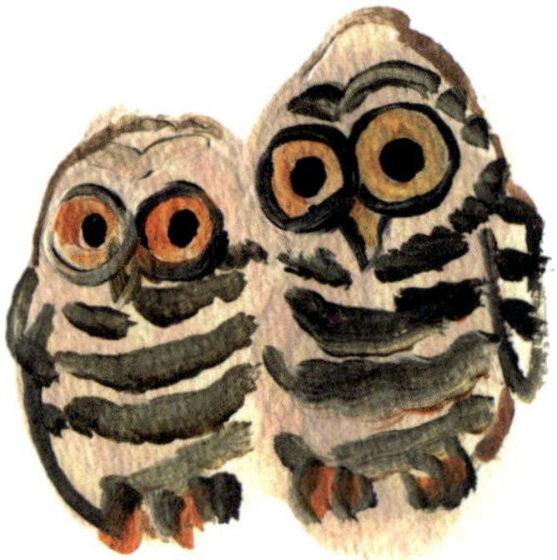

KRISTINA HELDMANN

printing analog magazine illustrations is "in" today, as a newcomer you would be well advised to look for another market niche. As in agriculture, production and distribution take a while – time enough for a seemingly lucrative market to turn into yesterday's market.
My advice therefore is to sometimes work diametrically to the supply. So, if today everyone claims that children's books are no longer worthwhile financially, according to the law of the pork cycle this assumption will create a situation in the near future where illustrations for children's books will be paid for well again because all the other providers will have focused on a different market.

So don't let it get to you, but use your head and analyze the market in detail. Then you'll find your way as an illustrator.

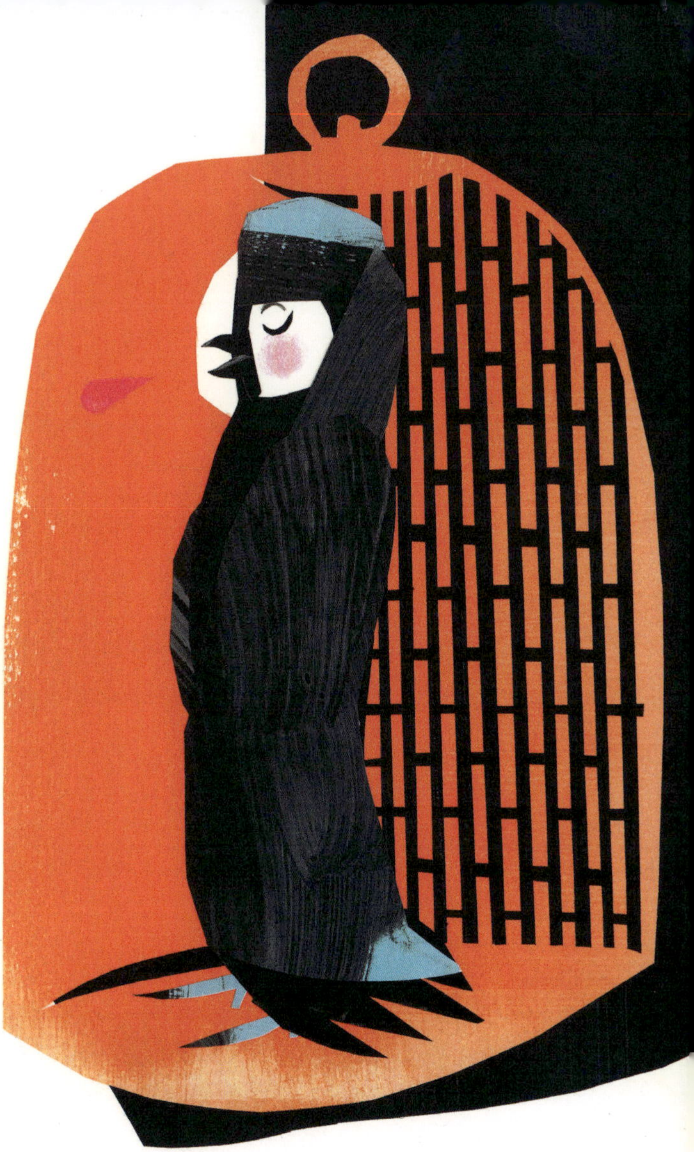

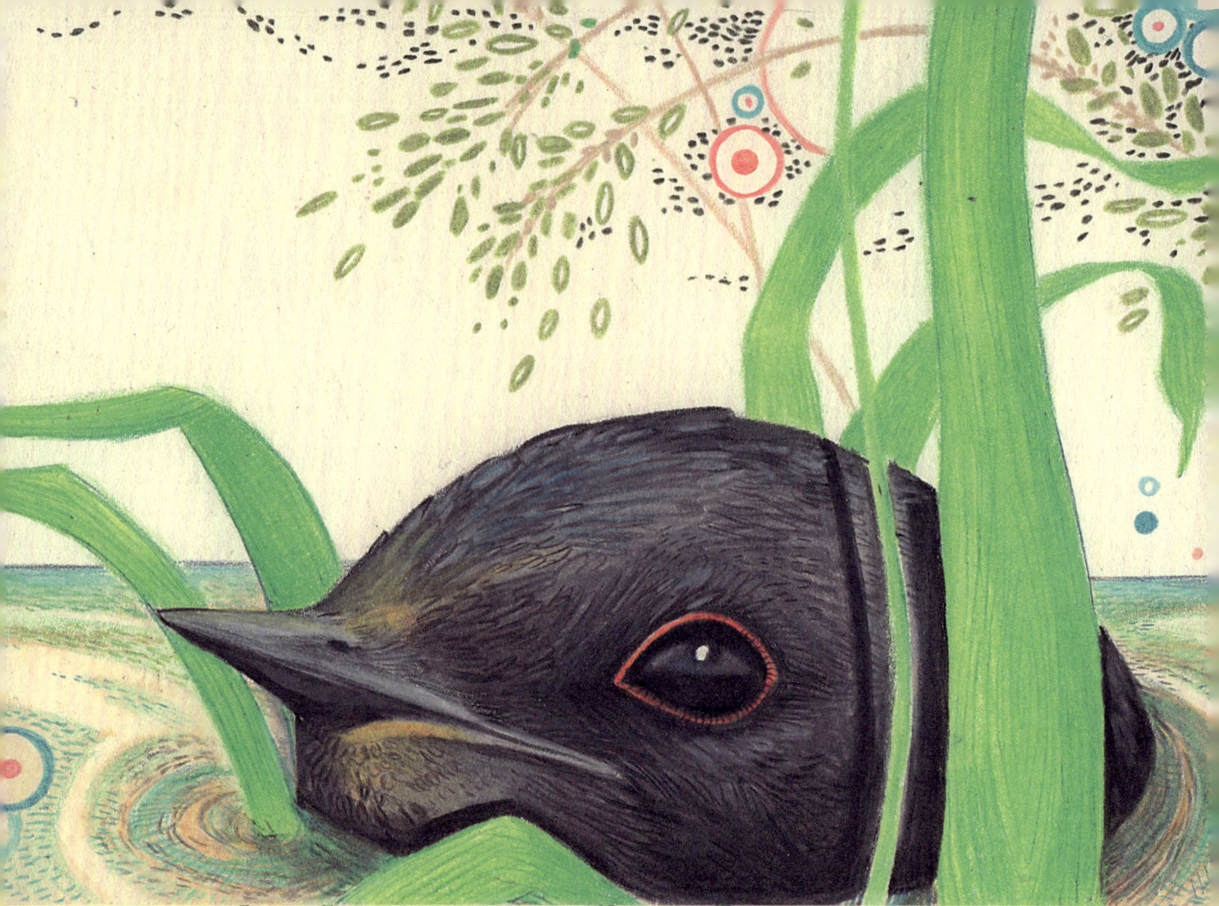

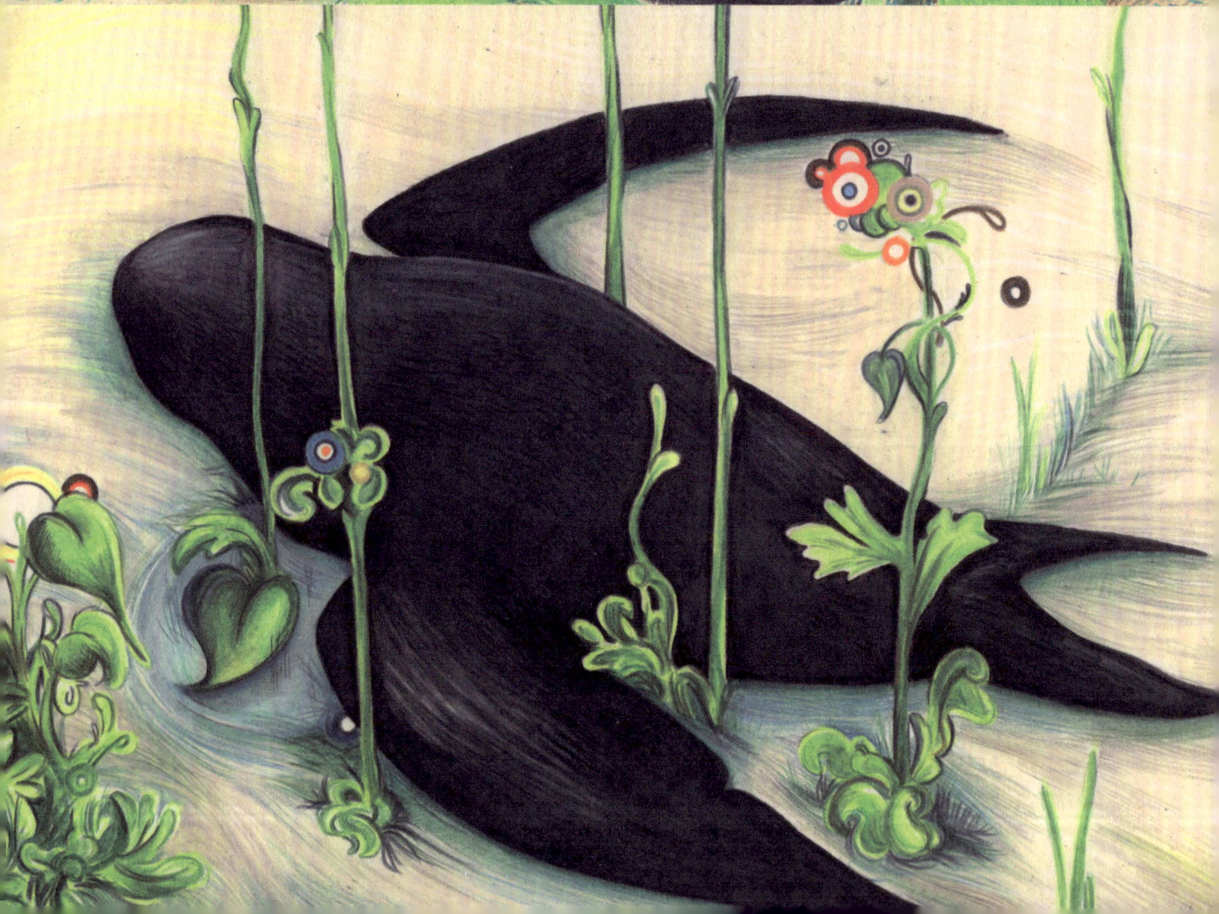

Ideas

The most difficult thing about an idea isn't having one, but recognizing whether it's good. CHRIS HOWLAND

The most important thing about an illustration is the vision it contains; the idea behind the illustration. The picture concept, style, content, design, execution, informative content, wit, aesthetic and sophistication – everything that makes up the illustration is based on a vision.

Ideas are the seasoning even in more dry subject matter such as science and informative illustrations. In areas relying on imagination – from editorials to children's books – they are the stuff that brings your picture to life.

The thing that makes a good illustration effective is the vision behind it.

Sometimes it's just a small thing like a picture concept or a design line. Sometimes it's exclusively the idea that carries the illustration. Indeed there are any number of examples of seemingly "poorly drawn" illustrations that work great in spite of it because the idea is just so good. It's little use if a picture is only "drawn well."

This is also the reason why it's not enough to focus solely on technical aspects. On the contrary, there are superb artists who cannot illustrate as well as illustrators who create wonderful things without ever having been perfect at drawing.

When visions are lacking, art becomes peculiarly trivial. It's like elevator music, like crying clowns or frozen pizza. Ideas are the soul of every illustration. If your picture is not based on an idea, it reaches no one. Ideas pull viewers in, pick them up and carry them along. Ideas are what generate the actual relationship between the viewer and the picture. Therefore the question of how to develop good ideas is not all that inconsequential. Paul McCartney once said that he simply dreamed the melody of "Yesterday." He woke up one morning, sat down at the piano and there it was – a gift of one night's sleep. Encouragement to simply dream a little more is not a bad tip for having ideas. But the fact that musicians are more liable to come up with melodies than, say, steamship captains are indicates that just more sleep alone might not be the whole secret.

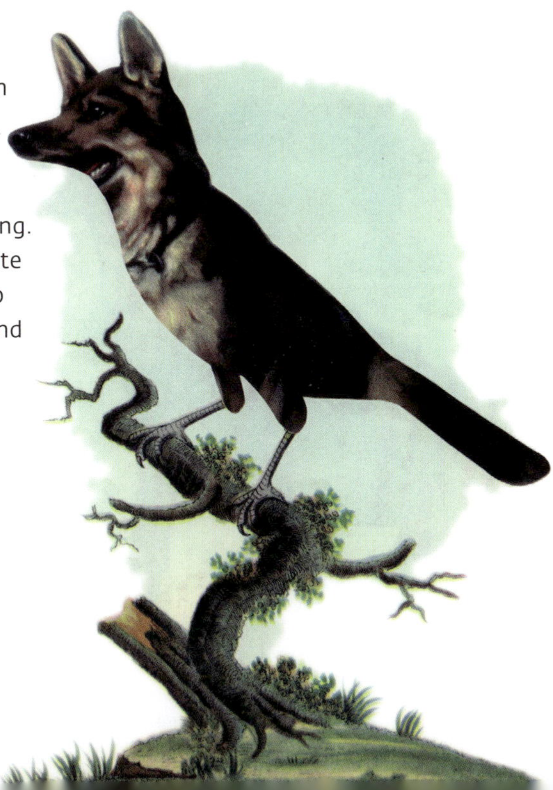

NORA MARLEEN

LOU BEACH

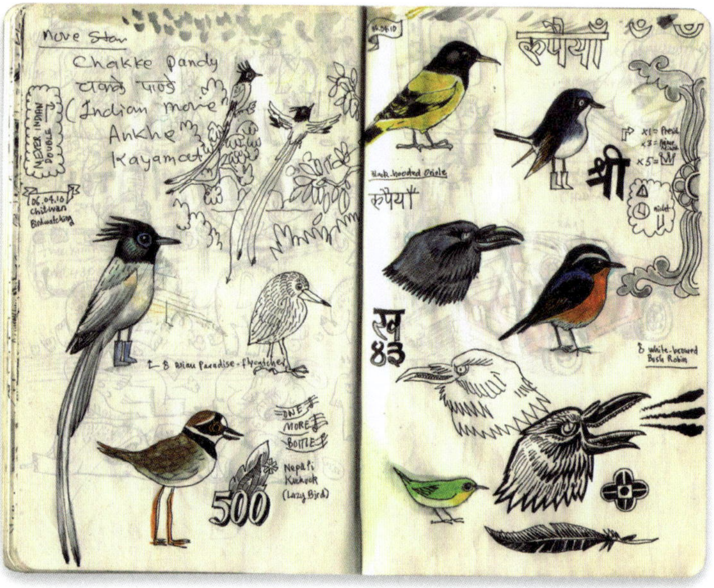

So how do you come up with good ideas? There are so many different ways to stimulate the imagination as there are different people on the planet.

Illustrating involves entering into a visual dialogue with a subject.

To start, take a look at the subject matter. Research it and question it. Take it in your hand, look at it from all sides, turn it around, knead it and re-compose it. Use a pencil and paper, build a copy of it or digitize it. Work conceptually or intuitively. Be open-minded and ready to forget all that if necessary. We are all different. It helps one person to constantly work on it and keep busy, it helps another if they take a nap or do some exercise.
Of course there are nonetheless methods for generating ideas, even for illustrators, and I'd like to present a few of the most important approaches to you here.

Research

In many cases, research is the starting point for the creative process. Researching means compiling material that may never be published but can or could contribute to the final work.
Generally, we divide classical research into four work phases: It begins with describing the problem (for instance, what is it about?), followed by compiling information, outlining what you've found and finally evaluating the results.

Let's be clear: You cannot illustrate something unless you understand it!

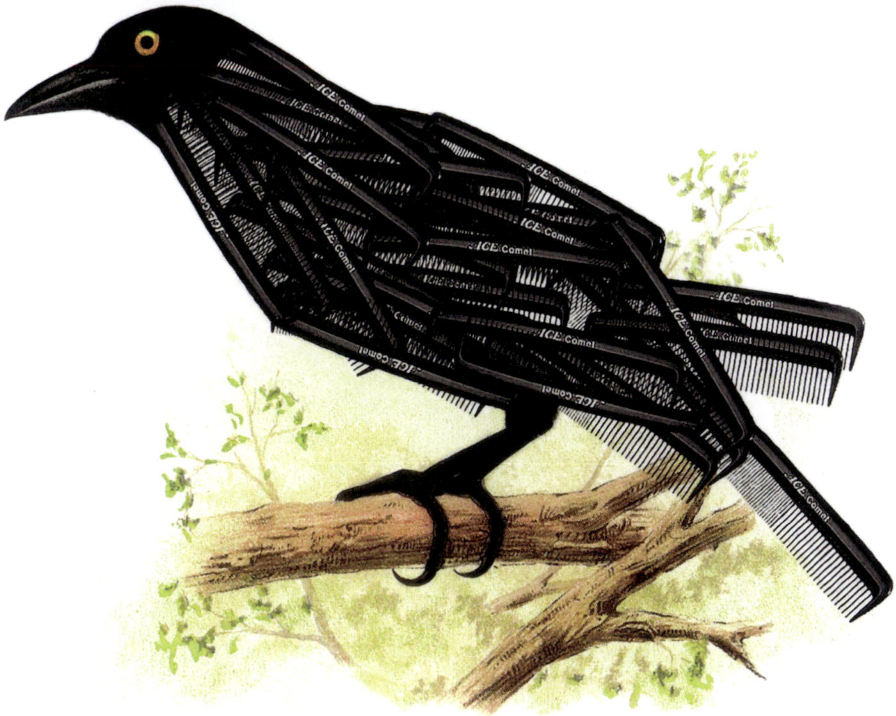

Brainstorming

This is why research is indispensable for the process of generating ideas. How intensively you undertake this depends largely on your way of working and the character of the job.
You can base your research on libraries, the Internet and other archives, experts and everything else that provides information on the subject matter. Your choice of sources alone will have an influence on your later work.
In illustration, at times the pathway already opens up your destination, since dealing with a subject matter usually results in a number of approaches for pictorial solutions.

Traditional brainstorming is group work. The term comes from the 1930s and the technique was a triumph in advertising in particular. Brainstorming thrives on free association. Every participant throws an idea out into the room and everyone else takes it, builds on it or put new combinations and terms into play. The basis for brainstorming is that everyone can just let go informally. What's important is only that the participants do not comment on or criticize each other (not even with raised eyebrows). The point is to inspire each other.

In a further phase, the results are then gathered and given shape.
To be fair, the result of a brainstorming session depends very much on the participants. Group dynamics can be inspirational, but they can also lead to roadblocks. In addition, the technique is not suitable for illustrators who work alone. Instead, they can try *brainwriting* – creating chains of associations in written form – or so-called mind mapping.

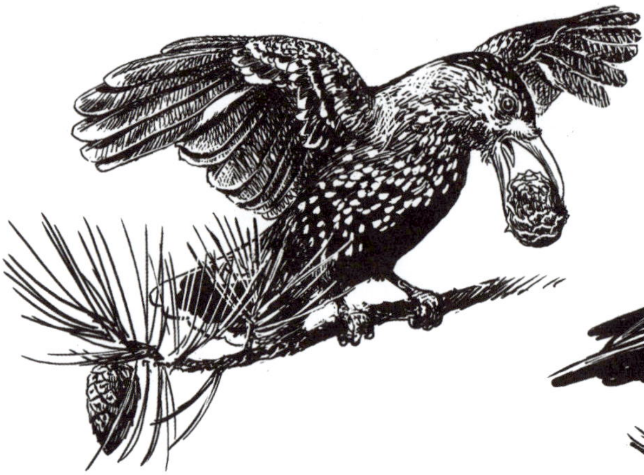

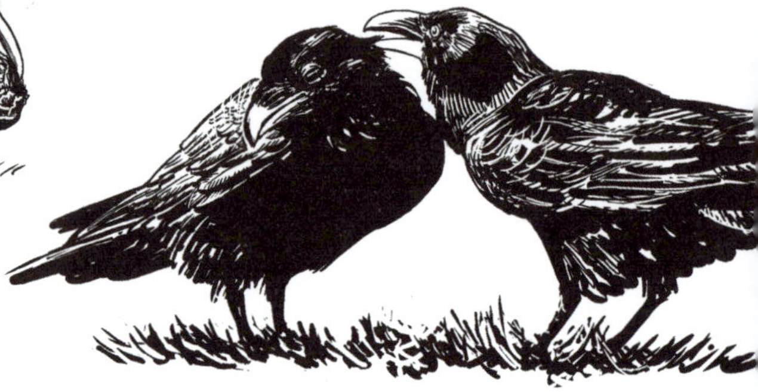

Mind mapping

Mind mapping is used to visualize thought processes as a kind of, yes, map. This method makes use of the fact that our thinking is not linear. On the contrary, thoughts crop up, our minds associate them and concoct them further rather than building on one another logically or hierarchically like a computer. You have to imagine it all not as a chain, but more as a cloud.

Using mind mapping, we attempt to visualize our thoughts and the idea clouds linked to them. You begin with one key word, for example the subject matter you wish to illustrate, and write or draw the next deepest thoughts around it. In turn, you can infer from these or continue on with them and connect the terms, themes or ideas with arrows and symbols. In this way a map is created that shows at a glance how the subject should be assessed: Promising approaches are particularly highlighted and offer structured ideas, while stunted branches either invite us to deal with them further or show us dead ends.

Mind maps can help us develop ideas, prioritize and shape them.

Inspiration

Besides doing research into the subject matter, a personal image archive is also helpful. Be inspired by pictures and compile your own analog and digital visual archive.

Collect pictures and photos that you like and that stimulate you. Comic books, magazines, lexicons and non-fiction books, toys and films offer inspiration as well as things picked up at flea markets, depending on your interests.

The collection should also contain your own pictures. Leaf through old sketchbooks. You'll be surprised at how many ideas are slumbering there just waiting to be awakened with a kiss.

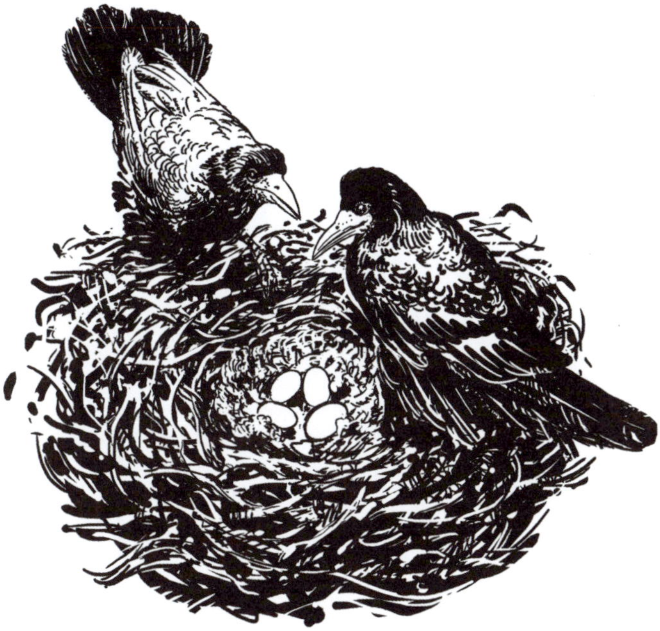

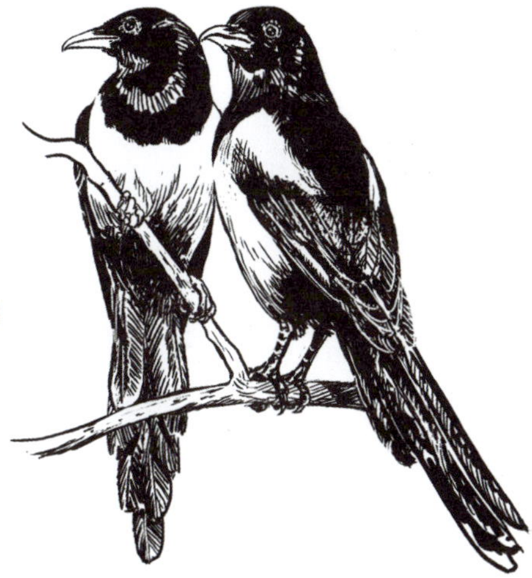

Conversation

One of the simplest methods of developing an idea is to talk with someone about it instead of thinking about it alone. In practice, mutual reflections open up new aspects and break down mental blocks.
The person you're talking with doesn't even have to say very much because talking about trains of thought and results you've come up with so far often uncovers new ideas and solutions.
So, just visit with a friend or a colleague, have a cup of coffee and chat about your current project. I am certain you'll go home smarter and full of new ideas.

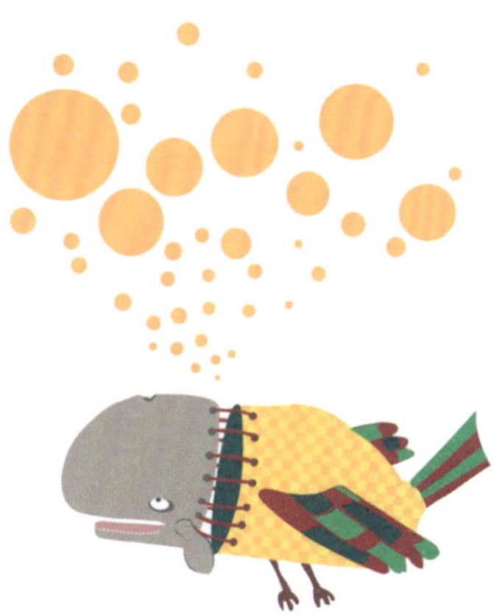

One more thing

Good ideas are fleeting, so write them down immediately! Just when you think the great new idea will come back by itself, it usually disappears. Good ideas sadly tend to dissipate if they aren't nailed down right away.
If you can't implement them right away, at least write them down. This is why creatives always need to have a pencil and paper on hand – when on the road and next to your bed. (Often the moments immediately after awakening are a creative goldmine!) It cannot be written in large enough letters:

Ideas are the most important part of every illustration.

KATJA KAMM

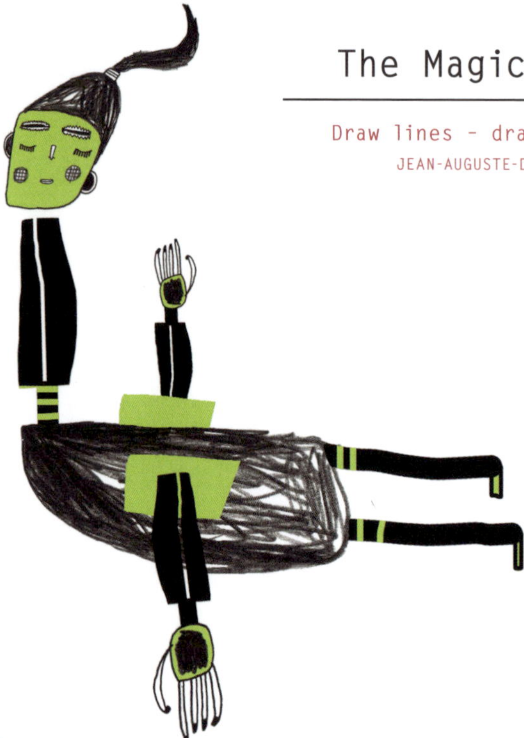

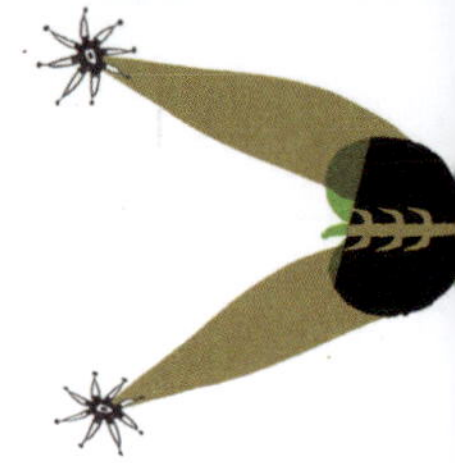

The Magic of Making

Draw lines – draw a lot of lines.
JEAN-AUGUSTE-DOMINIQUE INGRES

The truth is that you can generate ideas with research, with hard work and with cognitive processes, but it's not a *must*. On the contrary, one of the simplest ways to your idea is to just start *making*.

Start drawing. Pick up a piece of cheap paper and your favorite pencil and get going. Start with one small aspect or one little detail, with a sideshow or the main character. Start with whatever comes. You'll see: Almost every time, your first little visualization will be met with a full-grown visual idea.

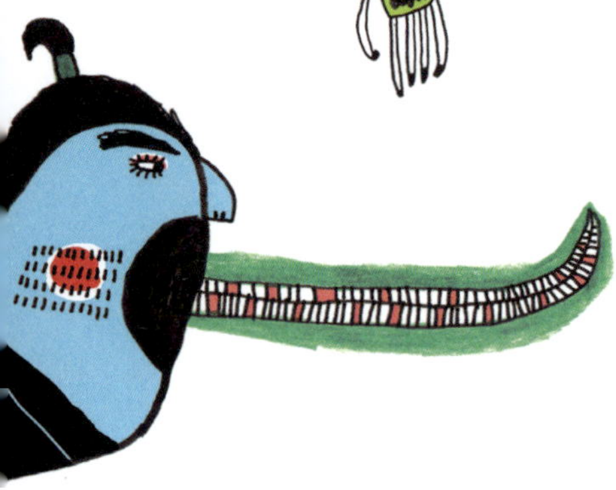

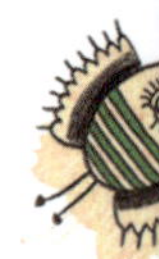

It's a little like magic: Making produces new ideas.

Every illustrator knows what I'm talking about. If you just draw away and let the pen flow, the ideas come flying in all by themselves. It has little to do with chance or luck. Visual ideas are generated through visual thinking. If you are searching for pictures in linguistic or conceptual structures, you will rarely find them. On the contrary, especially when it comes to picture ideas, to humor or to intuitive processes, too much rationality is actually counterproductive. You should rely more on your intuition here. And intuition in particular does not work very well under pressure. Therefore, allow your intuition to act as if it were having a friendly conversation rather than in a cross-examination.

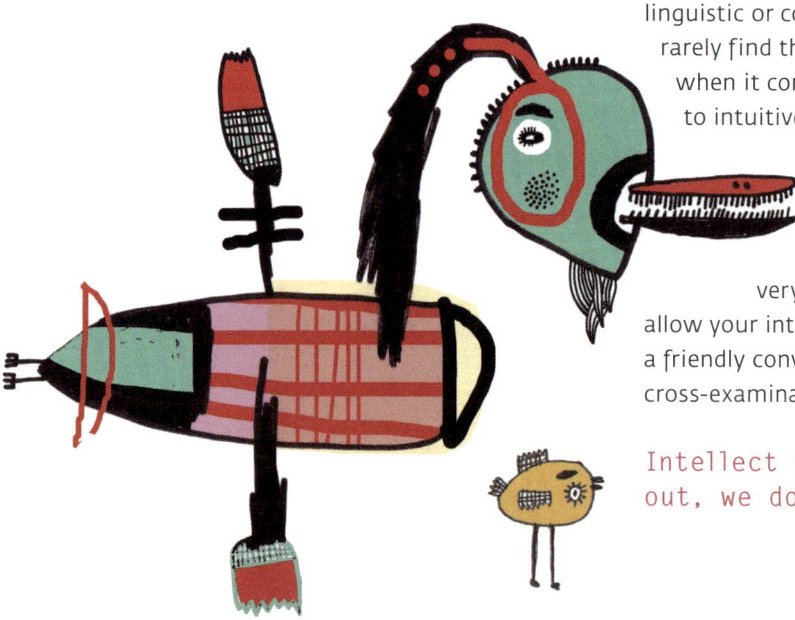

Intellect to intuition: "Spit it out, we don't have all day!"

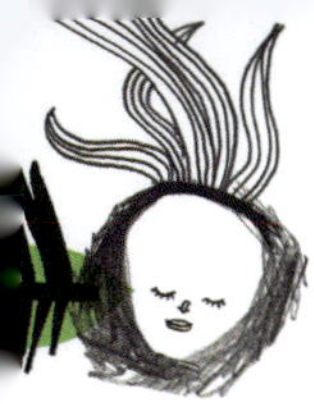

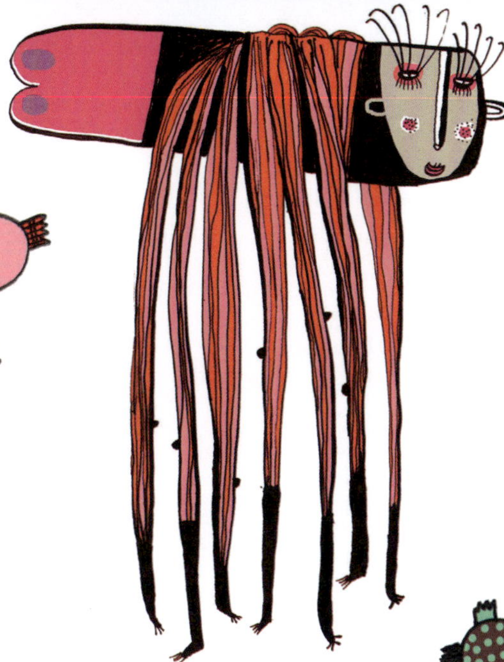

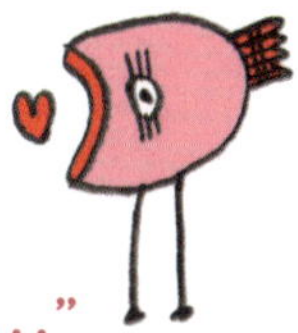

Intuition to intellect:
"I can't work under this kind of pressure! I'll say nothing without my attorney..."

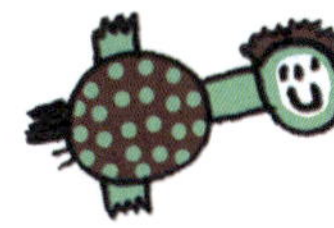

Instead, take advantage of the magic of making: just start scribbling. You will be dealing with the subject, but in a simple and playful way. For one thing, this lowers your expectations on the result. They're "only" first drafts. At the same time you activate unconscious processes via association chains. A dash, a dot, a circle; a deer, a deer, a dog, period.

The seemingly aimless drawing approach proves to be quite expedient. "Incidental" doodles like those we make while on the phone show the great ideas we can have when we don't try to force ourselves to have good ideas. They work so well because we're not always self-censoring. Self-censorship is toxic for creativity. Thoughts like, "I can't draw it like that; it's not smart or funny or creative enough," block any creative approach. In fact, we need the *unoriginal*, *unfunny* and *unintellectual* intermediate steps; most good ideas have *stupid*, *ugly* or *boring* forerunners.
If we don't allow ourselves to think in intermediate steps, we'll never move forward. This is where making is useful. Draw to see what you think.

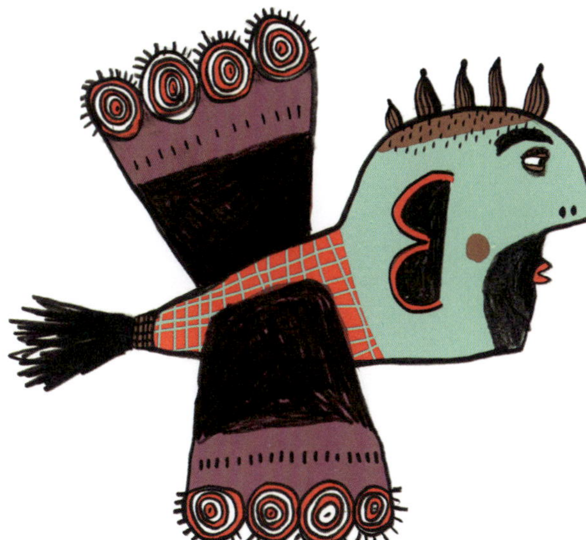

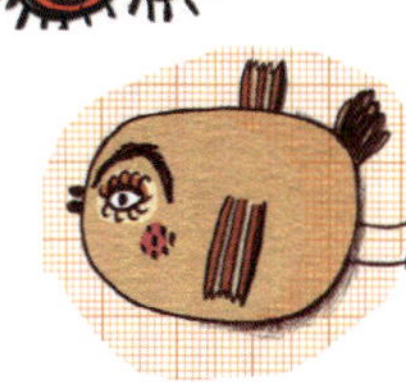

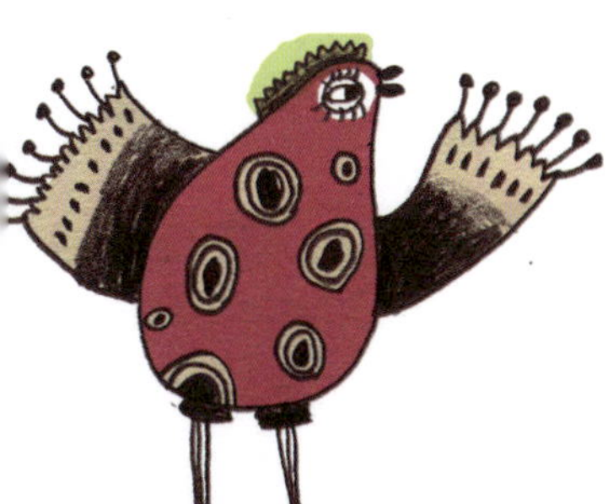

So my advice is: Just start. You'll see that after one or two detours, the really good ideas will appear like magic.

The Search for Your Personal Style

You can tell it's a good idea when it's stolen.
RUDI CARRELL

How do you discover your personal style? It ought to be different, new and distinctive! Refreshing and likeable, profound and have a high recognition value. A style that's not too superficial, perhaps a tad shocking, but also marketable. Sounds good. –

But how do we find our style? Do we have to search for it, like for a buried treasure or a lost sock?

Some explanation is in order here: Personal style is something that does not exist apart from us. It is inside us and is found not by *searching*, but by *doing*. Nevertheless, we often hear students bemoaning that they are already in their third semester and *still* don't have their personal style. Interestingly enough, a painter 500 years ago – say in the Dürer or Cranach generation – would not have thought so much about his personal style. They might have wondered if the way they represented something was appropriate, or deliberated over painting methods or the impact of an image. (It's even more likely that they wondered who would buy the artwork in the end.)

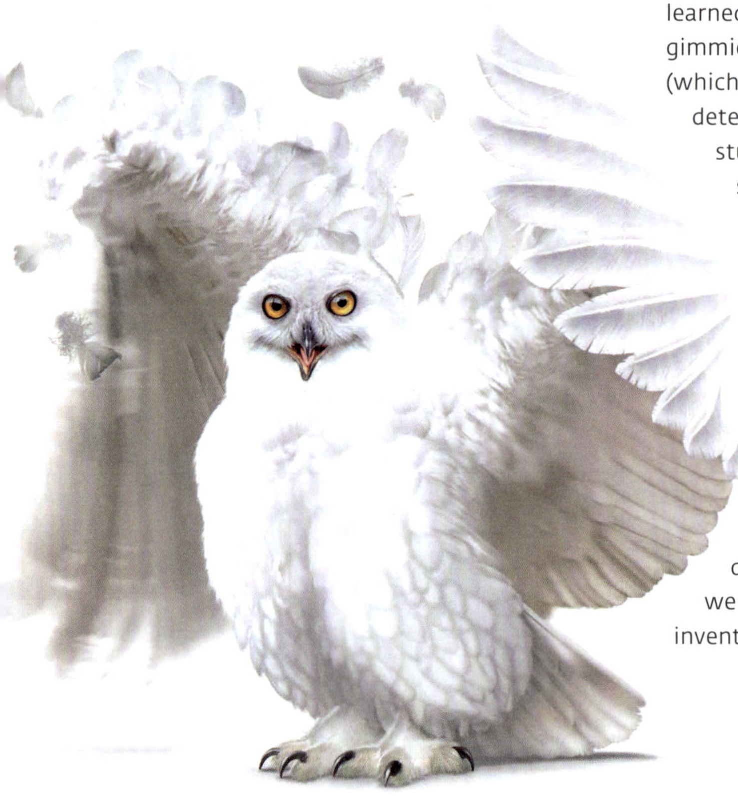

Personal expression would have been at most rated second or third in importance by them. In the painting schools of those days they learned to paint by copying. Tricks and gimmicks were passed down by the masters (which is why it's sometimes difficult to determine if a picture is by the master or student). For earlier generations, personal style was not a question. They would not have interpreted the remark, "that reminds me of ..." as criticism, but as praise.

The reason we think in terms of unique selling points today (and drive ourselves a little nuts doing do) is a cultural phenomenon: Our society has benefited from innovations in recent centuries. The technical and cultural developments since the Renaissance were only made possible by many inventions.

JÖRG SCHULTZ OLAF HAJEK

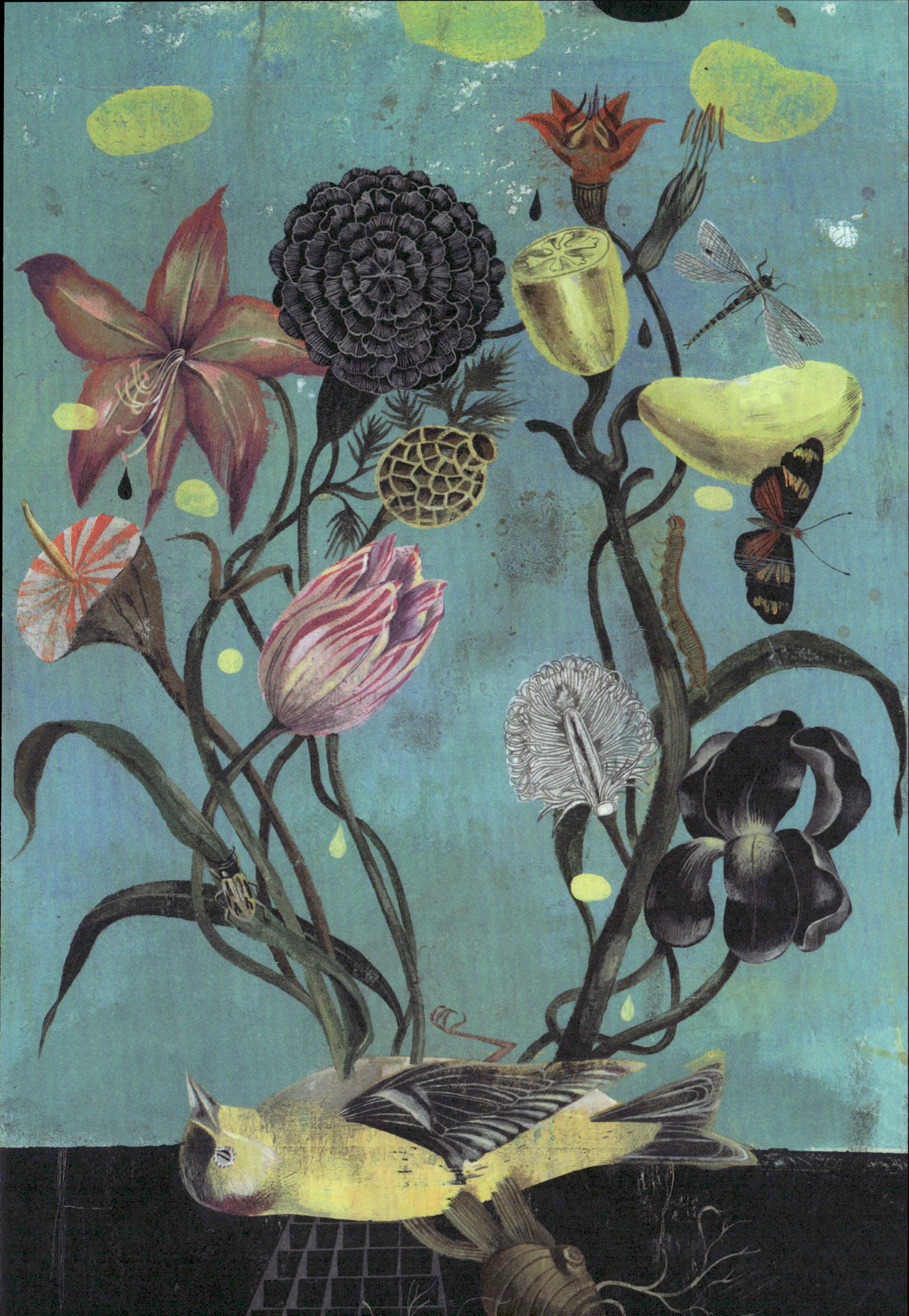

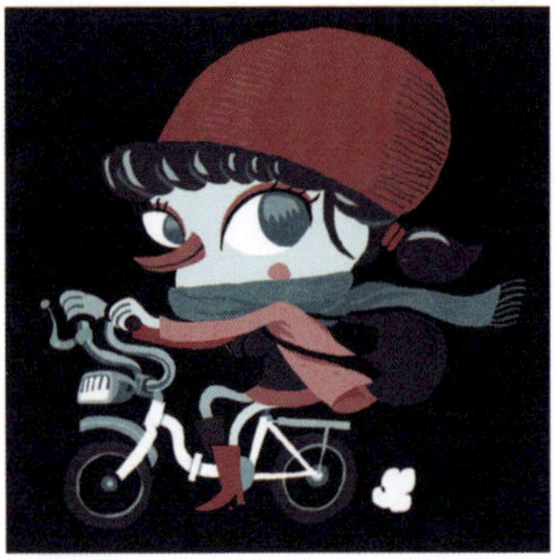

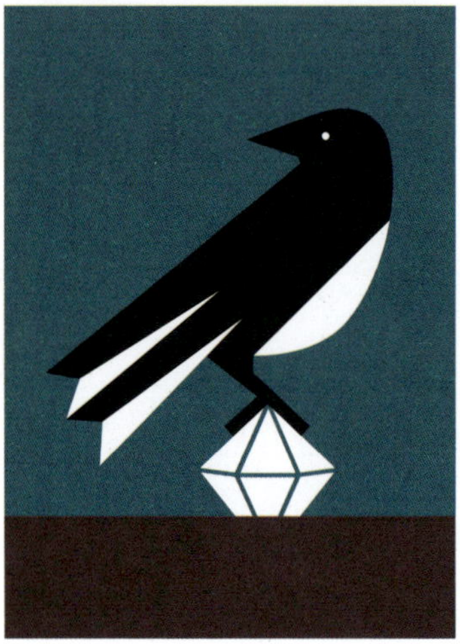

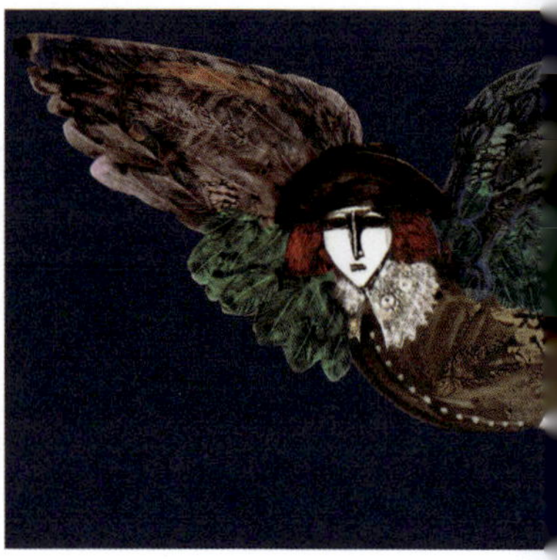

That is why innovation is seen so positively in our society. Galileo and Gutenberg, Da Gama, Newton and Curie determined the course of history. We, the witnesses of world history, then assign each new invention to one inventor simply because that is easier to communicate.

We therefore think in terms of "originators" who advance innovation.

In fact, developments, be they technical or cultural, arise quite differently: No art style simply emerges like a jack-in-the-box.
Cultural phenomena almost always build on one another. Art styles emerge as the result of viewpoints, tools, technological developments and fashions. They arise in a "climate," and usually they are created by several individuals who mutually influence one another. However, usually only the most decisive representatives of a movement are remembered. The viewer sees only the picture. For us "makers" that's different: Pictures aren't there all of a sudden, they have to be painted. For us, pictures are developmental processes. You scribble around, have or develop ideas, make sketches, experiments, devise protagonists, the foreground, background, build the picture piece by piece. So, we look at pictures as processes; we don't have the finished picture in front of us like the viewer does, simply because it doesn't exist yet. We work in intermediate steps. What color is the protagonist's dress, does the cat look to the left or the right, or should there be another building in the background?
Depending on which pen she chooses, which color she considers suitable or which frame she prefers, the illustrator determines how her picture develops. A picture is not a finished object for the maker, but the result of a chain of decisions and these decisions shape his or her style. For the process of creation is simply a matter of our preferences. We choose what we like or what our hands make well. We make our decisions according to these criteria and what we call a "personal style" emerges as an accumulation of all these minor decisions.
Personal style happens automatically. The longer we work, the clearer this style becomes.

For an artist, personal style is not something you can slip on like a jacket. There are, however, two factors that we can use to influence it: inspiration and experimentation.

MAX FIEDLER

KATHARINA J HAINES

HERBERT HOLZING

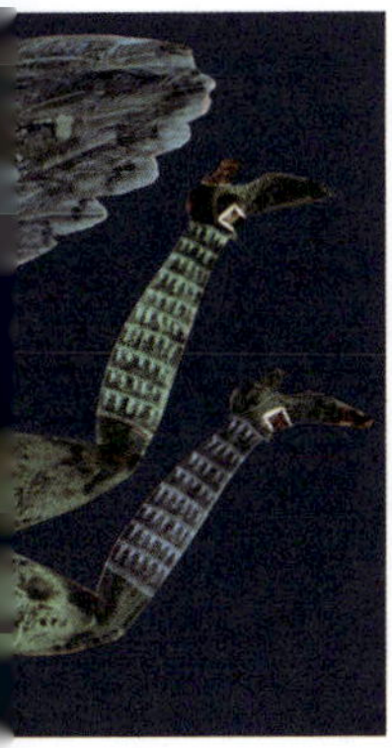 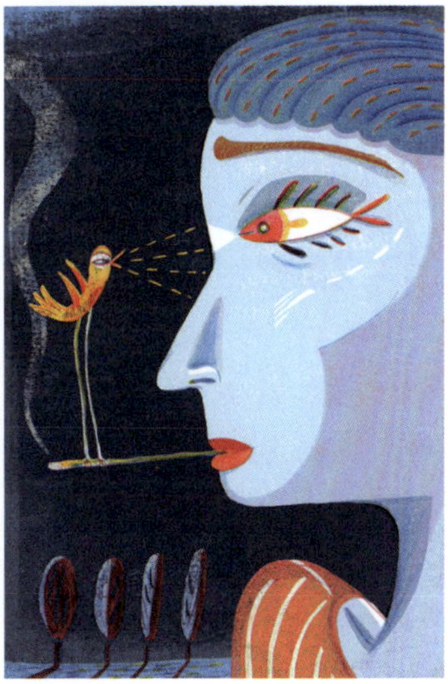 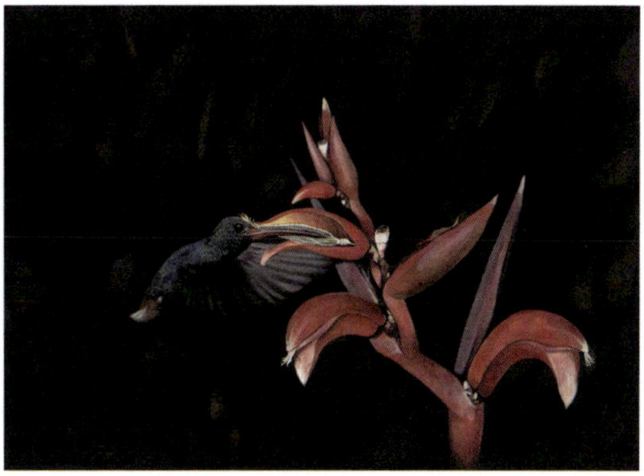

Let's start with inspiration. Dealing with the subject supports our decision-making skills and thus our personal style. Precisely because it is about decision-making processes, it is helpful to obtain input from the outside. This can involve a theoretical discussion, for example in talking to colleagues, visiting exhibits, specialist literature, etc. But it can also be the technique of another illustrator that broadens our horizons and therefore influences our way of thinking. You may like how someone else paints a nose, maybe a colleague's brush tips or how another person deals with a topic. If you don't make an exact copy of someone else's picture, but are just inspired by it, that's perfectly legitimate. Reinventing the wheel is a lot to ask.

The second important point is the joy of experimenting. Of course, we should not lose sight of the fact that to create something new we occasionally have to try something *new*. Taking up what others have been successful with is quite easy, because it will be appreciated by people's visual habits. But you are only innovative if you take a risk (even the risk of *not* pleasing others).

So, the bolder we advance our decision-making processes, the more resolute our personal style becomes. However, be aware that the term "personal style" is not a value in itself. I doubt you'd be happy with your personal style if it were a unique selling point for you but no one likes it – and even less if it had nothing to do with you at all.

The artistic dilemma is probably that we all want to be special yet still strive for acknowledgment. So, don't put the issue of "personal style" on too high a pedestal. Get to work, trust in your own taste and show us the world through your eyes!

Tip

Don't hesitate to try something new. You'll see that you're in good company. For example, the German illustrator Wolf Erlbruch used to be known primarily for advertising illustration, before he created a new style with his "little mole" in the 1990s and wrote illustration history. And before she brought her enchanting rabbit "Davy" to life in her relaxed watercolor style, the French illustrator Eve Tharlet was more known for detailed acrylic illustrations. As you can see, paradigm shifts are worthwhile!

ORIT BERGMAN

ANNIKA SIEMS

No Accounting for Taste?

Ninety percent of everything is shit.
A CLOCKWORK ORANGE, ANTHONY BURGESS, 1962

Taste – or what we call taste – is one of the most important basic skills an illustrator can possess.

Taste is that individual feel – an intuitive sense – for what's right and wrong in design.

Almost everything we do in this profession is based on it. Without good taste, we would lack the tool for deciding how to develop our illustrations. We would lack the ability to compare and, actually, everything we need to take an acceptable design stance. The feel for color, picture design, the feel for style, form and composition, as well as hundreds of decisions about content rely mainly on the oddly fuzzily defined notion of taste. But, what is this "taste" and how do we develop it? The awful truth is: there is no such thing as good taste – just personal taste. Because what we call good taste is by no means universally valid and there are no instructions that can teach you *good* or *bad*. This is because taste is a cultural phenomenon. For instance, if you were to compare books from Anglo-Saxon countries with those from Scandinavia, you'd discover striking differences in color schemes, layout and type. It becomes even more obvious if you take a look at Asia, at South America or parts of southeastern Europe. Beauty is not beauty, at least not if we look beyond our own noses. What's beautiful there is not what's beautiful here and my idea of beauty is certainly not the same as yours. Taste, also in illustration, is as diverse as the cultures of the world. It is associated with viewing habits that encompass all of human creativity. We find them in design, in apparel, architecture, art, etc. It's particularly noticeable in fashion. Perhaps what is considered sophisticated in Eastern Europe seems cheap and vamped up here at home while what we consider elegant understatement is perceived as scruffy in Eastern European countries (although this effect is losing some of its acuteness due to globalization and the Internet).

Taste is neither God-given nor genetically predisposed, but culturally experienced and influenced.

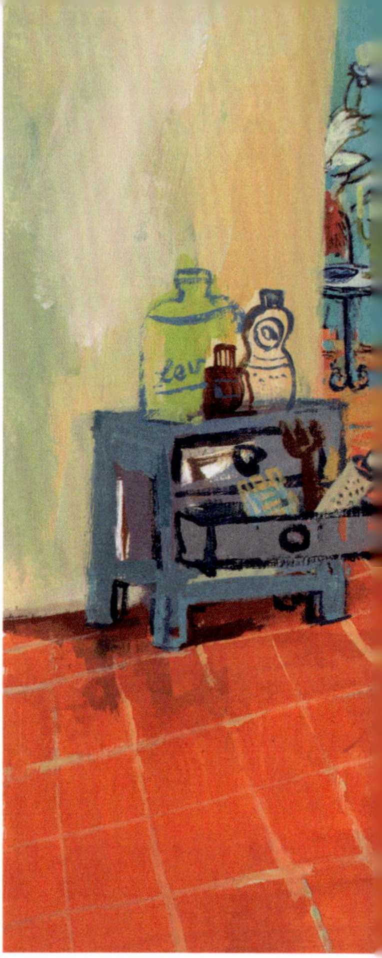

I imagine it might have all started something like this: One sweltering evening about 30,000 years ago, after endless wandering, the first humans finally reached the coast. Maybe they had come down from the mountains in search of food not long after they'd decided to stop being apes. So, here they stood on new shores, the Rift Valley of Africa behind them, swarms of birds above them and the ocean in front of them. Of course, they weren't familiar with the ocean since they had only ever seen lakes. So they decided to divide up the group. Half

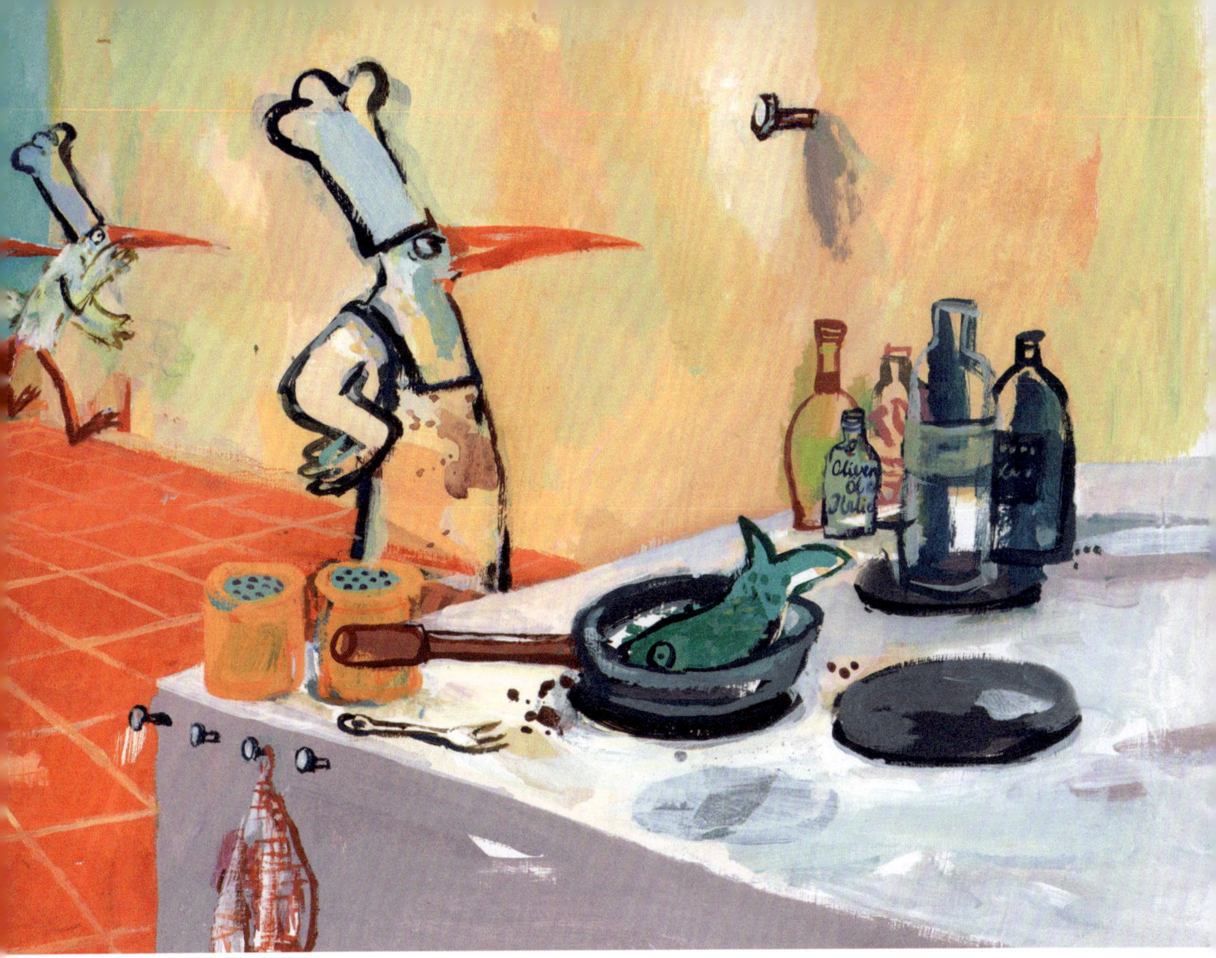

should walk to the left along the coast and the other half to the right. And when they had walked around the "lake," they would meet and sit down to decide which side of the lake they should settle on. They would celebrate a feast and sing their old songs together. And off they went; one group with the sun at their backs, the other group facing the glow of the setting sun. Alas, the lake turned out to be the ocean and it would take millennia before they had walked all of the shorelines and the many different descendants of the two groups met again and faced each other perplexed. For around the countless fires in the meantime they and their old songs had changed. The group that had crossed snow-covered mountains had perhaps added a verse about the cold. And those who had encountered wild animals had perhaps added one about the lions. They had continued to weave verses into their song, added to it, rewritten it, they had evolved other languages, rituals and arts and every one of them had forgotten the promise they had made to each other back then to celebrate a feast when they met again.

Now they stood facing one another as strangers and glared mistrustfully at the others without recognizing them...

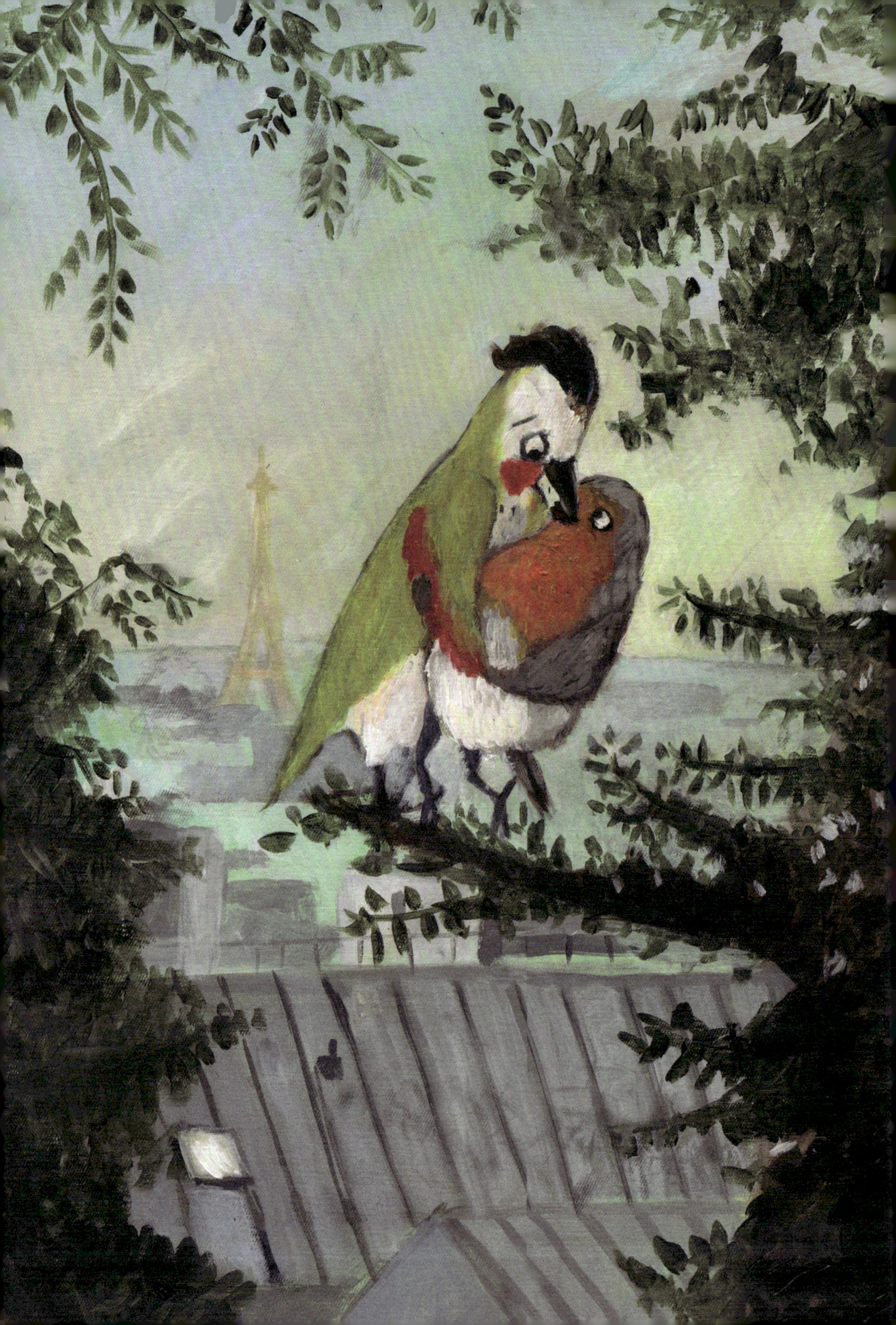

Viewpoints, including aesthetic ones, are related to experience. Life circumstances create preferences and aversions, societies cultivate beneficial ones or invent divisive ones because at one certain point in time their evolution benefitted from them. So taste is not universally valid because we humans have had different experiences at different times and in different places.

At the same time, every individual goes through a very personal and unique learning process when it comes to taste. For every individual can develop taste, more or less. It is a result of a conscious or unconscious examination of culture (one's own or foreign cultures, yes, even past cultures). The more you know about aesthetics, the more distinct your viewpoint about taste is.

Therefore, taste is equally personal and cultural.

Nonetheless, it is something all encompassing that affects practically every area of our lives. That's why you cannot train your taste sitting alone at your drawing table or computer. Taste thrives on interconnections. It is a fuzzily outlined phenomenon that resides simultaneously in many different areas.

We encounter taste in everyday life, in the designed environment, in architecture, art and product design, but it also at home in fashion, design and literature, in movies, accessories, in things we surround ourselves with, in music and even in cooking. Taste is just as personal as it is inevitably influenced by the zeitgeist. And in the way it helps us make aesthetic decisions; conversely our aesthetic decisions help us to further train our sense of taste. This is why it is important to surround ourselves – even outside of our own genre – with things that are "tasteful." "There's no accounting for taste," they say. But it's not given to us in the cradle. In reality, taste is a question of viewpoint, cultural evolution and the aesthetic development of each of us. Perhaps it could best be called "aesthetic intelligence."

And like every type of intelligence, we can also cultivate and develop taste.

We should always be willing to do so. After all, it's how we make our living.

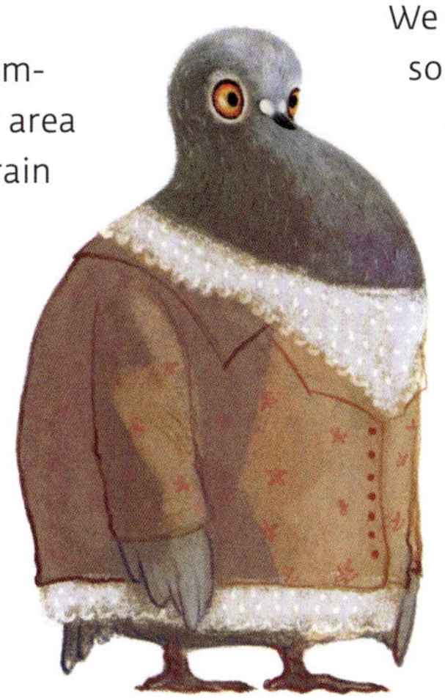

Bad is the New Good

What is new is seldom good; because a good thing is only new for a short time.
ARTHUR SCHOPENHAUER

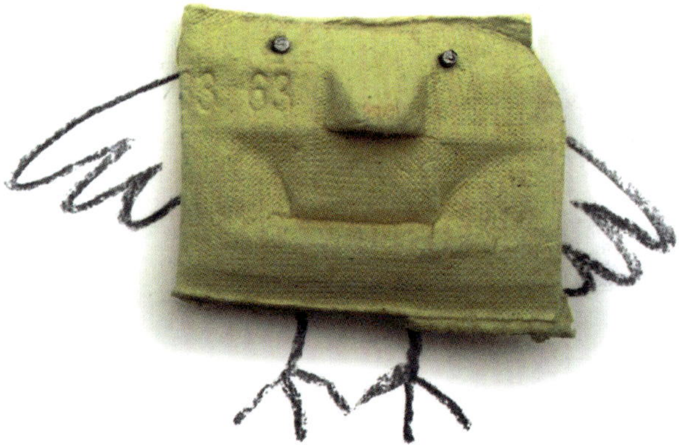

The recent advance of digital media stimulated a strange phenomenon: *charm* has become a new, crucial factor in design. The reaction to the ultra-perfected, high gloss illustrations of the 1990s and 2000s was to flirt with unfinished imperfection.

The scene is dominated by work that is a tad charmingly "slap-dash," a mixture of "inept" and "ingenious."

Bad is the new good. The gloss of the digital revolution seems to have promoted a counter-movement: the punk charm of the would-be authentic. Since it became possible to generate lifelike three-dimensional textures and slick pseudo realities, many designers felt the need for something more "real." The scene is in the grips of an analog renaissance: silkscreens and stencils, hand drawings and drafts.

Not by chance, an ever more predictable, overly modernized and rarely surprising reality has led to a call for authenticity. We yearn for true feelings and genuine ideas, for crocheting lessons and RVs, for Super 8, chickenpox and beer from a can, in other words, for real life.

It goes so far that we transition to generating a "genuine" and "authentic" aesthetic by, for example, layering smooth computer-generated

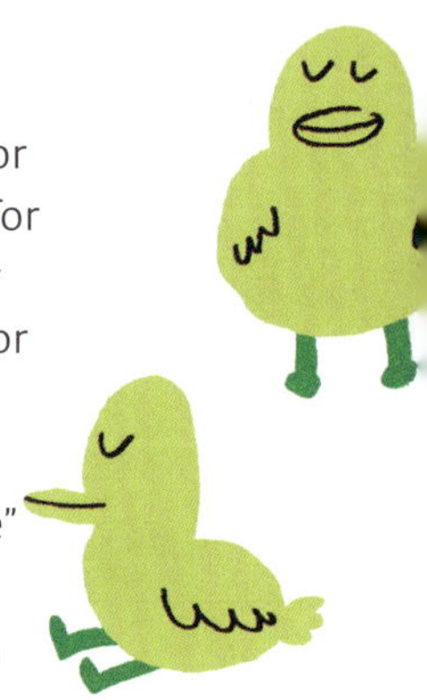

MEIKE STAATS

SARAH VARON

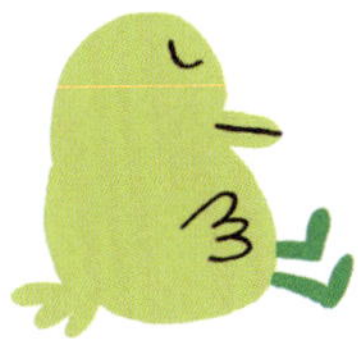

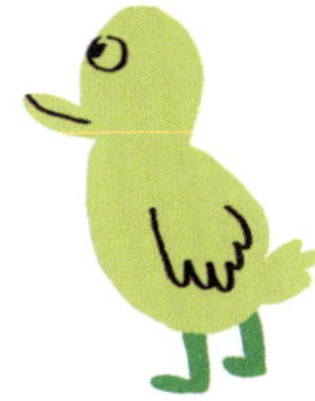

illustrations with a handmade old-style texture or by technically imitating imperfections in printing techniques. The success of photo apps like Hipstamatic speaks for itself. The trend is logical, but it also raises questions. For starters, it is good for us to distance ourselves from the excessive "polish" of the pure surface and to strive for substance. It is also understandable that the digital revolution focused on technicality and formality and thus promoted some empty content. From this perspective, a content renaissance is welcome.

Yet we should not allow this retro-trash aesthetic to become an end in itself. If we illustrators continue to neglect ideas and merely create *genuine-looking fakes*, we are at risk of making ourselves dispensable. It is quite thinkable that clients might soon decide to generate simplified design lines on their own. Agencies in particular will ask themselves why they are paying for a high-priced pro when the result can be imitated just as well by an unpaid intern.

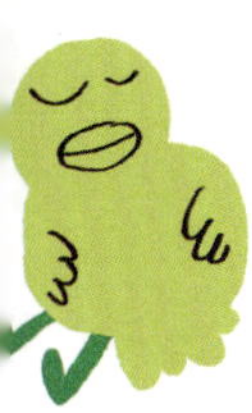

Therefore, it would be wise to remember what we as artists actually seek. Essentially, we long for authenticity, for genuineness in an ever more "phony" world. Retro alone won't lead us there. The problem is that this type of design was only genuine at that time. It was alive and truly the state of the art *back then*. Today, this style is genuine in a historic sense at best and has little to do with authenticity.

Art brut is doubtless enchanting, refreshing and charming, but it occasionally neglects the design basis.

> Therefore, don't forget that good illustration thrives on substance.

It needs both surface and depth. When bad becomes the new good there is always a risk that yesterday's new will rapidly become today's old. So don't rely on it entirely, but develop your own language. Then, I'm certain, you'll do your work well.

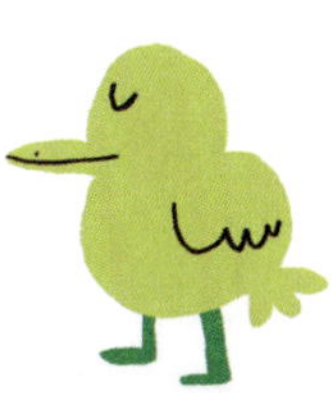

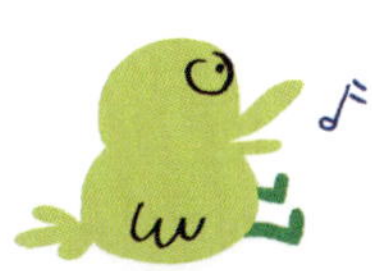

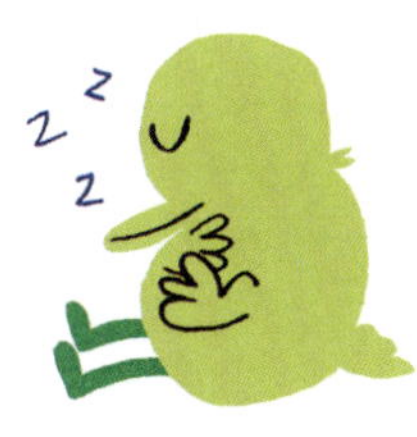

No Pain, No Gain

Today I'm an artist and that's wonderful, but originally I just didn't want to go to work.

FUNNY VAN DANNEN 1999

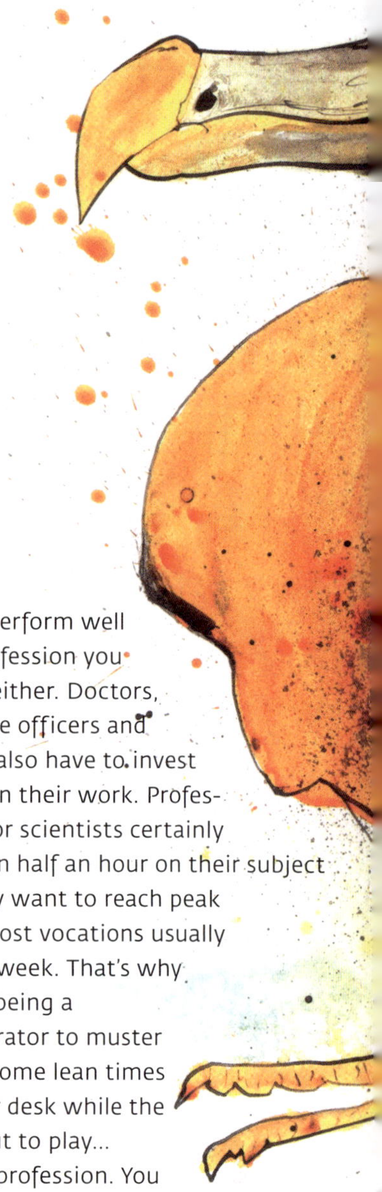

It may sound a bit hackneyed, but the phrase "Practice Makes Perfect" is nothing short of the truth. A lot of what we do is, alongside spontaneity and creativity, also the result of practice, diligence and intense examination. When we look at the (often highly virtuosic) work of our more experienced colleagues, we have to admit that for the most part it is usually so ingenious because the artists have been doing it for so long. Through years (oh, yes!) of practice and dealing with a material we internalize our way of working to a degree that makes its impact ever more accurate and playful. Practice *makes* perfect! In fact, only a few of us are born prodigies. On a closer look, most of the examples cited of this turn out to be less inherited talent than the result of hard work: Mozart would never have become what he was without the (sometimes very harsh) guidance of his father Leopold. Picasso's father was a painter who taught him at a young age. The composer Bach came from a composer dynasty. What at first seems to be the proof of inherited talent on closer examination proves to be a climate of engagement, constant, diligent work that made those artists what they are or were. No one is born a master. They are made or they make themselves. What may be sobering at first holds a great opportunity:

It doesn't matter where and when you start: sticking with it is what decides your career.

If you want to perform well in any other profession you cannot be lazy either. Doctors, musicians, police officers and dance teachers also have to invest time and work in their work. Professional athletes or scientists certainly spend more than half an hour on their subject every day if they want to reach peak performance. Most vocations usually have a 40-hour week. That's why it's also part of being a successful illustrator to muster discipline, overcome lean times and stay at your desk while the other kids go out to play... Illustration is a profession. You will only create good illustrations if you see illustration as work and do not misunderstand it only as something you identify with. The bad news: You have to stick to it. The good news: It's worth it.

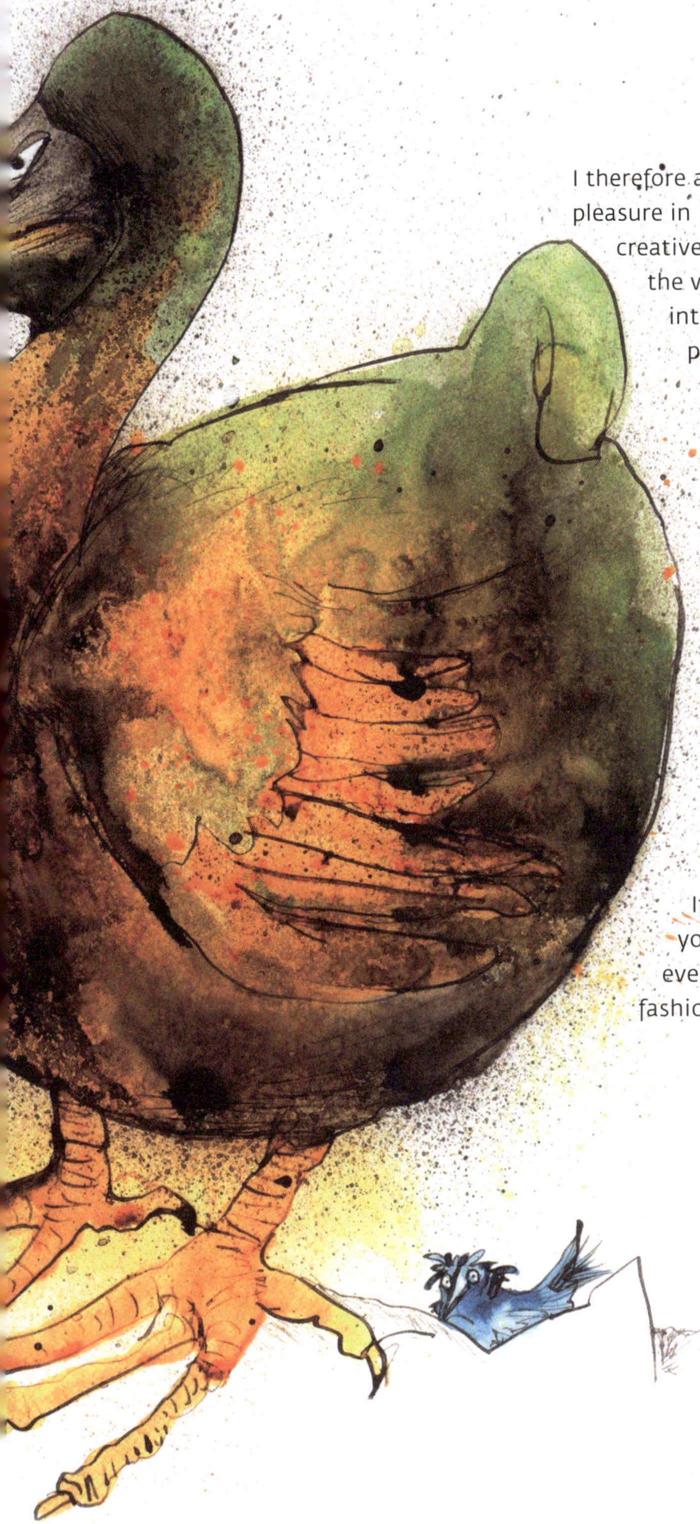

I therefore advise you to maintain your pleasure in it. After all, we have a wonderful, creative profession and thanks to our work the world is more colorful, beautiful and interesting. So try to maintain the passion and interest that you started out with and maintain the pleasure of illustrating as your engine. At the same time, don't drop your brush just because things aren't going well or you get stuck.

In reality, every successful illustrator I know possesses two traits:

1. They enjoy and love what they do.
2. They are disciplined on days when they don't.

If you maintain both of these traits you'll be successful in your field. So even if the phrase sounds terribly old fashioned, it's true: No pain, no gain.

Searching the Internet

"... a wealth of information creates a poverty of attention ..."
HERBERT A. SIMON

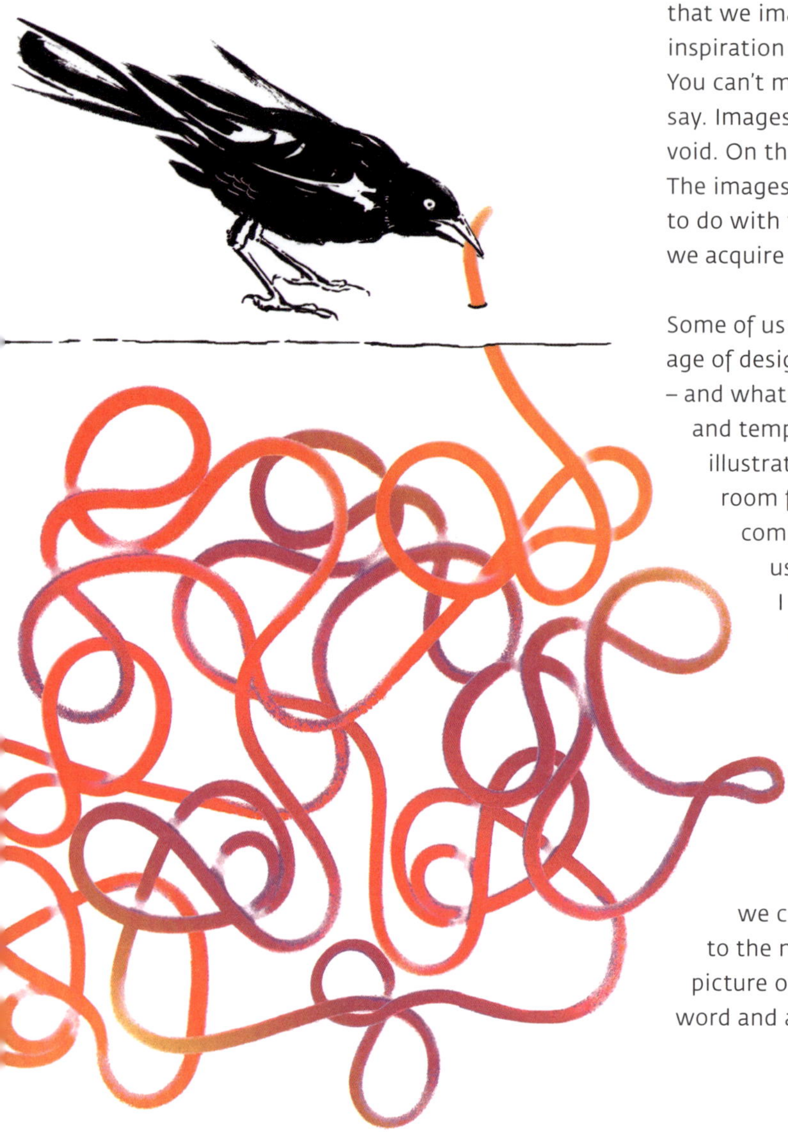

Images are omnipresent: images that surround us, images that caress us or harass us, images that inform us, delight us or entertain us. So it's not surprising that we image-makers often derive our inspiration for new images from other images. You can't make something out of nothing, they say. Images in particular aren't produced in a void. On the contrary, images beget images. The images we create always have something to do with the images that inspire us, so where we acquire our images is very important.

Some of us still remember of the Pleistocene age of design – the "days before computers" – and what effort went into collecting images and templates. Until only a few years ago an illustrator friend of mine still had an entire room full of archived clippings neatly compiled in file folders that he made use of when needed.

I remember that as a student I once had to spend about $45 for a specialized book on hunting because it was all I could find containing acceptable photos of foxes. At the time, that was a lot of money for me.

Digitalization has certainly made work easier for us. Two clicks and we can make our way from one image to the next. Today, if I'm looking for a picture or a template, I just "google" the key word and all I need is at my fingertips.

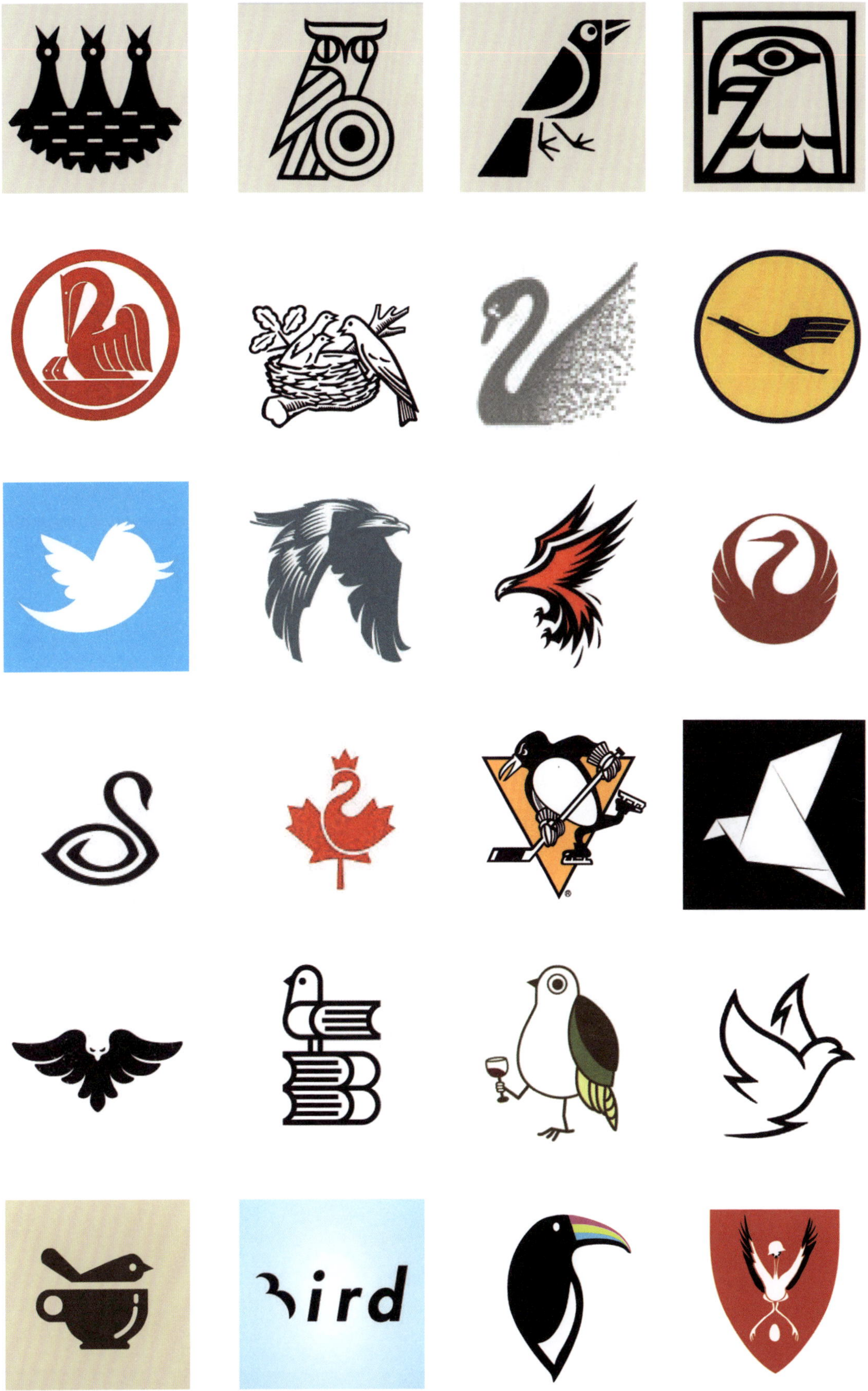

In spite of all these advantages, there's a minor catch: paradoxically, the millions of images that the World Wide Web provides us increasingly put us at risk of being visually impoverished. Water, water everywhere and not a drop to drink – why? Search engines are hierarchically arrangement according to the most frequent requests. This means we are always promptly supplied with the most-clicked-on images and they are always the same. To use my example from the Stone Age, if we all search for an image of a "fox," our screens will inevitably display the same fox. Hence, the Internet is stuck in the same dilemma as a public library where, in spite of its inventory of millions of books, the ones most often borrowed are those near the entrance. This wouldn't be so bad (boring at most) if we creatives weren't so urgently dependent on originality. When we always use the same templates we are always going to produce the same work. We repeat and create variations on only the familiar instead of really creating something innovative.

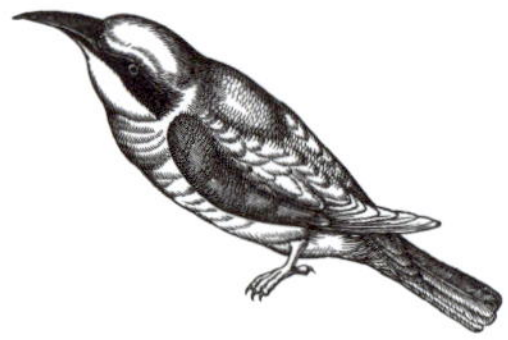

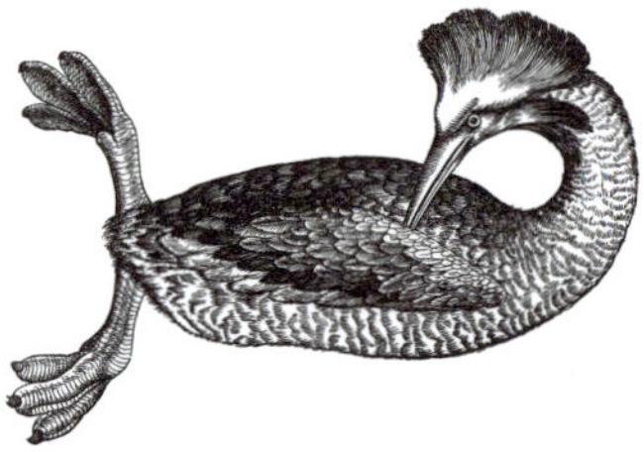

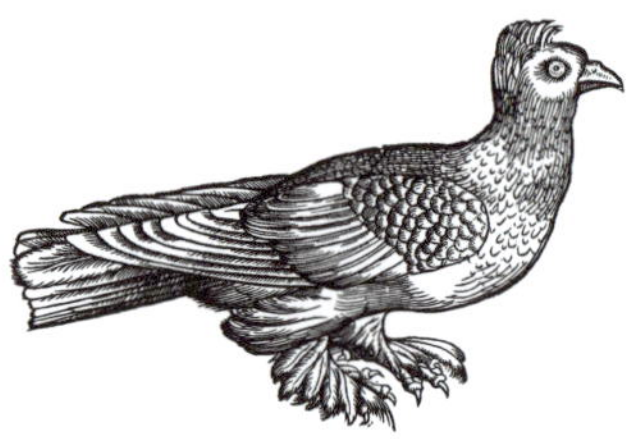

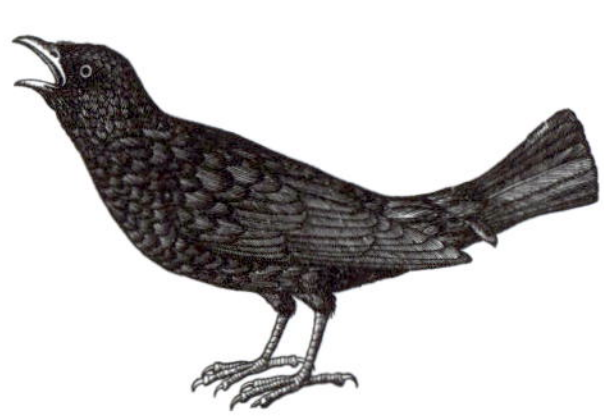

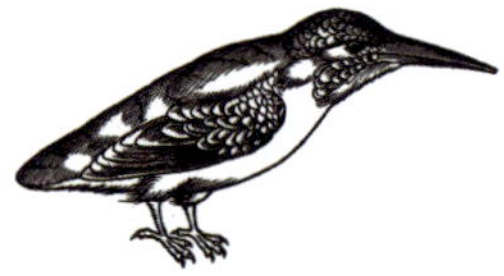

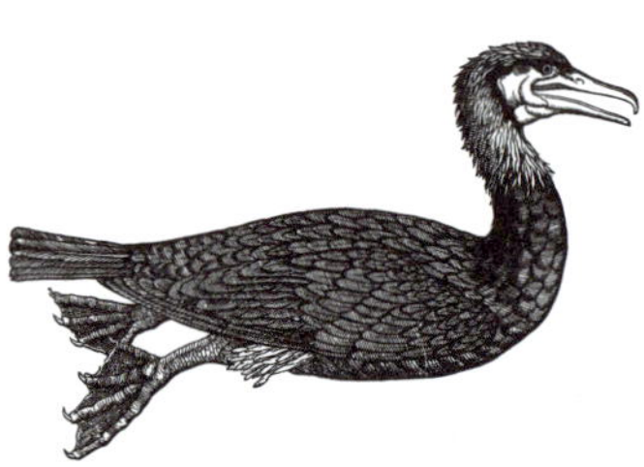

We won't find anything new on the Internet, but only what others saw, made or provided before us. This increases the probability that we will always be chasing after trends rather than setting trends ourselves. One way out of this dilemma is to leave the straight, fast and easy pathway now and then. On the old "crooked" pathway we meet our companions Chance, Error and Detour, but they offer plenty of creative potential.
Even in the digital age, we shouldn't underestimate how important chance finds, unplanned incidents and surprising encounters are for creative processes. When we draw something by hand we are creating something truly new that previously existed only in our own minds. When we enter into a creative process, research something unconventional or take an occasional step outside the front door, the change of perspective can often help us discover new territory. Consciously replace the mainstream now and then with your own wayside finds.

You can't google good ideas.

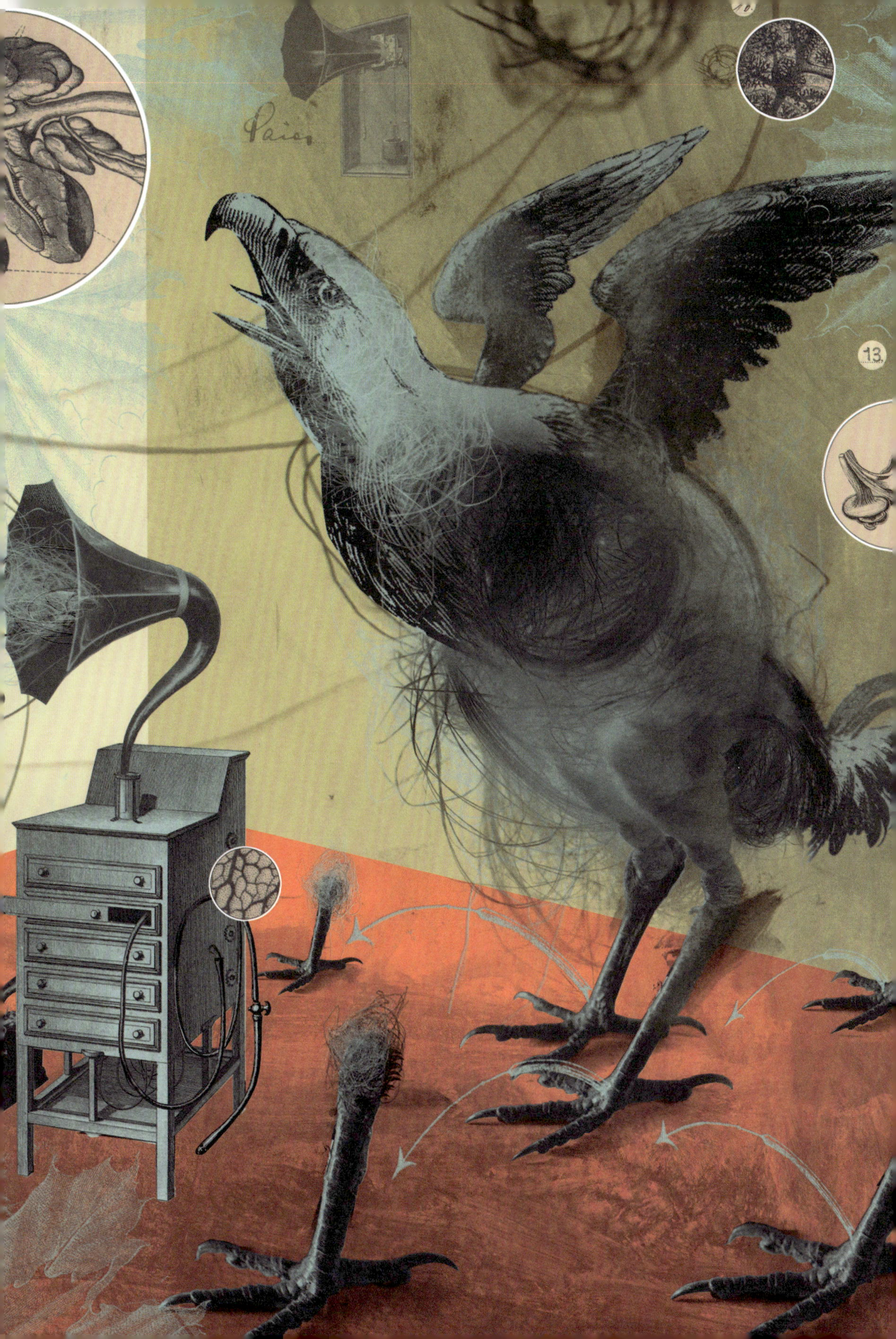
13

Truth Telling

It is the bright day that brings forth the adder.
JULIUS CAESAR, WILLIAM SHAKESPEARE, 1599

Illustrate comes from the Latin *illustrare* meaning *brighten* or *illuminate*. What we often disregard, though, is that pictures can also be used to obscure things and that illustration in particular can sometimes help to disguise the true state of affairs. We don't even need to look at the crude world of war propaganda, at evil images from past eras or totalitarian states; just look at advertising. There we'll find a nut-sugar-cocoa paste described as "vitamin-rich" (then in the small print that you'd have to eat pounds and pounds of it to cover the daily vitamin requirement) and many a sweet beverage passed off as "healthy."

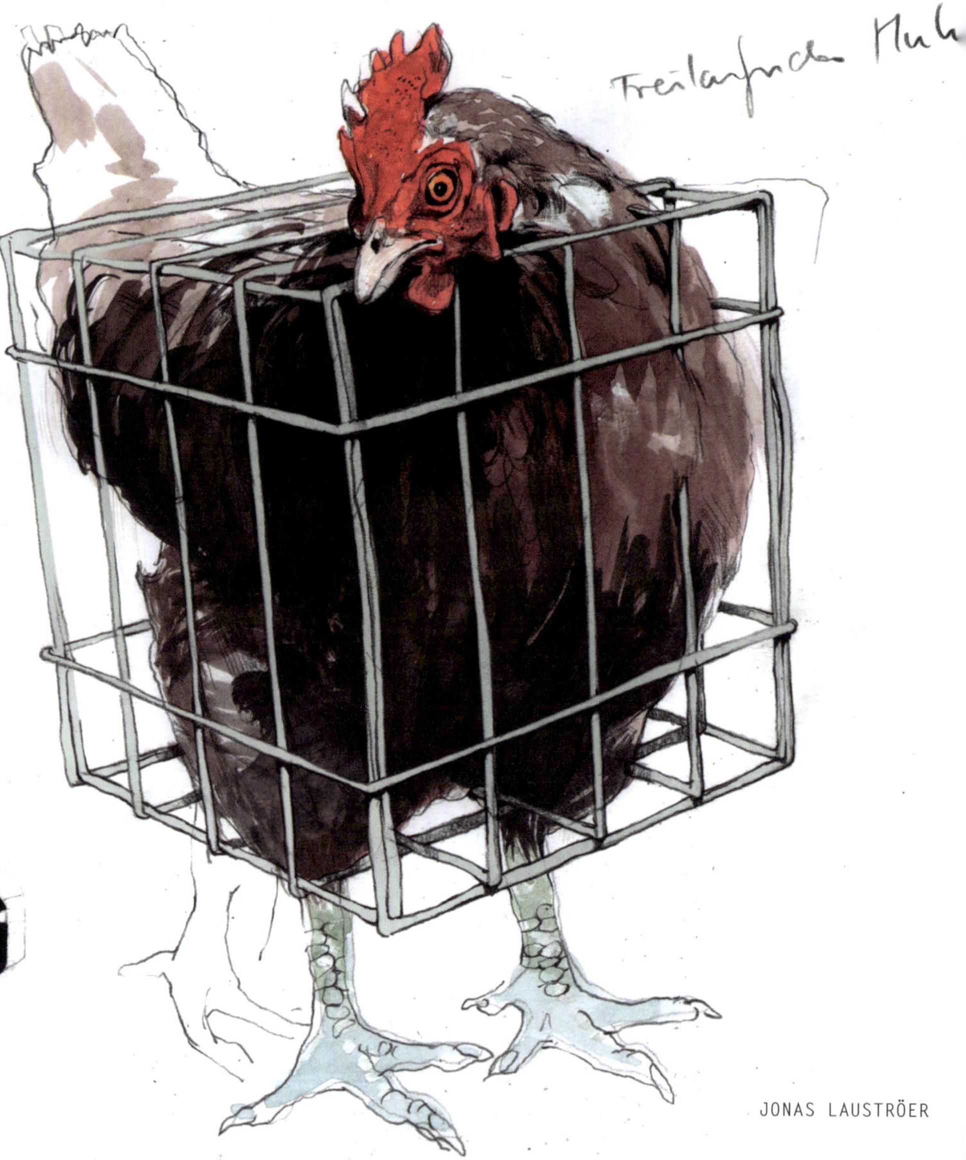

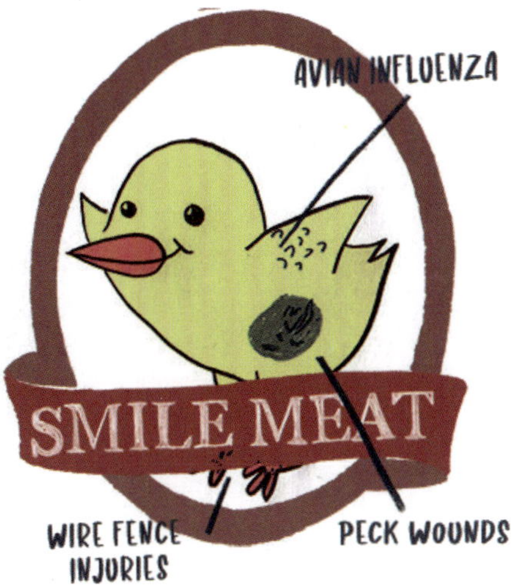

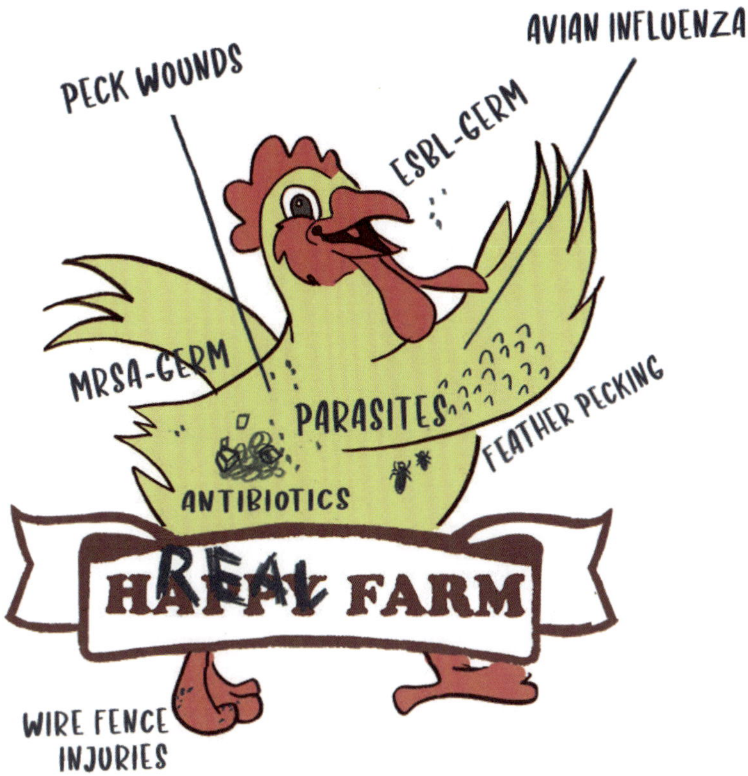

But it's not just the advertising messages that tell untruths, there are also pictures that lie. For example, when you pass a livestock truck on the highway, there are happy cartoon pigs sometimes waving at you from the back of the truck. However, if you should risk a side glance as you drive by, you will realize that the animals in the hold are by no means like the pink pictograph above the logo. They don't look very jolly at all.

So *what* is being illustrated? Images influence our point of view here, too. The cheerful cartoon pigs are what make the excesses of factory farming possible, because no one wants to see bloody or cruel pictures on a truck. On the contrary, it's the cartoon pig lies that create our tacit acceptance.

Illustration is by no means trivial. It is certainly also responsible. If your pictures lie for an evil thing, they become part of the evil thing. I know how difficult it is to give up jobs from time to time. Right away you worry that you will NEVER, EVER get another job. But my advice is nonetheless to say no if you're expected to play the devil's advocate as an illustrator. When we go on an assignment as illustrators with ethics, we also gain respect for our very own cause. And that will also pay off economically in the long term.

Variety

Variatio delectat.
CICERO

When was the last time you tried something really new? Routine is toxic to creativity. Very soon, you may be at risk of always composing pictures according to "Scheme F," of producing the same old same old illustrative soup. The fact that this is true has positive reasons: our preferences.

The same way that you might like to have cereal or a donut for breakfast, our artistic spectrum also contains likes and dislikes. This is normal and not a bad thing as such. We all have our own specific band-widths, be they preferred subjects, say, if you like animals or portraits; design mediums or techniques we like to use the most; or ways of framing a picture, color hues or pictorial ideas.

We are not always aware that we prefer certain things. (For outsiders, though, it's often quite recognizable – it pays to ask.)

We just choose these means, sometimes through routine, in part because of technical possibilities or simply personal taste. A little of what we call our "personal style" is behind this phenomenon. It wouldn't even be worth mentioning here if it didn't involve one little trap: It becomes an issue when we are not producing *one*, but a series of illustrations.

Pictures often appear in series. Many of the products we work for contain more than one illustration. For example, if we work for books, create a storyboard or draw for a film, we are talking about multiple pictures. And when pictures follow one another in a series – for instance in a children's book – it can soon get boring if you illustrations are too similar in structure. Then it's of little use if each picture is superbly drawn because:

Even a series of superbly drawn, similar pictures is a series of similar pictures.

Let's go back to the example of food. If you were to serve a meal to people every day made of the same ingredients, at some point they would begin to complain. Even if your dishes each taste delicious – your guests would get sick of them eventually. "Variatio delectat," said the Romans or, as *we* say, variety is the spice of life.

For this reason, it is wise to be aware of structures and then

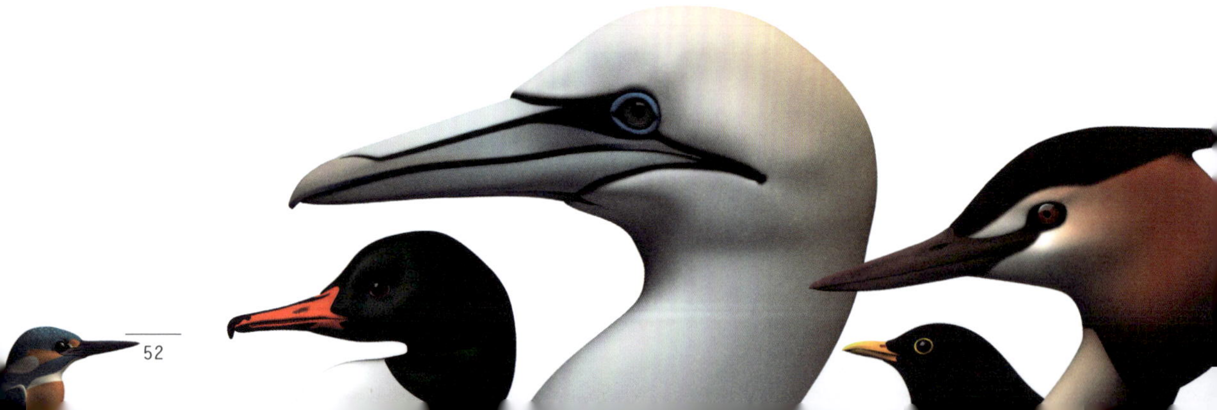

to play with them. And pictures in particular offer a great many possibilities for variation. You can use different colors: for instance if your last double page spread was mainly red, maybe its time for some green. There are also countless possibilities for the layout: a double page can be followed by a single page, a single page by one page of copy and then another double page. You can vary the subjects, perspectives and frames, you can depict different protagonists or play with the proportions.
So there are no limits to your imagination as long as you use it consciously. Small sketches are ideal for this. Series of illustrations need to be planned out for their entertainment value. First scribble your series and compare the pictures structurally. How often does the same character follow another? When is there a man, when is there a woman pictured? How often do you make a landscape and how often does the picture focus on details? Try following a wide view with a close-up and follow a close-up with a panorama view. You'll see: This will make your illustrations a lot more exciting than if you stage your picture series like a play where you are always sitting the same distance from the action like in a theater.

Tip

Get inspiration and practice. Variety is an attitude!
Try having something completely different for breakfast for a change. If you like cereal, maybe it's time for eggs. Try an exotic fruit you've never had and combine things in new ways: pineapple and Nutella or apples and peanut butter.
You'll see: Variety will not only pep up your illustrations, but your whole day!

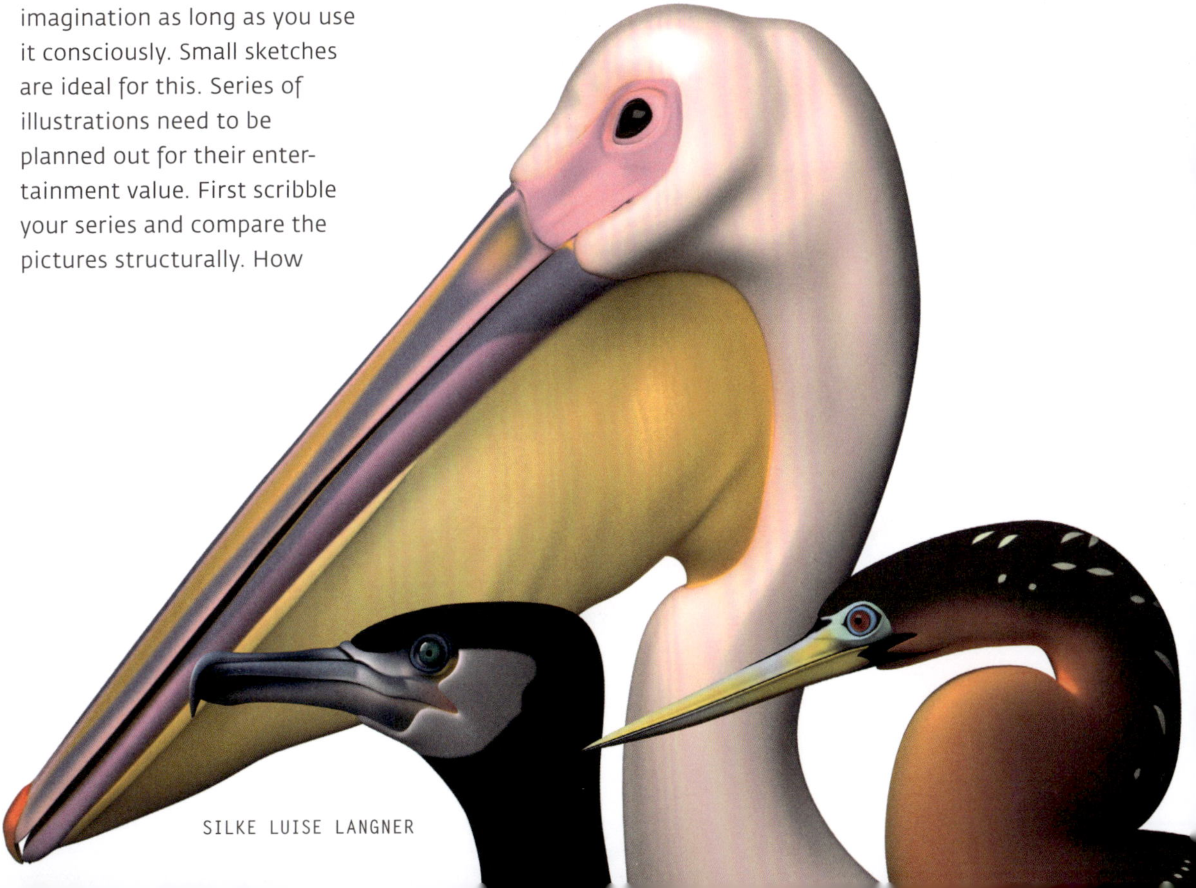

SILKE LUISE LANGNER

The Soul in the Sketch

Well, I've always liked simple rock. JOHN LENNON, 1971

Do you ever have the problem that sometimes your drafts look a lot freer than your finished illustrations? That the lightness and charm of the initial sketch seem to get lost during production?

Really, sometimes it's exasperating: Drawings that we just "throw down" are often so unique that we can't seem to reproduce them, try as we might. On the contrary, the more often you draw something new, the longer you work on something and the more finished and precise it seems to get, the more you endanger your work of losing its "soul."

It starts with the preliminary drawing. For instance, if you trace the first sketch for your illustration on a light table the results get worse with nearly every copy.

The original drawing was made briskly and directly, but every new version gets to look more and more routine. The illustration fades. Formally speaking, it may get better and more orderly, the details seem optimized – the nose gets better and the dog in the lower left corner – but overall the picture seems to have paled. It's mysterious. It gets even worse when we begin work on the actual illustration. As soon as we work on proper Bristol or watercolor paper and not on scratch paper, the picture seems to lose more and more charisma compared with the draft. It's almost as if it were jinxed: every hour we spend adding details and textures, our picture gets lamer and lamer. What to do? The easiest way to escape the dilemma might be to always illustrate as if we were sketching. But that would probably lead to a new crux: If you did, the sketches wouldn't come as easily and you'd be faced with the same problem – just sooner. Plus we can't very well declare sketches as "finished" and present them to our clients for:

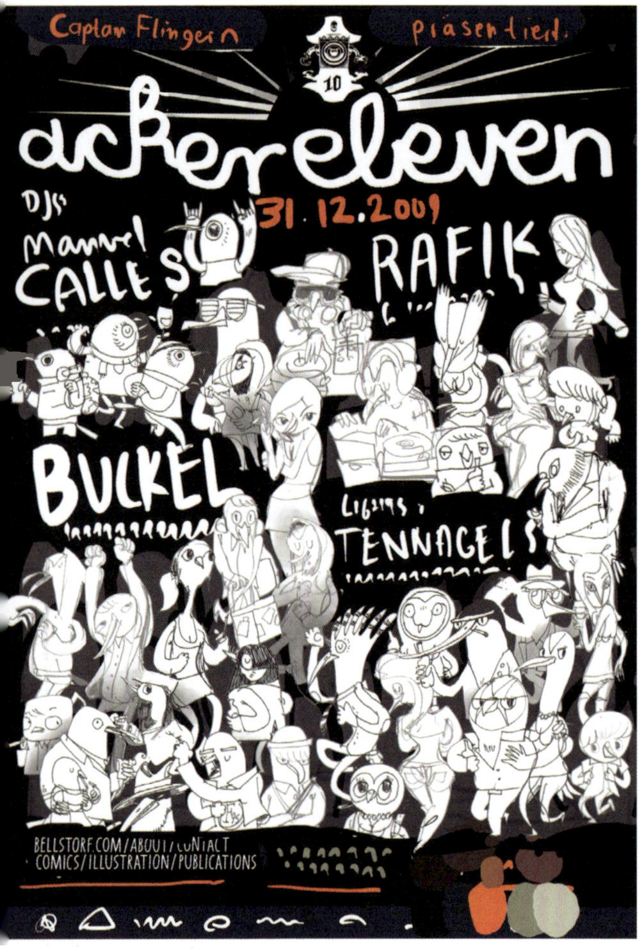

Preliminary drawing for an event poster

The care taken in production also creates quality.

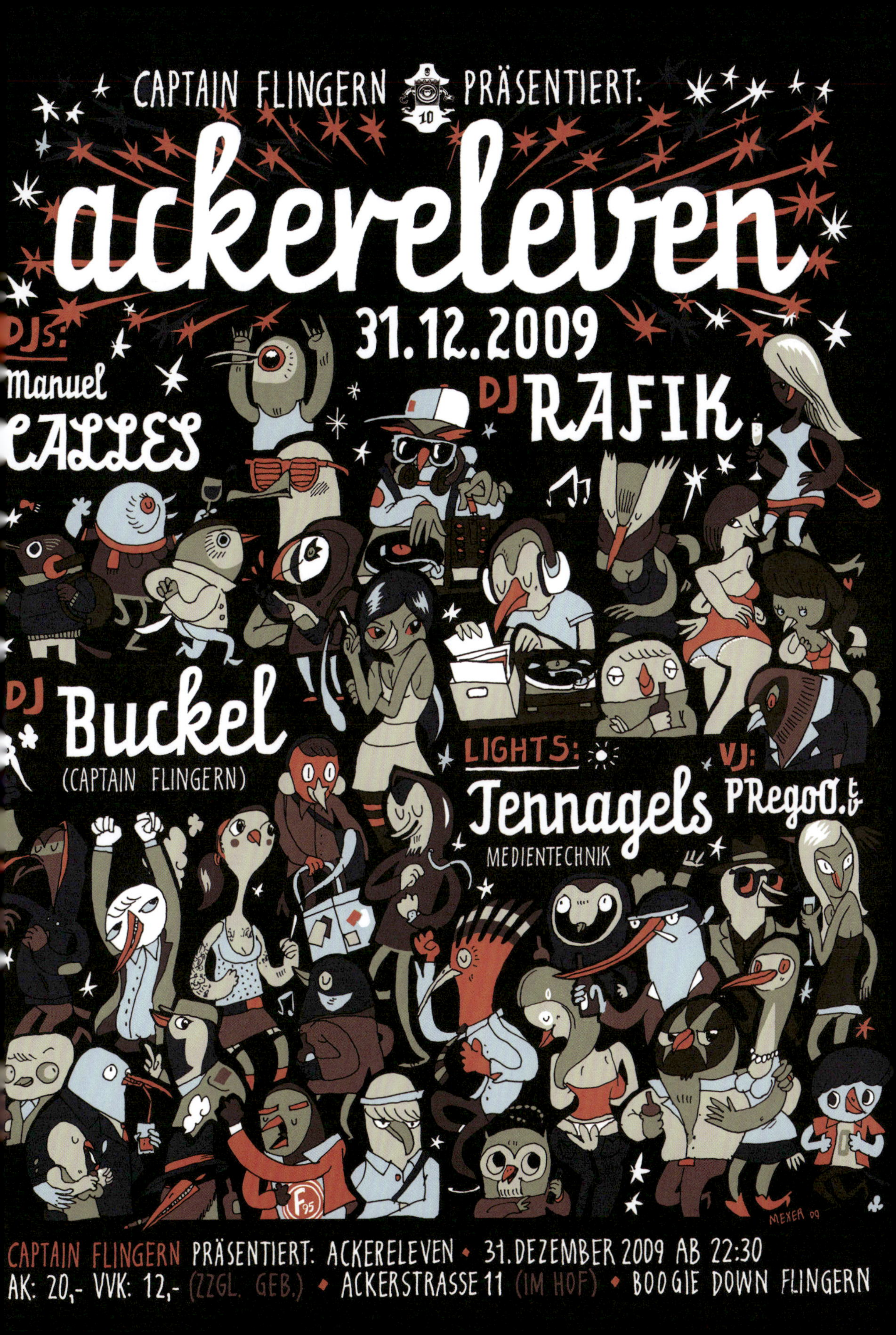
CAPTAIN FLINGERN PRÄSENTIERT:
10
ackereleven
31.12.2009
DJs:
Manuel
CALLES
DJ RAFIK
DJ
Buckel
(CAPTAIN FLINGERN)
LIGHTS:
Tennagels
MEDIENTECHNIK
VJ:
PRegoO.tv
F95
MEXER 09
CAPTAIN FLINGERN PRÄSENTIERT: ACKERELEVEN • 31. DEZEMBER 2009 AB 22:30
AK: 20,- VVK: 12,- (ZZGL. GEB.) • ACKERSTRASSE 11 (IM HOF) • BOOGIE DOWN FLINGERN

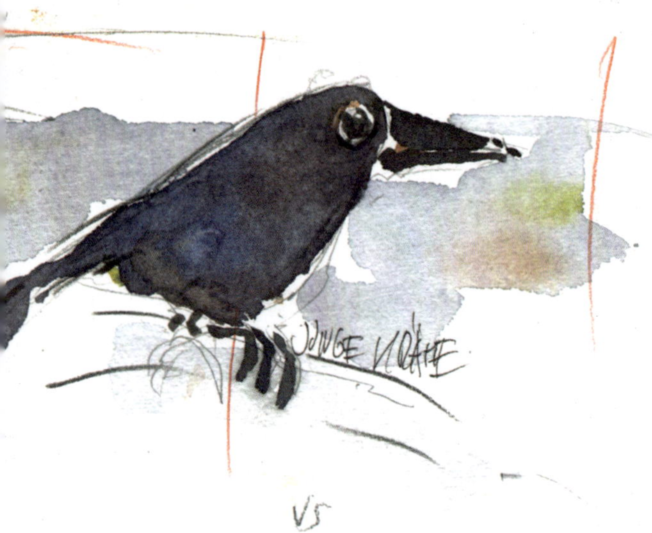

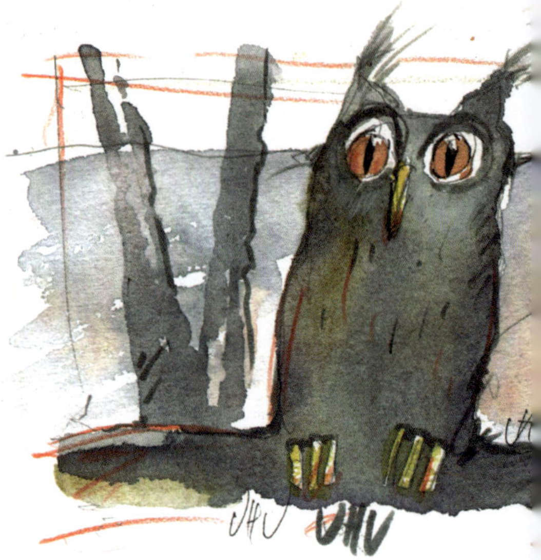

Preliminary drawing for an event poster.

It makes just as little sense to try and convince yourself "the illustration isn't finalized yet" (As a student I often used to have multiple versions of the same picture at hand that I worked on at the same time), as to try to rely solely on generative design so you can use preliminary drawings directly via Photoshop.

All these tricks won't solve the real problem that illustrations get "stiffer" the longer we work on them. The reason that finished illustrations often seem inferior to their drafts is simply that we *know* they must be turned into finished illustrations and aren't drafts anymore.

While working, we are, namely, very aware of whether "it's important" or not.

The reason your sketch flows so easily and loosely from your fingers is because the sketch *isn't meant for something yet*. It's the same reason why a song sung *in the shower* sounds so much better than if you were to sing it in an auditorium with critics in the front row: the more serious it gets, the more the playfulness is lost and replaced by the fear of failure.

Illustrations have deadlines; someone is going to assess them, criticize them and this is the decisive difference between them and the sketches. They will always be looked at as "just sketches," but your illustration is final. It will be submitted, looked at from all angles and possibly seen by thousands of people. You won't be able to run after every copy of the flyer explaining that it wasn't meant that way.

These are the processes that make you *worry your picture to death*.

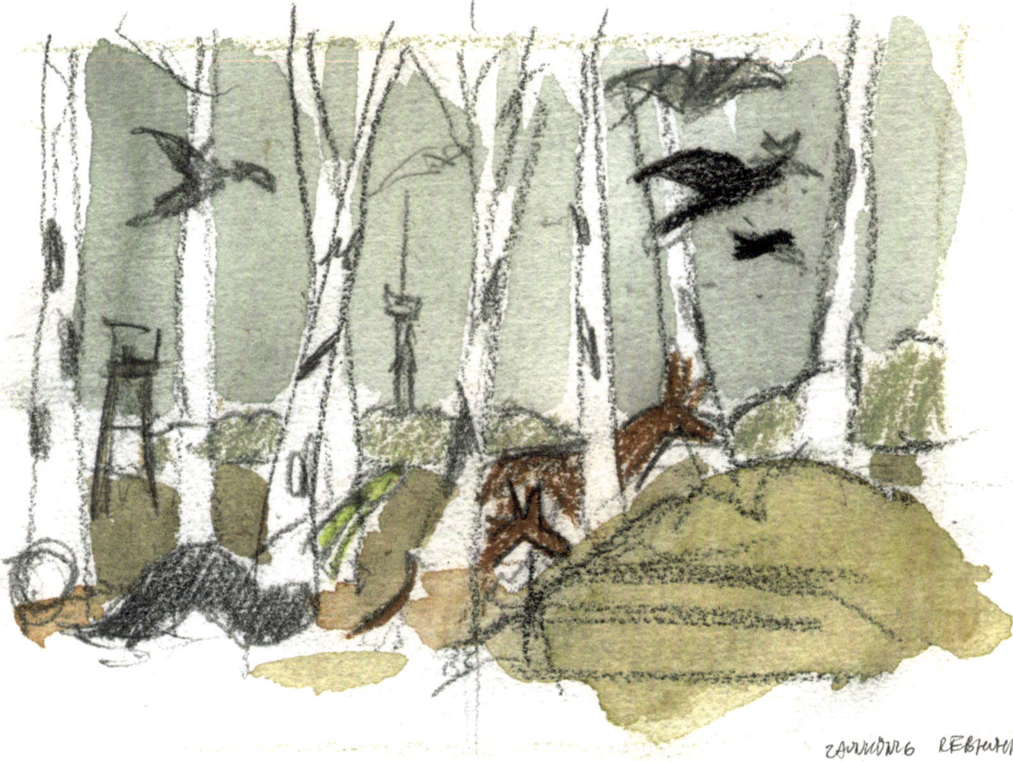

As long as we only produce something "at random," we are not offering evidence that we really have something to offer. Secretly, a role is also played by our fear of not being able to live up to our own demands. It's easier to hide behind sketches and that's why they're easier to produce.

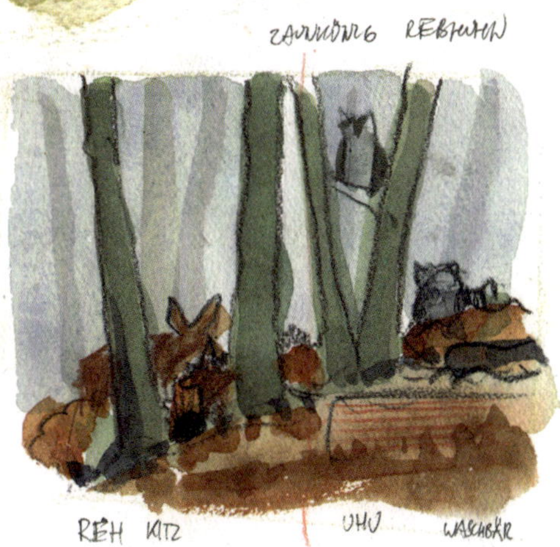

It's the fear of failure that's killing your illustration.

Recognizing this might not take away the anxiety, but it may be the *first step* out of the dilemma.

As illustrators, we need to learn to stand behind our work.

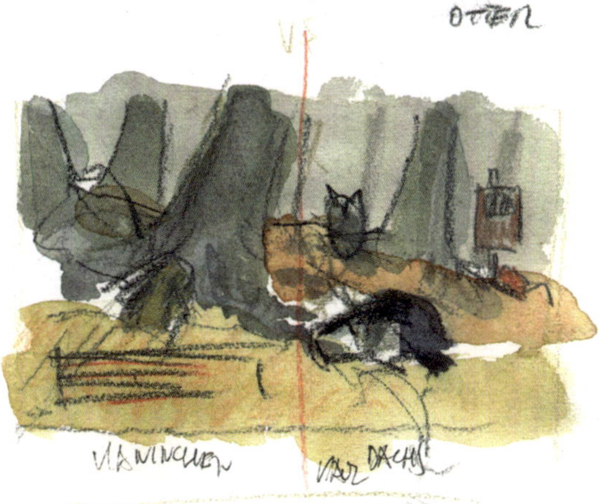

And not draw pictures for assumed later critics. You'll see that when you internalize this, the discrepancies between your drafts "for nothing" and your final illustrations will begin to disappear. Little by little, your pictures will retain their soul.

Dominant Colors

It's not easy being green.
It seems you blend in with so many other ordinary things. KERMIT'S SONG, SESAME STREET

If you were to alternate using all the colors of your palette while painting a picture, you would only create a multicolored jumble. Your picture would be colorful, but without any color tone. My first advice for the successful use of color can therefore only be: Less is more. Especially at the beginning, it often turns out to be helpful to work with only one, at most two basic colors. *Dominant* colors make working immensely easier.

Have you been to the movies lately? Did you notice the colors? Color systems are extremely important, especially in big productions. Take a close look – you can learn a lot about the dominant colors principle from films. For example, if a young sorcerer's apprentice in the movies is wearing the reddish-brown colors of his sports team, it's no coincidence that this scene is shot in front of gold-patterned wallpaper, which brings the reddish brown to its best advantage. Or when the princess in a historical drama appears in the Blue Salon in a turquoise evening gown.

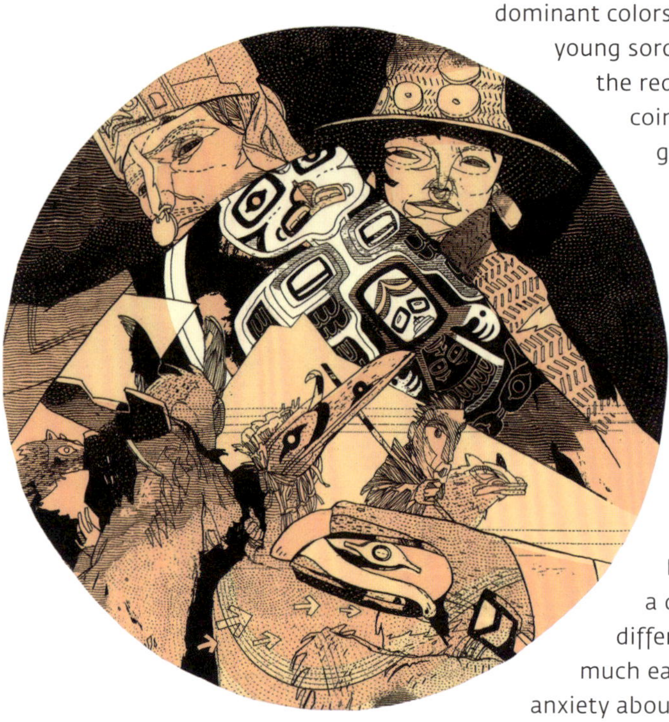

Tip

Make little color sketches before you begin. It's wise to test the color tone with a series of little splotches before using them in your picture.

If you deliberately let your picture be led by a dominant color or a color space (for example, different shades of blue), you'll be surprised how much easier it is to work with color and lose any anxiety about it.
This is ideal especially for emotionally accented use of colors, because dominant colors can be delineated much more clearly. Color spaces convey your message more clearly. Thus, a picture

will look completely different with a red/golden color mood than if it consisted mainly of cold blue tones. In addition, dominant color systems are extremely helpful for creating eye-catchers. For example, you can set a complementary color shade within a dominant color tone to direct the eye. In a movie about knights (to stick with the example), if the blood of the murdered victim appears dark red in the surrounding green of the water or the queen flits past complementary, pale blue castle walls in a bright orange dress, the effect is immediately far greater.

Dominant colors thus offer us a good start in working with color. They draw the attention of the observer and help us to easily solve the problem of variety. Because nothing is easier in a sequence of pictures than to have a predominantly red picture follow a predominantly blue or green one. Even a movie is nothing but a series of pictures. Let yourself be inspired from time to time by the movies. Because it is by no means the color as such that lends feeling to our illustrations – it is the deliberate use of color.

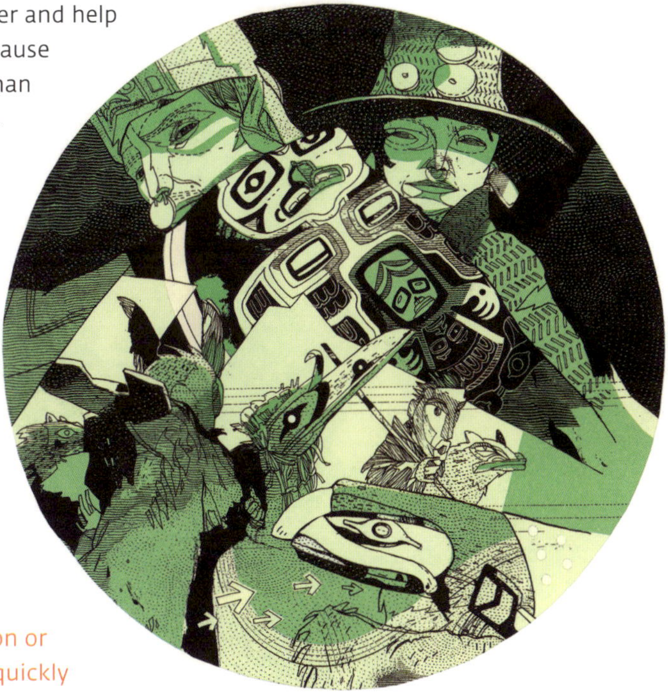

Tip

You don't have to reinvent the wheel. There is nothing wrong with being inspired by others to use color tones. It may make sense to make a note of "good color tones." This can be a color tone in a picture, but also in nature, a house, in fashion or in something completely different. You can quickly conjure up a sketch of the color tone with a few daubs of watercolors. And you can use this tone later in your own work.

Details and Perspective

If there were only one truth,
you couldn't paint a hundred canvases on the same theme.
PABLO PICASSO

Another subject area where you can learn from the movies is that of angles, details and shot settings.
Camera angles and shot settings create narrative elements because they define the observer's point of view – or ours. And this is one of the most important factors in the composition of pictures.

In the early days of cinema – in part also in the early days of painting – pictures were always presented more like big puppet theaters. Viewers looked at images frontally at an average distance of about ten to twelve feet. The central character in the picture thus looked like an actor on a stage; he was visible in full size and the surrounding space was also sufficiently presented. In shot settings, this is called a "long shot," where we can see *all* the important things.
This perspective works well for *one* picture. But as soon as we use repeated long shots in a series of pictures, things soon get boring.
There's an anecdote from filmmaking history about how different shot settings found their way into our way of seeing.

During production of the first Western in film history, *The Great Train Robbery* in 1903, a mistake is said to have revolutionized movie making.

Legend has it that a cameraman accidently kept his camera running when the actors, who normally were at the stage distance of ten feet, happened to walk past. While watching the resulting "ruined" material, the producers suddenly became aware of the effect of shot settings. The main characters were suddenly very close and seemed emotionally much more present because they filled the frame.
According to the legend, the new discovery was promptly implemented: In the closing scene of the western, in a close-up the actor Justus D. Barnes aimed his weapon directly at the camera and fired it. The effect is said to have been tremendous. During screenings of *The Great Train Robbery*, the audience ran screaming out of the theater.
Although the effect of our images is likely to be less drastic today, shot settings still play a tremendous role in illustration.
It begins with the entertainment factor. For example, if you illustrate a children's book with twelve double pages, it would not be helpful to have twelve sequential identical shot settings. On the contrary, it would be more interesting to open the *scenario* with an extreme long *shot*, to present your protagonists on the next page in a long shot or a *close-up*, to switch again in the narrative strand to a *knee-shot* and then, in the thrilling finale, to jump to a *close-up* ... or any number of variations of that. You understand what I mean; you do go to the movies now and then.
Shot settings not only make a scene more vivid, they are also of narrative significance. A close-up conveys a whole lot of feelings, while an extreme long shot naturally creates visual and emotional distance. This makes shot settings tools in the narrative thread, which one should not underestimate.

The same applies to camera angles. You can look at something from the front, but you can also shift the viewing

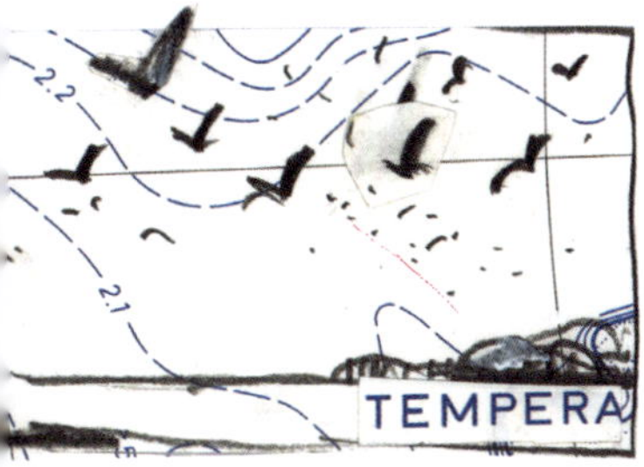

Extreme long shot

The picture is dominated by the landscape. The focus is on the surroundings, the birds disappear as tiny dots in the sky. Good for opening scenes.

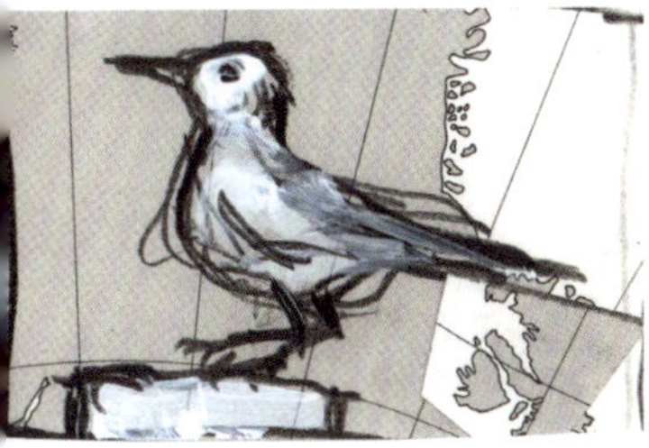

Long shot

The bird in its direct environment. The picture is dominated by both the main character and its surroundings.

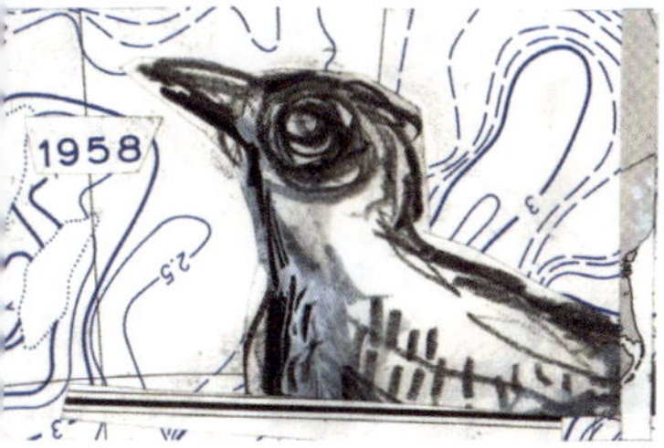

Medium shot

Part of the bird is visible. In movies, this setting is often used in interior scenes, for example for conversations.

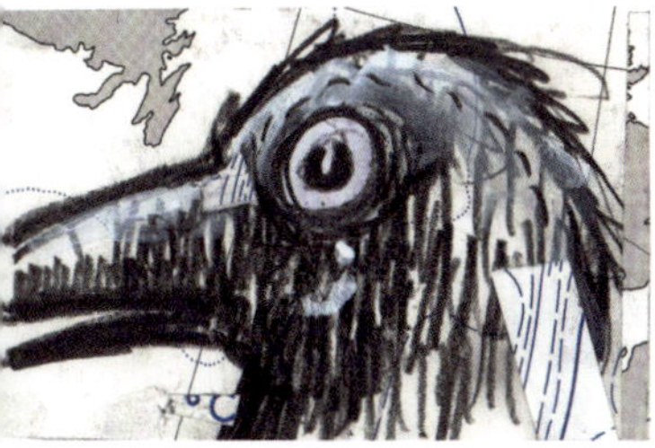

Close-up

The bird is very close; the focus is on details and enlargements. In movies, close-ups are often used to show the faces of the main characters ("eyes").

horizon. Low- and high-angle shots are famous examples. Again, it is not only (but also) about entertainment: a low or worm's-eye view makes the other person look bigger and, for example, more dangerous, while with a high-angle or bird's-eye view we can create emotional distance.

As you can see, when we draw pictures, it is very helpful to be familiar with the way perspectives work. Points of view, shot settings and camera angles are important variables for us as illustrators because they not only determine the viewer's perspective, they put us in *relation* to the images and thereby create a relationship between them and us. A minor hint for your tax return: *Never go to the movies for pleasure*; you are doing *essential media research*. ;-)

Illustration techniques

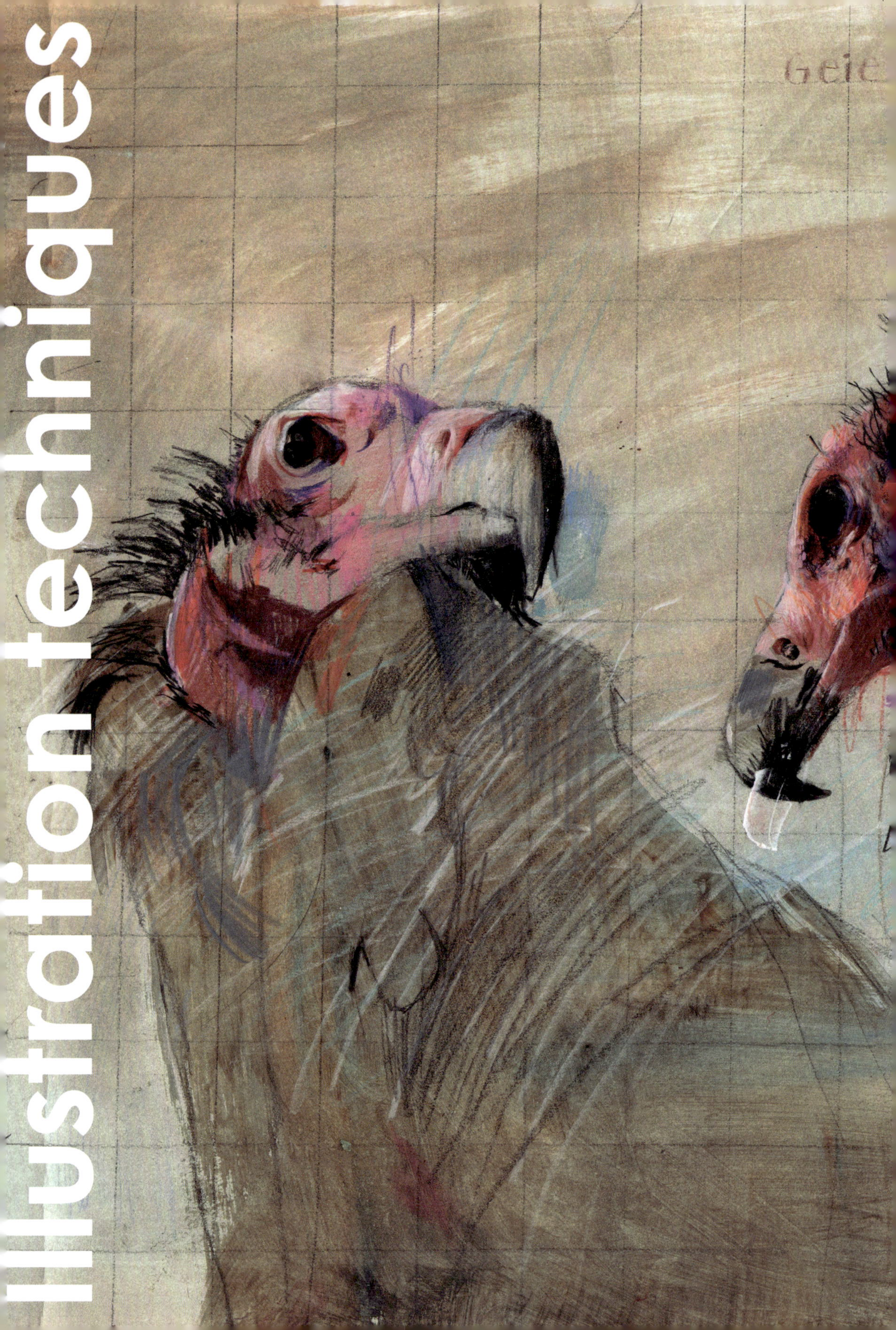

nd keine Grifftöter, gehören trotzde

zu den Greifvögeln.

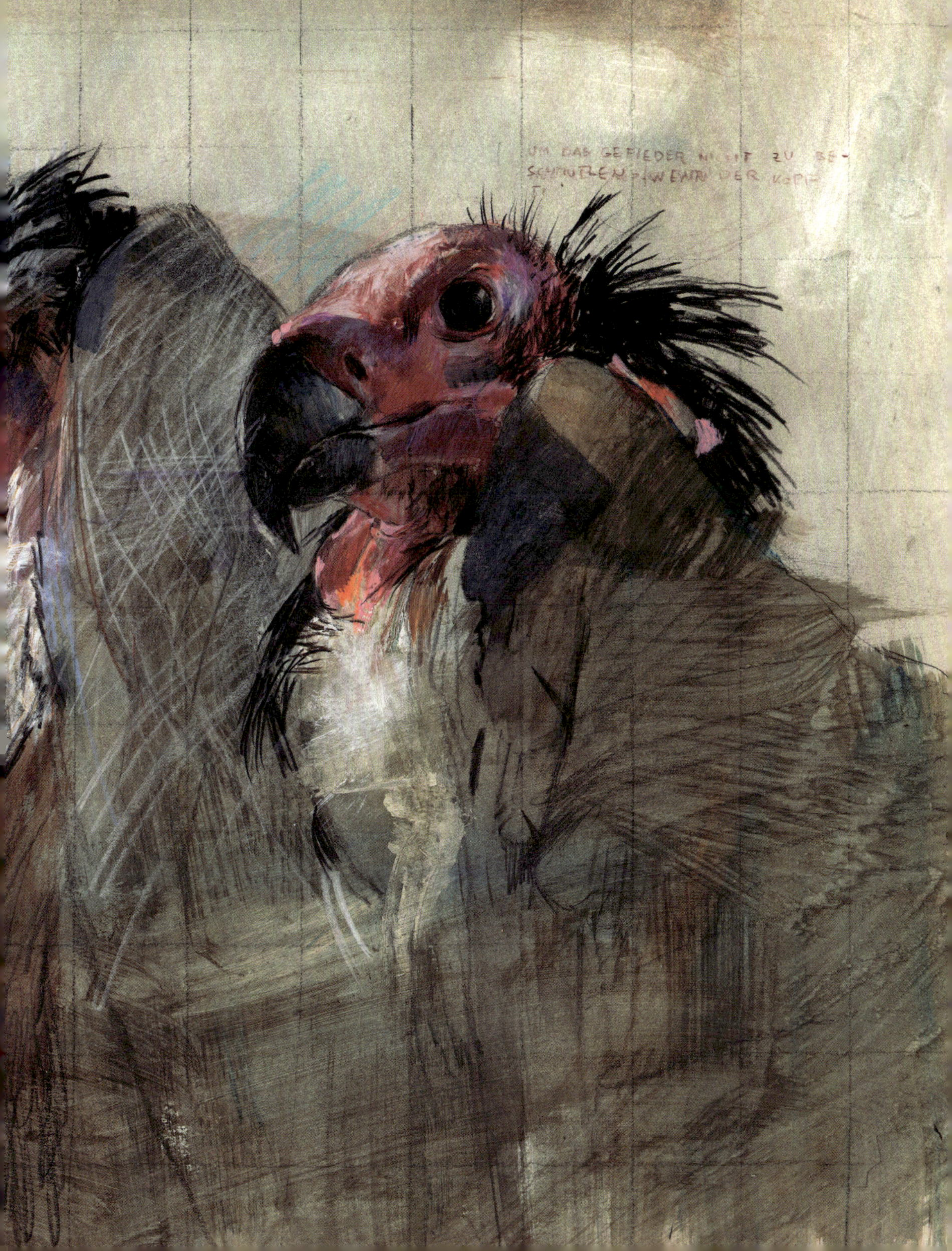

Pencils

I want to arrive at a more deliberate and exaggerated way of drawing. VINCENT VAN GOGH

We all are familiar with pencils. They're the all-rounders among drawing utensils. 2B, 3B, HB? With an eraser or without? There's not much more one can write about them...but I'll try!

The leads of modern pencils are made of graphite and clay. The first of these modern pencils emerged in England in the sixteenth century after they discovered large graphite deposits in the north of the country.

So, why are they called leads? Pencils don't contain lead, at least not nowadays. But even in ancient times people used lead styluses. In the Middle Ages, the lead was replaced by silver or a silver tip since the precious metal had even better abrasion properties. Drawing with them was, however, still quite laborious since the writing surface had to be pretreated. Graphite, which is crystalline carbon, is much more suitable for drawing, and the abrasiveness of the pencil can be controlled by adding clay. The mixing ratio determines whether the lead is hard or soft: the higher the clay content, the greater the hardness of the pencil (B = soft, H = hard).

Which pencil you use for illustrating is a matter of taste.

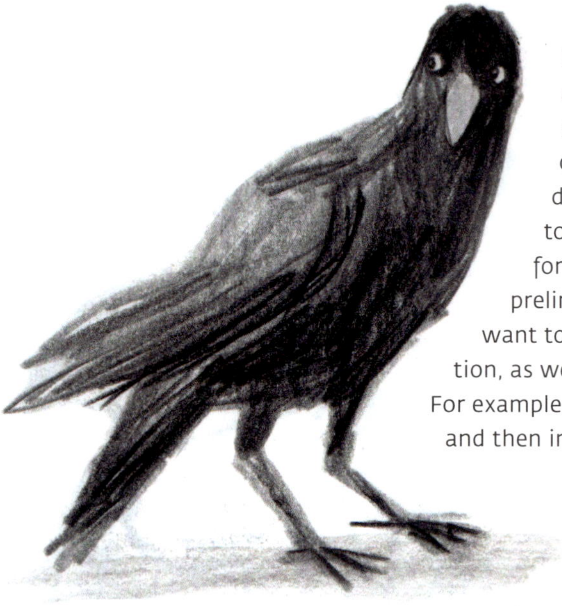

But on principle softer pencils are better suited for artistic drawings (I always recommend 3B for loose sketches, nudes, for example). Hard pencils, by contrast, lend themselves to accurate, detailed drawings and technical applications. How *we* want to use the pencils for our illustrations also matters for the choice of hardness. A pencil used only for preliminary drawings is a different one than one we want to use as the sole medium for an image. Pay attention, as well, to how easily the lines can be erased.

For example, comics are traditionally drawn with soft pencils and then inked in a later step with pen or fineliner. The underlying pencil stroke is then erased.

← JONAS LAUSTRÖER NORA MARLEEN

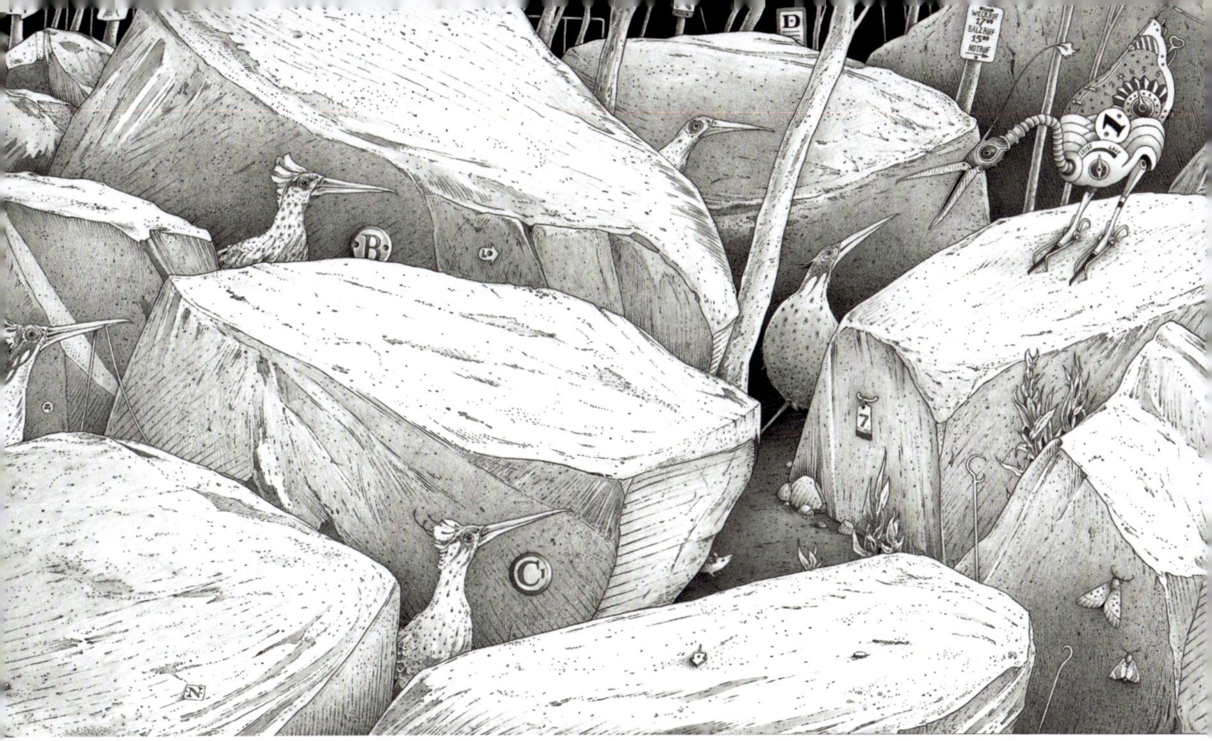

Of course, you can leave preliminary pencil drawings in illustrations as well, because pencil strokes are great for mixing techniques. In reproduction, their stroke varies from gray to black depending on abrasion and in combination with glazing techniques (for example, watercolors) they are *the* medium of choice. It is useful to know, though, that pencil strokes are fixed by watercolors. Once you cover your drawing with a layer of watercolors it can no longer be erased.

Tip

To avoid smearing old pencil lines on the paper with your hand while drawing, place a clean sheet of paper between the palm of your hand and the drawing surface.

Blurring or shading the graphite in pencil strokes can also be used wonderfully for illustration. In contrast to the clearly contoured stroke of pens, fineliners and such, the broken line of the blurred graphite offers particularly appealing effects. In addition, you can easily create transitions and gradations. Some illustrators use proper smearing tools such as blenders or erasers to control gradations in detail. In this way you can create almost photorealistic images from a blackened pencil surface with an electric eraser.

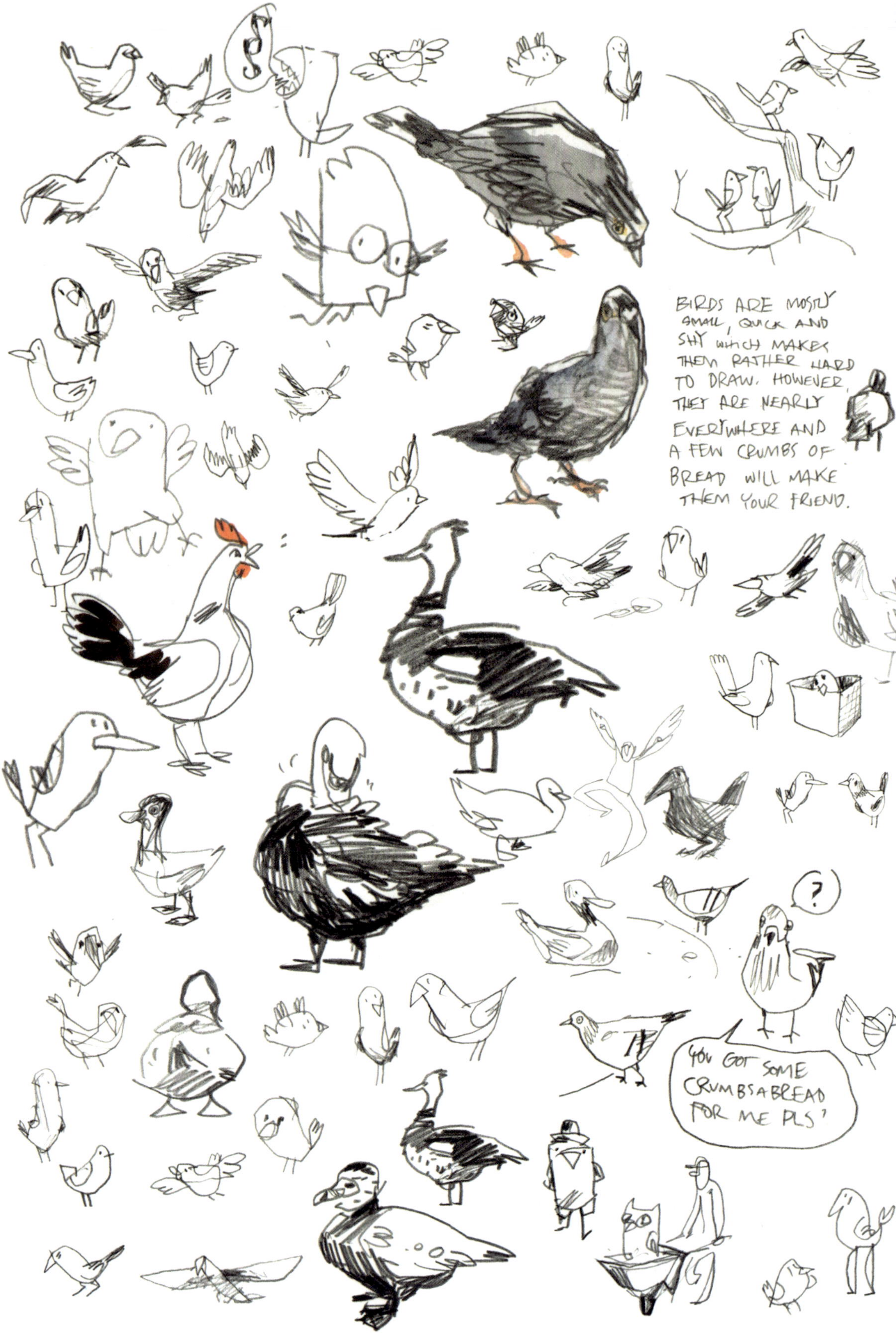
BIRDS ARE MOSTLY SMALL, QUICK AND SHY WHICH MAKES THEM RATHER HARD TO DRAW. HOWEVER, THEY ARE NEARLY EVERYWHERE AND A FEW CRUMBS OF BREAD WILL MAKE THEM YOUR FRIEND.
?
YOU GOT SOME CRUMBSABREAD FOR ME PLS?

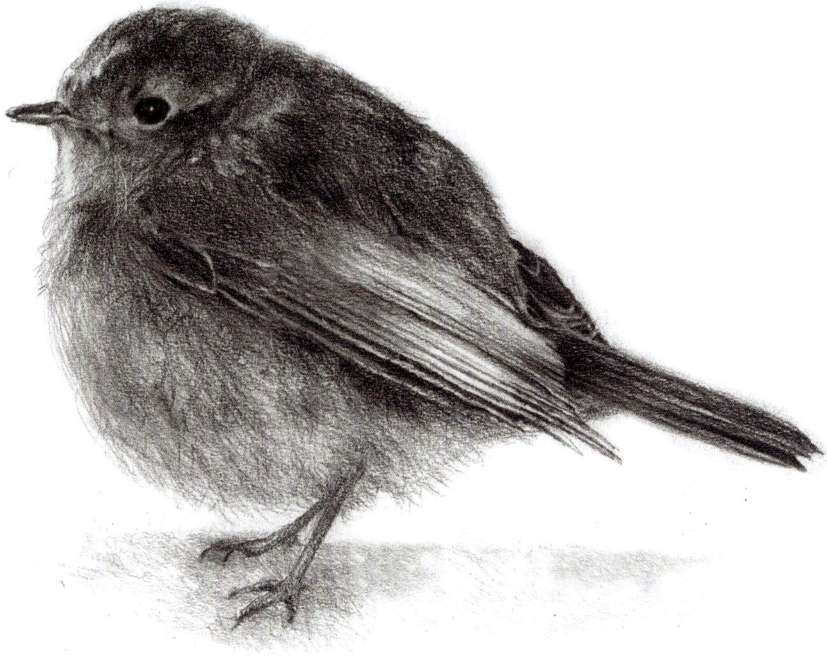

In addition, the easy blurring favors rubbing techniques. For example, using graphite surfaces, it is very easy to trace originals.
Funnily, the pencil is one of the analog "profiteers" of the computer age. *Today* pencil drawings serve as templates for digital work. Whether lines that are later colored, preliminary drawings, sketches or basic designs for the pixel or the vector field: As a rule, everything is done with a good old-fashioned pencil.
Two types of pencils are sold: retractable pencils and pencils made of wood. The latter are made of soft cedar, because it has few knotholes and can therefore be easily sharpened. Retractable pencils have the advantage that they don't need sharpening and they are available in much finer thicknesses. Mechanical or TK pencils have also proven useful.

Erasers

A pencil needs an eraser. Erasers work because the adhesion force of rubber is greater than that of paper. So when you rub an eraser over the paper, the graphite particles adhering to the surface move to the substrates due to the adhesion.

Colored Pencils

My favorite color is colorful.
WALTER GROPIUS

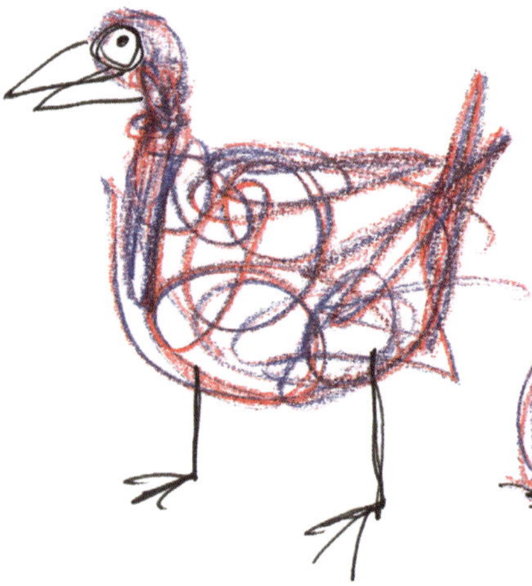

A colored pencil is made just like a regular pencil: they take a piece of wood, mill a groove in, fill it with glue, and insert a lead. From the other side they take another piece of, also grooved, and glue it against it so that the lead is completely enclosed. Then the pencil is shaped and it's ready to go.

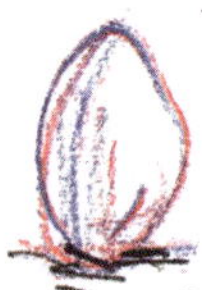

The difference to regular pencils is that the lead is not made of graphite (crystalline carbon), but of colored pigment. In addition, the binder with which the pigment is bound to the lead is different. In pencils it's usually clay, but colored pencils are often quite mysterious.

Some are probably oil-based (like Caran d'ache from Switzerland), while others (like American Prismacolor) probably contain acrylic or wax. The different binders are responsible for the different properties of colored pencils. The binder determines whether the colored pencil can be painted with water or oil as well as eraser resistance, hardness or the amount of abrasion. And every manufacturer uses their own, top-secret recipes.

The quality of colored pencil leads partly determines their stability. Unfortunately, colored pencil tips often break off when the lead inside is broken, which happens when they are dropped. (Incidentally, that's why many colored pencils aren't round but octagonal: so they don't roll off the table.) A broken lead makes a colored pencil unusable.

You always have to sharpen them and you're always dealing with chunks that leave ugly streaks on pictures. Although some manufacturers try to glue the leads with acrylic, this is not good for the drawings. So take care of your pencils.

In addition to processing and binder, the major manufacturers' colored pencils also differ in the selection of colors offered.

Tip

Colored pencils with multi-colored leads, so-called rainbow pencils, are a nifty gimmick for drawing. They contain different, adjacent color layers, so that their color always varies slightly.

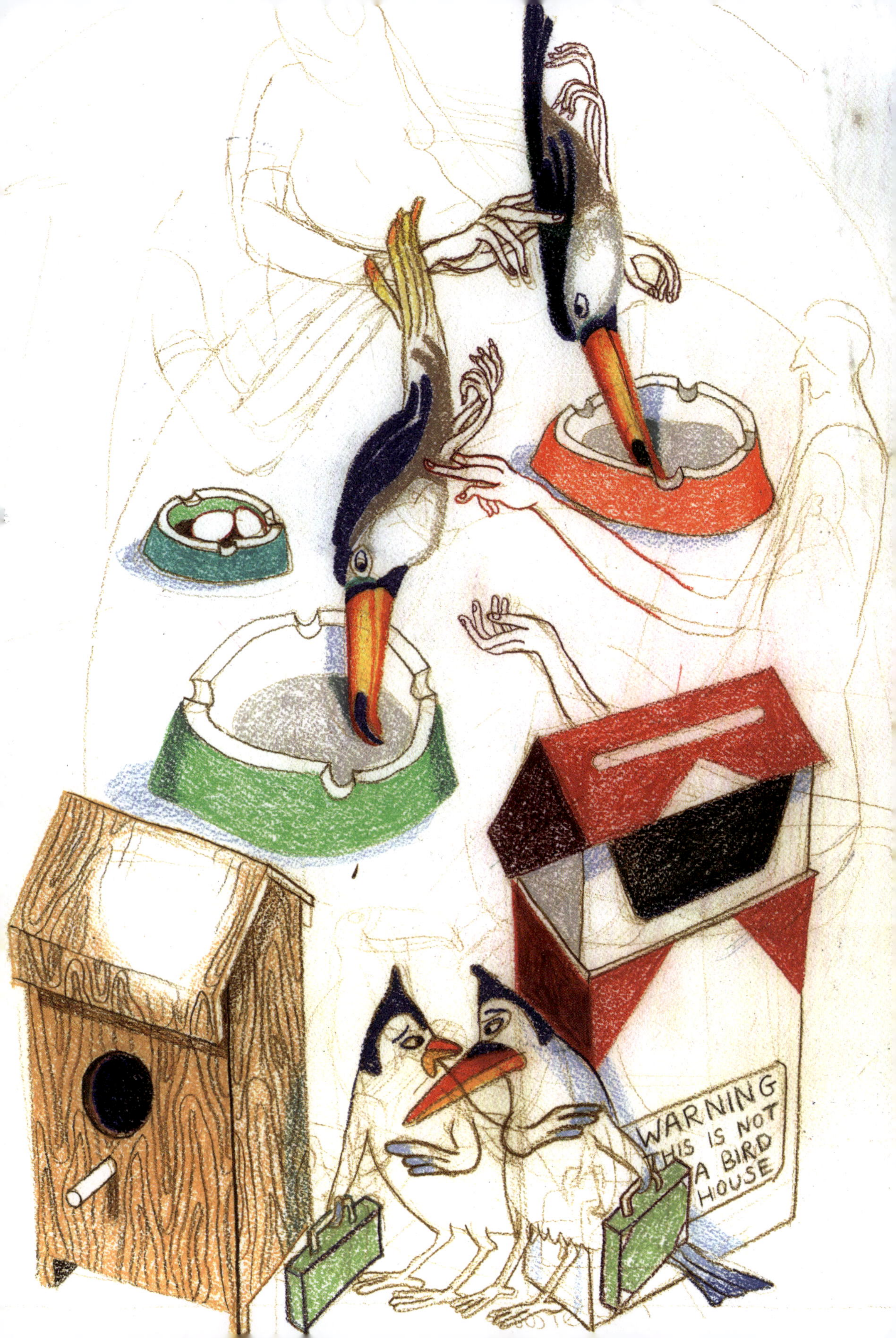
WARNING
THIS IS NOT
A BIRD
HOUSE

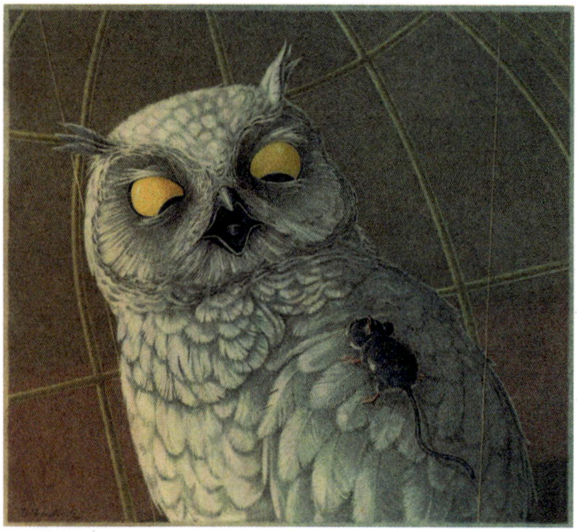

Prismacolor from the USA offers the largest assortment. They currently produce 156 hues and have announced another 50 for the future (Polycromos by Faber-Castell is available in about 120 hues). Prismacolor is also available in different degrees of hardness: *soft*, *hard* and *erasable*.

In general, the brands of colored pencils are quite different, and that has a major impact on our way of working. For example, harder colored pencils – such as Faber's Polycromos, which are very popular in Germany – are particularly suitable for mixing techniques, to use over watercolors, or for detailed, precise illustrations. Colored pencils with softer abrasion (i.e. with wax or acrylic in the lead), on the other hand, are favored by many illustrators for loose drawing work or for large format pictures.
The so-called watercolor pencils (i.e. chemically water-soluble wax-based colored pencils) are especially popular among hobbyists, but also reveal their strengths used for accents in watercolors or in mixed techniques.

It's best to just pick up a few individual pencils and try out which ones are best for you before you decide to buy a costly assortment box. Incidentally, you draw with colored pencils just like you do with regular pencils. You can create depth by hatching and overlaying, and create transitions by shading and blurring. In addition, you can produce painterly effects by applying several different colors on top of each other.

Colored pencils are the perfect bridge between drawing and painting.

What's also nice about colored pencils is that they aren't only suitable as a pure drawing technique, but, as I said, also excellent as a supplement technique. Depending on the ground, you can create wonderful accents with colored pencils, for example in watercolor, gouache or acrylic paintings.
But colored pencils are also great for pure, unmixed drawing and illustration techniques. As with pastels, the drawing surface plays a major role with colored pencils, as its structure may show in the illustrations. As a rule of thumb, the more precisely you want to work, the less texture your paper should have.
Many artists prefer to use a knife instead of a sharpener to sharpen pencils. This is because the ratio of the wood to the tip of colored pencils is unfavorably shaped for commercial sharpeners. Ideally, *a little* wood should surround the colored pencil tip, because that makes the tip more stable.
Unfortunately, commercial pencil sharpeners do the exact opposite. A lot of wood covers the tip at a shallow angle. So using a knife may be a solution to this problem. Another option is

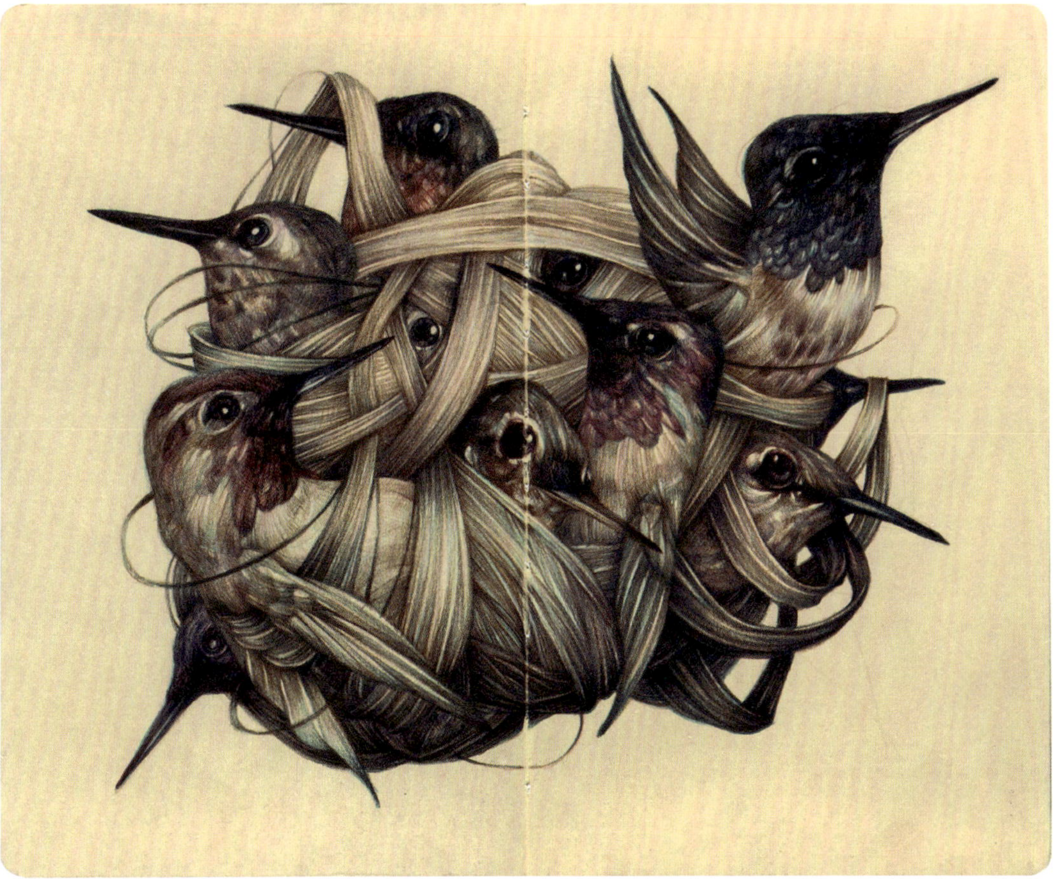

provided by the cosmetics industry. If you use an eyeliner sharpener, you'll notice that your colored pencils break off less readily because of the shallower cutting angle.

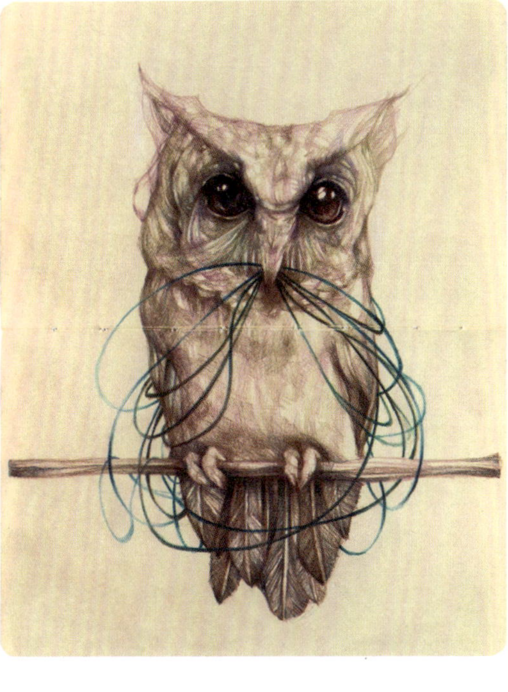

By the way

Faber-Castell is currently the world's largest manufacturer of colored pencils and pencils, producing over two billion each year.

Chalk and Charcoal

Drawing is still basically the same as it has been since prehistoric times. It brings together man and the world. It lives through Magic.

KEITH HARING

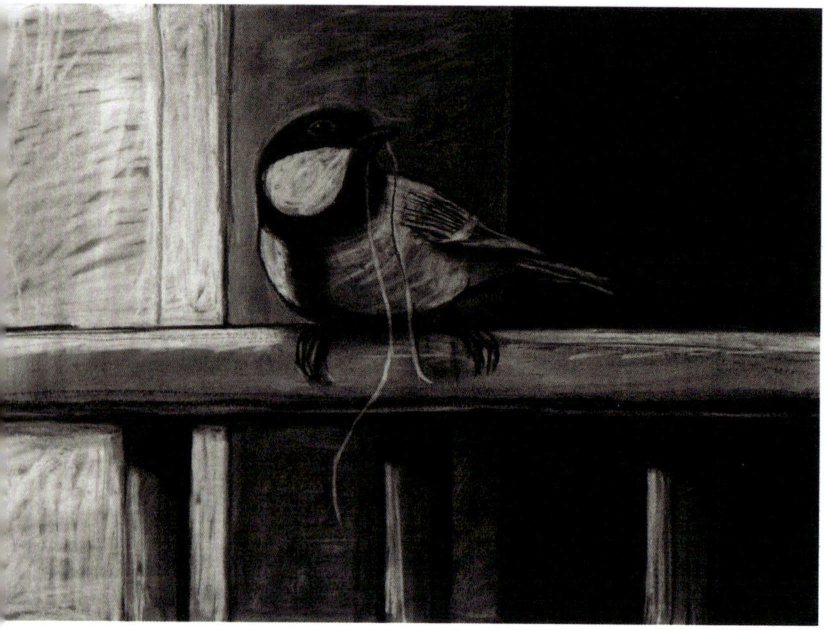

Red chalk, white chalk, charcoal ... to delve into the traditional drawing techniques, you actually have to go very far back as far as the cave in Altamira where the oldest known drawings were made on the walls with charcoal and red chalk; to the Neolithic dead covered with red chalk; to the red ships of Ancient Greece and to the Himba of Namibia, who rubbed their bodies with red chalk and fat to protect themselves from heat and mosquitoes. And of course, we can't forget Leonardo da Vinci, his self-portrait as a bearded old man, and his friend and competitor Michelangelo, who executed his sketches for the Sistine Chapel with red chalk.

In fact, you have to go back a long way, because red chalk, white chalk and charcoal have been with artists for quite some time. And with good reason:

Chalks are non-toxic and easy to handle, they are inexpensive, lightfast and of simple beauty.

So it's time to take a closer look at the three techniques.

Red chalk (also called *sanguine* because it resembles the color of dried blood) crayons are mineral; originally they consisted only of clay and iron oxide. There are even smooth, soft iron ores that can be used by cutting square crayons to draw with.

Today, red chalk is mixed, for example from clay, white chalk and hematite as a pigment.

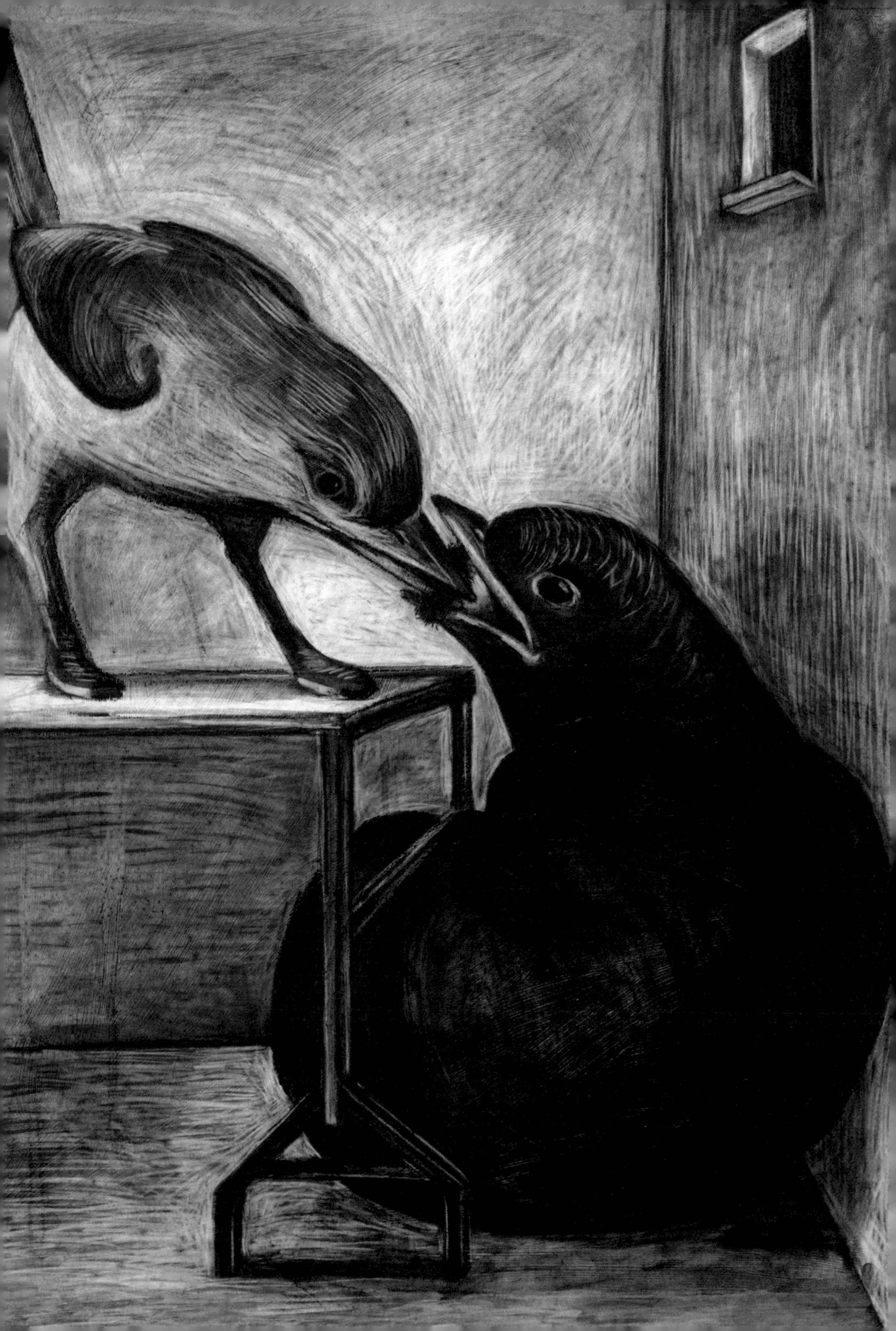

White chalk is very similar. For good reason an entire geological age (the Cretaceous Period from Latin *cretaceus*, from *creta* 'chalk') is named after it. In the past, white chalk consisted exclusively of a particularly fine and white form of limestone, but today it is also produced from gypsum or magnesium oxide.

Charcoal occurs as bituminous coal or charcoal. We usually use charcoal for drawing, available as inexpensive sticks. In addition, you can even make them yourself by slowly burning cut wood in a sealed clay pot.
With charcoal you can produce very black fields and lines. In contrast to the usual graphite pencil, it doesn't reflect light and its color is actually jet black. (Charcoal from bones or burned ivory was once used as a pigment because it's even blacker than charcoal.)
In drawing, red chalk, white chalk and charcoal are applied in quite similar ways. All three have in common that they are easy to work with, create good gradations and blur fabulously. However, they blur so much that the drawings we make with them have to be fixed. Today, all three are mainly used for studies and sketches (they are especially popular with students in the nude drawing course), but there are also a number of illustrators who use the three dry techniques for finished works. Red chalk, white chalk and charcoal have a somewhat old-fashioned, but very appealing aesthetic. Similar to colored pencils or graphite pencils, they can be used to create both lines and gradations as well as create transitions by shading using the side of the chalk. The techniques

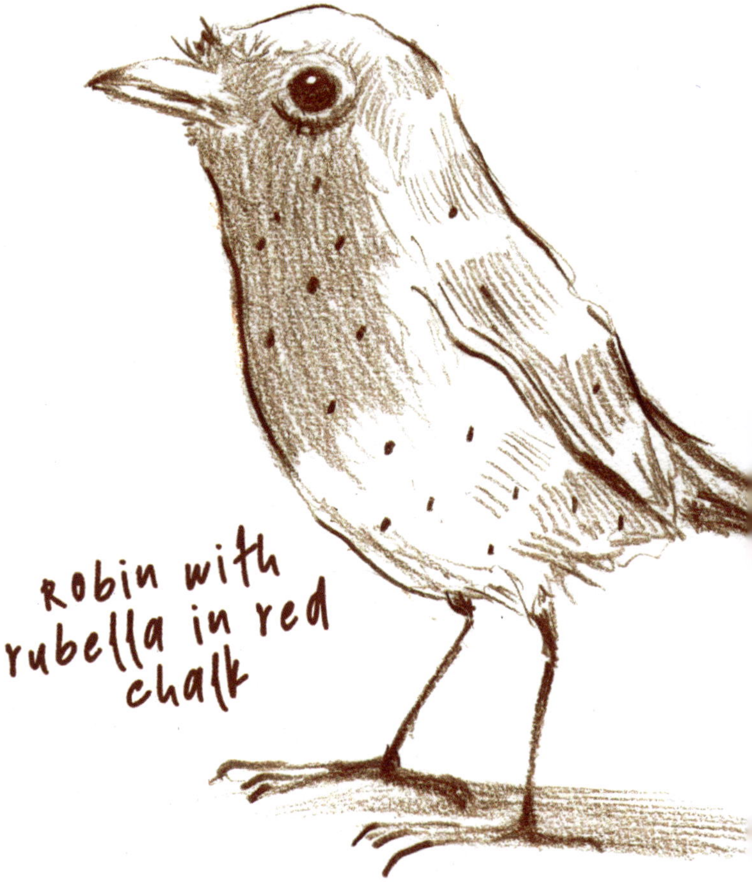

can also combined very well, especially if you're not working on white paper but, for example, on colored Ingres paper. A mixture of red *and* white chalk, which can be used to simultaneously produce multiple depths in a drawing, is particularly effective.

White chalk, red chalk and charcoal can be employed in an impressive number of ways to make wonderful drawings.

Finally, I would like to reveal a secret about a somewhat unpleasant feature of the "dry" techniques: White chalk and red chalk sometimes emit a strange, unpleasant noise while drawing. If you've ever made a line on a stone with a piece of pottery or roof tile you know what I mean.

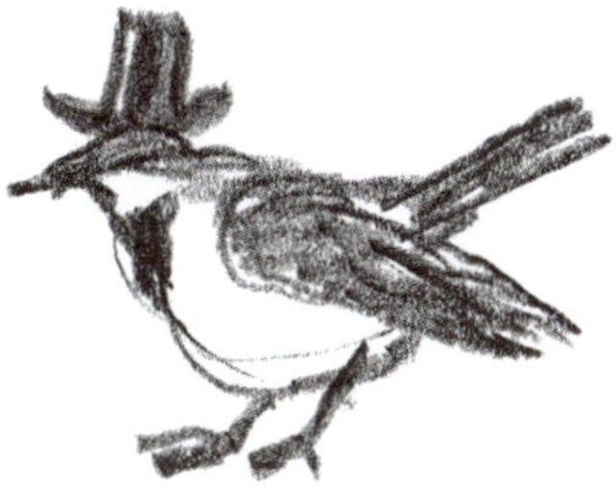

And everyone has flinched at the squeal of white chalk on the blackboard.

The reason for this is the natural frequency of the material. Red and white chalks are minerals and therefore occasionally begin to vibrate audibly due to their internal structure.

The friction caused by drawing causes it to vibrate and the material begins to "squeak" at its natural frequency. To prevent this, there is a very simple trick: You need to shorten the sound box, the resonating body. If you break the chalk into shorter pieces, this natural frequency rises into a range that is no longer audible and the squeaking is gone.

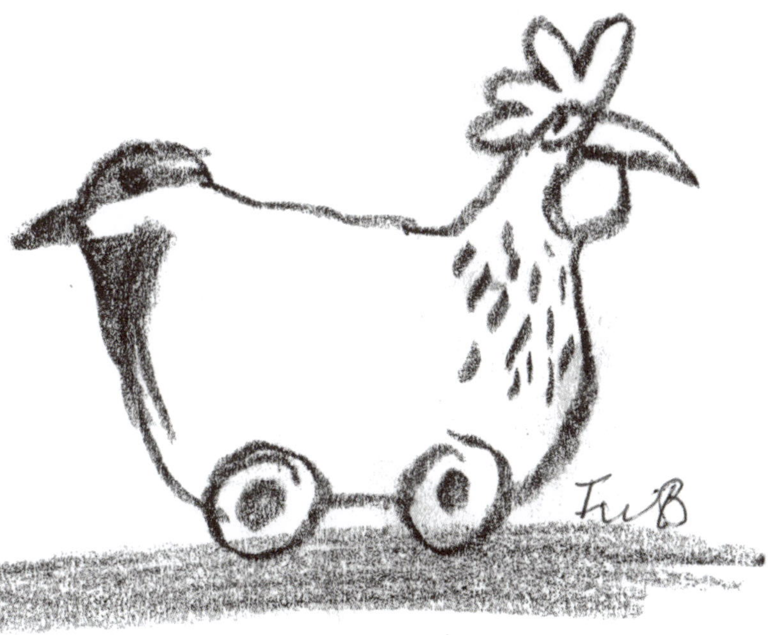

Pastels

"Pastel" comes from the Italian word for "paste."

Opening a box of pastels is like eating a glazed donut: your hands get sticky before you've taken a single bite. You merely touch the box and you've got colored fingers.

The word "pastel" is actually a little misleading. When we speak of *pastel hues* in painting we mean very delicate, soft under-colors, or shades with a high white content and low color density. The ratio of pigment to binder or filler is very low.

Pastels, though, are usually the exact opposite: they contain an incredible amount of pigment. You can tell the first time you open your pastel box: It's a treasure chest full of brightly colored chalks the brilliance of which is only exceeded by pure pigments.

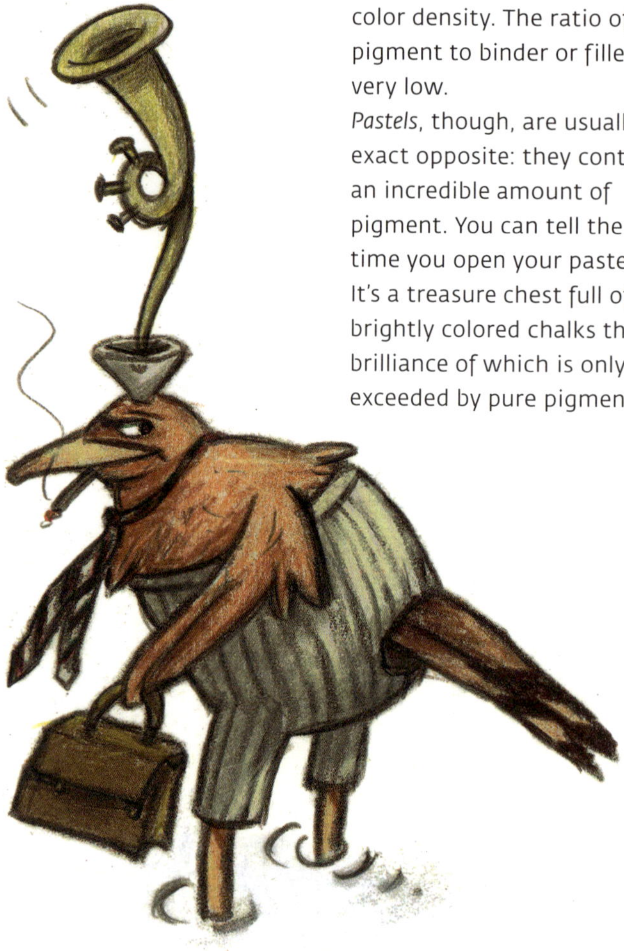

The color intensity of pastels is due to their lack of binder. They only have enough binder to keep them in shape, but as soon as they come into contact with the drawing surface, they crumble. Interestingly, the word "pastel" comes from the Italian word for "paste." This has to do with the earlier manufacturing process, because pastel is a relatively old technique: there have been brown, black and red pastels since the 15th century and today's brightly colored version has existed at least since the Rococo.

Pastel is among the most color-intensive art techniques. Since there is no adhesive between the pigments and since you can only layer a certain amount of loose pigments, pastels are also sold in every imaginable color. The more color we apply, the less it adheres to the paper.

This dilemma is solved when working with pastels by regularly adding fixative to the intermediate steps of the illustration. Conventional fixatives are suitable for this either as a spray or in liquid form. The latter is sprayed using a pump spray bottle that produces a vacuum when pumped (its use requires a little practice otherwise the fixative will leave spots). In spite of this minor drawback, this technique is exceedingly popular today because of its ease of use and its incredible color intensity.

Working with pastels can best be described as a mixture of drawing and painting.

The chalks are used like colored pencils for drawing or blended to color fields. The special thing about pastels is that the dusty fields, when not fixated, can be blended incredibly well, thus allowing for the most delicate of transitions. The colors are mixed with the fingers, brushes or a special blending stick called a *tortillon*. The biggest shortcoming of the pastel technique is its rather rough lines. Although the chalks can be used to make the most delicate of transitions, they don't make very fine lines. To circumvent this problem, pastels are now also available in pencil form with which finer details can be drawn. There's also another, very clever and less expensive trick: since pastels are a somewhat chalky affair, little, fine bits naturally crumble off while working. You can use these for fine lines using the following method:

Are you familiar with mechanical pencils that you can push regular pencil leads into? Not the very fine ones, but the ones with a 0.5-millimeter diameter. First you remove the lead. Now, when you push on the back, three jaws that usually hold the lead emerge at the tip. You can pick up your pastel crumbs with these jaws and then use them like a fine pencil for making accents.

The choice of the right paper also plays a major role when working in pastels. To ensure that the pigments adhere to the paper, it shouldn't be too smooth. Therefore, specially textured papers are sold (for example Canson or Ingres papers). The color of the paper is also important. Many use colored paper for their pastel illustrations so that the color of the background can affect their images.
Although many call them "pastel chalks," the white pigment of real chalk is rarely used for shading. Usually lithopone, zinc oxide or titanium dioxide is added. Colored glue, resins or kaolin are used as binders, but the exact mixtures are well-kept secrets. In early days, oatmeal gruel was used as a binder, but I assume that's passé. Still, with those well-kept secrets, you never know. :-)

Tip

Pastels are as brilliant as they are sensitive. You will need to use fixatives and protect presentations with glass frames or mats.

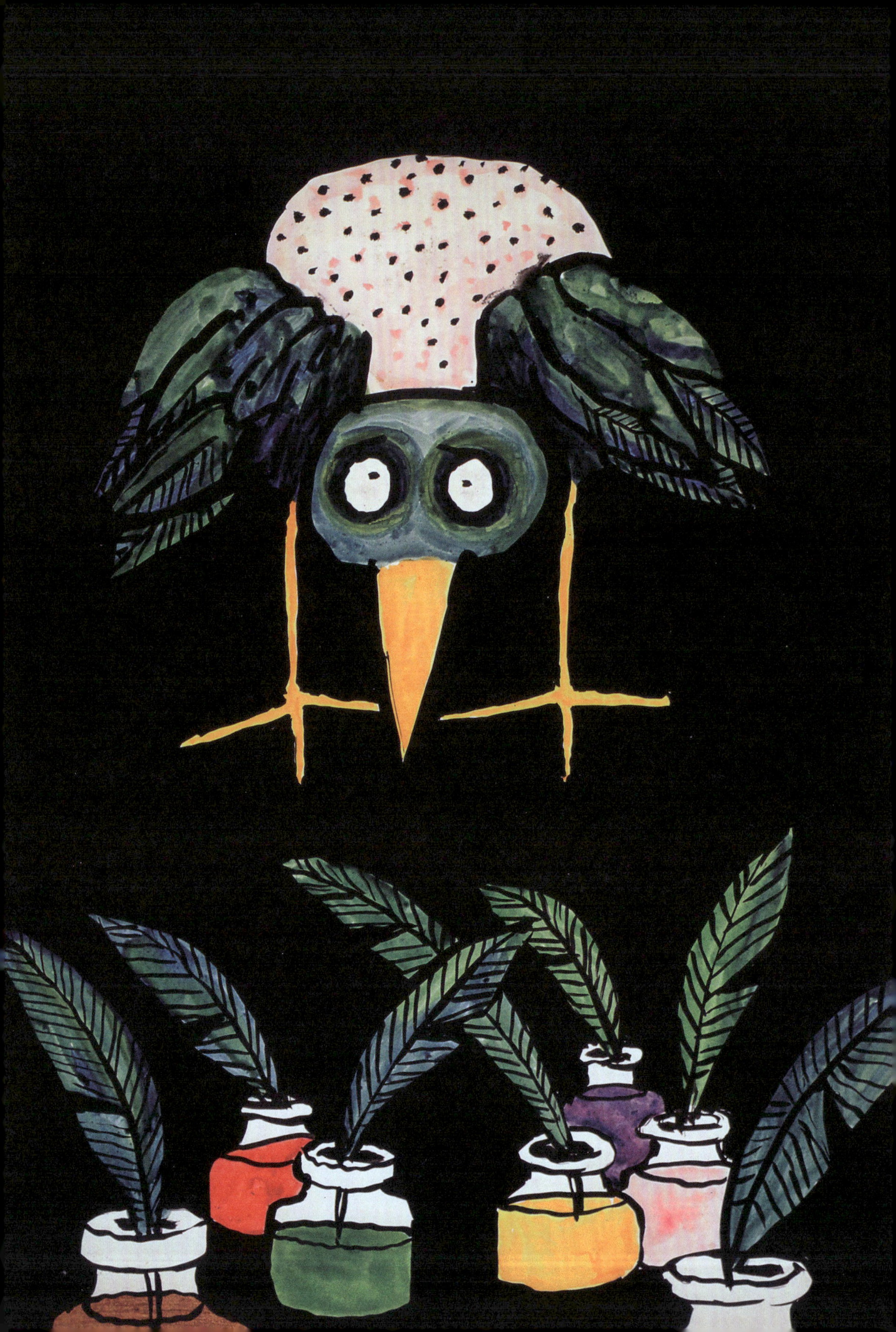

Ink

It is marked with a curious instinct - the taste for India ink. When a person sits down to write, the monkey squats cross-legged nearby with one forepaw folded over the other, waiting until the task is over. Then it drinks what is left of the ink, and afterward sits back on its haunches, quiet and satisfied.

THE MONKEY OF THE INKPOT, WANG TAI-HAI 1791

Ink has always been a powerful fluid; used to write love letters and sign death sentences, make declarations of war and sign peace treaties. Ink and paper made volumes of poetry and bibles, spell books, encyclopedias, promissory notes and laws. Because of ink, Mozart's fugues and Shakespeare's dramas survived. Ink shaped Dürer's armies and Picasso's doves of peace. Ink preserved art and poetry, errors and knowledge and ink destroyed kingdoms with a stroke of the pen.

Ink is one of the most important inventions that we humans ever created. Very soon after fire, the wheel and writing came the inconspicuous, dark black fluid. People have been drawing with ink for at least 5,000 years. Egyptian officials used it as well as Chinese painters, pious Hebrews used it to write the first Bibles, and Roman chroniclers sharpened their pens to report on political trickery. Technically speaking, ink is usually a mixture of water and dye – whether soot, charcoal or iron sulfate – and a binder like gelatin, acacia gum or acrylic resin. The main difference between ink and India ink is that ink can be re-dissolved with water after drying, whereas the addition of shellac makes India ink waterproof. However, the terms are not trademarked and by no means clearly defined.

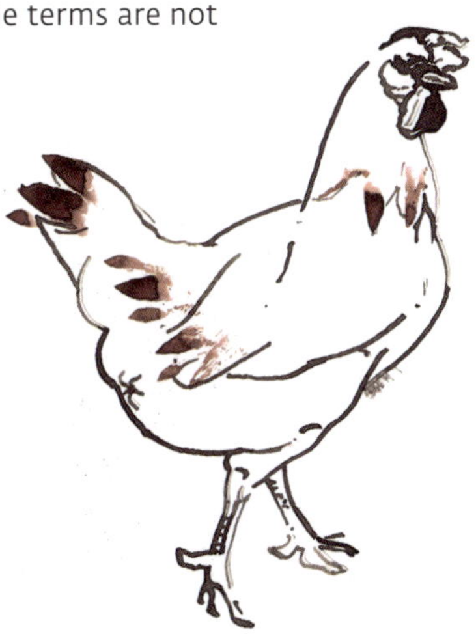

TOMI UNGERER

ERHARD GÖTTLICHER

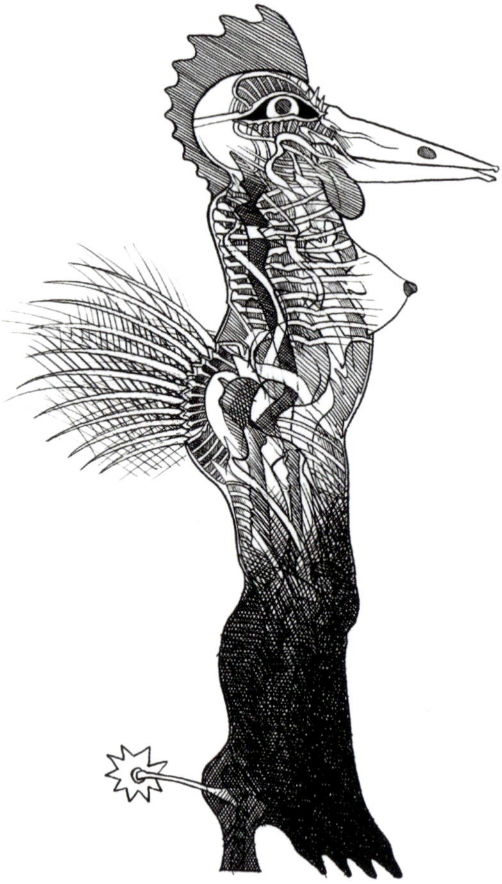

Some things sold as India ink do still run after wetting again, so it is always worthwhile to take a look at the packaging. "Waterproof" is the most reliable term. For us illustrators this is not insignificant, especially if you want to color line drawings, for example with watercolors.

In addition to the black India ink made of soot or "lampblack," there are many colored inks, mostly acrylic-based, and many manufacturers offer dozens of shades, so there are no limits to your imagination. Brown inks, sepia (originally made from cuttlefish ink) and bister (made from the charcoal of beech wood) are particularly noteworthy for drawing. Both are perfect for drawing and illustrating because they have their own charms and create much softer contrasts than their black counterparts. What makes inks and India inks particularly interesting for us illustrators is their universality:

The fantastic thing about ink is that you can both draw *and* paint with the same ink.

Diluted, ink is wonderful for glazing surfaces: to color your drawings. As with watercolors, you can apply the paint in layers or let it blend together wet. In this way, you can make one picture with a single material. And especially when you're working with brown ink, you'll be amazed at the multitude of gradations contained in a single inkwell. This makes ink a thrifty and incredibly versatile material. But, just as important as ink are the tools we use to put them on paper.

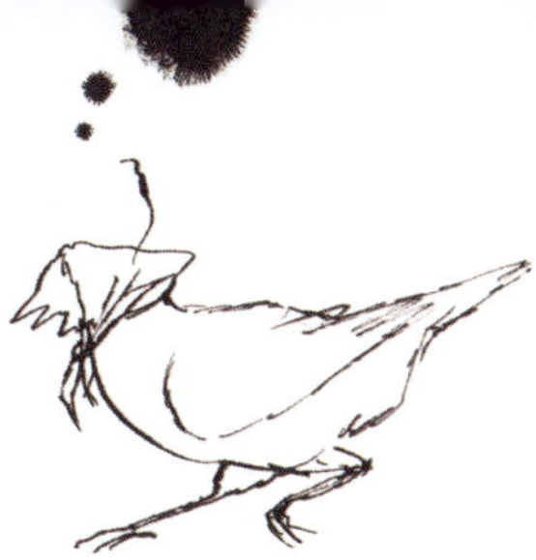

ALJOSCHA BLAU

Ink and pens belong together: The pen is mightier than the sword, Edward Bulwer-Lytton wrote in the middle of the nineteenth century, and he was quite right, but we might add that it is also mightier than a fineliner. The lines that you can draw with pens beat all the technical pens in terms of beauty. That's reason enough to dig out the old implements again.

Pens are basically the individualists of drawing. They are not standardized like inks and fiber pens, they have no standardized thicknesses – instead, they respond to our feelings. The special thing about pens is that their stroke has no uniform width, but varies. With every increase in pressure, it widens! In addition, the line reacts to the respective direction you draw in: Depending on the direction you lead the pen, the stroke width, especially of broader pens, changes. The lines are lively and elegant, becoming unmistakably what we call typical pen strokes.

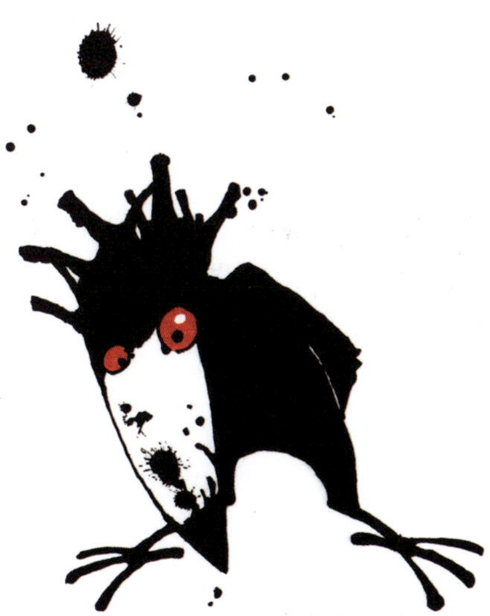

HANS BALTZER

Pens

The "classic" pen is of course, a real feather. In our case, a goose quill, the flight feather of a goose.
Goose quills were used for writing and drawing for centuries, and it was not until the invention of the steel quill in the eighteenth century that they were almost completely supplanted. Only the name "feather pen" has remained. Goose quills are quite suitable for drawing, but the feathers of other large birds, such as birds of prey and ravens, swans or ducks also provide useful material. (Feathers from factory-farmed birds are generally useless because of their one-sided diets.)
Raw feathers should be hardened before cutting. To do this, first push the marrow back with a wooden stick, cut the pen roughly (a diagonal cut) and hold it carefully over a flame (but don't let it burn). You can also put it in hot sand that has been heated in an oven. This causes the material to harden. If you want, you can burn in an ink reservoir with a hot nail. Just as with reed pens, burn in a hole about two inches above the tip of the pen. In the end, you split the pen, sharpen it a bit – and you're done!

To process a raw feather requires some practice. But, skillfully made they are a great writing and drawing utensil.

Steel quills

Steel quills are available in all sizes. There are nib and calligraphy pens; ornamental, writing and drawing pens in a wide variety of designs. Smaller steel quills are best for drawing. The pen itself is placed on a penholder made of wood or plastic and carefully cleaned after working. Which pen you like best is a matter of taste and the assortment available at your local art supply store (since steel quill pens have been supplanted by indelible pencils and ball-points, the selection has dropped sharply). But dip pens, steno nibs, Bremer Börsenfeder and of course, classic drawing pens are all well suited for drawing.
When working with the different pens, you will soon find that certain pens feel good to you. This is partly due to the pen itself, but partly also because you "break in" your drawing utensil while working. In other words, you give your pen a certain "edge" with the angle with which you usually guide it. The effect of this is that it always feels better to draw with your old pen than with a new one. That's why I recommend:

Handle your pens with care and look after them well.

Wipe off the old ink and don't let it dry. You should also occasionally remove dried remains with a steel brush. You can also burn the pen with a lighter after buying it to make it softer.

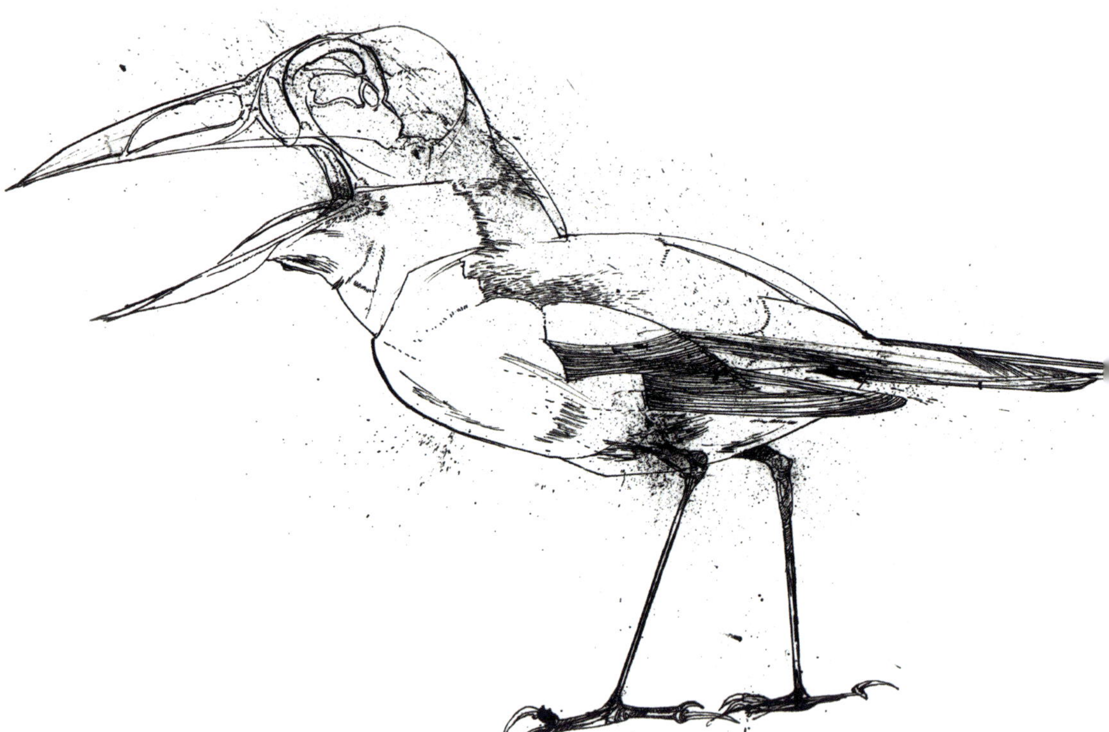

Reed pens

Reed pens are also wonderful to draw with. You cut the end of a short piece of reed or bamboo at an angle with a knife. An angle of about 30 degrees is good. The roundness of the reed creates a curved cut, much like a fountain pen's. Next, split the tip and then sharpen it from both sides so that two even sides are created to the right and left of the gap. (If you want, you can harden your reed pen in the oven.) The stroke of a reed pen is wonderfully soft and lively and cannot be imitated using any steel quill.
Another trick is to carve a small ink reservoir in your pen before splitting it: Drill a tiny hole in the long side of the pen tip where the ink can collect so you don't have to dip your pen in ink as often. The hole for this should be a little less than half an inch above the pen tip, right where the slit begins. But beware: Bamboo splits quickly so you should scrape the hole rather than drilling it, very carefully, with a sharp knife and with very gentle pressure. You'll see it's worth the effort. Reed pens with reservoirs create longer, more powerful lines.

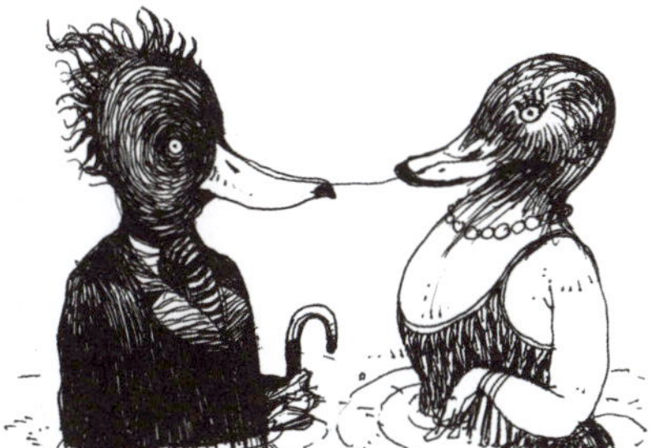

HANS BALTZER

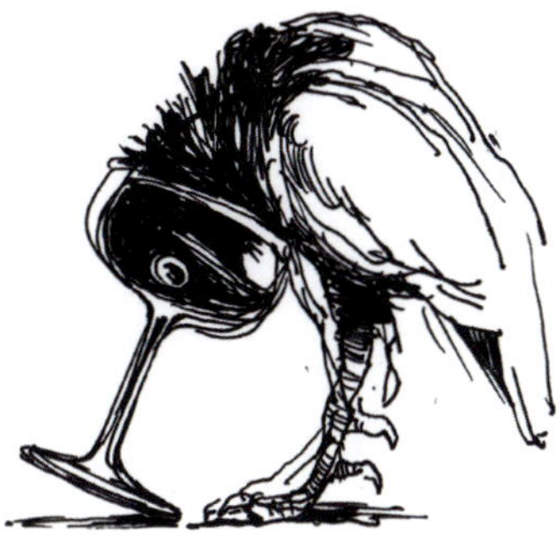

Glass pens

Glass pens have a spindle-shaped twist at the end that serves as the tip. Glass pens are easy to handle, they produce a pleasing line, which, however, corresponds little to the pressure you use. The advantage of the glass pen is its easy handling. Its disadvantage becomes clear when you drop it. Then you have to buy a new one...

Drawing pens

Drawing pens are mechanical pens that are predominantly used for technical drawings. Their big advantage lies in their simple construction: They basically consist of two isosceles steel tips, which are held apart by a screw. The ink collects between the two tips. With a drawing pen you can make straight lines or circles since it can be combined well with rulers and compasses unlike normal pens. Because they are less suitable for freehand drawing, they are mainly used for graphic elements, fonts or construction drawings.

JONAS LAUSTRÖER

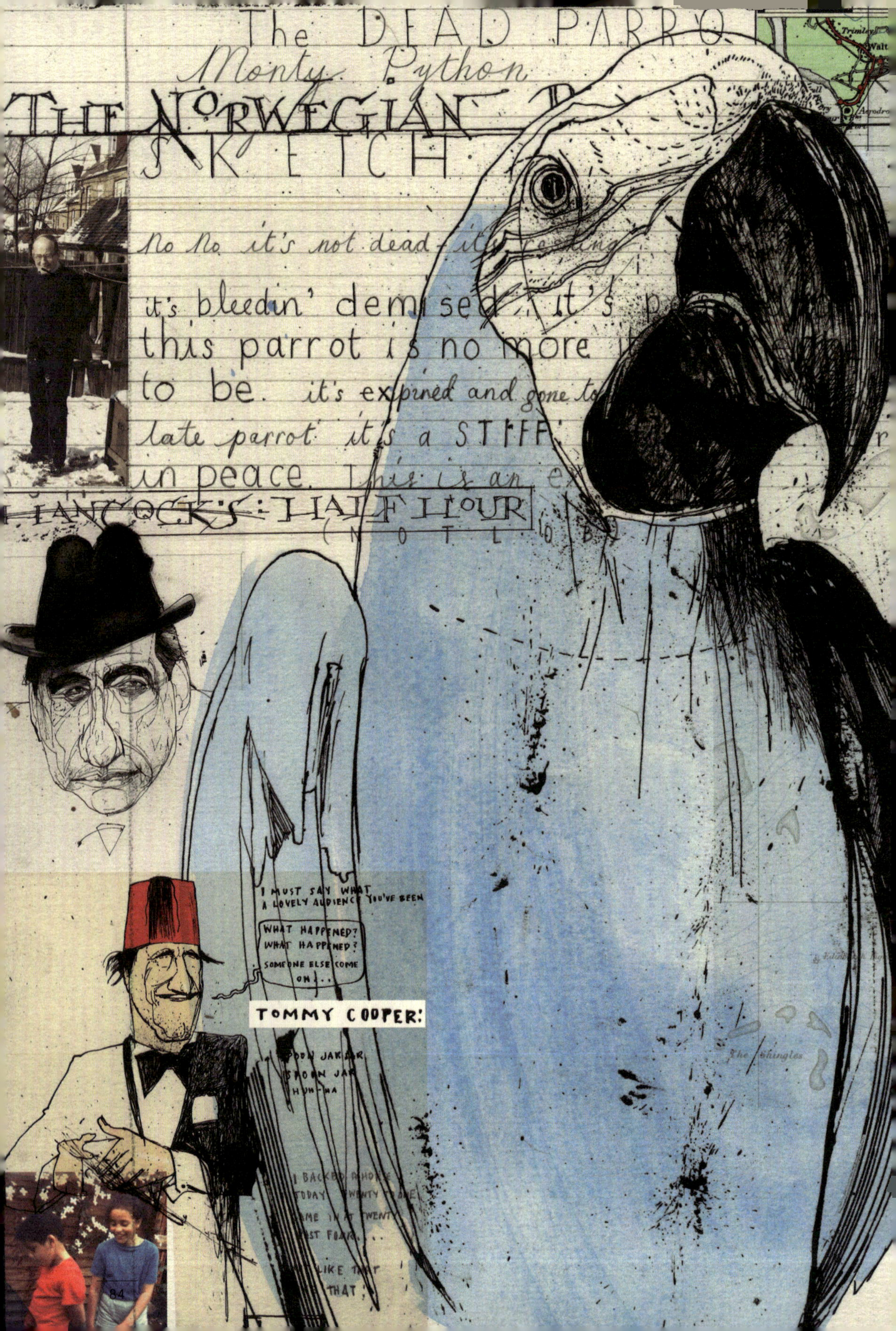
The DEAD PARRO
Monty Python
THE NORWEGIAN
SKETCH
No No it's not dead
it's bleedin' demised
this parrot is no more
to be. it's expired and gone
late parrot it's a STIFF
in peace. This is an
HANCOCK'S HALF HOUR
I MUST SAY WHAT A LOVELY AUDIENCE YOU'VE BEEN
WHAT HAPPENED? WHAT HAPPENED? SOMEONE ELSE COME ON...
TOMMY COOPER:
HUH-HA
I BACKED
TODAY
THAT

Fountain pens and technical pens

Fountain pens are the evolution of steel quills. Basically, a small tank of ink was added to the steel quills. The first fountain pens contained a piston mechanism used to suck up the ink. (You occasionally come across such fountain pens at flea markets, but unfortunately most of the gaskets and containers were made of rubber and in most cases they don't work anymore.) Fountain pens with interchangeable cartridges are much more common. They are very well suited for drawing, produce the usual beautiful, variable pen lines and, compared to fineliners, are cheaper in continuous operation. The disadvantage, however, is the fact that these fountain pens as well as technical or Rapidograph pens contain water-soluble ink. So if you want to color your drawing, cartridge pens will not provide you with a good foundation.

Rapidograph pens are technical drawing utensils that are filled with cartridges much like fountain pens. Their drawing style resembles that of fineliners and they produce a hard, clean line. They are especially suitable for technical drawings and for final artwork made using rulers. Like fountain pens, they contain water-soluble ink and are thus difficult to use as a basis for coloring.

Tip

To avoid ink spots, after each immersion you should make a short stroke with your pen on the edge of the paper or an extra sheet of paper (which is useful to have under your writing hand anyway) or classic blotter paper. Only full pens drip. It is also advisable not to wear your very best T-shirt when working with ink and India ink.

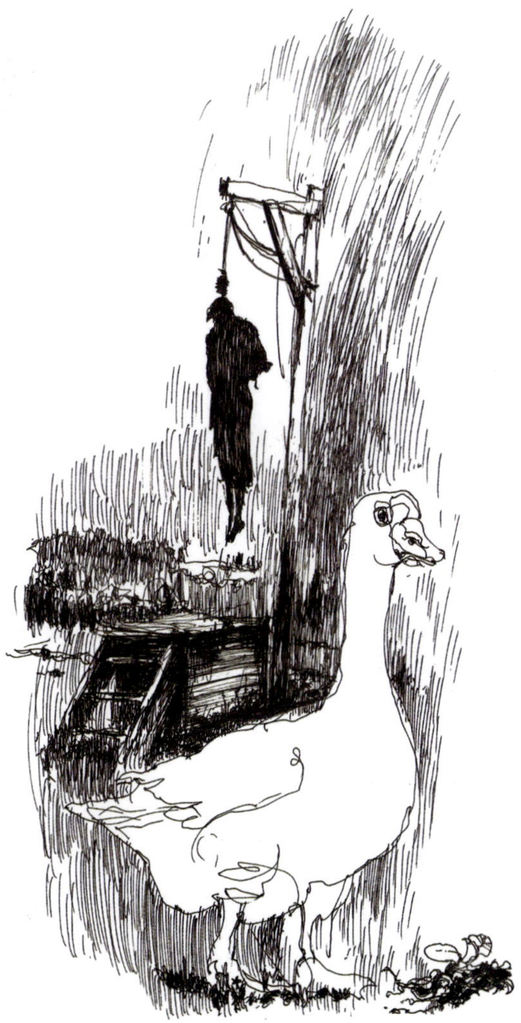

DAVID HUGHES

DAVID VON BASSEWITZ

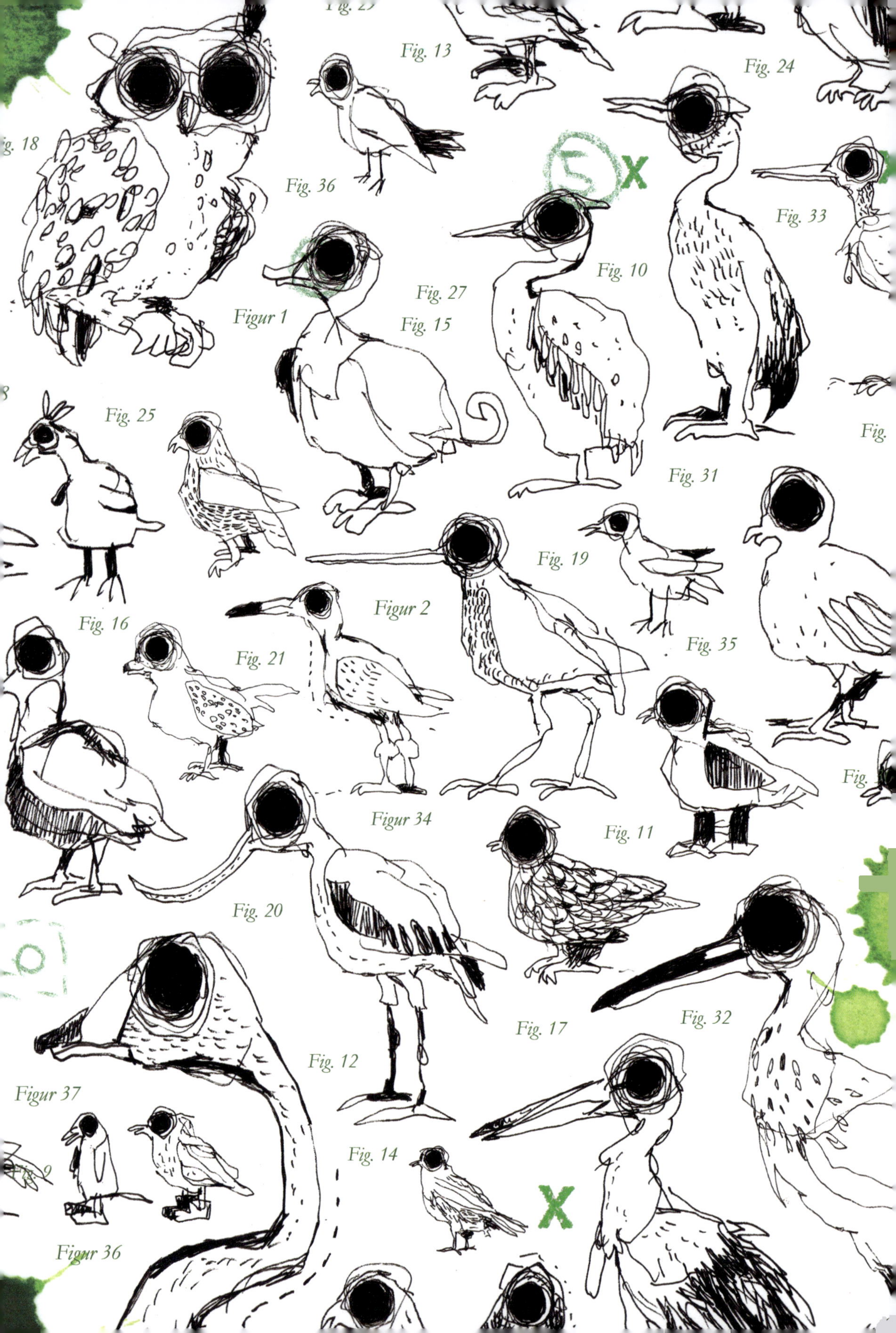
Fig. 13
Fig. 24
Fig. 36
Fig. 33
Fig. 10
Fig. 27
Figur 1
Fig. 15
Fig. 25
Fig. 31
Fig. 19
Figur 2
Fig. 16
Fig. 21
Fig. 35
Figur 34
Fig. 11
Fig. 20
Fig. 17
Fig. 32
Fig. 12
Figur 37
Fig. 14
Fig. 9
Figur 36

Ballpoints, Fineliners and Their Ilk

All artists are willing to suffer for their work.
But why are so few prepared to learn to draw? BANKSY

While traditional pens (whether steel or reed) undoubtedly create beautiful lines, they do have one crucial drawback: They have to be dipped into liquid ink while working. To remedy this, drawing implements that carry their own ink were invented long ago. Even Galileo Galilei is said to have devised a forerunner of the ballpoint pen and at least since the dawn of the modern age numerous patents have been devoted to solving this problem. Piston-filled fountain pens, indelible pencils and ballpoint pens of more or less suitable quality were invented.

Anyone entering an average stationery store today can marvel at the countless consequences of this ingenuity: pens, pens, pens in all colors, shapes and sizes. Nevertheless, most of them still work according to the same old principles: liquid ink is stored in a reservoir or carrier and flows through a pressure-sensitive closure (as in ballpoint pens) or directly over the core of a fiber body (like a felt-tip pen and fineliner) onto the paper.

They are all wonderfully suited for drawing and illustrating, but with some peculiarities that I'd like to describe in this chapter.

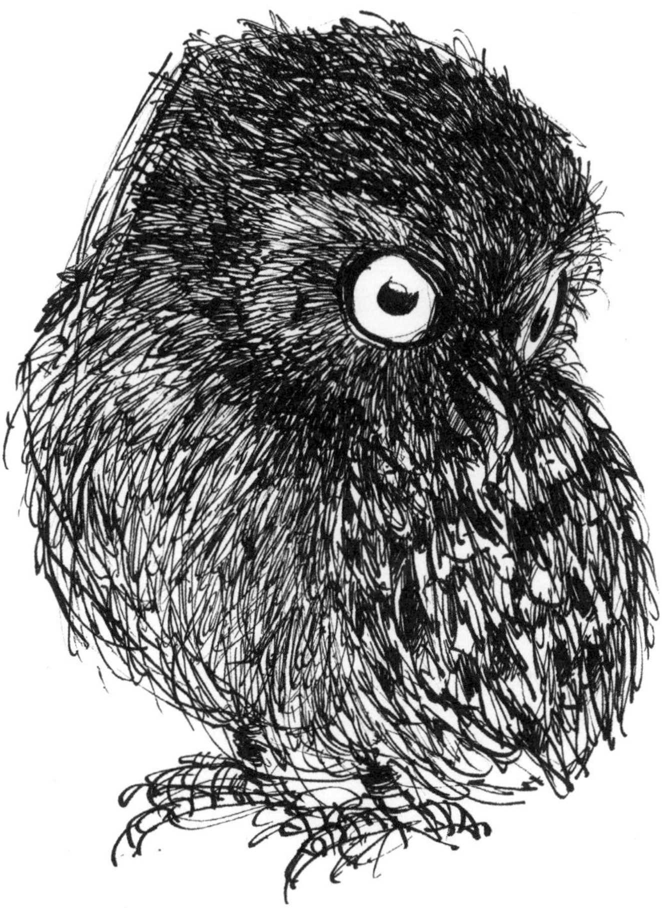

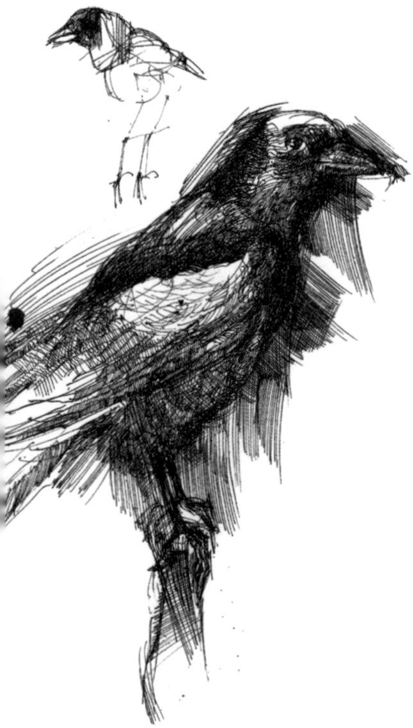

Ballpoint pens

Ballpoint pens have existed in their present form since the 1930s (the story that they are a by product of space exploration like the Teflon pan is mere legend). Their inventor, László József Bíró, fled Nazi persecution of the Jews during the Second World War and took his idea to South America, from where his "Eterpen" conquered the world.
Ballpoint pens work with an ink reservoir, at the end of which is a small metal bead. While rolling across the paper, the ball picks up the ink on the inside and then transfers the ink to the paper. This leads to uniform, non-spattering ink application.

As an economical product, ballpoint pens didn't catch on right away among artist circles, but are now an important part of almost everyone's pencil case. Their advantages lie above all in a good price-performance ratio and the fact that the quality of their lines remains the same throughout their "lifetime" and does not gradually decline as it does with fiber pencils. In addition, with ballpoint pens (unlike many other pens), you can also create something like grayscale: if you only press very lightly, the stroke reacts dynamically and gives off less ink.

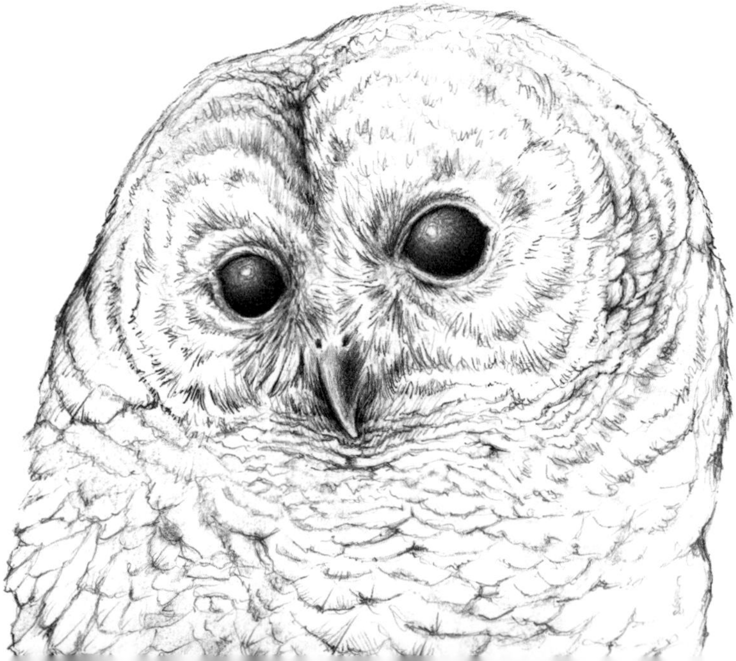

ABOVE:
BORIS RÖHRL

BELOW:
CLAUDIA HAHN

RIGH:
UTE HELMBOLD

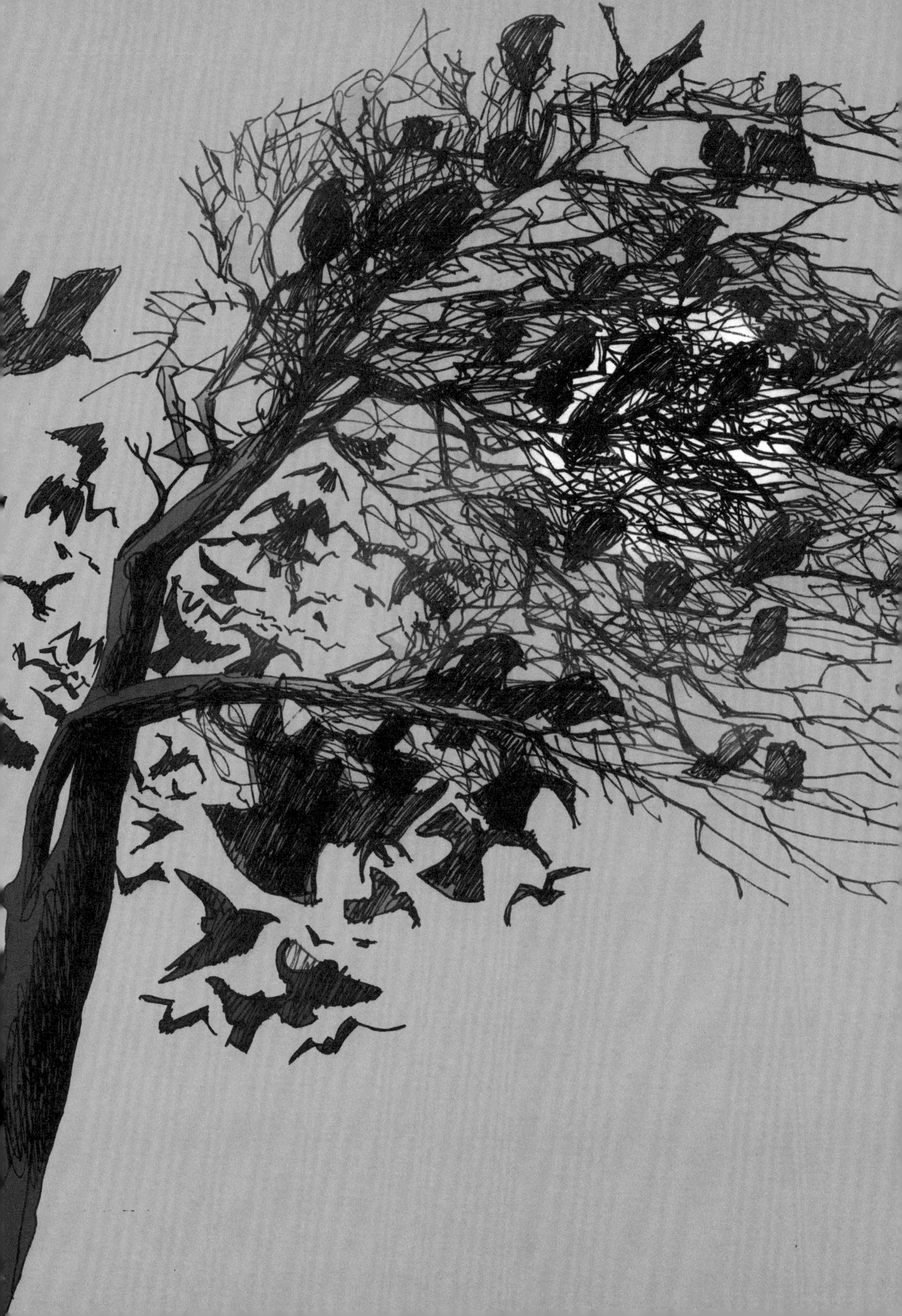

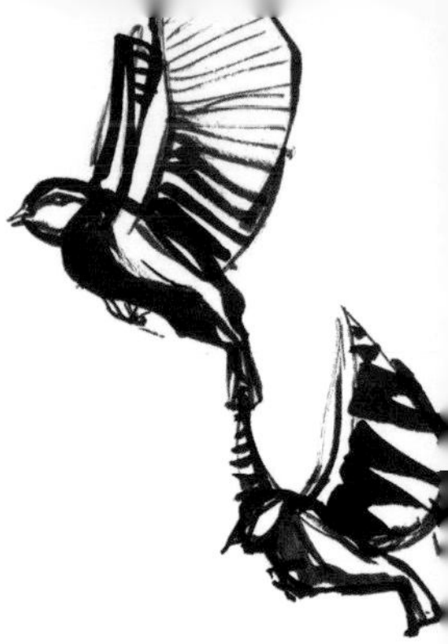

Fineliners

Fineliners are technically felt pens; they work on the principle that the color is held by an absorbent carrier material (usually polyester fibers), from which it moves forwards via a fiber tip to the paper.
This facilitates a good flow of ink, but with the disadvantage that the ink stored in the fiber becomes less over time, since the largest capillaries always empty first. Therefore, the more you write with a fineliner, the worse it writes and you are forced to spend a lot of money for more and more new fineliners. To prevent dehydration, the fibers are protected with an airtight cap (do not leave it open or the quality of a fineliner diminishes quickly).

Fineliners are offered in all sizes and qualities. For working with them you just need to decide whether you want a pen with water-resistant or water-soluble ink. This is important if you want to color your drawings afterwards with watercolors (although sometimes "blurring" is intentional, try it with water...). Otherwise, the selection of your fineliners is a matter of preference.

Presumably, all illustrators have a whole bundle of one or the other favorite pen in a drawer.

For example, I have been using the 0.5 mm Edding Profipen for years. Of course you can use everything from neon colored pens to sepia tones for drawing.

Rollerball pens

Rollerball pens are sort of a compromise between fountain pens and ballpoint pens because they have a reservoir of liquid ink but their tip is also made of a ceramic or metal ball. The main difference between them and ballpoint pens is that their ink is many times thinner, which allows for light, flowing drawings.
Remember, though, that almost all rollerball pens contain water-soluble ink. Unlike fine-liners and ballpoint pens they are not suitable for preliminary drawings under watercolors.

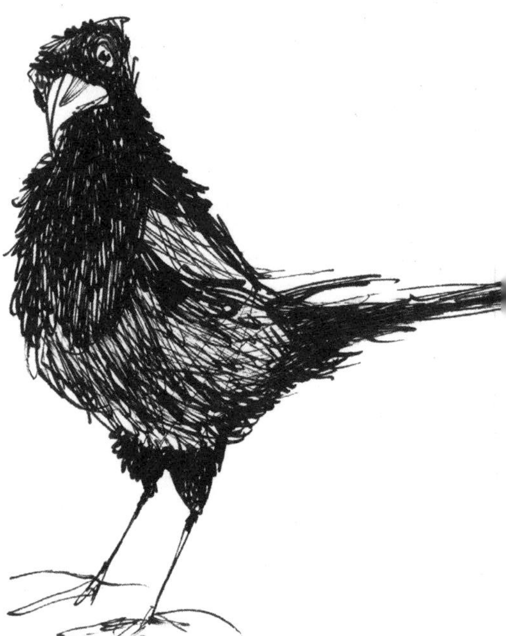

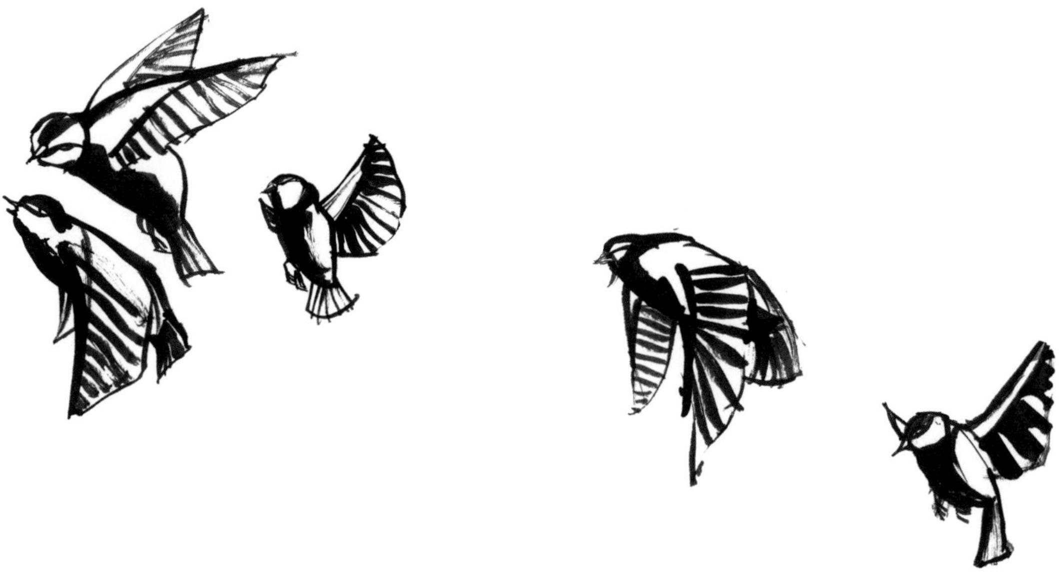

Brush pens

A special drawing utensil comes from Japan. Brush pens originally developed for calligraphy combine an ink reservoir with a brush tip, or a "proper" synthetic brush.

Brush pens are a brilliant invention. They are portable, refillable and you can basically work just as you can with a conventional brush. They create a very aesthetically pleasing stroke (which varies from very fine to very thick depending on the pressure used) and create rich, deep colors.

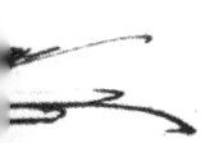

Once only made as black brush pens, Pentel has added product ranges in all colors. There are now also alcohol-based brush markers from their competitors Copic and Faber. Even the disadvantage of the earliest models that the brush pens used only water-soluble ink (water-resistant paint made the brush stick together) has been fixed in some models: They are now also available in a waterproof version.

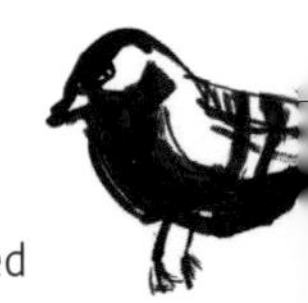

In fact, brush pens are just as well suited for quick street-side sketching in the café as for professional work in the studio (I like brush pens with light grays, for example, if I want to add a quick glazing tone to a sketch).

So it's hardly surprising that so many illustrators (especially in comics and manga) swear by brush pens, because they combine the advantages of pens and brushes in one product. In a word: Buy!

Markers and Felt Pens

What I need is a big fat magic marker.
JOHN TRAVOLTA IN "PULP FICTION" 1994

Every child knows that felt-tip pens are great for painting and drawing. We usually forget about it, though, while growing up.
That's a mistake, as some designers discovered in the late 1970s. They took the conventional sets of felt-tip pens with their few child-appropriate primary colors and added a broad, nuanced color palette, and suddenly far more was possible.

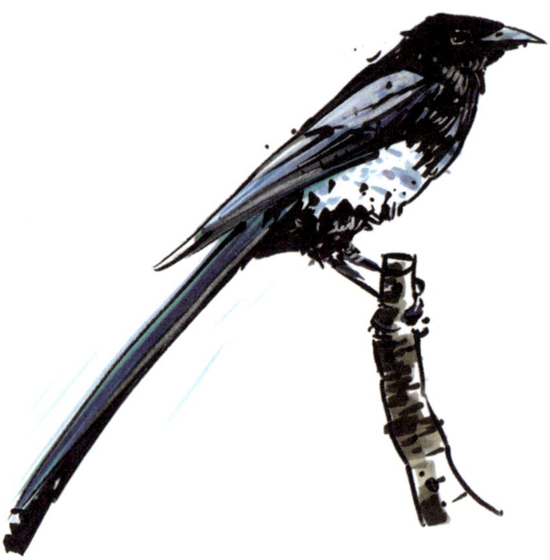

The new generation of felt-tip pens – markers – created a new genre that revolutionized layout techniques and scribble illustrations (once the domain of liquid tempera and watercolor paints).

Like all other felt-tip pens, markers originated in Japan. They contain a core made of polyester fibers (or comparable fibrous material), which absorbs the color or ink and evenly dispenses it at the nib. Many professional-grade pens (which we usually understand as "markers") are refillable and have replaceable fiber nibs.
The most common solvent is alcohol, which enables even application and dries quickly. Alcohol-based markers can easily be used on copies without smearing the drawing. The chief brand is Copic, which sells a variety of models in hundreds of colors (currently 364) and with a variety of fiber nibs. We differentiate between *flexible* brush nibs for loose, organic drawings and replaceable, *stiff* nibs more suited for technical drawings.
Copic markers can also be sprayed with a compressor or a handy airbrush system and there are also very wide markers for sketching on flip charts.

The chief advantage of markers is their short drying time.

Their second big plus is their beautiful, colorful strokes. They are particularly suited for clearly accentuated areas, for instance for coloring drafts, storyboards or advertising sketches.

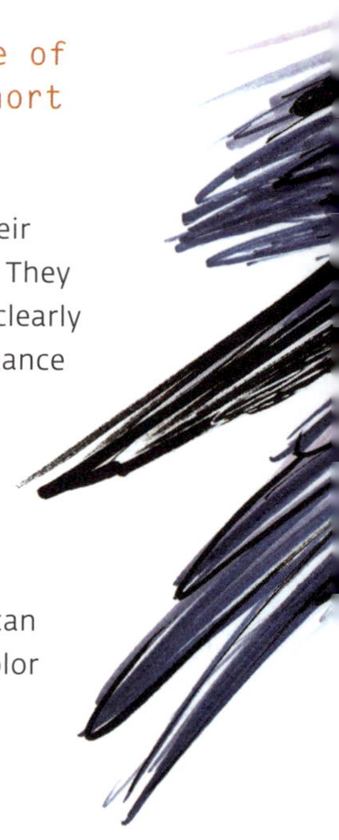

Working with markers is a glaze technique, so you can employ your basic watercolor skills because the fields of

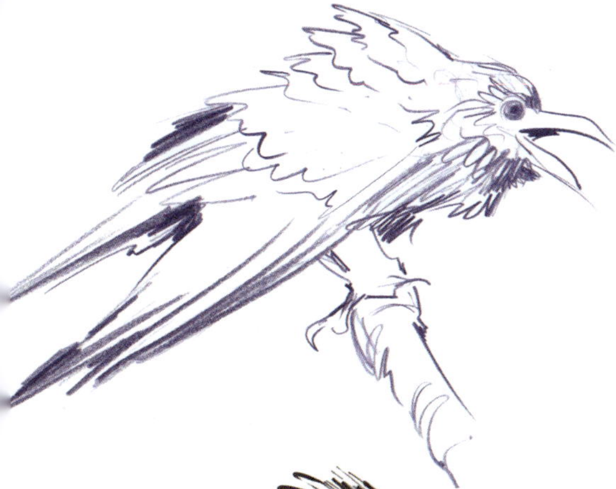

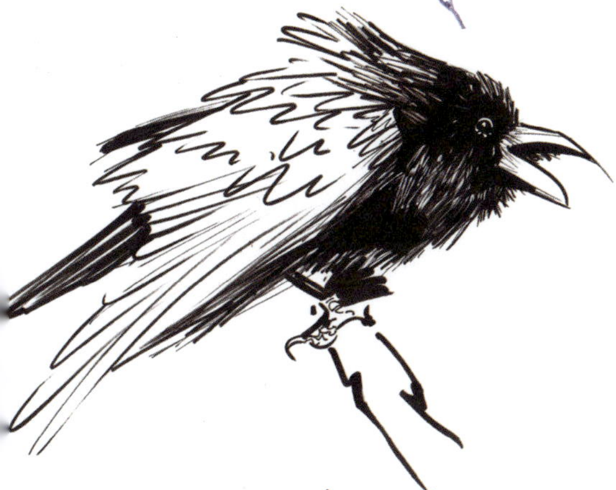

color also shine through the layers. As in watercoloring (or "multiply blend" mode in Photoshop) the layers of color multiply to create darker shades. If you go over the same area a number of times (layering), the color darkens. Therefore, just as in watercolors you work from light to dark and use the white of the paper as the lightest area. You can also use markers to achieve exciting results like multiple color nuances or a mixture of other shades.

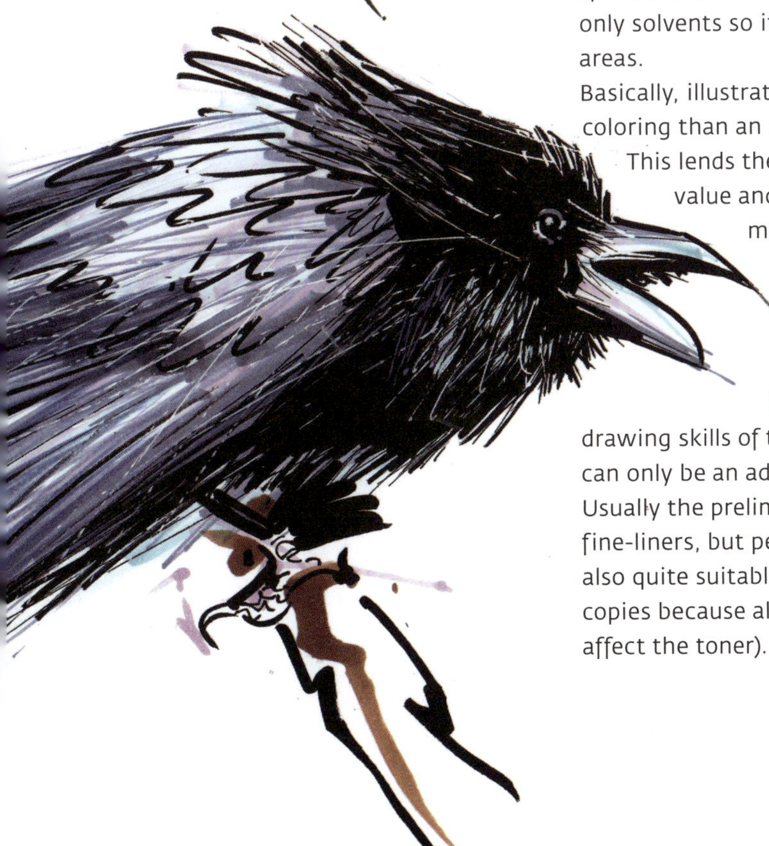

You can produce soft color transitions using special "blender" markers. A blender contains only solvents so it dissolves the bordering color areas.
Basically, illustrating with markers is more like coloring than an opaque painting technique. This lends the underlying drawing huge value and turns layout, scribble and marker illustrations into very drawing-based styles.

But this also means that the quality of a marker illustration relies on the drawing skills of the illustrator. A confident line can only be an advantage in markers.
Usually the preliminary drawing is done with fine-liners, but pencils or ballpoint pens are also quite suitable (you can even color photocopies because alcohol-based markers don't affect the toner).

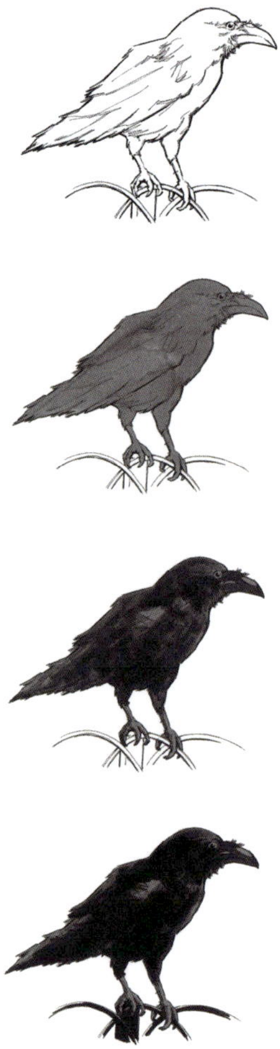

But markers are great for far more than just scribble illustrations or layouts: versatile felt-tip pens are also good for "real" illustrations. Many illustrators use markers for nearly everything, from the first step to the final artwork. Just note that some shades lose their luminance and brilliance in reproductions.

Markers are especially popular among comic and manga artists.

Their ease of use and good painting properties speak for themselves. Nevertheless allow me to mention two minor drawbacks of fiber pens.

You'll notice the first as soon as you start shopping: since they are mainly marketed to professionals, markers aren't exactly cheap. If you plan to buy a complete set of them you'll be making a small investment. So think carefully about what color palette you plan to begin with and how it can be best supplemented over time.

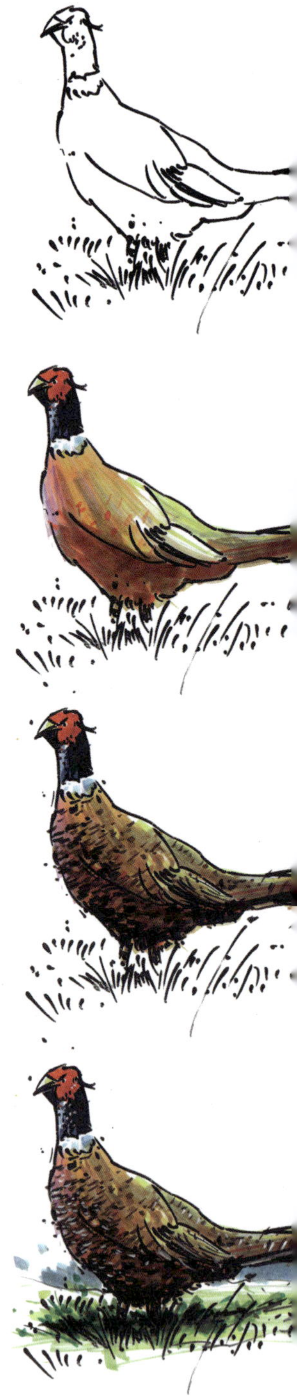

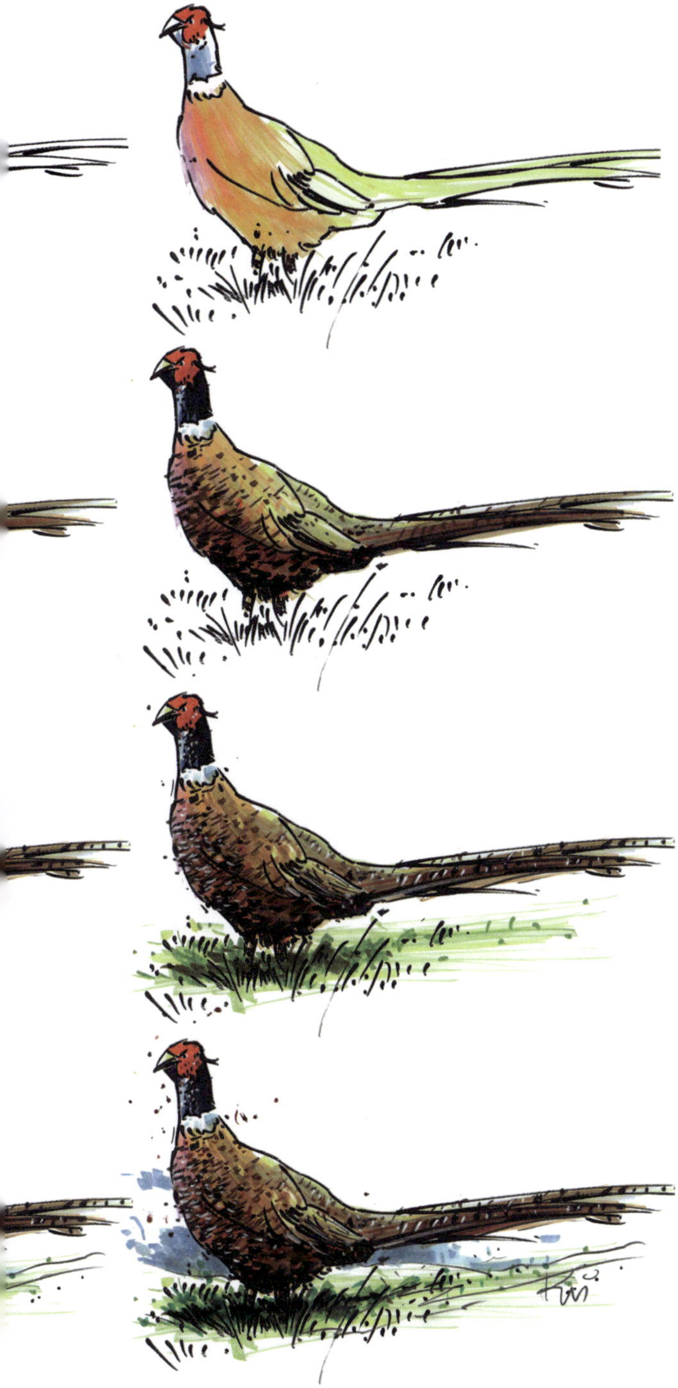

The second is a more long-term problem: most marker inks aren't lightfast. You cannot create pictures to hang on a wall with them because marker images fade with time.

Tip

The paper is exceedingly important for work with markers. For example, if you use regular copy paper with markers the colors "bleed" quite a bit. This blurs the edges of the colors and the illustration loses luminance. Many manufacturers therefore offer specially coated, bleed-proof layout paper. So if you plan to use markers to color photocopies, it's best to make the copies on this special marker paper.

Watercolors

Watercolors is the first and the last thing an artist does.
WILLEM DE KOONING

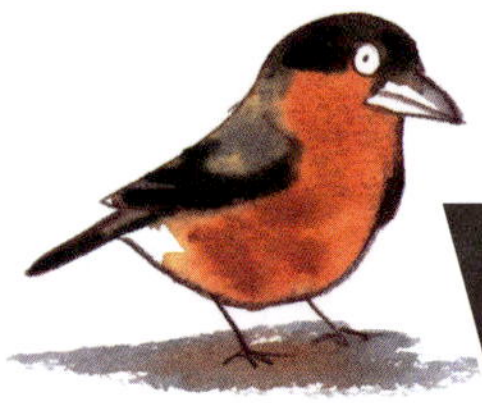

Watercolors have a strange reputation. Like they're actually only for children, a hobby for Sunday painters, a technique used by bored dentists' wives on vacation in Tuscany and similarly silly notions. That is nothing less than nonsense. Anyone who has seriously worked with watercolor will confirm that it is a very complicated and demanding technique.

Watercolor is one of the oldest paints used by humanity. It is based on the vegetable binder acacia gum (an African resin), glycerin and honey. It's water-soluble and can be re-dissolved when wetted. The appeal of the watercolor technique lies in its strong translucency and its delicate character.
As with all glazing techniques, for watercolors we use the color of the paper for painting. This means that there is no white paint, but you simply don't paint white and light spots in your picture. This requires extensive knowledge of light and shadow. If you don't paint the white, you have to know the lighting conditions right from the start. There is not much room for trial and error. Once a piece of paper is covered with paint, it becomes difficult to remove. This makes watercolors a challenging technique.
If you paint an oil painting, for example, you can simply lighten a spot that is too dark in the picture with white – that's not so easy with watercolors. In addition, the water used while painting soon flows everywhere except where you want it. The paint eludes direct control by the painter.

You could say watercolor is the anarchist of painting techniques.

It always does what it wants. Using less water doesn't help: When working with watercolors you mustn't be economical with the wet element.

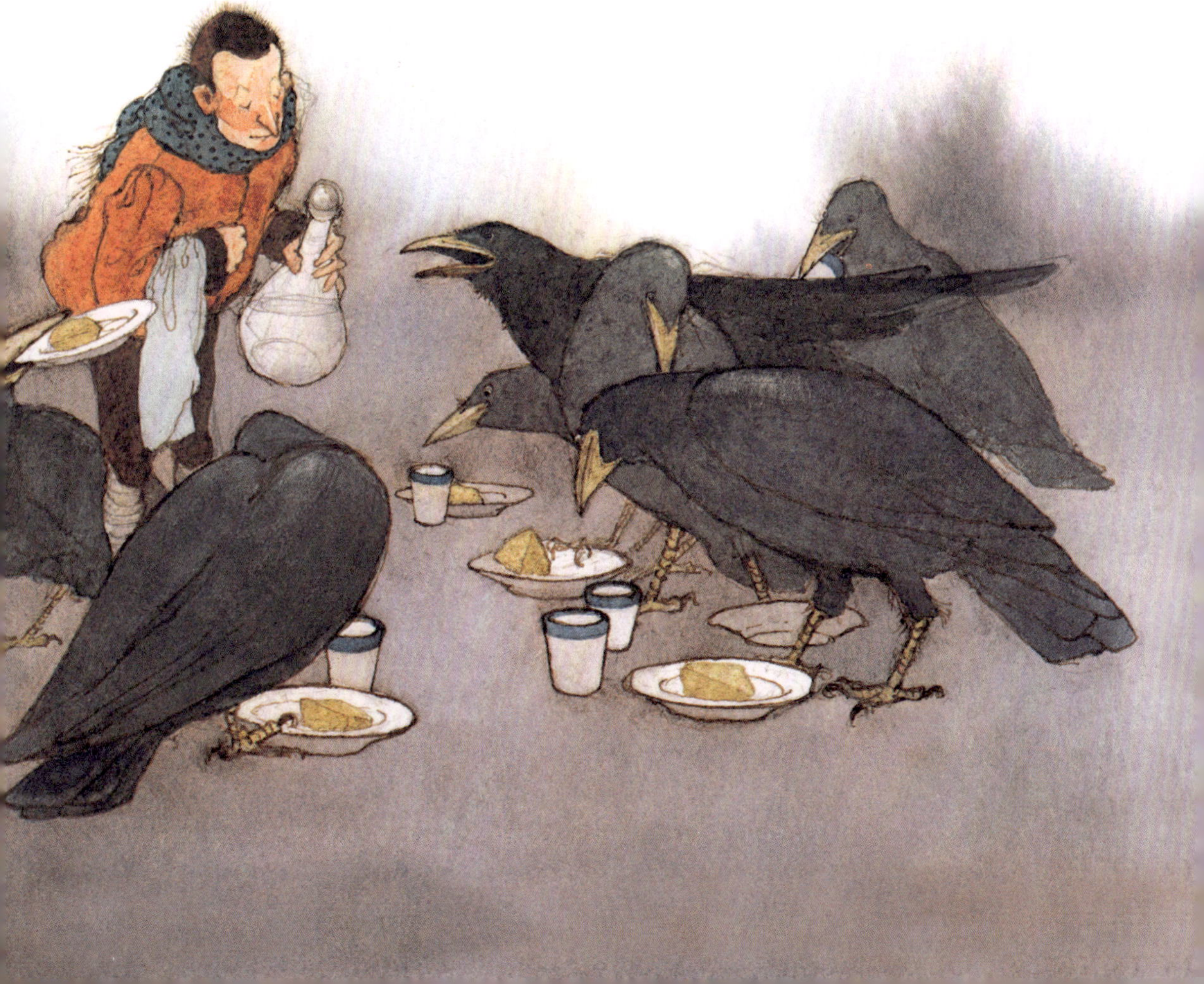

Watercolor paint lives through thin layers applied with lots of water. If you use too little or the paint is too thick, it loses its luminosity. That's why working with watercolors requires a lot of practice, because its inherent unpredictability actually makes watercolor one of the most difficult techniques ever.

Watercolor is tricky, but believe me, it's worth it!

The first and most important tip for dealing with watercolors is to break down the many different ways of painting with watercolors to the two main applications.

Basically, we only differentiate between two techniques when working with watercolors: the glaze, or the work with thin, superimposed layers of paint; and the wash, or working with wet paint, which is allowed to run together wet.
All other techniques basically come under one or the other technique – or a combination of both. But, honestly, you have to have some experience for both of them.
Let's have a look at their application:

The glaze

The painting technique of glazing is based on the phenomenon that with thin layers of paint, we see the underlying layer shining through. One can imagine a glaze like several layers of colored slides. With each additional layer, the color darkens. (The technique is similar to multiply mode in Photoshop.) This effect is used to create spatiality and light and shadow by, for example, painting over areas of the picture with the same color after the paint dries.
When glazing, we lay layers one by one, wait until they are dry, and repeat the process in the parts of the picture that need more color.

The advantage of the glaze is its easy manageability and, for watercolors, good control.

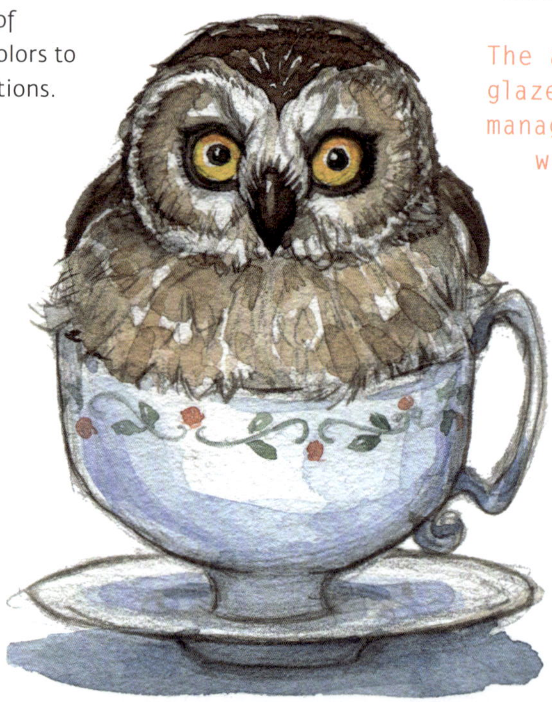

TIMOTHY BUSH

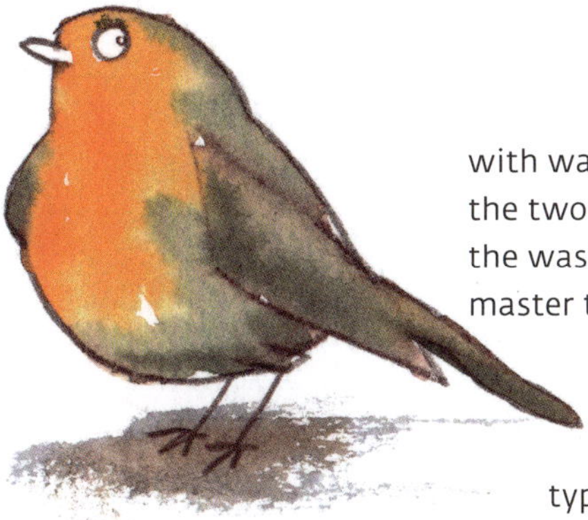

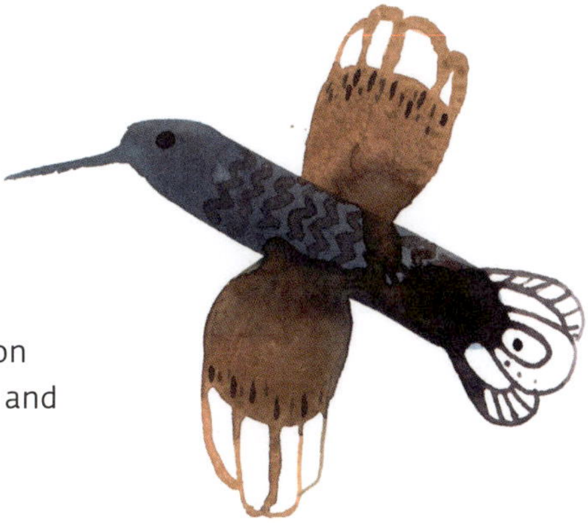

The wash

With the wash, we take advantage of the fact that wet paint runs when it encounters other spots of wet paint. In this case, we carefully let color surfaces abut one another or add paint to areas that are already wet. We try to control the inevitable resulting blends by skillful dosing and directing with the brush to create the desired effect in the picture. Obviously, you have to factor in some failed attempts, but practice also makes perfect here.
The big advantage of the wash is that we can use it to create incredibly smooth transitions. Especially for organic forms, for lighting moods, for water, clouds or the like, the technique is therefore indispensable.
So we are dealing with only two basic techniques. All work with watercolors is based on the two pillars of the glaze and the wash, and once you master these two basic techniques you master watercolors. Depending on what type of picture you're painting, you decide on either or a number of combinations. For example, in one picture you use the wash technique for the sky, while you may paint the house in the foreground using the glazing technique.

Watercolor remains an anarchist. It's a little chaotic and takes time and patience to control. At the same time, it's a great technique: not only because it's relatively inexpensive and you can carry watercolors in practical boxes while traveling – for example for your sketchbook or for picturesque memos. Above all, watercolor is a wonderful painting technique. Delicate and powerful, full of lightness and depth, it is certainly one of the most beautiful ways of bringing color into play. So give it a chance!

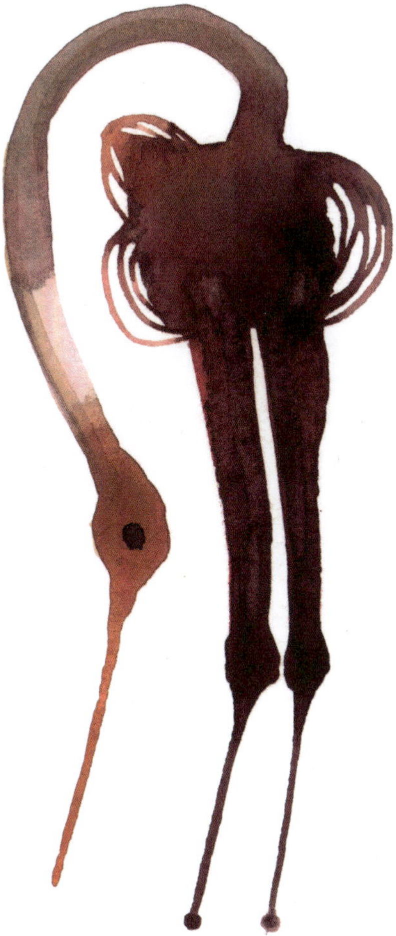

Gouache and Tempera

Gouache is a really strange sounding German word.
GONG LONG YU, GUEST STUDENT FROM CHINA

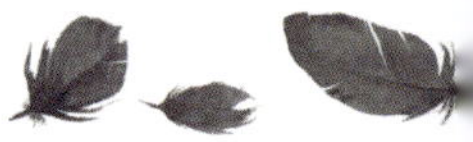

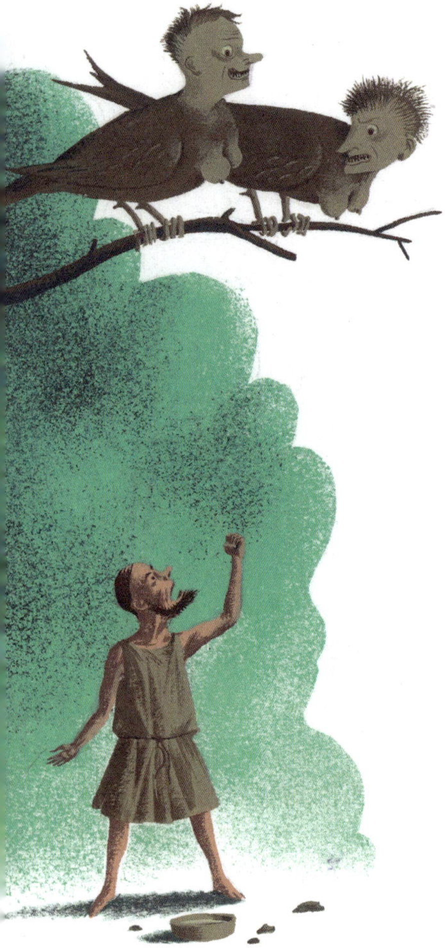

Gouache and tempera are the oldest of painting techniques. Long before oil or watercolors (at least in its current transportable form) and very, very long before acrylic, the two binders were almost the only ways to put color on supports.

To understand what I mean, let's take a look at the theory of painting materials: What is the difference between all the paints? What makes oil oil, acrylic acrylic and differentiates a colored pencil from a crayon? In fact, the actual differences are not the colors themselves. The red you find in a colored pencil, in a watercolor box or in ink is often exactly the same red pigment. The real difference between the painting techniques lies in the glue, the material that holds the pigments together and ensures that they do not simply fall off the picture after drying. In painting, this adhesive is called "binder" and it's this binder that defines the different techniques depending on its makeup.

Let's take a closer look at the two oldest paints and the binders they contain. For tempera, they once used one of the simplest binders in the world: an egg. Since late antiquity (and even before that, for example on Egyptian mummy portraits), tempera was *the* paint of choice. In addition to egg tempera there were related types of tempera paint containing casein, starch or similar binders. What they all have in common is that they are processed in a water-soluble form, but after setting they are relatively resistant to abrasion due to the traces of oil they contain.

Tempera is usually applied in layers, which has the disadvantage that soft transitions are difficult to achieve. The main advantage of the tempera is therefore in smooth, monochrome colored surfaces. It is very well suited for this, which explains why tempera is still used frequently in schools. When dry, however, tempera tends to change in hue a great deal. This is a negative characteristic it shares with gouache paint.

Gouache is not dissimilar to tempera in terms of the color effect. In fact, gouache painting evolved from tempera painting. It is also soluble in water, but it can be slightly dissolved when moistened again (with the emphasis is on "slightly" – because that's all it is). Due to this property, gouache can be used in a more painterly manner than rather simple tempera. The gouache binder is basically the same one that also lends watercolor its durability: acacia gum, the resin of North African acacia trees. In fact, we could say that gouache is nothing more than watercolor paint with chalk added.

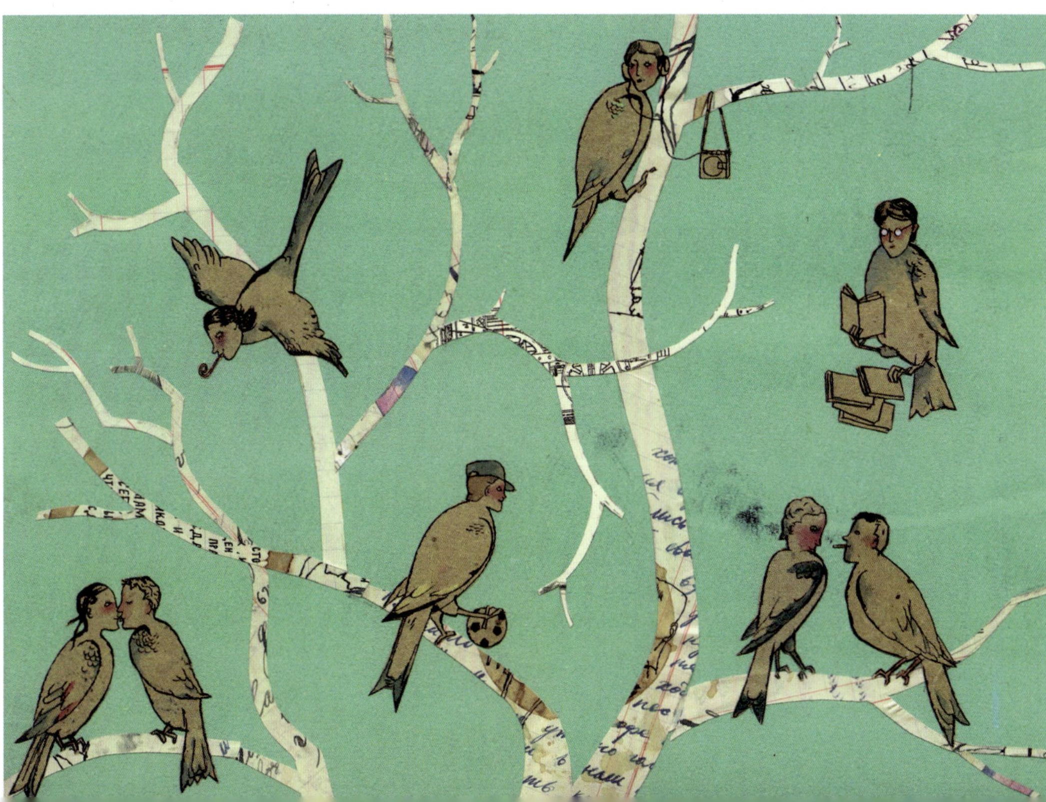

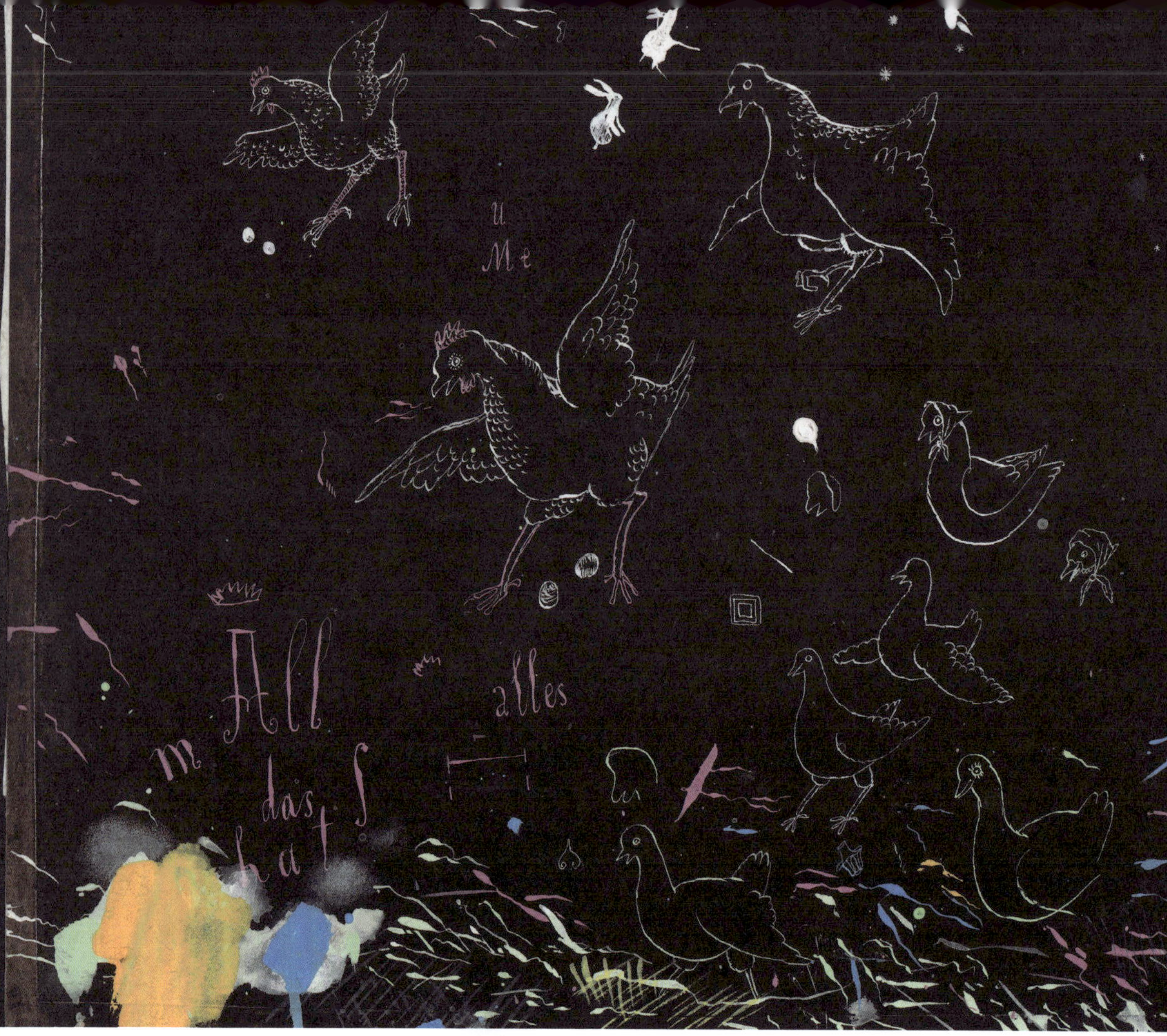

The invention of gouache dates back to the early Middle Ages and was originally used primarily for book painting.

The advantage of gouache is that with it you can combine the painting methods of paste-like and glazing paints.

You can work with it like with oil paint as a technique that covers well, but also like with watercolors in glaze technique. After drying, gouache has a velvety-looking surface. Both of gouache and tempera have lost much of their appeal due to the development of acrylic paint, as their colors tend to change quite a lot when they dry and their use requires a great deal of care and attention. In addition, they are much harder to store than acrylic paint. In fact, tempera and gouache paints can spoil like old egg salad.

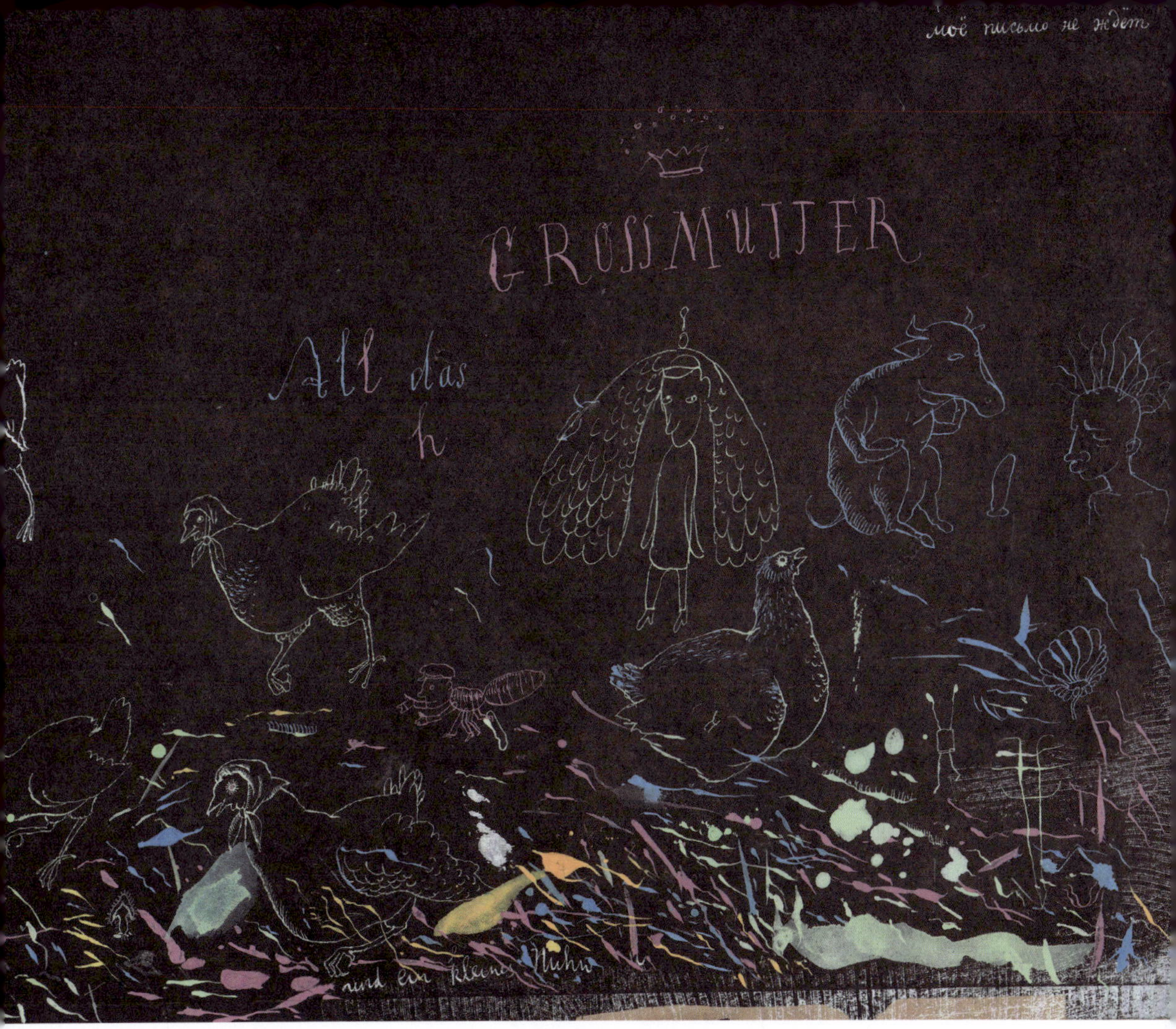

Nevertheless, more than a few illustrators like working in tempera and especially gouache. Their inherent roughness, their crumbliness, their randomness and their obvious "vintage" look are the boons of these techniques. Particularly if you want to create an "old paint" effect, the "oldies" are worth discovering.

Gouache and tempera may be old, they are alive and well.

Tip

Gouache is a natural paint so it can go bad like old milk. Store it in well-sealed jars or use it up immediately.

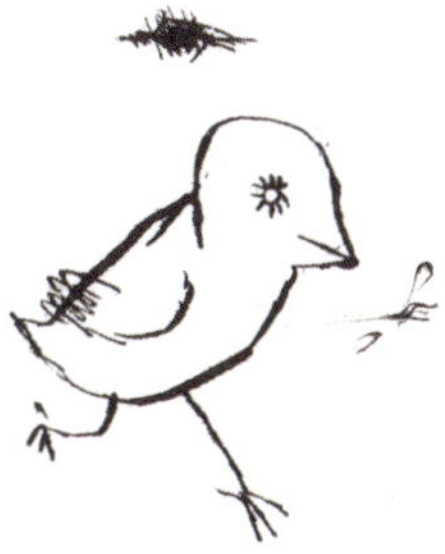

Oil

The best artwork is the most expensive artwork.
OBIAS MEYER, SOTHEBY'S CONTEMPORARY ART DEPARTMENT SPEAKING WITH "DER SPIEGEL"

For a long time, oil paint was considered the paint of *paints*. Oil connotes nobility, quality and solidity, oil sounds like value and continuity. If you had asked my granny, she would have assured you that a *proper* oil painting would be much more valuable than, say, a pen and ink drawing; that oil painting is the best and most difficult of all techniques, the "supreme discipline." Probably most people would agree with her. But should they.

Let's take a closer look at the miraculous stuff: Oil paint is by no means as old as its reputation would have us believe. It was not until the end of the Middle Ages that it entered the painting stage, which had been shared by its competitors gouache, tempera and watercolors since antiquity. In the fourteenth century, Dutch masters (for example Jan van Eyck) replaced the customary tempera paint with the new medium, which soon became *the most* popular paint in art.

Oil paint consists of various oils, such as hemp or linseed oil, resin varnish, turpentine and, of course, pigments. The paste-like paint is usually sold in tubes (in the olden days, it was stored in little bags made of pig's bladders) and in

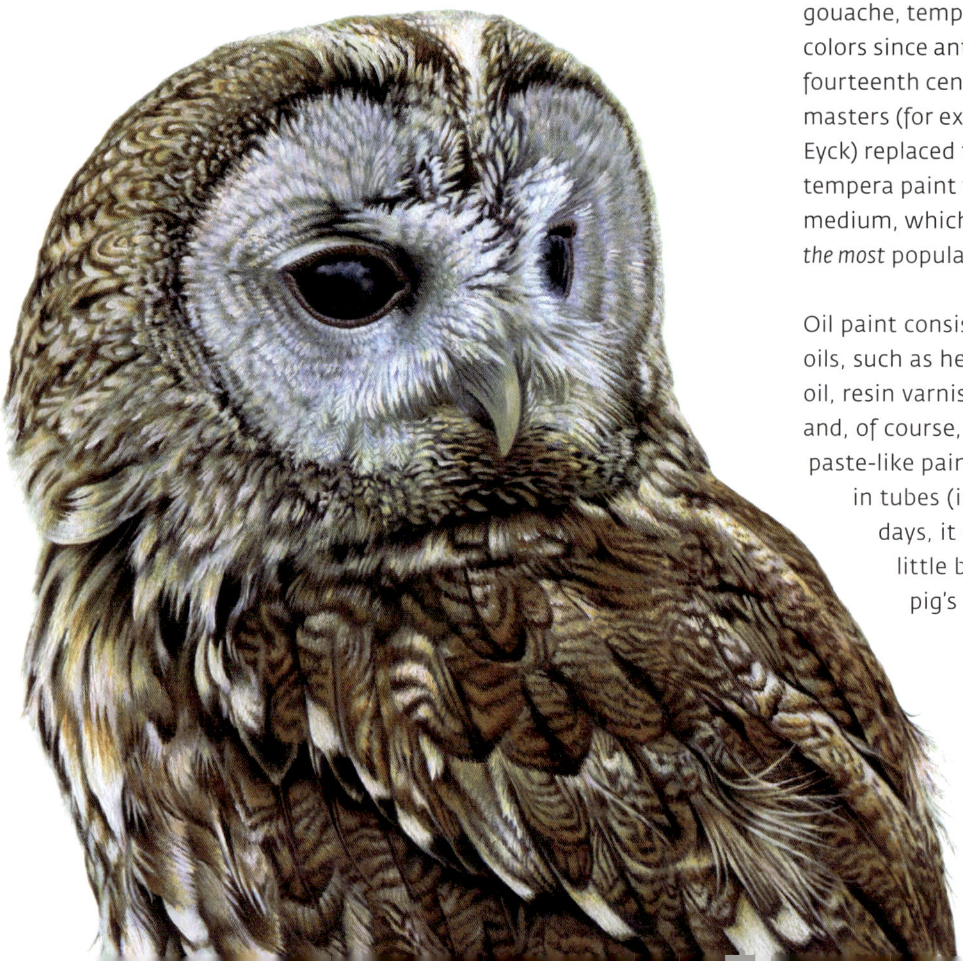

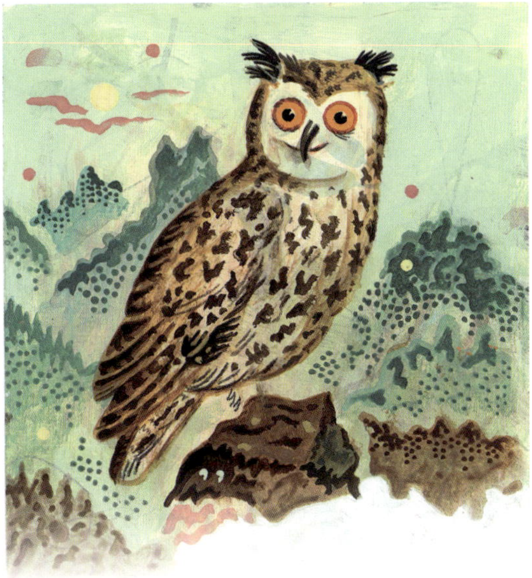

its consistency is a little like toothpaste. It can be used both as cover and as glaze, and its advantages lie in its extremely good painting properties, its ability to cover and its color intensity.

One disadvantage of oil paint is that you cannot combine it very well with other paints.

Water-based paints in particular are not compatible with water-repellent oils. They are therefore usually combined by what is called underpainting. This means that the water-based technique (such as acrylic paint) is applied first and painted over with oil after it dries.

Oil paint can be applied to almost every support. The traditional canvas is not particularly recommendable in illustration. Oil paint also adheres very well to cardboard, wood, cardboard or thick, non-absorbent paper.

Incidentally, in traditional painting, the support did not necessarily have to be white: Thanks to its good coverage, oil paint allows for a variety of painting styles. So you can prime the whole picture first in one color, laying the background of the picture first in a color other than white (which is highly recommended, give it a try ;-)). Oil paints can also be applied directly to the support. You can work from a mid-tone, "raise" it out of a dark background with light hues, or build up your picture in thin layers. In a nutshell, the good painting properties and the coverage of oil paint justify the technique's good reputation.

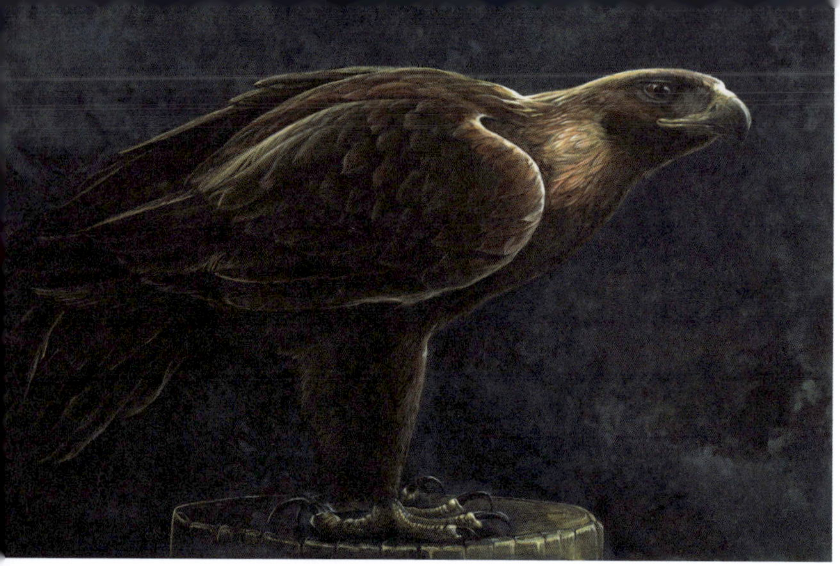

however, not all that's squeezed out of a tube is gold. The first drawback of oil paint reveals itself while you're working: it stinks of turpentine. This is not only annoying; turpentine oils and cellulose thinners needed to work and to clean brushes and materials, are by no means harmless to health. In addition, the great advantage of oil paint at the same time its major drawback: Oil paint dries very slowly.
For painting – particularly precise and detailed painting – that may be a distinct advantage since it allows a painter to work on an oil painting for a long time. An oil painting with thick layers of paint takes days, sometimes weeks or months, to dry. This is good because you have a lot of time to work out details or make corrections.

On the other hand, a long drying time is not so good if, as is often the case with illustrations, it's commissioned work under time pressure.

Deadlines and oil paints will probably never be reconcilable.

For illustrations that have to be finished quickly (e.g. in the editorial sector, if you are working on the next issue of a newspaper), oil paint is highly unsuitable.
But if you have time and are work on a longer-term project (for example on a book), oil paint remains a wonderful technique that still has plenty of adherents today.

In conclusion, we could say that given time, my granny would have been right in her assessment...at least this once. :-)

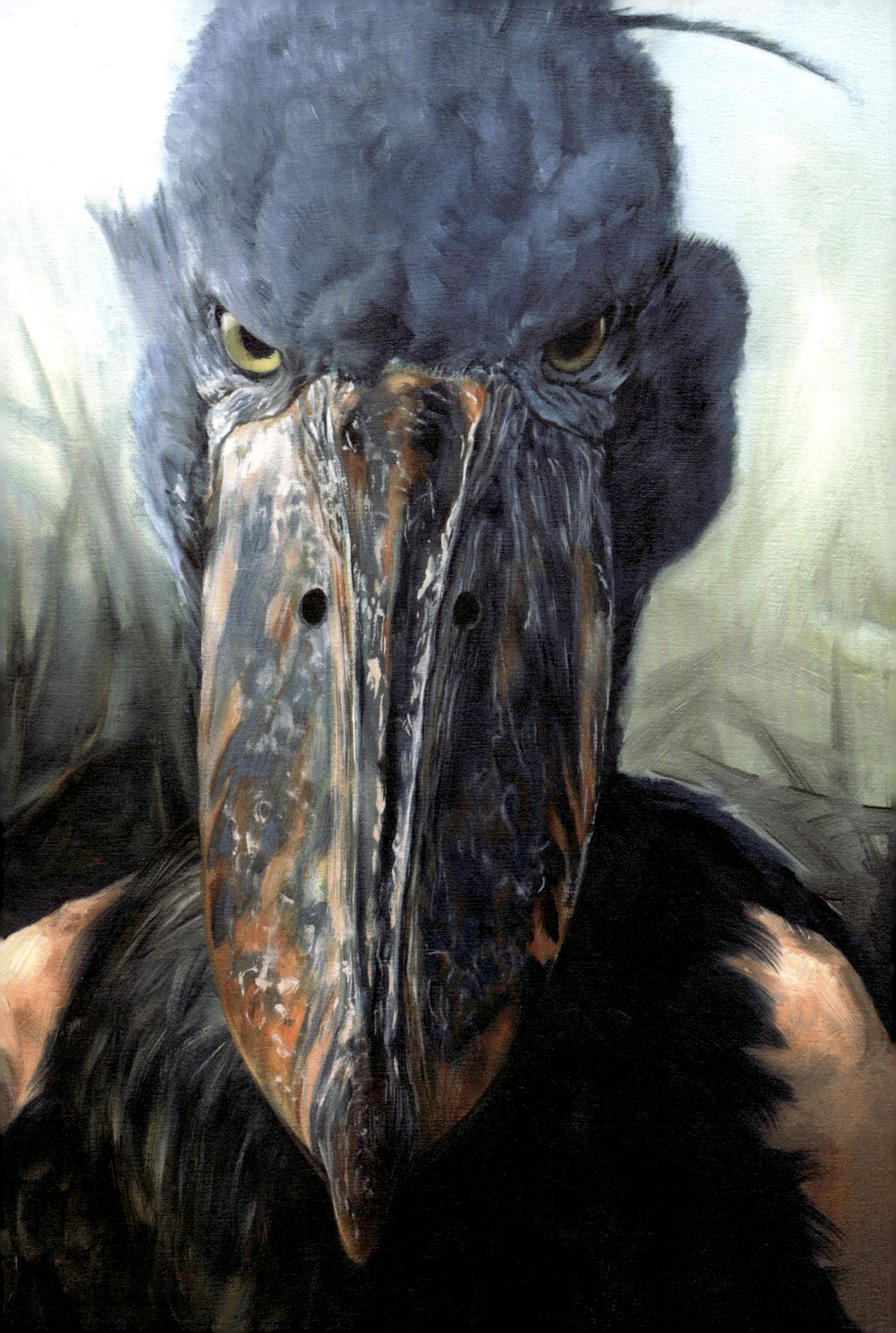

Acrylic Paint

$CH_2{=}CH\text{-}COR$

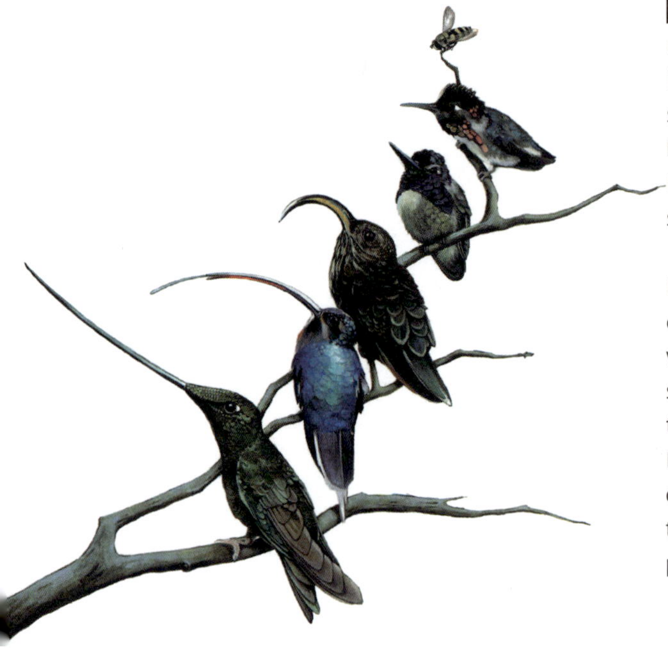

Painting was revolutionized over sixty years ago by the chemical industry's introduction of acrylate polymers. Acrylic paints were first devised for murals and made their way into the art world in the early 1950s. Based on a pigment suspension in acrylic polymer emulsion, the new paint had the incredible advantage over oil paint that it could be diluted with water – eliminating the stench of turpentine.

Its drying time also differs hugely from that of oils. Acrylic dries quickly and thus enables rapid work. It also adheres excellently to almost all surfaces and you can, if needed, apply it in thick layers.
No wonder then that this new paint – in spite of all the reservations aired by artists about the new "plastic paint" – has outranked oil paint over the years.

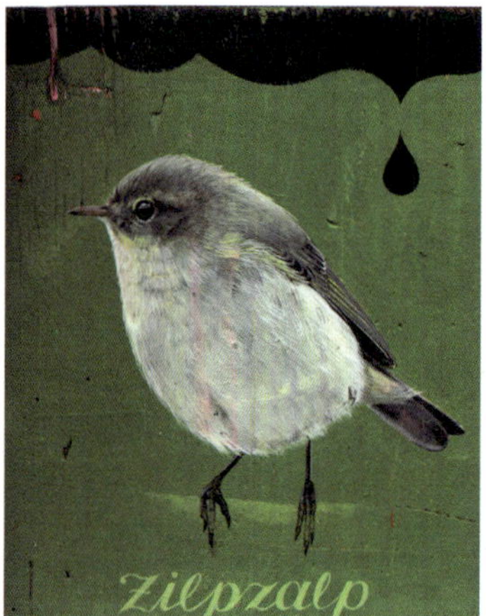

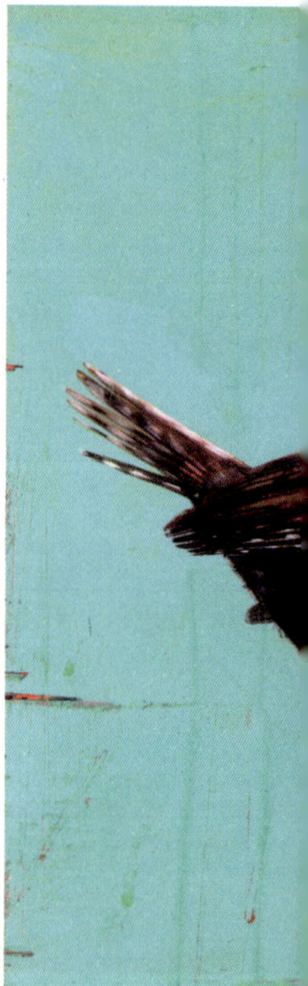

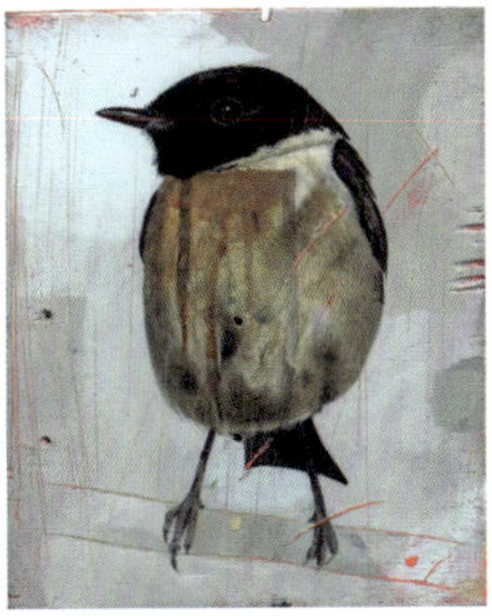

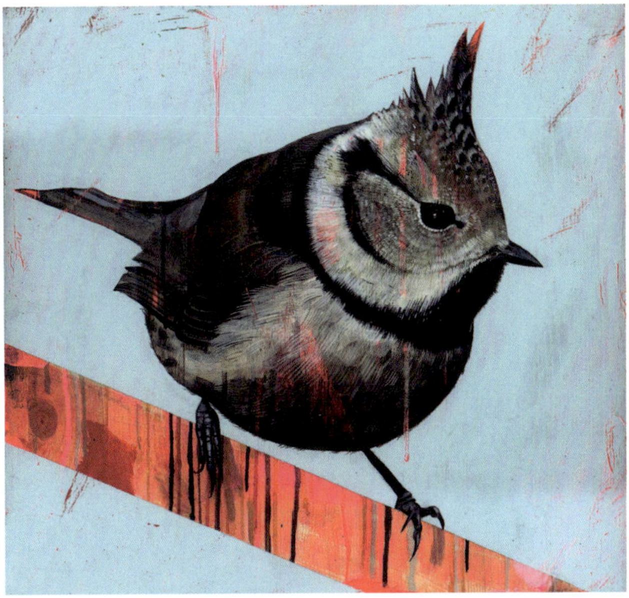

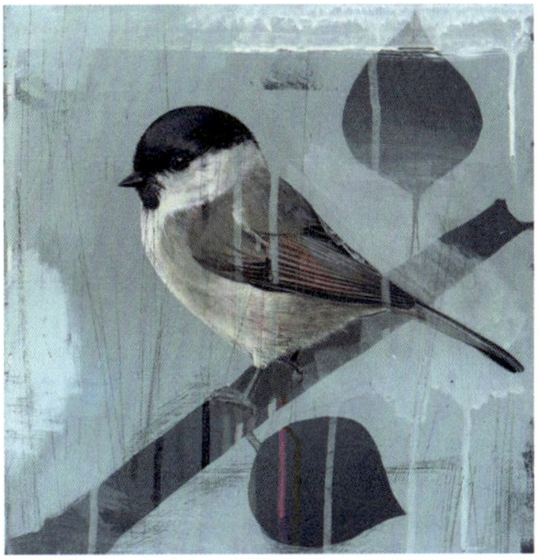

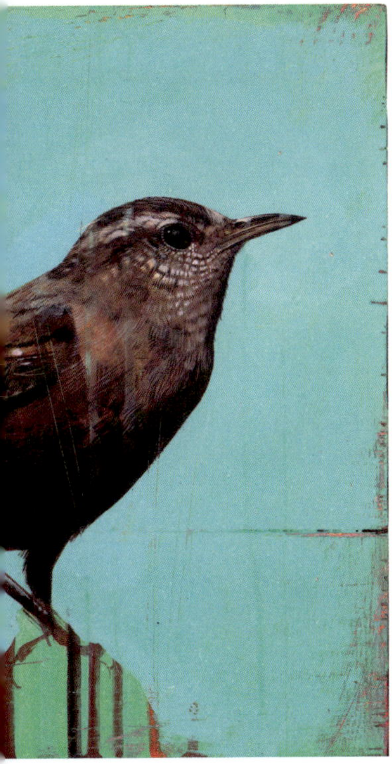

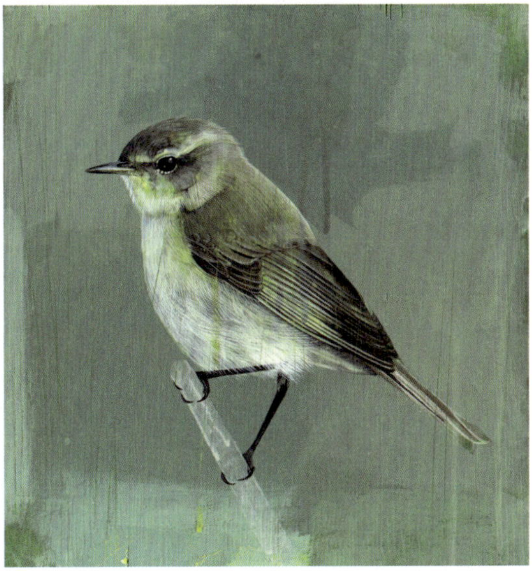

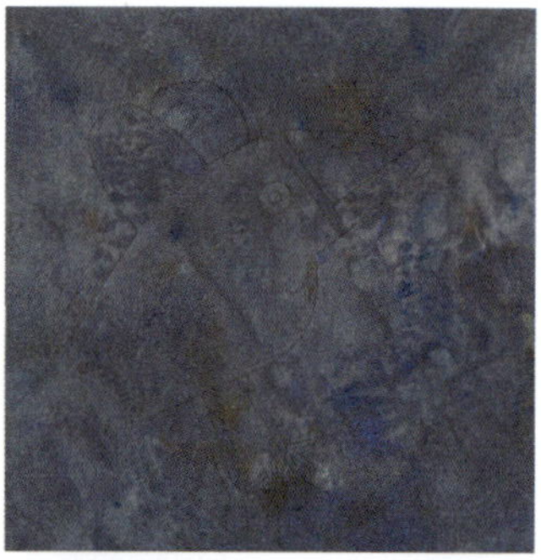

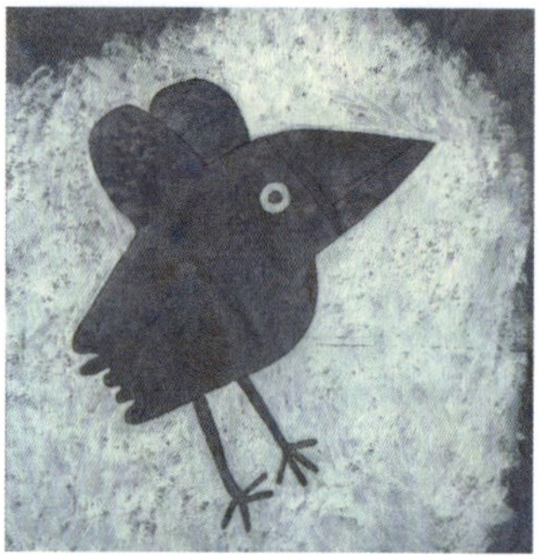

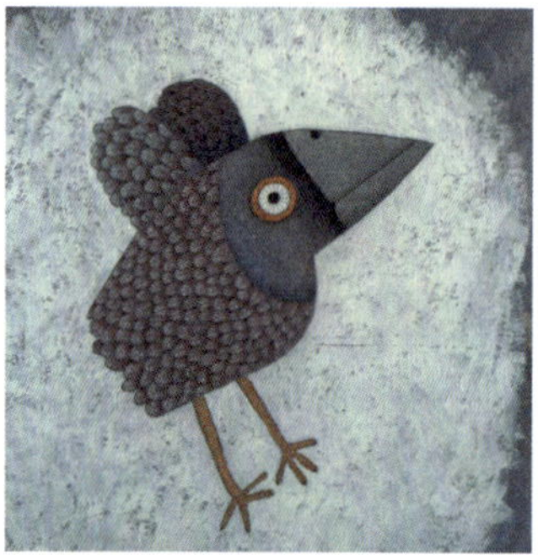

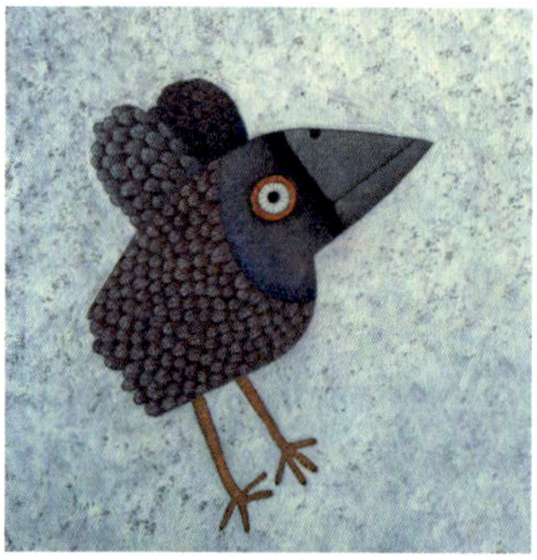

At first glance, acrylic paint does look like oil paint. It has similar coverage properties and has the same toothpaste-like consistency as its oil-based relative.

The main differences are that it is used with water – acrylic paint doesn't become water-resistant until it dries – and it dries much faster. The advantage of this is that you can paint a number of layers without blending them. The usual priming coat needed for oils is not necessary. Otherwise, its painting properties are quite similar to oils. Both paints are equally suited for directly applied brushstrokes, palette knife and sanding techniques, as well as the gradual method of layered painting.

Due to their odorlessness and high pigment density, acrylics are also excellent for glazes and washes in which the colors, like in watercolors, are highly diluted and used wet-in-wet (quite unlike oil paints which would necessitate considerably unpleasant odors, making this practically impossible).

The invention of acrylic paint was a true advancement for painting, comparable only to the breakthrough of oil paint in the 14th century. Regardless of what kind of illustrating you do – from photorealism to loose sketches to roughly surfaced, luminous expression – acrylic paint can be used for almost everything and in a far more timesaving way than oil.

Acrylic paint is thus an all-rounder from the chemistry set. Versatile and combinable with almost every painting technique and with a good price-performance ratio, acrylic is so popular because it is the paint-of-all-trades.

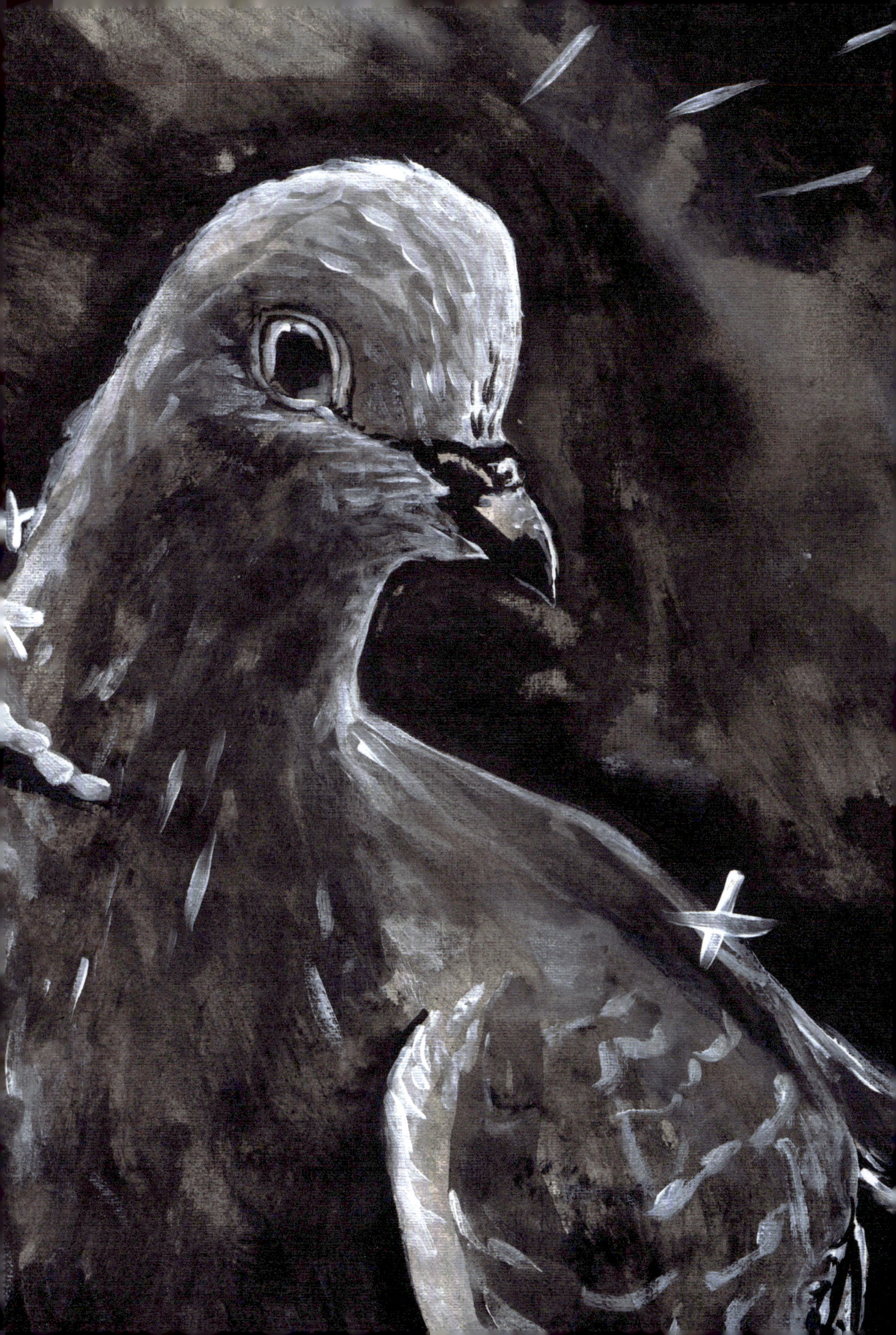

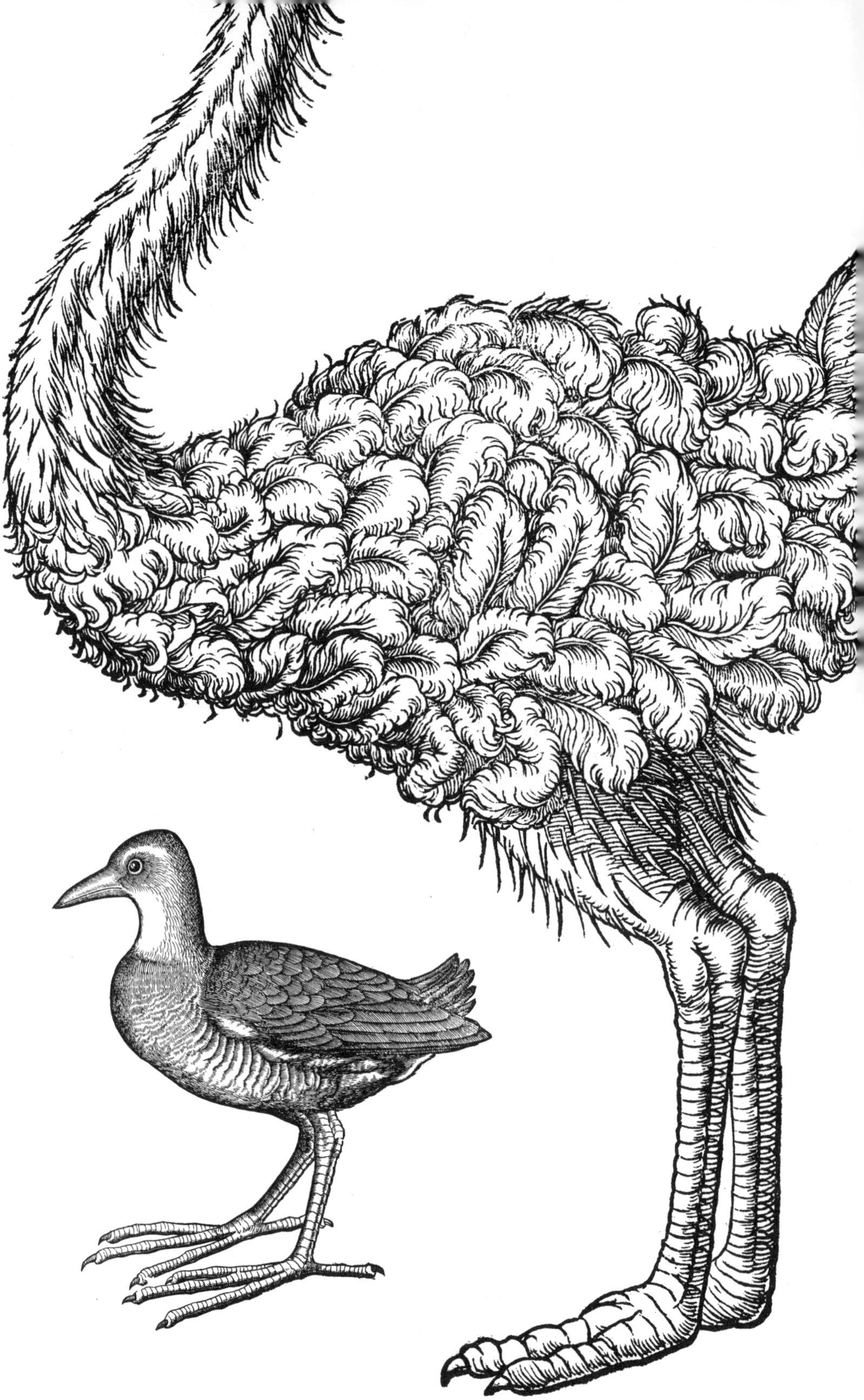

Woodcut

Truly, art is embedded in nature;
he who can extract it, has it.
ALBRECHT DÜRER

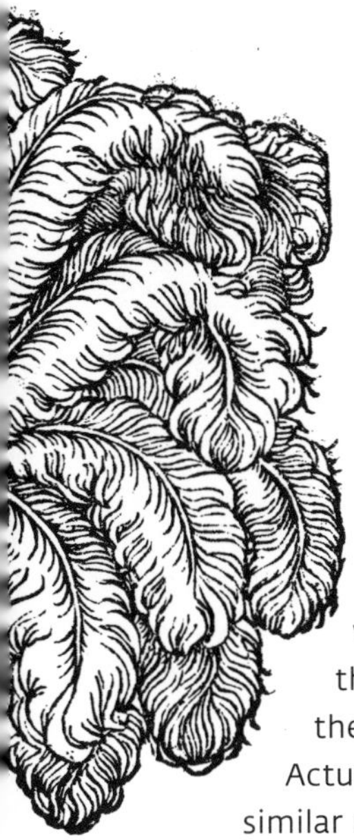

What's the use of exploring an ancient technique like woodcutting? Can't we illustrate today without descending into the handicrafts dungeon of the Late Middle Ages? Actually, we can achieve very similar results using scraperboard, and obviously we can use a computer to create the aesthetic of a woodcut. So does such an antiquated technique belong in a book about illustration? You guessed it: the answer is *yes*. Allow me to mention two chief arguments for it. First of all:

With an original graphic print we create value.

The topic has always driven us and, after all, the question of value is one of the fundamental concerns of our art. What is our work worth? Is it paid fairly and does it receive the appreciation it deserves?
One part of the answer may lie in originality. An original graphic artwork has a market value, just as a book of original graphic artwork has collector's value. Secondly, and perhaps more importantly:

The creative process stimulates our imagination.

Always knowing the outcome beforehand has little to do with creative processes. The creative process expands our artistic horizons via the factors of coincidence and discovery. So it's not at all absurd to master the old techniques. Plus, art printing is fun! So let's take a closer look at the old hat – pardon me, the woodcut.

Woodcut or "xylography" is one of the oldest graphic techniques. The ancient peoples of the orient reproduced images using wooden prints. Along with metal type and linocuts, woodcuts are one of the relief techniques in which the raised surfaces of the plate are used for printing. Woodcuts can actually be made with any type of wood. Only particleboard and pine are not particularly suitable. All you need is a board, a few sharp woodcut chisels or knives and some chalk for preliminary drawing.
In addition – and this is very important – you need something to attach your wood to the table. You should *never, ever* hold the wood in one hand and use a knife with the other hand! That's the quickest route to the emergency room. Woodcutting tools are infernally sharp and slip quicker than you'd imagine.

CONRAD GESNER

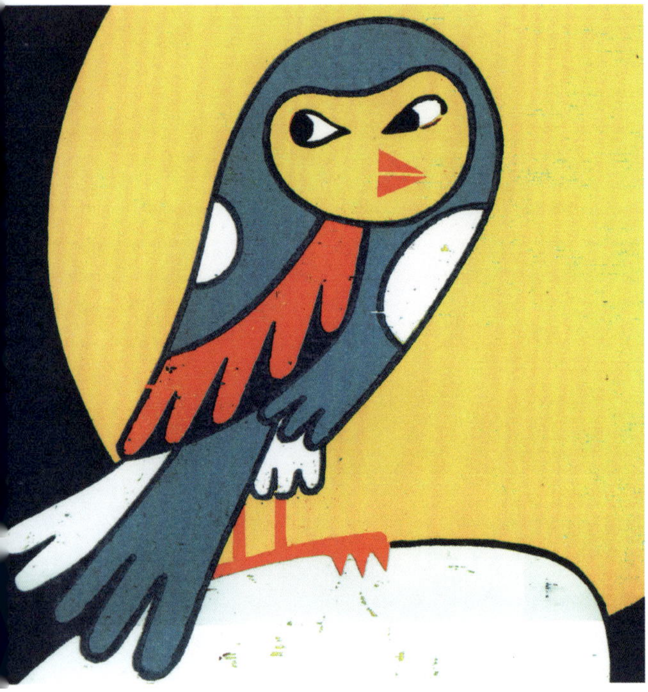

Commonly, wood thicknesses of about one to one and a half inches are used that can be planed or sanded smooth if necessary. Then you begin! First draw your preliminary drawing right on the wood with chalk. If you want, you can darken the block with ink to make it easier to see which sections later need to be cut away. Don't cut straight into the wood, but with two opposite cuts going diagonally from the printed lines to remove the non-printed areas. You can also use various sizes and widths of U and V-shaped gouges, knives shaped so that they carve furrows, grooves or lines from the wood, sliver for sliver.

The detail of the lines depends on the wood you choose.

It starts with the variety of wood. For example, the wonderfully filigree Classical Japanese woodcuts were made on soft wood, while the European Expressionists preferred the hard, splintering traits of coniferous wood. The grain also plays a role. End grain blocks cut at right angles to the grain are easiest to cut. You also have to note imperfections, like knots in the block. Wood is a natural material with very different features than, say, linoleum. Interestingly, this is what makes the material so appealing. Unpredictability stimulates creativity, even in color, because:

Tip

Woodcutting tools are extremely sharp. To prevent injuries, always cut using outward motions and firmly fixate the wood with a clipboard or a screw clamp.

Woodcut is by no means just for black and white.

People have been creating color woodcuts for centuries and there are two different techniques for making them.
The first way is to use multiple printing plates made with transfer lithography: You print a sheet from the first plate and then press the wet reproduction facedown onto a clean plate of the same size. Now you've transferred the first mirror-inverted onto the second plate. Now, you can use this print as the scale drawing for cutting your second color plate. Thus every additional color is cut onto a separate plate and the templates are repeatedly transferred to the wood.
The second method is even more impressive and as simple as it is brilliant: reduction printing. This is a color printing technique using only one block by progressively layering from the lightest to the darkest color.
In this method, you first ink the entire surface of the block with the lightest color and make one print. You then cut away all the areas of the block that will contain this *first* color. So, when you ink the printing plate with a *second*, darker color and print over the *first* print with the modified printing plate, the second color will match perfectly since the newly cut areas omit the first color you printed.

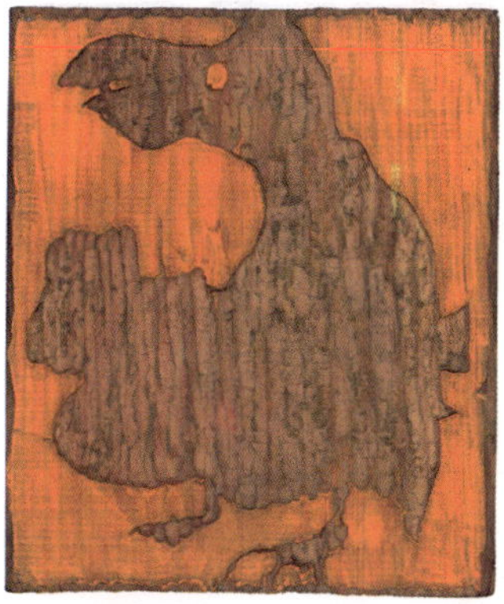

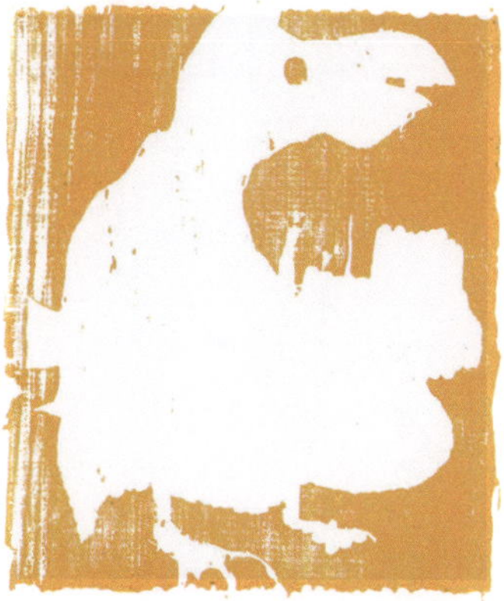

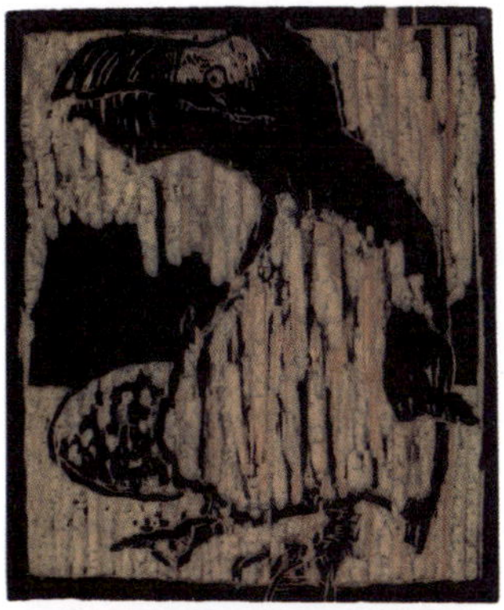

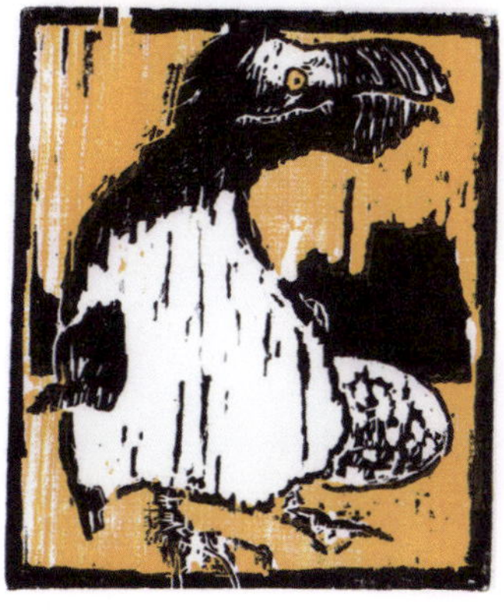

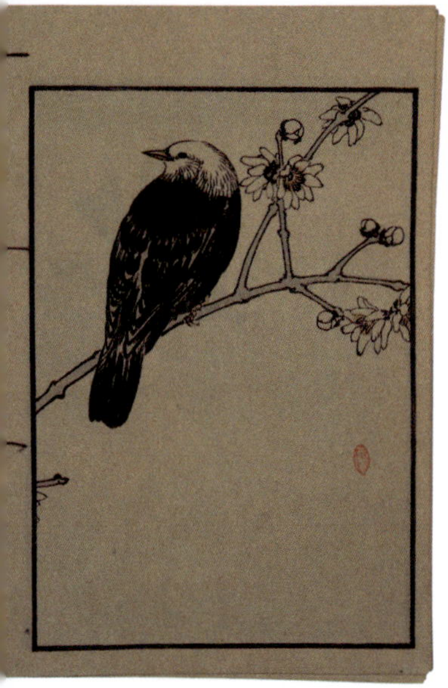

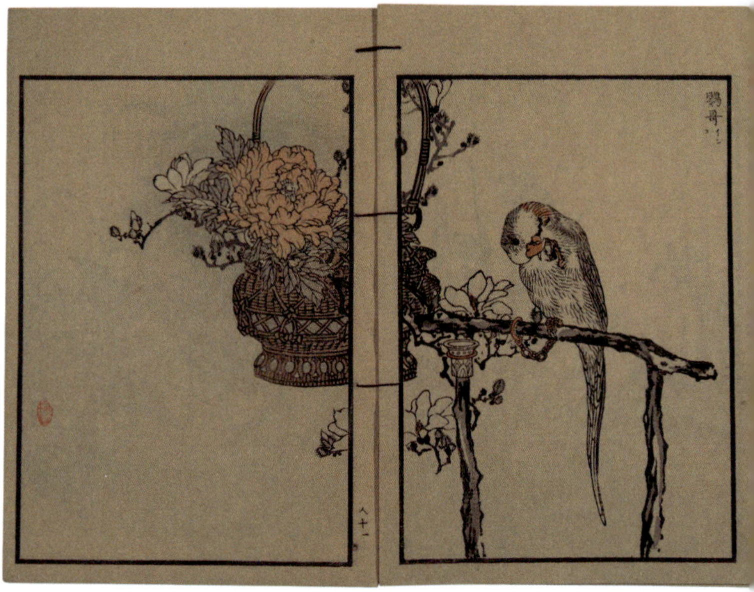

In simple terms this means that each color is cut from the plate after printing. With every consecutive printing, the previous color is covered and the original color remains only in those places that you have cut away before the next layer. You can repeat this method as often as you want because with every new cutting and over-printing you can conjure up more, ever-darker shades. The only thing you can never do with reduction printing is to re-print an edition. The number of copies must be decided in advance because the production process gradually destroys the printing plate.

Printing is very simple: First you ink your printing plate with an inking roller and then lay a thin sheet of paper (for example Japanese paper) on the printing plate. Now you can transfer the ink to the paper by pressing on it using the heel of your hand, the back of a spoon or a folding stick. Larger editions can be printed in roller or book presses.

Media, old and new, frequently accelerate social upheaval. The woodcut in particular is a technique that initiated and accompanied a cultural revolution in Europe.
The history of this revolution began about 150 years ago with the art and antiques dealers who imported Asian vases for European courts and bourgeois parlors. Ceramics and costly porcelain in particular are very fragile. Before ending up in Europe's salons, the porcelain and clayware had to be well packed for transport across many borders, deserts, mountains and shipping passages. To protect them from breakage the Japanese and Chinese dealers wrapped the vases in old woodcut prints.

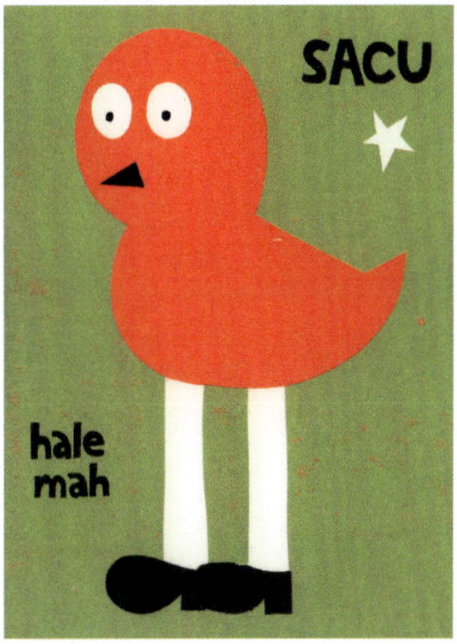

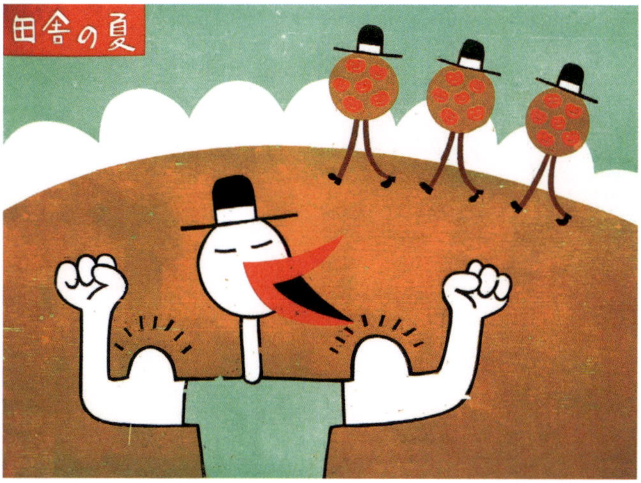

Colorful Japanese prints, views of Mount Fuji, everyday and even erotic scenes, called Shunga prints, made their way to Europe as packaging materials.
At first they were thrown away, but it did not take long before these works attracted interest. Indeed the woodcuts from Asia by artists like Hokusai and Hiroshige with their unusual compositions and new aesthetics had a magnetic effect on budding modern European art. Inspired by the new perspectives and the interplay of the colors, European artists began to experiment in the manner of these woodcuts. The techniques of painters like Van Gogh, Gauguin and Munch as well as many German Expressionists were greatly influenced by these luminous prints from China and Japan. (In some of Van Gogh's painting we even see Japanese woodcuts hanging on the walls of rooms.)

The impact of these woodcuts is almost inestimable, but the powerful and luminous lines of modern classical art would have been very different without the influence of these prints from the Far East. Japanese woodcuts hidden in shipping crates were the pebbles that triggered the avalanche of modern art.

Collage

I believe more in the scissors than I do in the pencil.
TRUMAN CAPOTE

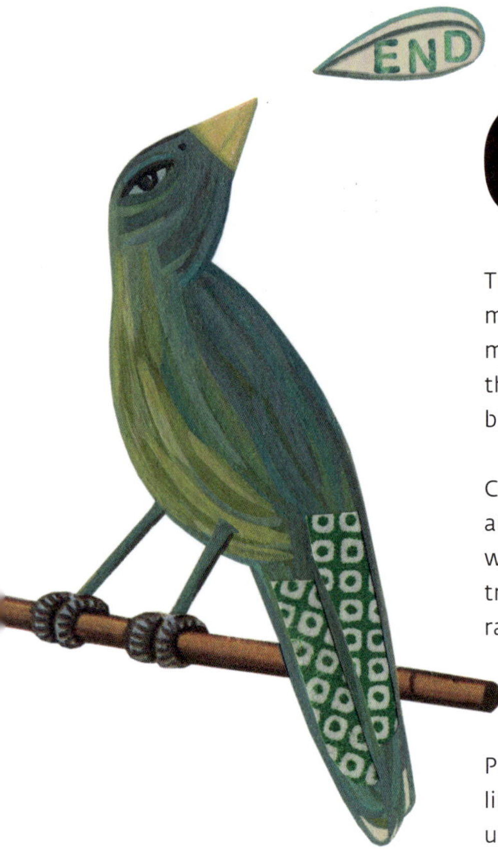

Collages make things easy. They're easy to like and they're easy to make. That's because collage is a tremendously modern technique – even if it has been for over a hundred years.

The word collage comes from the French verb *coller*, which means "to glue." A collage is the combination of different materials, of paper, textiles, photos, found objects, snippets, things from daily life, tickets, newspaper clippings and memorabilia of all kinds.

Collage is an entertaining medium that always seems a little anarchistic. The technique unites fragments of the outside world with inner impressions without having to produce a traditional picture. This makes collage a fresh and contemporary technique. It's not surprising that it is a child of early modernity. The first collages in art are from the beginning of the twentieth century and made by (who else?) painters of classical modernism like Kurt Schwitters, Max Ernst, Pablo Picasso and John Heartfield. For these pioneers, collage was liberation from bourgeois constraints, a mobilization of creative unconscious forces. At the same time it was an attempt to capture the sensory overload of the new era. Collage was a new artistic concept. It was playful and created new content by putting things in completely different contexts. In addition, the collage was not concerned with pictorial illusion (i.e., spatiality or perspective); it allowed the eye to pause and thus always remained a bit abstract.
In fact, collage fit perfectly into a new, overstimulated and accelerated modern age. No wonder it has been up to date since its beginnings and has never gone out of style.
One could even argue that we still live in something like a "collage age."

Tip:
Collages sometimes bring up copyright issues. If you use someone else's material, you should ask permission first. The legal argument is usually that a collage is only a free of the need for permission if the impression of the original fades in the new work. – So take care!

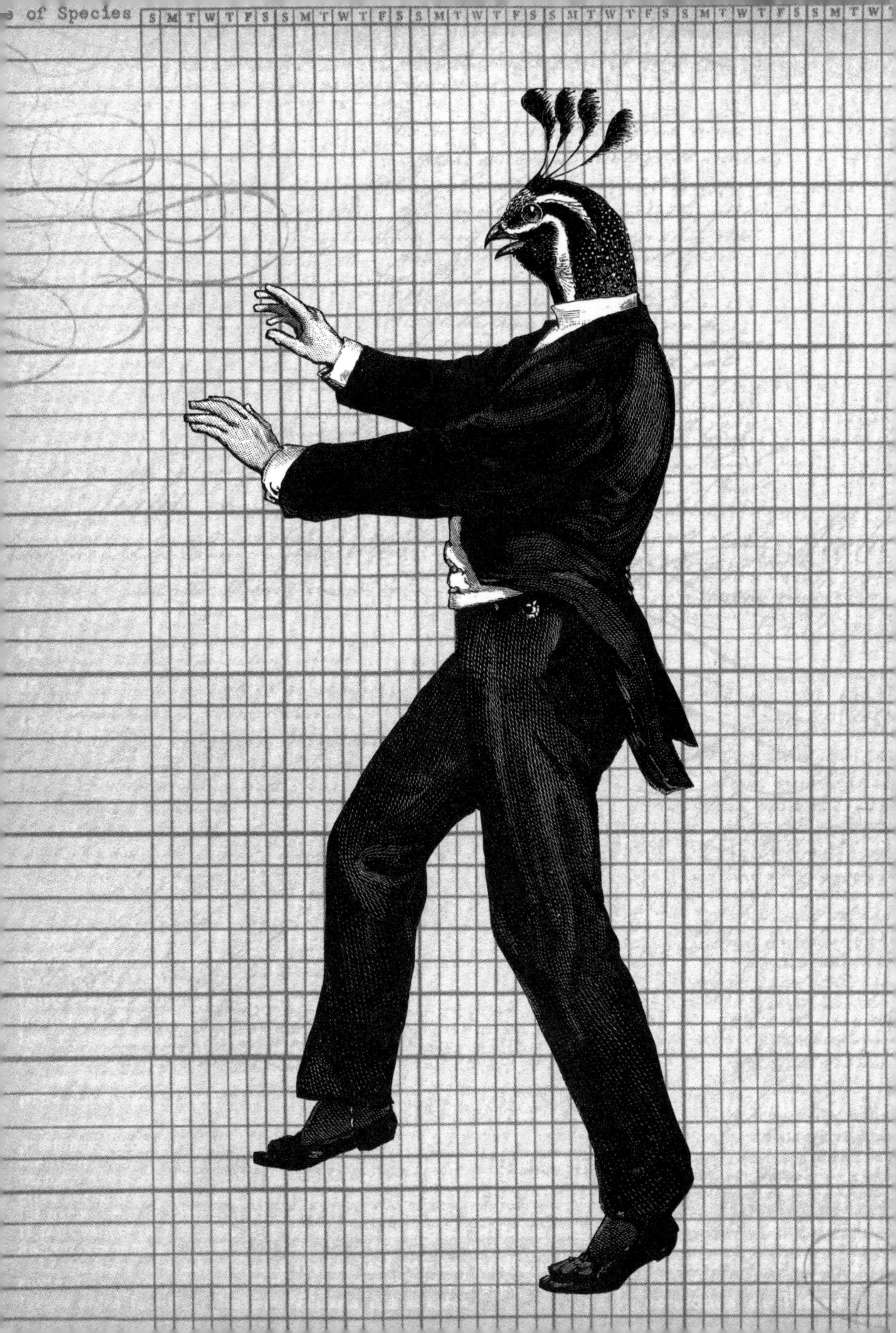
of Species

Many media products that surround us are at least partially collage-like. Nothing seems more normal to us today than merging very different elements in a collage, such as pictures and writing, although it was regarded as unnatural two generations ago.

In fact, collages are everywhere: We encounter them in poster art, in advertising, in campaigns, in editorials and in book illustration. They are at home in both commercial and free art.

In addition, the technique of collage is also a popular means of expression in other arts such as music, movies, literature, the theater, etc.

The fascination of collage is its playful anarchism.

You can tell how much creative pleasure it gives not only the viewer, but also the artist. It starts with the fact that before every collage, there is a phase of collecting. The pieces come from a variety of sources and transform designers into hunter-gatherers: waste products, scraps of paper, wallpaper scraps, instruction sheets, photos, picture fragments, unfinished drawings, writings, sketches, advertisements, old papers and new labels and a thousand little things are good raw materials for any collage. And because the individual elements have different sources, they can also be interwoven with completely unrelated things to form a new whole. For example, you can combine drawings, paintings and collage elements in a great way.

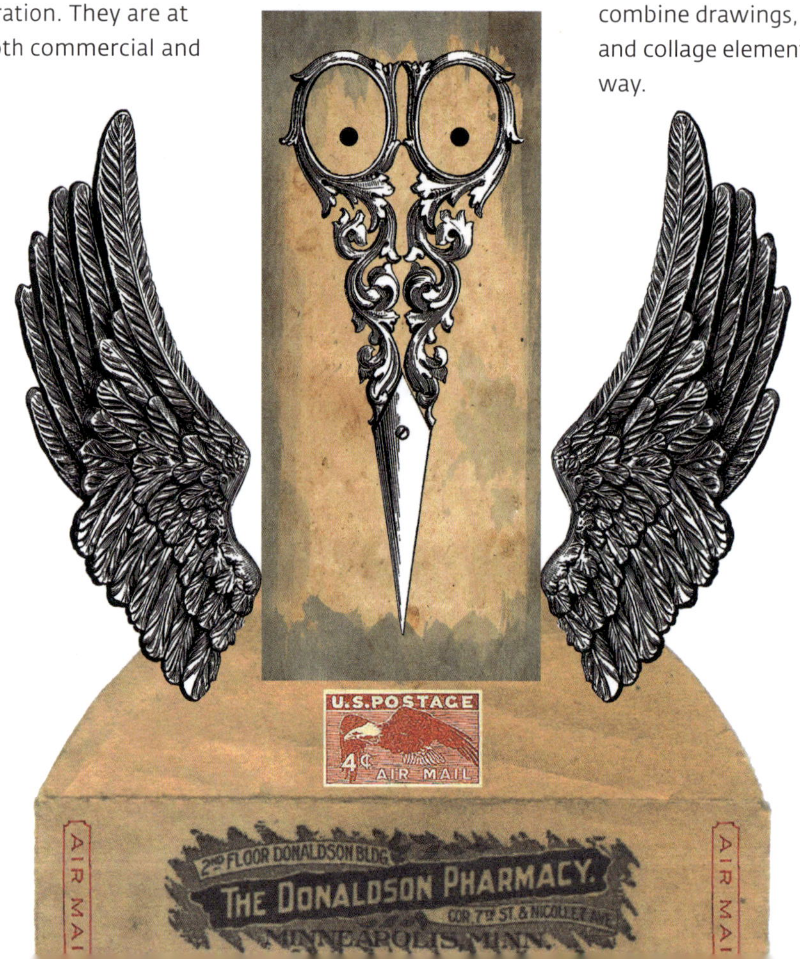

JIM COHEN

In addition, proportions and picture elements do not necessarily have to be realistic, which is precisely part of the illustrative added value. In addition, the collage-making process is wonderfully fluid. In contrast to pure painting or drawing techniques, one can deal in many ways with the pictorial elements in a collage. This makes collages a great (and simple) experimental field for picture design – at least as long as they're not glued.

Trial and error are the soul and starting point of any collage.

And all you need is a cutting machine, a pair of scissors and a little glue.

Maybe collage appeals to us because, strange as it may sound, it resembles our way of thinking. I believe that collage owes a good deal of its power to its associative, detached structure. The "classical" picture describes a moment: a tree, a house, a landscape, a protagonist, a scenario and a narrative moment. This makes the classical picture a snapshot. A collage, on the other hand, is more spatially and temporally indefinite. It doesn't describe our way of seeing as much as our way of thinking. It intuitively interweaves the most diverse levels of reality, much as we do in the flow of thought (and it doesn't matter if they are analog or digital collages). Casually speaking, any of us could make a landscape, but only the artist can make a specific collage. The fact that it thus describes much more the individual and internalized as an "objective truth" makes collage a tremendously modern medium. In collage, intuition and individuality are combined with playfulness and creative precision. And that's why it's hardly surprising that it has been used in art and illustration for so long.

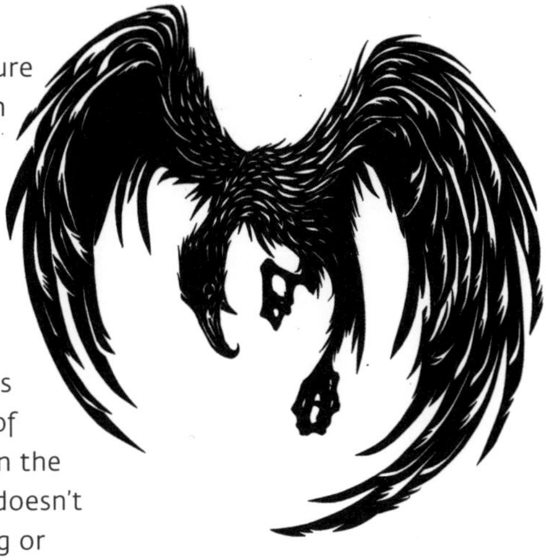

Paper cutting:

Paper cutting or *Scherenschnitte* is a precursor to collage. It came from China and was widespread in Germany – hence the German name – in the eighteenth and nineteenth centuries.
For Scherenschnitte, paper is cut to make an ornamental or realistic picture. Paper cuttings are often presented on a contrasting background – say, white on black – and occasionally used in illustration (especially as a collage with colored papers).

Computers and Generative Design

I've seen things you people wouldn't believe.
BLADE RUNNER, RIDLEY SCOTT, 1982

Power on, power off – who knew that this infinitely simple process would revolutionize the world – and with it the world of pictures? Ever wonder how computers work (and I don't mean how to turn them on :))? The answer is simple: A computer basically works like a switch. Power on, power off, on, off, on, off, on, off. Everything displayed on your computer is based on code showing the status of these switches.

But how does "on and off" become a picture, a text, a porno or an illustration?

Imagine a row of switches, let's say eight. These eight switches, looked at in a row, could be on or off. By combining the individual switches, a numerical code can be generated in a row of switches the meaning of which changes depending on the position of each of the switches. So the positions the eight switches are in express something.

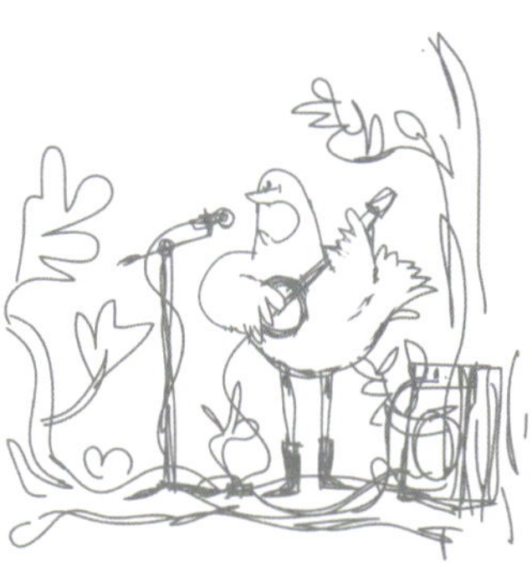

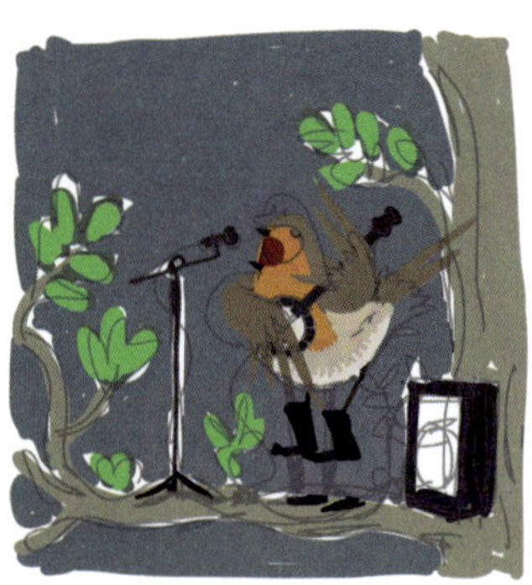

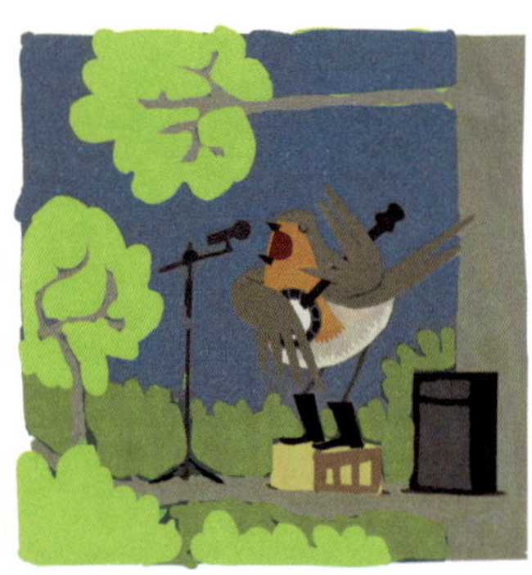

SYLVAIN MAZAS

In this code, the letter "A" could be represented by the switch position 00000001, a "B" by the switch position 00000010, "C" would then correspond to 00000011, etc. The information in our computers is thus coded symbols of the status on/off. Got it?
In fact, number codes are not a new invention. Forerunners of the principle from which today's computers developed already existed in ancient times, for example, around 1000 BC in the abacus developed in India or China. But not until the binary number system discovered by Leibniz in the eighteenth century created the mathematical foundations on which our present computers are based: power on, power off. Except that the "on and off" in our computers, of course, is a little faster. Actually, a lot faster: on the latest MacBook, 2,300,000,000 times a second.

The reason computers have to be so fast these days is partly because of our profession: because of images.

Pictures are what really need computing power. A pocket calculator needs virtually no memory. But images are made up of tens of thousands of pieces of information. And the position of each pixel is also determined by binary codes.

To understand how a picture is created in computers, it helps to look at a digital camera. A digital camera consists of a housing with a lens and shutter, except that instead of film, a photosensitive plate (a silicon chip) is attached to the rear wall. This chip is made up of millions of individual photosensitive cells that change their electrical charge when exposed to light. Each light point is assigned an electrical voltage. While taking photographs, each cell is now queried for its voltage and the information successively ("sequentially") is stored under a special address. As we saw above, computers can only store electrical digits, such as "zero" for no voltage or "one" for voltage.
The images are rasterized and cuts into strips. This replaces the two-dimensionality with one-dimensional information associated with an address (pixel no. 7 has the information "0," pixel No. 8 has the value "1" and so forth). The computer puts everything together.

In fact, our eyes work the same way: for each pixel there is a light (and color) sensitive cell, which is not requested digitally, but all analog at the same time. So, not two nerves go to the brain from the retina, but a nerve connection for each light-sensitive cell.

Our eyes see colors like a digital camera does. For the colors red, green and blue there is one cell especially sensitive to each color (and an additional one for black and white). If only red and green are stimulated, the color "orange" is stimulated, if all three cells are stimulated at the same time, the result is the color impression "white," etc.
When the stored image information is displayed on a computer, the computer moves the pixels to our monitor and switches them, depending on the information, on or off. Here, the light is composed of three colored points of light, which "mix" different colors depending on the combination.

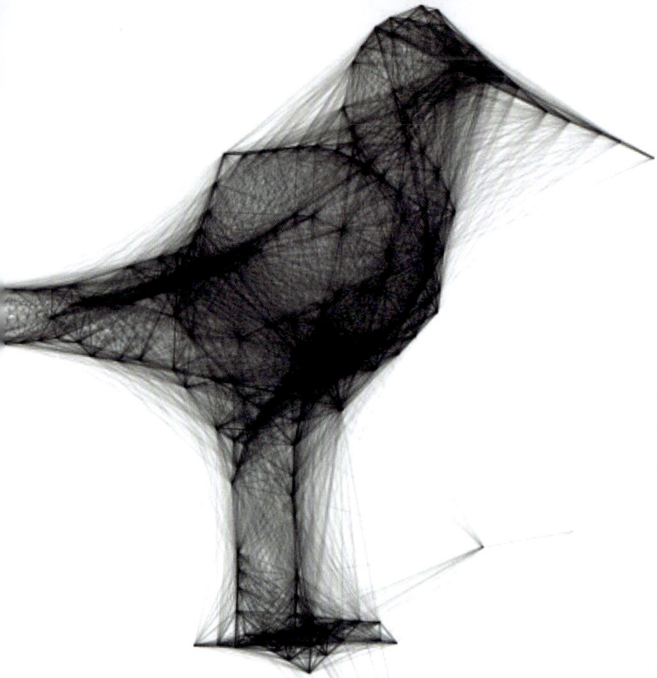

So we're dealing with information about light that has been converted into a number code. This applies to all images, movies and games, and it explains why we as the "image makers" need so much computing power and storage space. Of course, a huge number of binary codes have to be used if you want to put together a picture or a movie.

From there it's just a small step to software-driven design. Because, of course, binary codes with their pixel information can be easily converted.

Using software, we control the pixels directly and change their parameters and thus the image, the font or the color information composed of them.

This change can be made individually and specifically; but you can also write special small programs or use ready-made codes that carry out these pixel changes independently and iteratively.

Such programs, such as Processing or vvvv, generate images according to predefined parameters. This is called "generative design" (the example on this page was created that way). Most illustrators today work with vector or pixel-based programs (we will hear about the main representatives, Illustrator and Photoshop, in the following chapters), but a combination of different software is also becoming increasingly popular, since almost every program has different strengths.
For example, Painter is great for imitating the realistic look of traditional painting techniques (such as oil or watercolors), while many 3D programs are perfect for building basic shapes.
In daily use, we illustrators also have "haptic" interfaces: digital tools such as graphics tablets, Wacoms, Cintiqs, Inkling, iPads and their ilk, with which we can paint as if with a pencil or brush or communicate with drawing programs.
Looking back, it seems hard to imagine that the triumphal procession of the computer was only very recent. Many illustrators still remember the late 1980s when the first computers appeared in agencies and their awe at these new machines that cost as much as a house.
Computers really have changed the world as not many technologies have for a long time. And they literally turned the world of images inside out.

Photoshop

I'm the guy ... who makes you dream of things you'll never have.
FRÉDÉRIC BEIGBEDER, 9.99

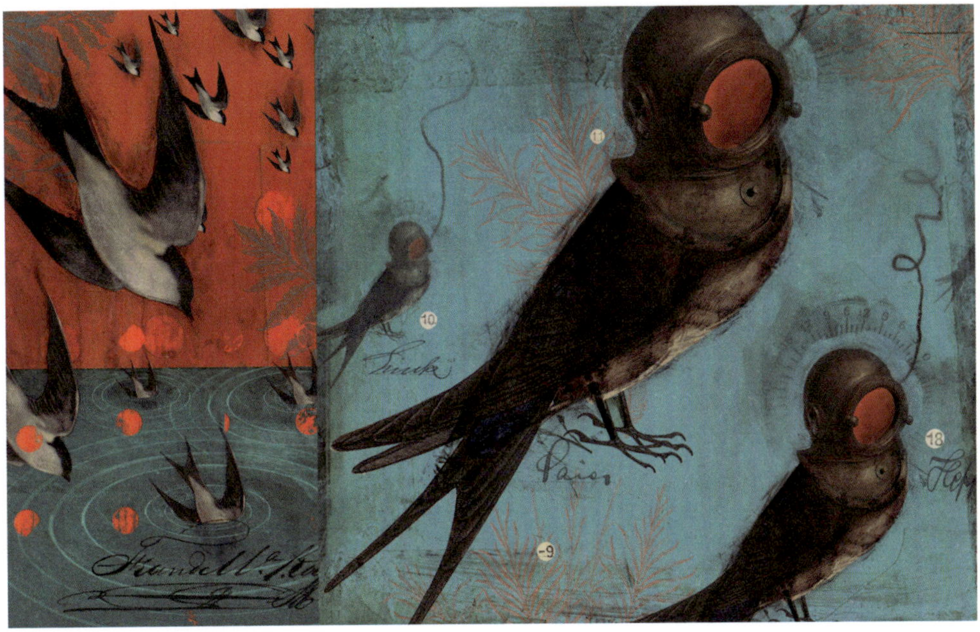

I still remember how fascinated I was as a young boy looking at blurry black and white photos of the Loch Ness Monster. I sat on my bed on the second floor of our house with a cup of cocoa, a piece of paper and pen, and dived into my favorite fantasy of becoming the first explorer to pull the mysterious creature out of his blurry photos into the light. I constructed traps, designed Nessie Observation Stations and debated with my (very patient) father how to drain all the water from the loch.

Of course, I was Nessie's biggest fan. I had a small library about the fabled Scottish beast – thick, pseudo-scientific concoctions (presents from my English aunt), packed full of theories *and photos* of striking significance: Wasn't that a fin in the unfocused mess of graininess? Didn't a *long neck* clearly emerge from the faded blackish-gray of a blurred snapshot? That was long ago. I drank the cocoa up, the loch has been proven to be uninhabited (much to my regret) and even our house no longer stands today.

Most importantly, though, photographs have lost all that was once considered of evidential value. For as strange as it sounds, photos were once actually considered a sort of proof. Even back then, they were faked (by analog means), but not so long ago photos were still testimonies of a truth that has become as doubtful today as the famed Scottish crypto-zoological subject.
In fact, today photos prove nothing. They owe that to a program that raised its head from the digital floodwaters in the late 1980s.

In 1987, Thomas Knoll was annoyed that his new Mac couldn't render grayscale. He therefore wrote a program to fix the problem. Together with his brother John, who created visual effects for movies and used the program in James Cameron's science fiction film *The Abyss*, he further developed Photoshop for Adobe.
Today, Photoshop is the best-selling (and most commonly pirated) computer software for image editing. About 90 percent of all professional designers use it. The significance of the program is clear from the fact that people no colloquially longer speak of "edited" but of "photoshopped" images.

Originally designed only as a program to edit photos, it evolved tremendously within just a few years:

One of the most revolutionary developments in Photoshop was the introduction of the layering technique.

It ensures that different images can be superimposed like slides and can be edited independently. This made complex collage techniques possible.

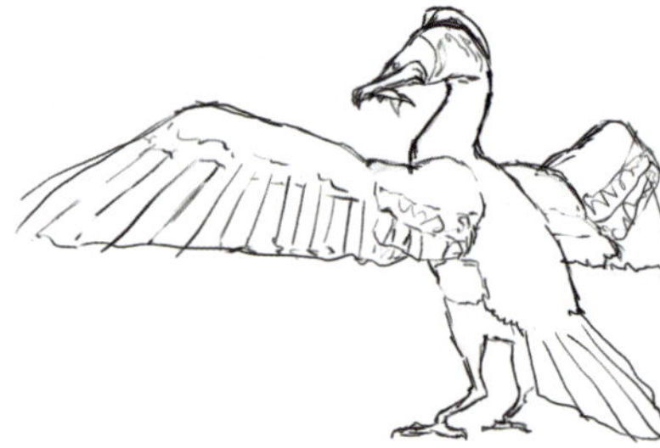

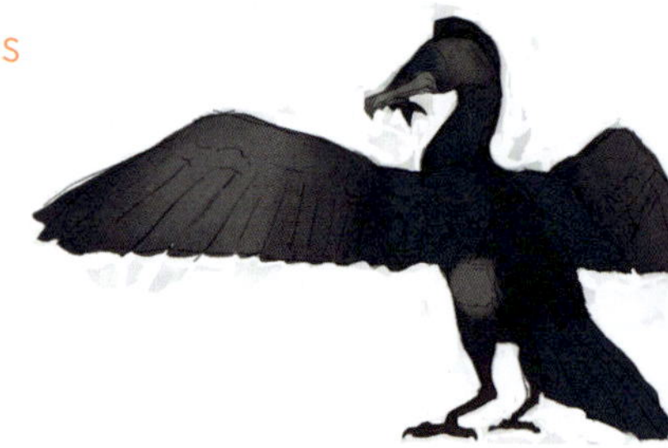

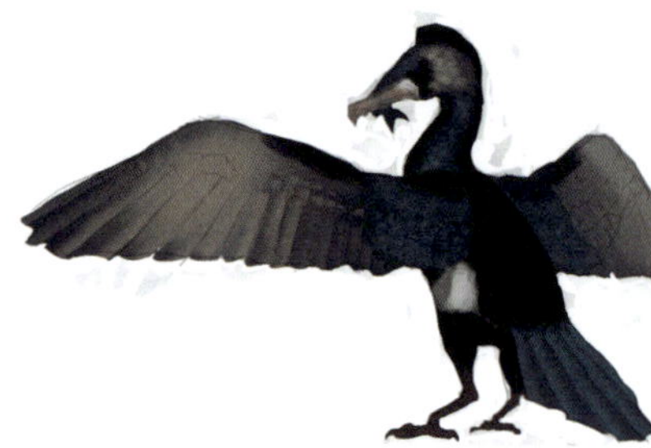

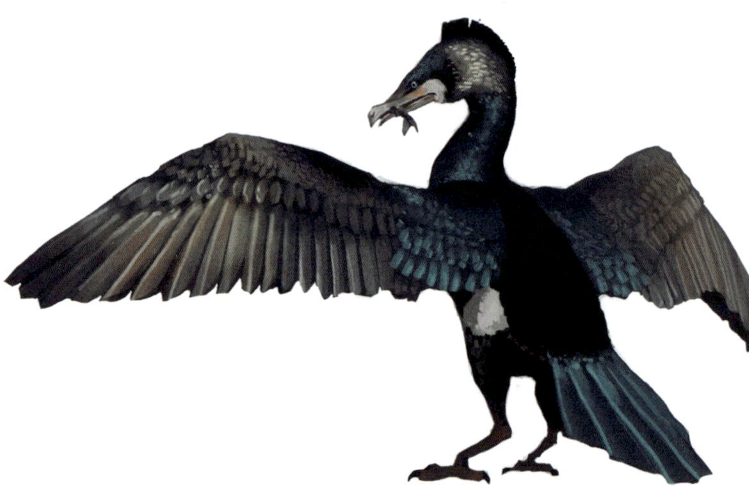

In fact, with Photoshop you can either simulate or generate almost every thinkable technique and visual effect today. That makes it universally useable for us designers.
Photoshop is one of the most powerful image editing programs ever made. It allows us to rotate, distort, recolor, change proportions, insert image elements (like sea monsters ;)) or to delete, paint, copy, render, and so forth.

Photoshop helps us reinvent images, is a painting palette and toolbox in one, the "Swiss army knife" of image editing.

The program is universally applicable and indispensable for anyone who wants to edit or create pictures.
This is all the more remarkable as the program's chief potentials only grew from the addition of extra tools. During the initial phase, these were mainly added functions that could also be used to create images. But with the growth of functions, many extensions were developed that are now independent. Quite a few illustrators today use the once additional processing functions, such as *brushes* (formerly a correction tool) or the *lasso* (formerly a mere selection tool) to just create images.
Layer functions are now used to insert or to paint on structures directly. In fact, the exciting thing about the program is its complexity. It enables us to solve visual problems in a thousand different ways and to find ever-new solutions by combining a wide variety of editing tools.

In addition, a program like Photoshop is indispensable for the prepress stage. Print shops demand precisely defined files to guarantee high-quality reproductions. And for this, too, Photoshop has become indispensable: The image size can be edited in no time. Trim, tone and color can be modified with just a few clicks.
And if something doesn't turn out just right in the original, Photoshop also has a tool for corrections.
Presumably, this is one of the program's recipes for success. It is usually hard to correct mistakes in analog illustrations, but Photoshop stores a history that you can use to go back in time step by step (or just press cmd+Z).

However:
Digitally generated illustrations have one minor drawback. As much as they make the work easier, you cannot produce a (sellable) original with it.

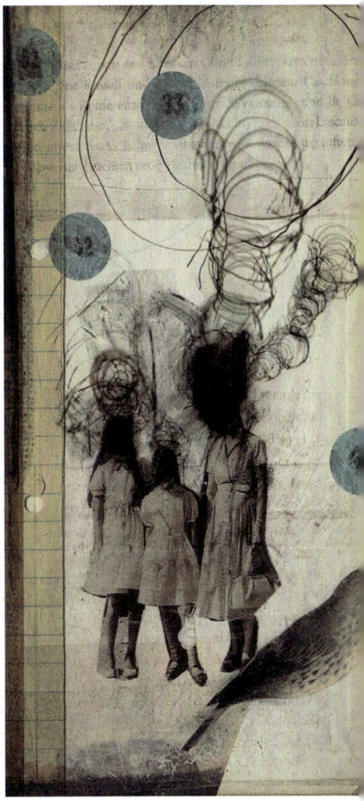

In fact, Photoshop not only revolutionized image editing and illustration; it turned our way of looking at pictures upside down. Because of it, photos have lost their authenticity. And I'm not just talking about the Loch Ness Monster. In fact, the extent of this development and how it is changing the way we look at the world in the long term cannot be foreseen today. For our profession, illustration, the effect has been enormous.

Some of the success and revaluation that illustration has experienced in recent years may well be due to this as well.
Illustrations have an advantage over photographs that their author remains tangible. Due to subjective positioning, a recognizable style, the person behind the illustration stands for the authenticity of the picture. So a monster I create exists at least *in my imagination*.

The fact that the art of drawing is currently going through such a renaissance is probably partly due to a program that was originally invented to portray grayscales better.

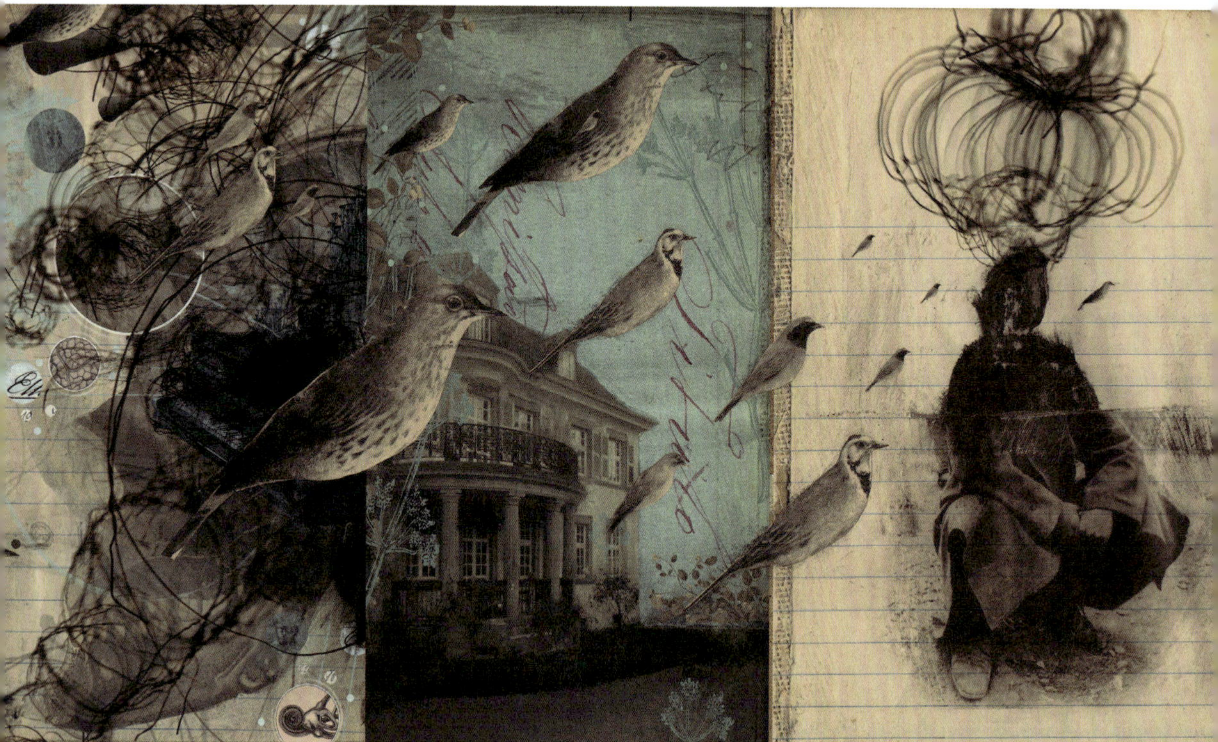

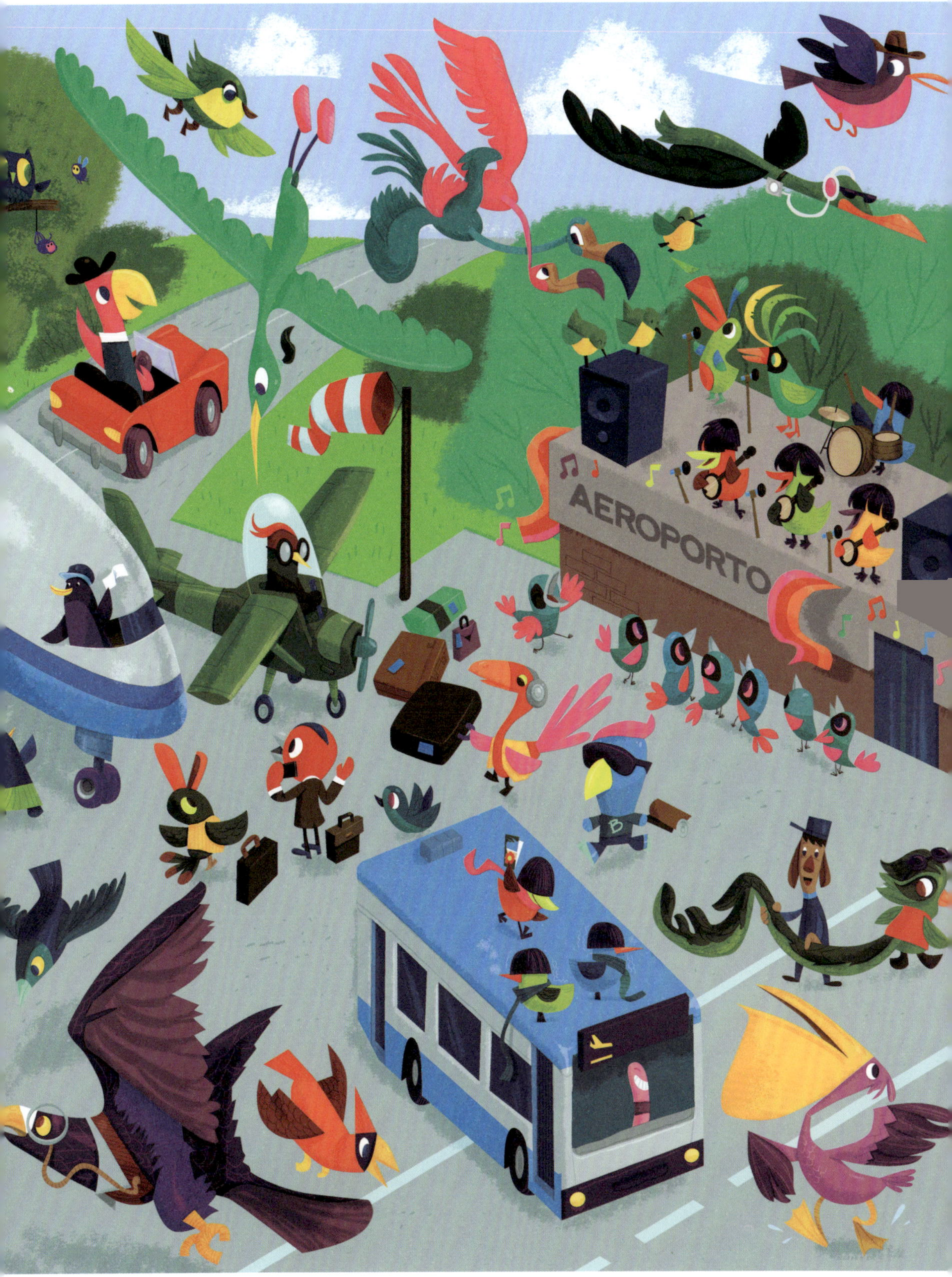
AEROPORTO
B

Illustrator

A very nice drawing, Dave...
HAL9000 COMPUTER IN A SPACE ODYSSEY, STANLEY KUBRICK, 1968

As we saw above, Photoshop's strengths are the limitless capabilities for editing pixel images. This is done by manipulating the color, brightness and transparency properties of the underlying pixels. The downside (aside from limitations related to the resolution dependency of the files): Photoshop does not recognize objects. It is therefore not possible to select part of an image, like a chair, and assign it a different color. To do so, part of the image, which is a chair for the user (but only a mass of pixels for Photoshop), must be isolated using the selection tools. Only then can this pixel area be edited, for example, recolored. If you cancel the selection, the area once again blends into the surrounding pixels and would have to be selected again for further editing. Over the years, Adobe has developed methods and tools to offset these drawbacks. Nonetheless, this is the fundamental difference between Photoshop and object-oriented programs like Illustrator.

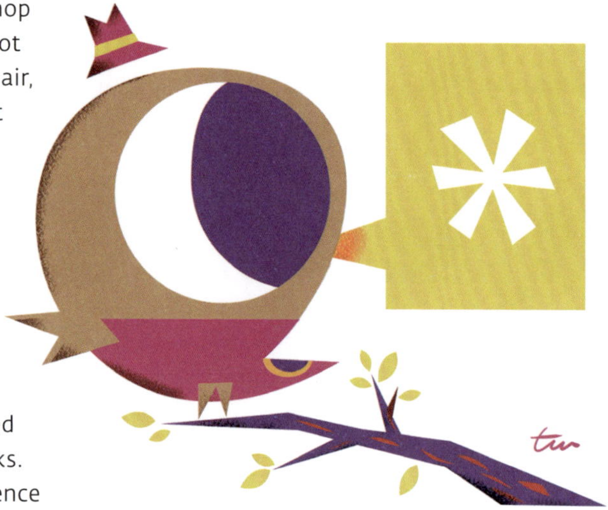

Illustrator has been part of Adobe's product line since 1987. It was added to the Adobe Creative Suite, which combines and coordinates a wide variety of graphics programs, in 2003. This greatly facilitates the often necessary and meaningful collaboration between Photoshop and Illustrator. Illustrator is object-oriented and vector-based. The vector technique is based on an invention that originated from automotive development. At about the same time in the 1960s, two French engineers, Pierre Bézier at Renault and Paul de Casteljau at Citroën, discovered a model with which curves could be represented in a mathematically relatively simple (and visually very appealing) way. Since Citroën kept the invention a secret for almost ten years, the "Bézier curve" was named after Renault's engineer.

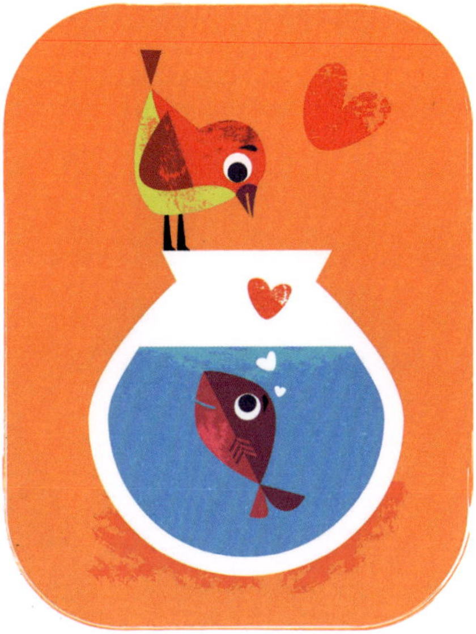

Simplified, the method can be described as follows: To depict a line in pixels, the entire area of this line must be filled with individual pixels. You can imagine how many pieces of information such a picture contains. But the same line can also be described using only two points: beginning and end point. In this way, all of the contours are displayed with comparatively little effort in Illustrator. You need less computer power and memory and the drawings remain scalable. In addition, lines can be selected as individual objects and given properties. For example, line thicknesses can be used as properties, which make work much easier. And in Illustrator you can work with layers just as you do in Photoshop. The advantage is that you can construct complicated graphics better. Layers can also be faded in and out if necessary, you can hold them in place (very handy if you don't accidentally want to mess up something good), and you can rearrange them over and over again.

Layers are very helpful for creating multiple versions of a drawing.

Illustrator supports both RGB and CMYK color modes, making it ideal for viewing on the web as well as for printing. For us illustrators, there are two working methods: For the first, you scan a sketch or a finished drawing and then edit it in Photoshop. Then it can be vectorized and further edited in Illustrator. For the second method, you create the drawing using Illustrator. Special symbols and construction tools are available for this, which can also be used quickly and effectively with a graphics tablet.
By the way, Illustrator can undo an infinite number of operations. That's why even the most adventuresome illustrators don't need to be afraid of ruining their work. For even in Illustrator, in an emergency, you just press cmd+Z.

How to survive as an illustrator

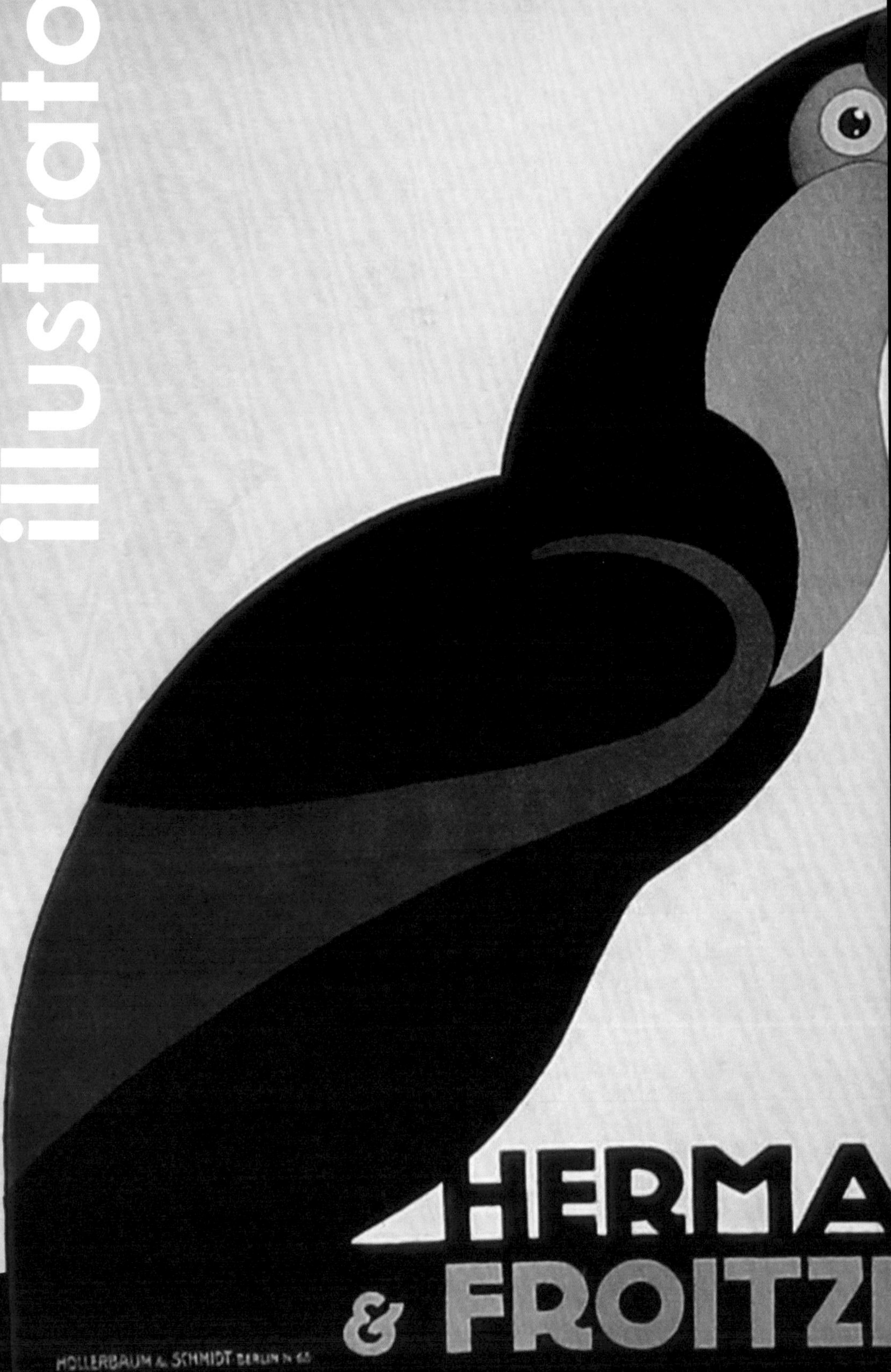

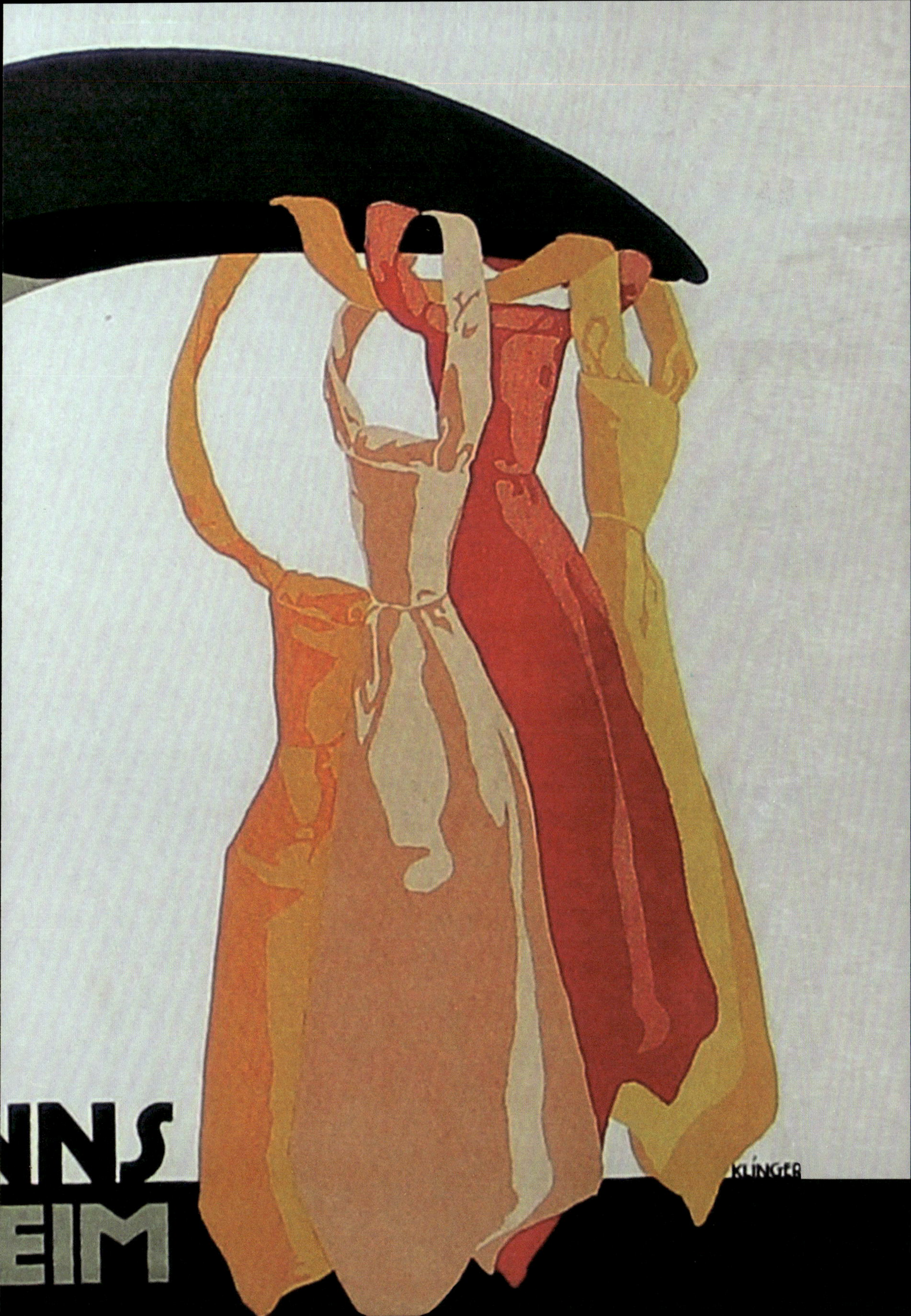

NNS
EIM
KLINGER

Material Fetishism

Only the best for your artwork?

One thing is certain: Good materials are a must. The trappings of any medium-sized art supply store will make you think your illustrating career will go nowhere without taking out a small business loan. They have sable brushes costing hundreds of dollars and 555-pound watercolor papers for $40.00 per sheet. Art supply stores in particular are purveyors of material fetishism topping English royalty and Saudi princedom.

Which leads us to the question: is it really necessary? Can we really not paint any decent pictures without expensive materials? Is there no hope for us poverty-stricken artists? The answer is: less is more.

Tip

It may sound trivial, but you're better off investing in a high quality, spine-friendly chair and a good lamp. These will pay off far more in the long term than buying a new generation computer every 18 months or piling up a huge assortment of sable brushes.

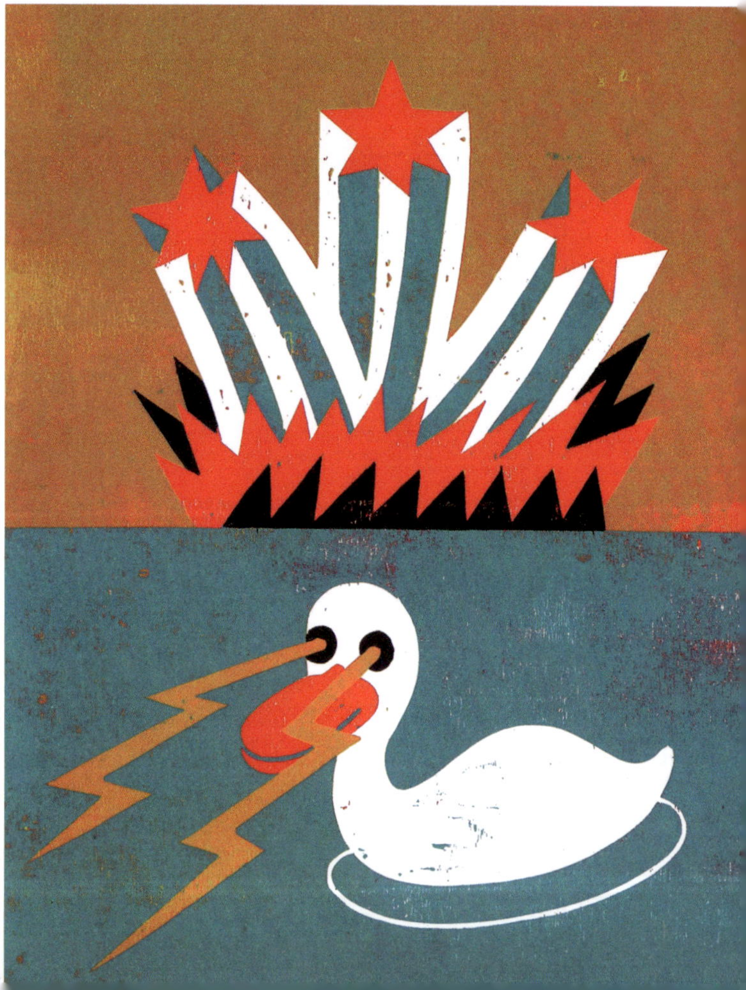

← JULIUS KLINGER

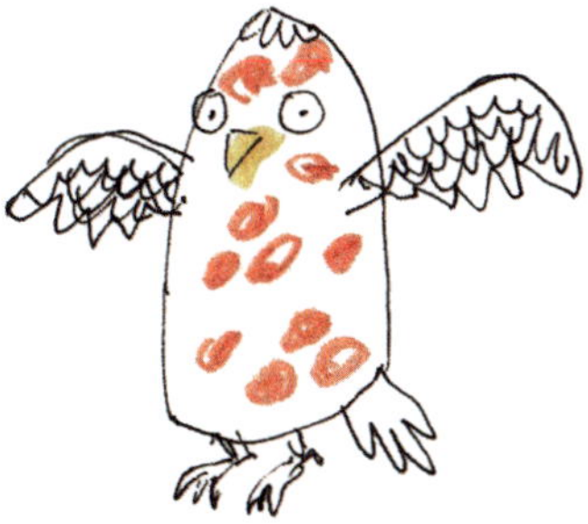

As paradoxical as it may seem:

Exquisite material makes it harder to create good pictures.

Such things actually tend to distract us rather than promote creative results. How helpful can it be if we are plagued from the very first stroke: What if it doesn't turn out well? What if I'm wasting my forty (even ten) dollar sheet of paper? Hand-bound sketchpads, pre-glued watercolor pads and luxury painting boxes aren't going to loosen up your stroke. On the contrary, you might start worrying that your artistic skills can't live up to the expensive material.

I advise students to start with inexpensive materials. A good sketchbook needn't cost more than 12 dollars and at first you don't need more than a pencil, an ink pen or a ballpoint. Not only will all the fancy materials raise your expectations, but you'll have to lug them around with you, too. Worst case, the weight of your bag will determine how much time you spend searching for a good subject. So there are good reasons to focus on the essentials and to ignore the overabundance in art supply stores, particularly in the early phases.

The same goes for digital hardware and software. In this age of ever newer and bigger it may sound heretical, but high-performance computers and top-shelf programs don't make good illustrations. Expensive material can't replace ideas; computing power won't give you a feel for pictures. My advice is:

Don't drive yourself nuts.
Less is more.

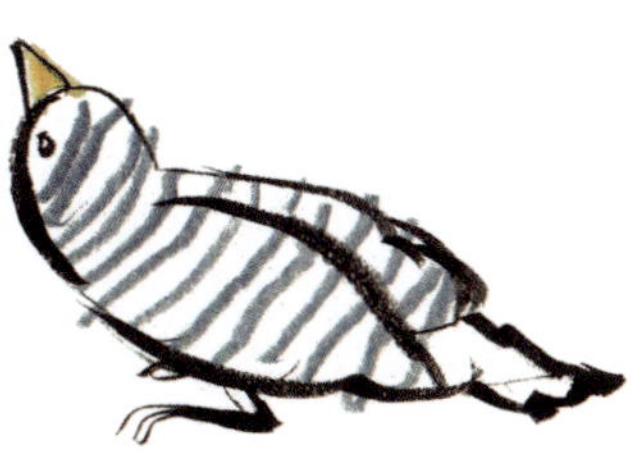

ROMAN KLONEK

JULIANE WENZL

Workplace and Studio

There are two things that I will not put up with during working hours. One is liquor and the other is men. SOME LIKE IT HOT, BILLY WILDER 1959

Oscar Wilde's *The Picture of Dorian Gray* describes what an ideal studio looks like: A bright room with a huge front window, the view into a rambling garden, through which the late summer scent of roses streams in. Dancing sunspots, the sounds of a piano, a cup of tea and inspiring muses complete the pleasant atmosphere. Maybe a velvet-covered divan, a painter in a smock and the ensemble is perfect.

So, a simple tip might be to simply orientate yourself to *that* when choosing your workplace. If, however, such a studio doesn't happen to be at hand, I would advise you to focus on the really important aspects. For although the scent of roses may not have a bad influence on our workflow, light and space seem more crucial.

In fact, the choice of your workplace plays an important role because, after all, you spend most of your day there. Ideally, you should avoid a desk covered in junk as well as some cold shed in a backyard full of filth, noise and nasty neighbors.

Your workplace should be a place you feel good in.

It doesn't have to be an all-round feel-good haven, but you can certainly demand a minimum of ambience. At the beginning of your career in particular, you have to cut corners, but even having a good café around the corner or a decent taco stand nearby can increase the quality of a studio by far.

Much depends on taste and life circumstances. Nevertheless, I would say that you should not work for the long term at home at the kitchen table. Working at home may seem very practical, but you have to have a good deal of discipline to really work hard there.

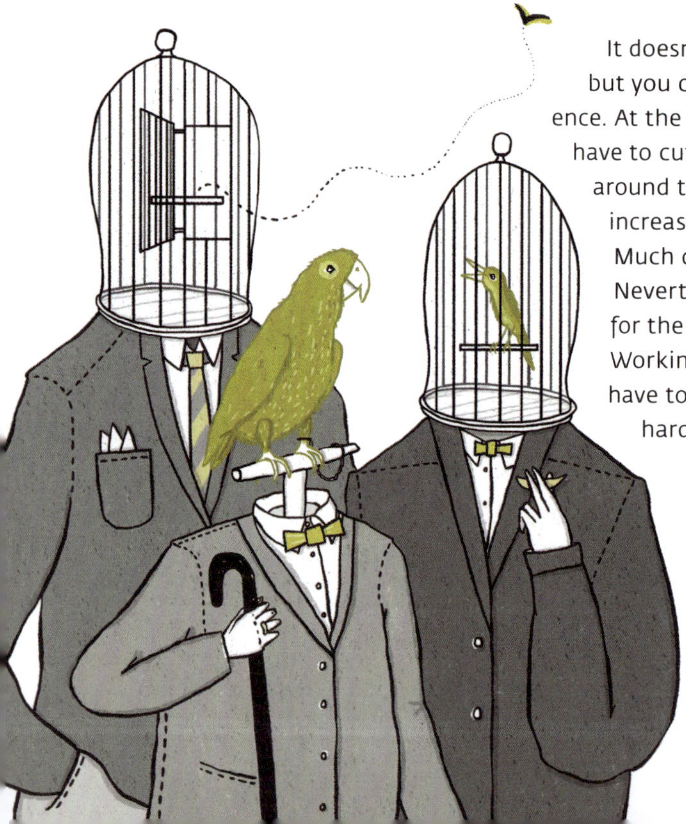

At home there are too many big and little distractions. You run the risk of squeezing a thousand domestic things into your working hours. You need at least a study, but the aim is to have an outside studio. The advantages are obvious: The spatial separation helps you divide work and leisure time; if not you cannot function in either properly. As a beginner, you should answer the question of whether or not to share a studio with a YES. In fact, it would be a waste to work from home to avoid a studio rental since you're also doing without friendly co-workers, inspiration, break companions and technical support.

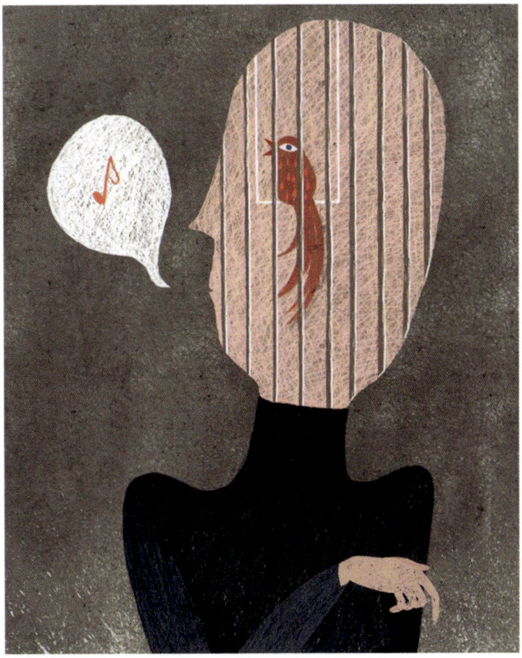

Shared studios are worth their weight in gold.

You're not sitting there alone, you can help and motivate each other and ask for opinions. Many professionals are familiar with the dilemma: If you work on an illustration for a long time, after awhile you become "blind"; that is, it is increasingly difficult for us to judge how to move forward on an illustration. Here, too, a quick glance from a colleague or sitting down over an espresso with them helps us to gain the necessary distance.

In addition, shared studios occasionally generate jobs. For one, because you can outwardly sell yourself as a community very differently (for example via a shared website, group exhibitions, etc.), but also because you can take over jobs from colleagues who may need help or simply have no time and therefore have to turn them down.

Of course, the establishment of a shared studio requires that you have enough colleagues with whom to share a studio. In large cities, it is relatively easy since shared studios usually already exist – just look at notice boards in art supplies stores.

However, if you live in a rural area, the search is certainly less easy. But here, too, there are ways. It is conceivable to share a workspace with members of similar professions, such as graphic artists, architects or designers of any kind. The most important thing is that the "chemistry" between you and your studiomates is good. If you can't stand each other, having the same profession won't help either.

Perhaps we can say in general that one should strive for a good atmosphere in the workplace and that it should be designed as best as possible. A good atmosphere pays off, for example in increased work efficiency. Better working conditions help you concentrate better and generate more money, so that the investment in a studio quickly pays off. You should like your workplace. If you hate it, your work will show it.

Finally, I would like to dispel the stubborn myth about artists thriving amidst "creative chaos." I'm afraid that's mostly nonsense. Although there are artists who work in studios that defy description (look up photographs of the English painter Francis Bacon's workspace), we can assume that they have accomplished something in their workspaces *despite* and not *because of* the chaos.
To put it bluntly, it is usually better to work in organized, handsome workplaces. You spend less time searching (say for materials, etc.) and you'll simply prefer working if you straighten up your desk – and your computer desktop – now and then. Piles of unfinished work load you down.

> Finish your work and straighten up your workplace. You'll see how much more capacity that will gain you in every respect.

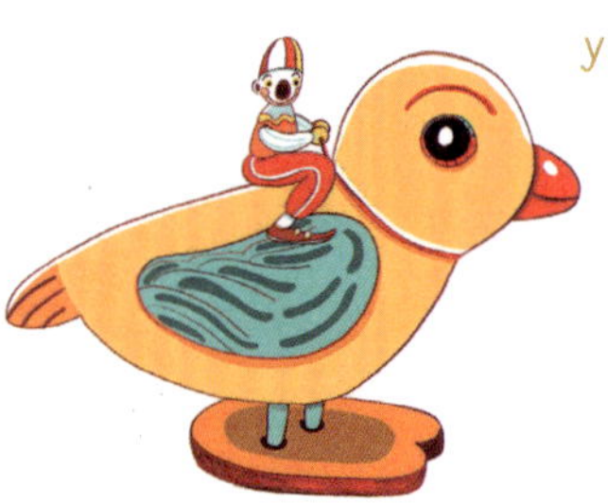

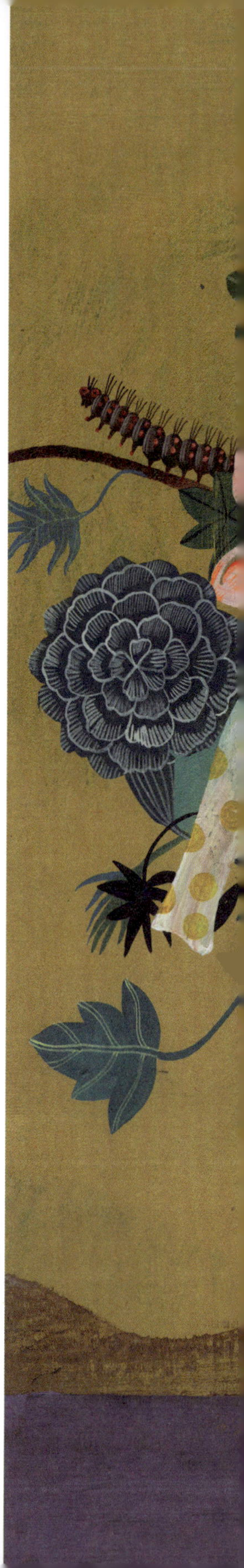

ORIT BERGMAN

OLAF HAJEK

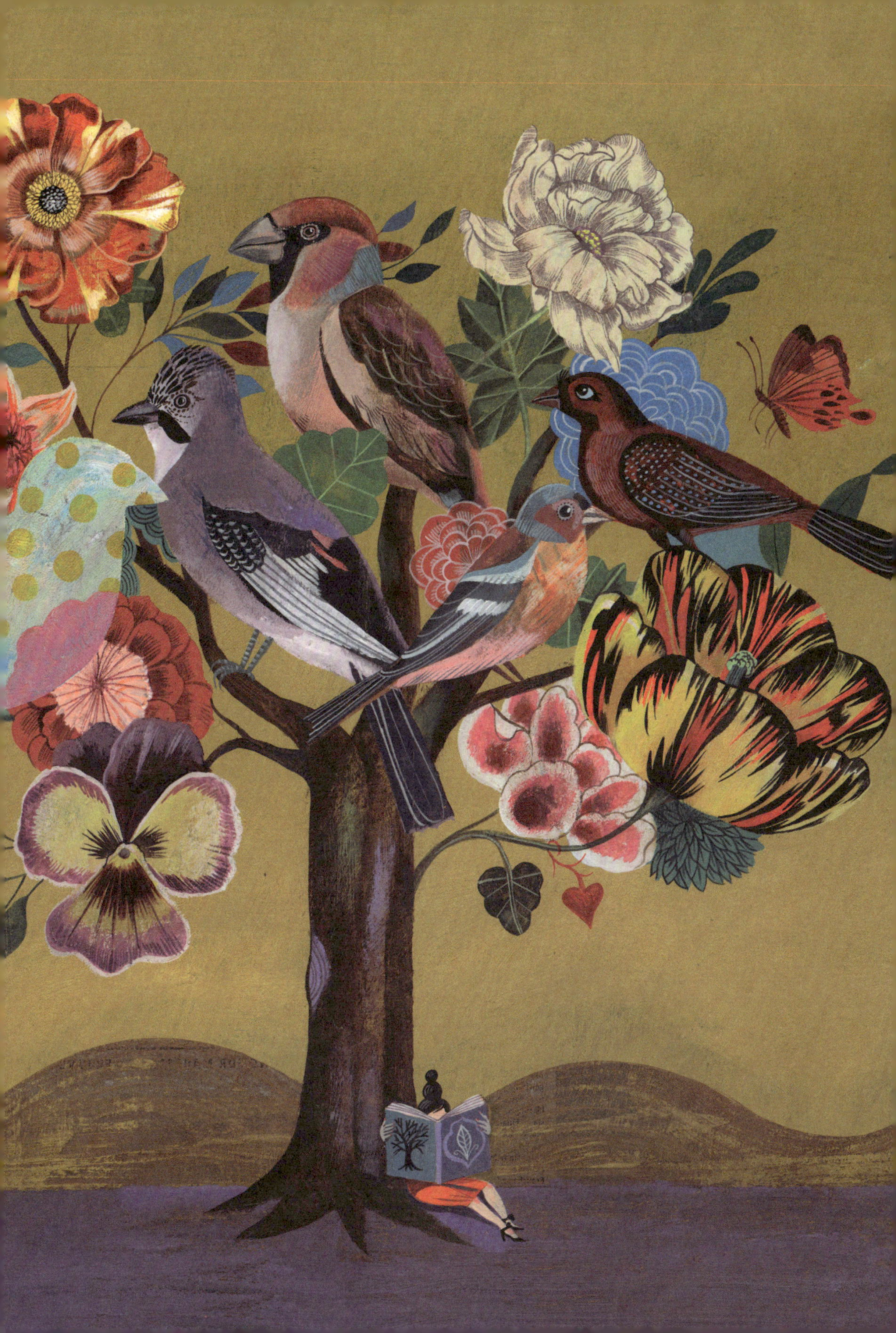

Presentations

My name is Bond. James Bond.
SEAN CONNERY, 1962

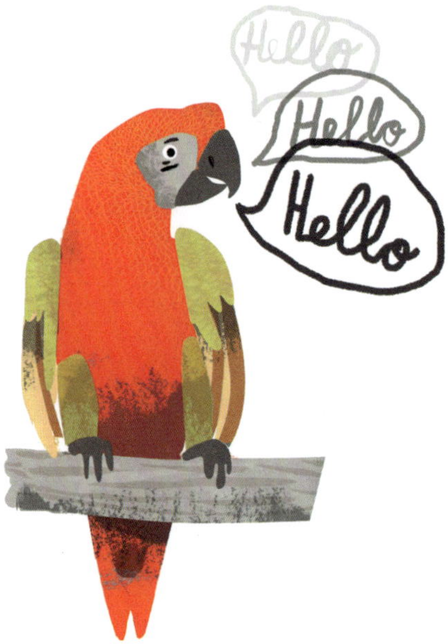

Imagine you're at a restaurant – candlelight, pleasant music and good company. And imagine the waiter comes over with the spaghetti you ordered looking very unhappy.
He stands there indecisively and announces feebly, "This was just an attempt; it may not be the final version ... You know, scallops are difficult ... if you want anything changed, just let me know ... and, yeah, I hope you enjoy it anyway!"
I suspect that you wouldn't dig in quite so bravely than if the waiter had simply bade you enjoy the meal.

I'm using this example to say that *the way* you sell yourself and your work has an impact on your career success. It starts with the fact that you simply have to arrive at agreed appointments on time – whether it's for a presentation, a briefing or a job interview. Allow yourself more time, because something can always happen even if it's just a missed subway.
But most of all, your demeanor itself plays a big role.
I'm sure you also prefer to work with people who you like. A little courtesy never hurts. And although you may be there primarily to talk about your pictures, friendliness builds bridges. So show yourself from the best side. This is especially true if it things don't go smoothly right away: Deal with criticism constructively and do not be overly complacent when praised. Above all, it's helpful to check what your attitude is when you enter into a conversation:

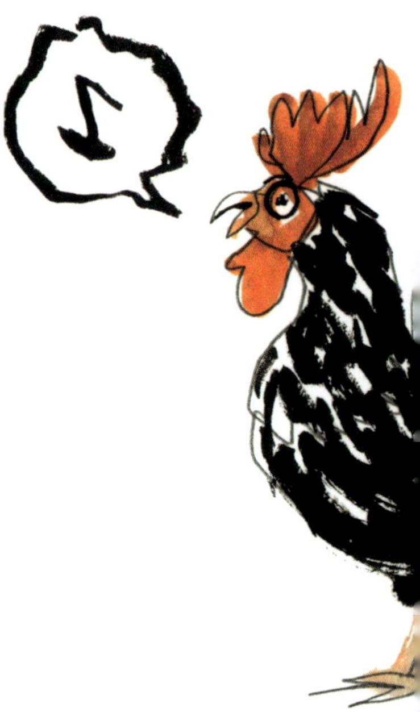

Do you go in expecting a good discussion or are you already hunkering down in advance for fear of criticism?
Most of us illustrators tend to hide our light under a bushel. And the moment when we present our work is simply a moment of truth.

We all know the feeling – whether at a trade fair meeting, in an application, a job interview or when presenting a commissioned work: Until we get the okay, we're insecure. How will the other person react? In our mind's eye, the client bursts into tears of joy – or he has a tantrum. The range of possible reactions that we imagine reveals the extent of our insecurity.

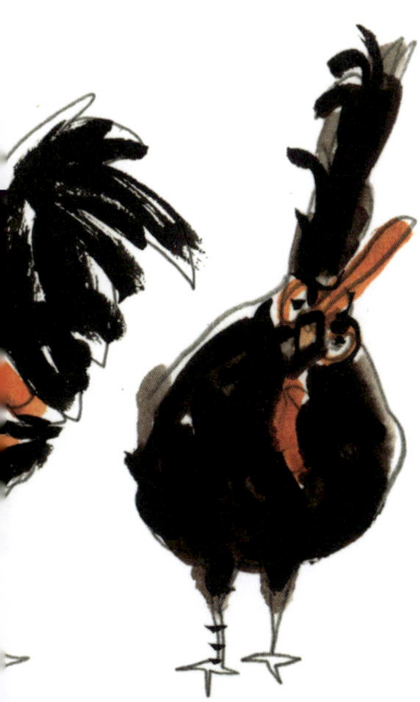

My clear advice here can only be this:

Stay cool.

In reality, the criticism you fear is often caused by the fact that you don't present your work with enough self-confidence. Uncertainty often tends to make us make ourselves smaller than we are. And we often – as a kind of unconscious reflex – get into the trap of taking the side of possible critics in advance. In other words: we criticize ourselves because we fear criticism.
This kind of behavior is anything but helpful and you have to learn to not allow it to break through in the wrong moments.
It is of little use to your cause if you stammer through a presentation, claim it is "not meant that way," or admitting that a toothache and lack of time stood in the way of your doing your best work.

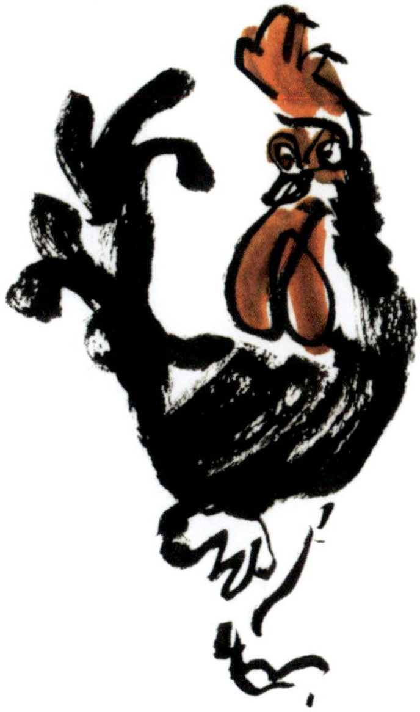

To put it briefly: That's not your job.

The critique is the other side's concern.

Then again, this doesn't mean you should be bursting with self-confidence and fling the gauntlet at the slightest correction.

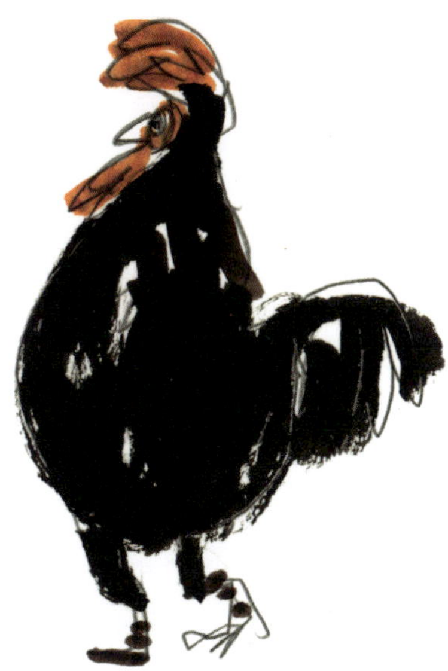

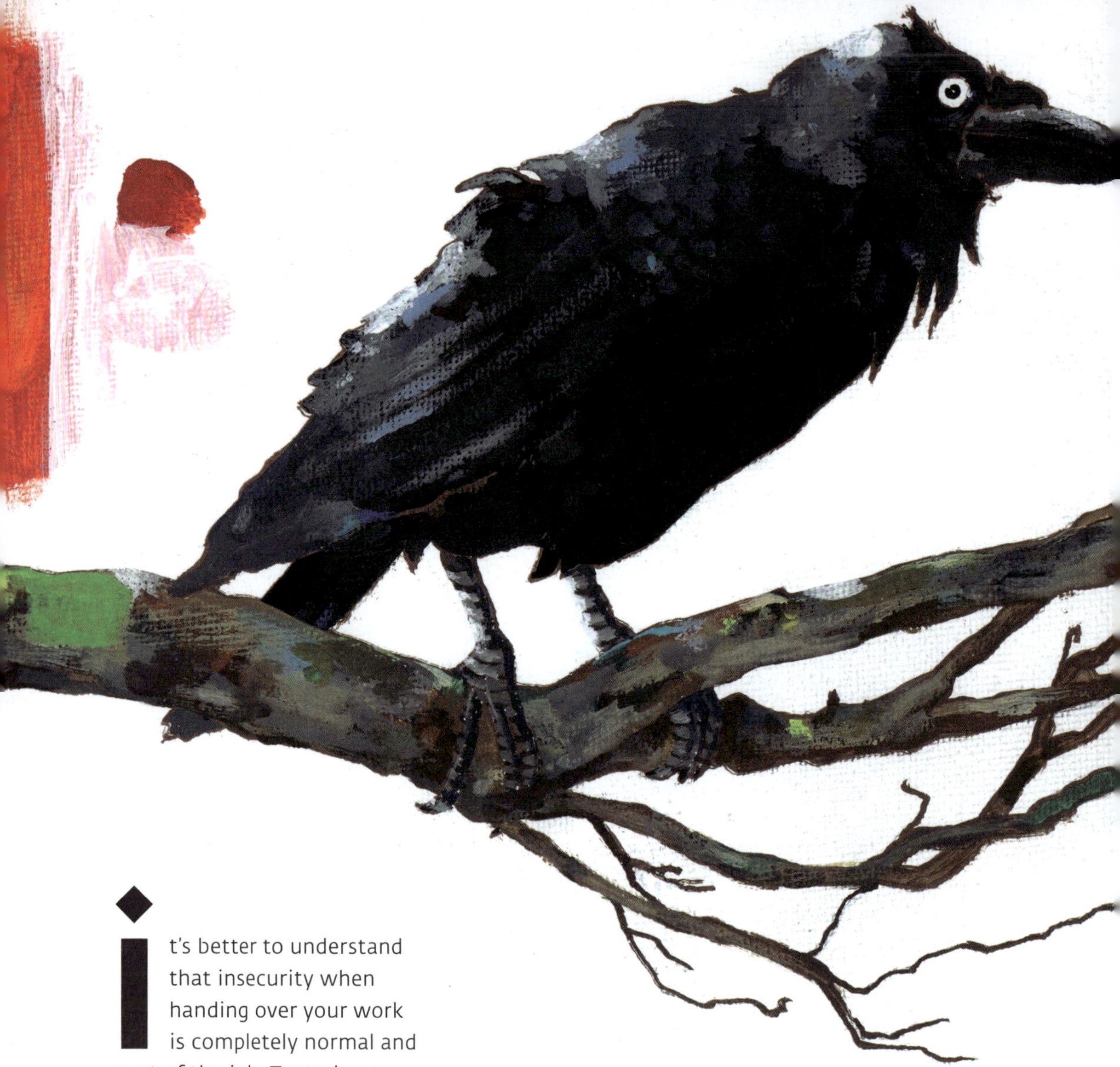

It's better to understand that insecurity when handing over your work is completely normal and part of the job. Try to have a healthy attitude about it. In other words, simply choose a friendly, brisk and objective tone of voice.

Presentations are only something between you and the client anyway. They are important for the sale, and as such they have to be taken seriously. We don't have to overrate them by making ourselves smaller than we are or by thinking we can accomplish anything by bluffing alone.

Instead, learn to represent your work professionally. Your finished illustrations must ultimately work without explanations. Once your pictures are printed, you can't chase after every book or magazine to explain what you really meant.

Be brave!
(And put a nice shirt on, would you, and take your hands out of your pockets.)

Business Sense

If you only knew the power of the dark side!
DARTH VADER, THE EMPIRE STRIKES BACK, GEORGE LUCAS, 1980

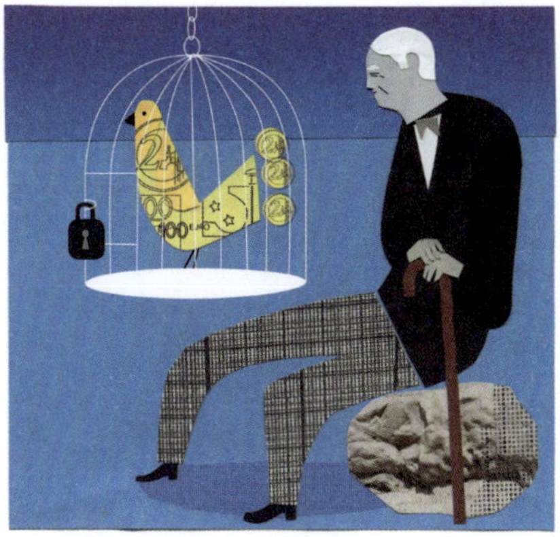

It may sound hackneyed, but to survive as a designer you ought to learn some business basics. The reason is – and I cannot say it clearly enough – *because* it is something we are not very good at.
It's true. We illustrators consciously work with beautiful things. We spend a lot of time bringing our creativity and imagination into the world, often neglecting vile things like earning a living and thinking about retirement. We're not good businesspeople. The idea of actually only becoming an artist because you're "not good with numbers" is much more common than is generally known. Sometimes it almost seems as if this attitude is an elemental part of us.
The problem with that is that we naturally do not learn to master things that we avoid as well as the things we enjoy and therefore do more diligently. This would not be so bad if the world were populated by honest, generous and altruistic business partners. That this is not the case is demonstrated by a look at the main topics of almost any forum on the subject of illustration. As the O'Jays song about money goes, "For a small piece of paper, it carries a lot of weight."
That's why I'd advise you to take time on this subject now and then and *practice*.

Since we basically neglect our business sense, we have to purposely train it.

For example, turn it into a little game: Try to haggle whenever you can. Go to flea markets or try to get better prices in stores. Learn mental arithmetic. Learn all the basic arithmetic operations. It's good practice to regularly add up all the prices of the items you've put in your supermarket cart or occasionally find out the percentage of a sum.

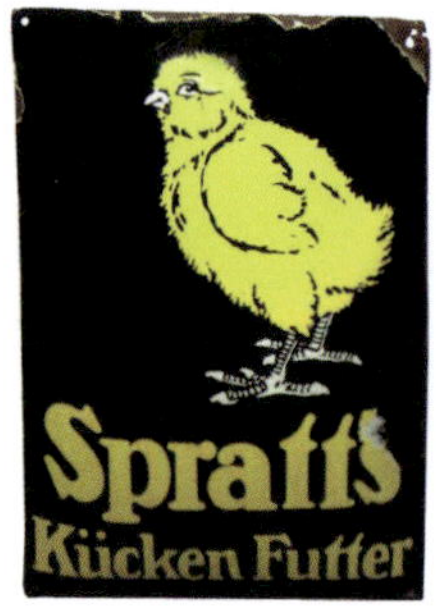

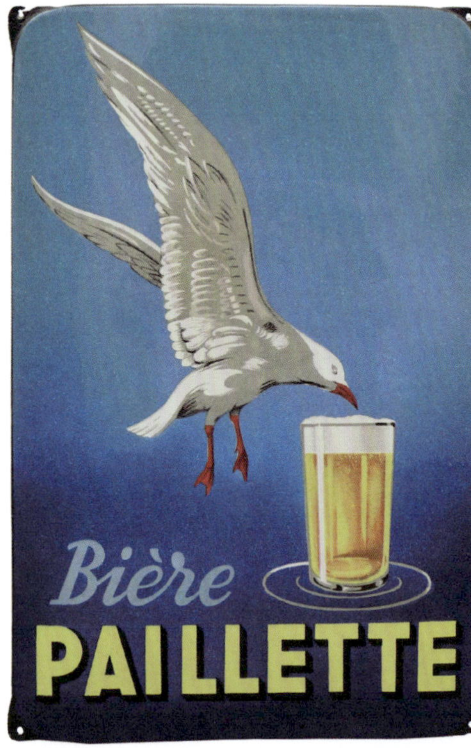

not everyone is born with business sense. Still, it's like a muscle: if you exercise it regularly, it grows on its own.

Now, this doesn't mean that you should join the "dark side of the Force." You don't want to build a real estate empire or become a hatchet man. First and foremost, we want to make the world more beautiful with our work. Nevertheless, the framework conditions have to be right. Even in a more beautiful world, you have to eat.
So don't neglect such things too much. Business sense enables us as artists to simply do our work better.

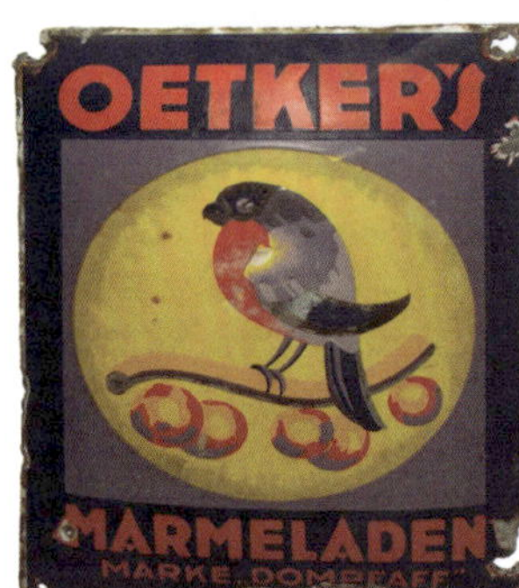

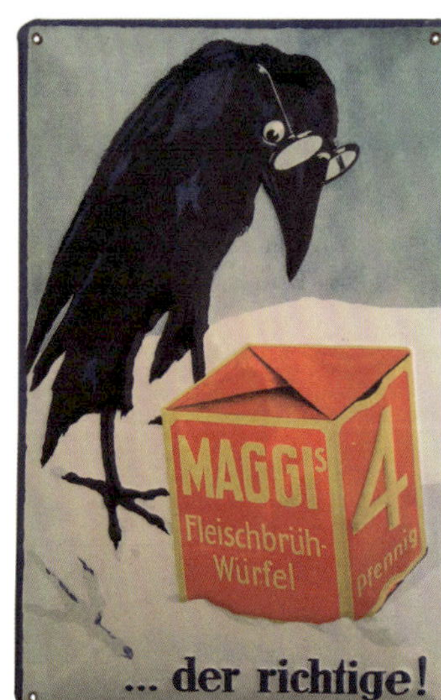

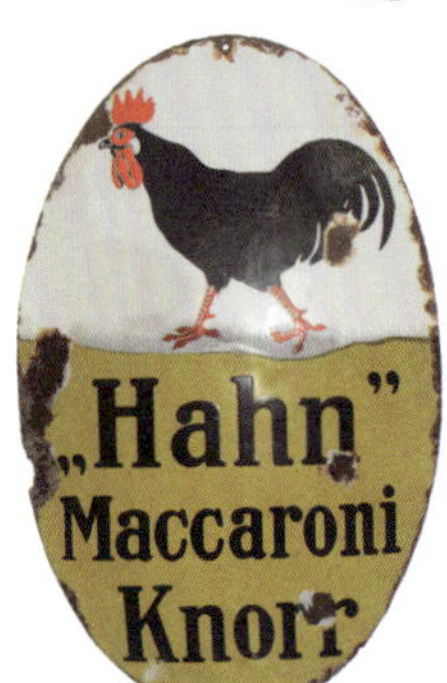

Enamel signs, ca. 1920

Contests, Pitches and Sample Illustrations

You wouldn't have won if we'd beaten you.
YOGI BERRA

The best way to get a clear estimation of whether it's worthwhile to take part in contests is to ask your local fortuneteller. One brief glance in the crystal ball and you'll know whether pitches, contests and sample illustrations pay or not. If you don't have an all-knowing sphere around, though, I can offer you my opinion on the subject:

I would first try putting the cart before the horse: Why, you might ask yourself, do potential clients hold a contest instead of just grabbing a phone and calling *you*?
If your answer is, "Because they don't know me yet," then, I'd say, you have a good reason to take part in the pitch. If your answer is almost anything else, I'd be skeptical about it if I were you.

In illustration, contests are usually very badly paid. It's another thing with pitches for architectural commissions or advertising budgets in the millions, but if we're talking about the usual prize monies in our sector, illustration pitches are sometimes more like acts of desperation than strategies.
Because you'll be footing the bill for a pitch in most cases and that before the order comes in. For one thing, you're being asked to spend time and energy on something that probably wouldn't have interested you anyway. For another, the anticipated yield for your effort can only be found in the above-mentioned crystal ball.

By the same token, a contest is a pretty safe bet for the client: They only pay the winner. Everyone else goes home empty-handed, but they offer the audience a spectacular show. To put it briefly, contests should mainly serve for scouting purposes and consider their target group to be career novices and students.

Since the advance work is yours, you should put it in relation to the expected success. If you neither like the subject nor already have finished drafts in your drawer, it would be best to think twice about whether or not you really want to take part.

Sometimes it's better to instead invest your time and energy in your own projects and ideas.

In the book and editorial sectors in particular, it's worth an illustrator's while to push ahead their own projects. Clients are usually interested and open-minded, for example if you present your ideas at a tradeshow. So budget your energies and focus on what really interest you.

In the case of so-called "sample illustrations," things aren't as clear. There are times you might be asked for a sample illustration by publishers or agencies when the client is not so sure whether you or your style really suits the job. For instance, the client would ask you for one page or one chapter for a specific project.

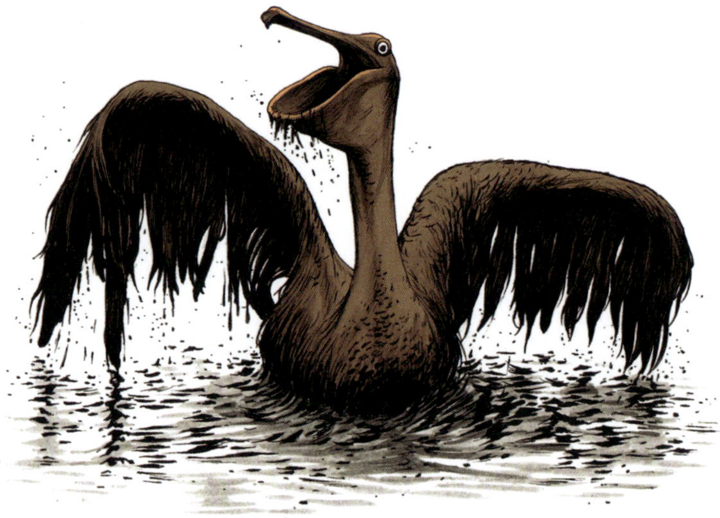

Sample illustrations could therefore be called little internal contests. The difference being that you are already on the shortlist. In such a case I would advise you – especially for jobs that could bring in lots of money or lots of renown – to put in an advance payment here. In many cases it really is worthwhile and it is occasionally also quite understandable (for example for career novices) that the client doesn't want to buy "a pig in a poke."
Nevertheless, with sample illustrations you soon run the risk of working for nothing, especially if the client asks several illustrators for a sample at the same time. Therefore, in my view, it would be correct to ensure that your submitted works are remunerated, if only by a recognition fee. And that has three very practical reasons:

Firstly, you actually *increase* your chances of getting the job if you demand payment even for sample drawings. It is simply unprofessional to work for nothing. You'll out yourself as a beginner if you don't demand a recognition fee.

Secondly, you should consider this: If you do not ask for a cancellation fee in case of rejection, for example because you think you are being accommodating to your prospective client, you will usually achieve the exact opposite. Because without a cancellation fee, *you* are the one who can be rejected by the client for *free*. This is important if your competitors are getting a cancellation fee if they are rejected. In this case, you can easily calculate *who* the potential customer will tend to refuse if they have the same qualifications, even if only to save money.

And thirdly, it's so that if you are rejected in spite of all the effort, you at least have a consolation prize in the cancellation fee. Be brave! Even that is better than nothing!

Competition

Still alone in o-hell-o – see the deadly nightshade grow.
"AISLEY OF PLENTY," GENESIS, 1973

I remember very well that while I was a student, doubts often crept over me when I looked at my classmates: Everyone else always seemed to be further along, better, more talented and more cunning than I. For the life of me, I couldn't imagine how, among such a grand bunch of rivals, I had even the slightest chance of finding my way as an illustrator. Funnily enough, years later all of my former potential competitors admitted when asked that they saw it the same way. Just *the other way around*.

To understand this, I would like to briefly take you into the world of perceptual phenomena. Does this situation sound familiar, for example? It's Saturday afternoon. The supermarket is packed and, as always, there are not enough cashiers. You steer your shopping cart towards a line, but as soon as you get in the line, it slows down as if by magic.

And while you wait, you can see how all of a sudden everything is moving very quickly two cash points away. Should you move? Move! But again your new line slows down. It's like being jinxed. Is it jinxed? No, it's statistics!

In fact, on average the lines are progressing at the same speed. But there are always a few outliers with an average value. And since you are standing in line, but at the same time are *observing* five or six others, it is more than likely that another is moving faster.

Interestingly, we then usually pay particular close attention to those lines. We hardly notice lines going the same speed or slower than ours. The effect is that in the ranks of competitors it always has to look like someone else is faster or more successful.

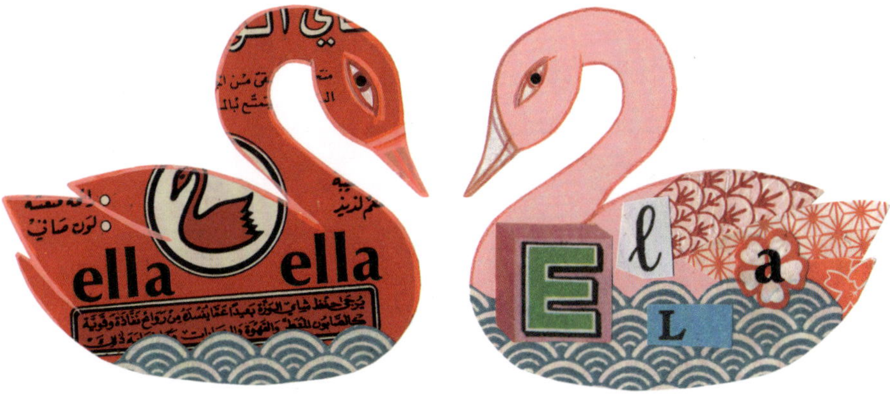

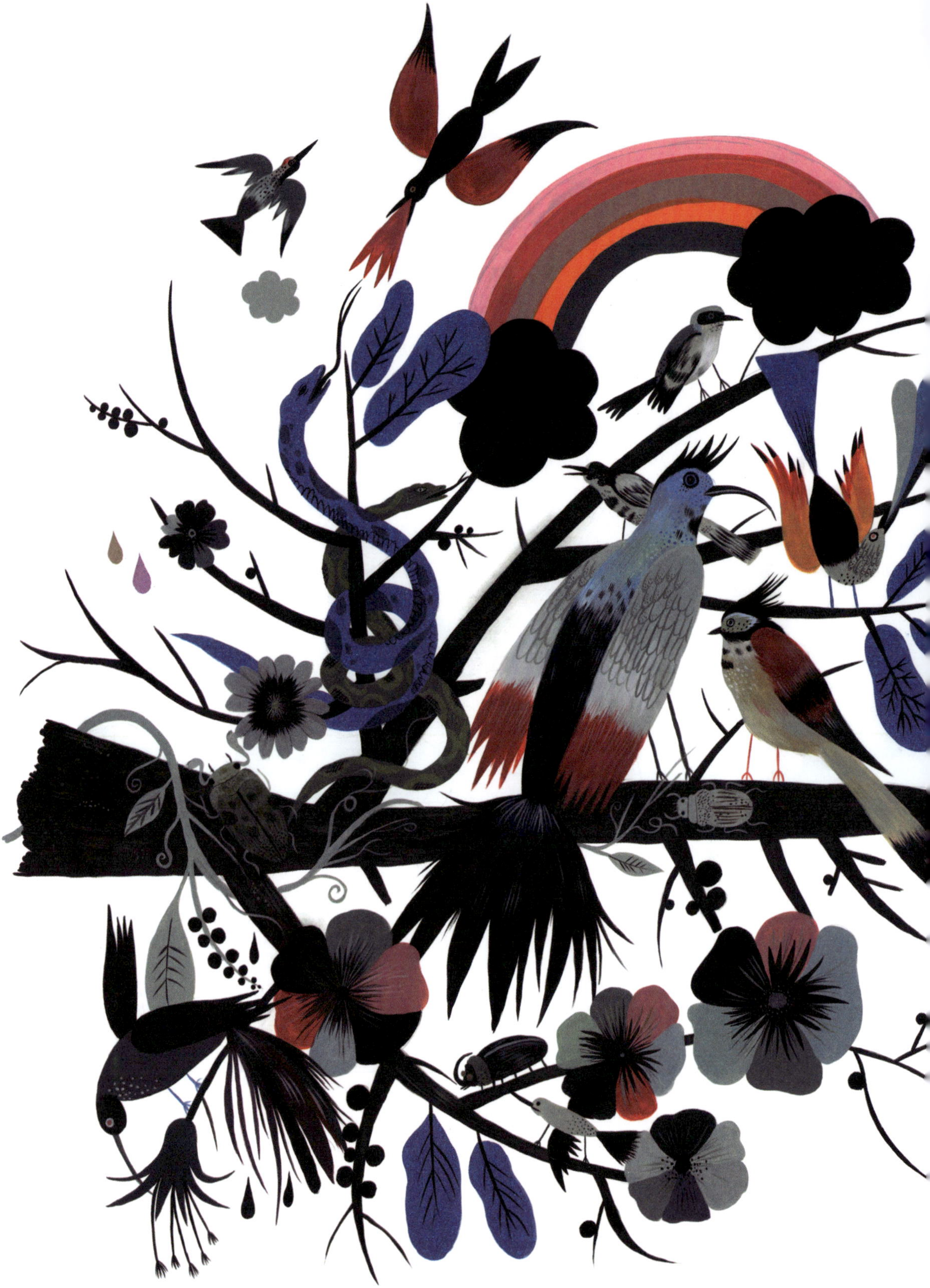

Competition is a strange phenomenon, and the reason why others sometimes frighten us is as complex as the fear itself. One of the explanations for this is that we usually perceive others and their accomplishments differently than ourselves. That's because we simply cannot relate to the work of others, in spite of our interest. When observing the results of the efforts of others, we can hardly judge how difficult or easy it was for them to reach it. We can't imagine the process of the making and thus it seems at first (and at first sight) better. Every cook knows what I mean: A dish you cook yourself it is far less enjoyable than one that others serve to you. Plus, everyone is trying to look as good as possible to others. You don't post failures on Facebook. The result is that we count our own failures, but notice them less in others.

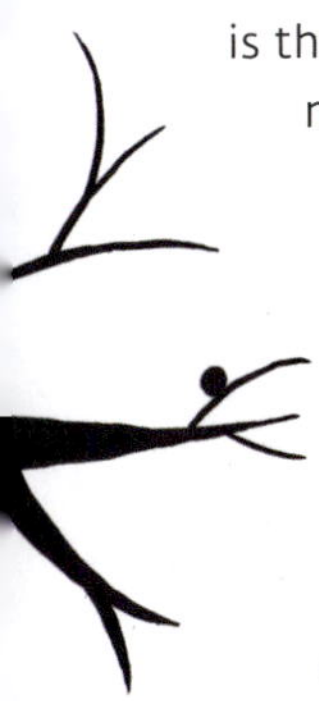

From a distance, everything looks more appealing. Our own achievements also impress us less than our own weaknesses. We are usually more worried about deficiencies than elated over good things. An overdrawn account unsettles us more than being in the black calms us. So, we quickly book the successes of others to their credit while we would only do that for ourselves with reservations. All we see is that they were published, whereas in ourselves we mainly see what we did not succeed at doing.
Therefore, competition frightens us even if the reasons for this are less due to the fact than to our idea of it.

They say, "The grass is always greener on the other side of the fence."

But is it?
There's an old rule of economics: "Competition fuels business." We all crave what we see. And a market for illustration is created only if illustration is on the spot. Markets have to be made, so there is no reason to fear competition. On the contrary, since there *are* other illustrators and you're not alone, you have many advantages. You can hardly establish a shared studio on your own, you can pass on experiences, learn tricks and stratagems from one another, and associations and professional associations work together to strengthen where we alone would be weak.
In reality, the advantages and disadvantages balance one another out and the market usually proves to be many times larger than one would expect. So, if you do not see it so grimly, you won't just be doing yourself a favor: you'll get support and nice co-workers where, seen the other way, you only see competitors.

By the way, in spite of all my fears, I did find my way as an illustrator.

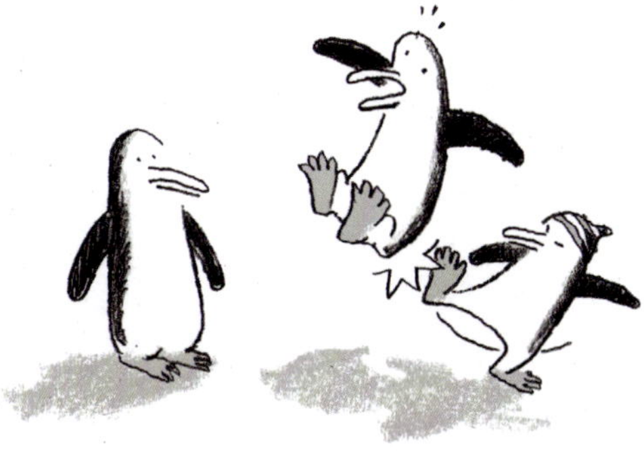

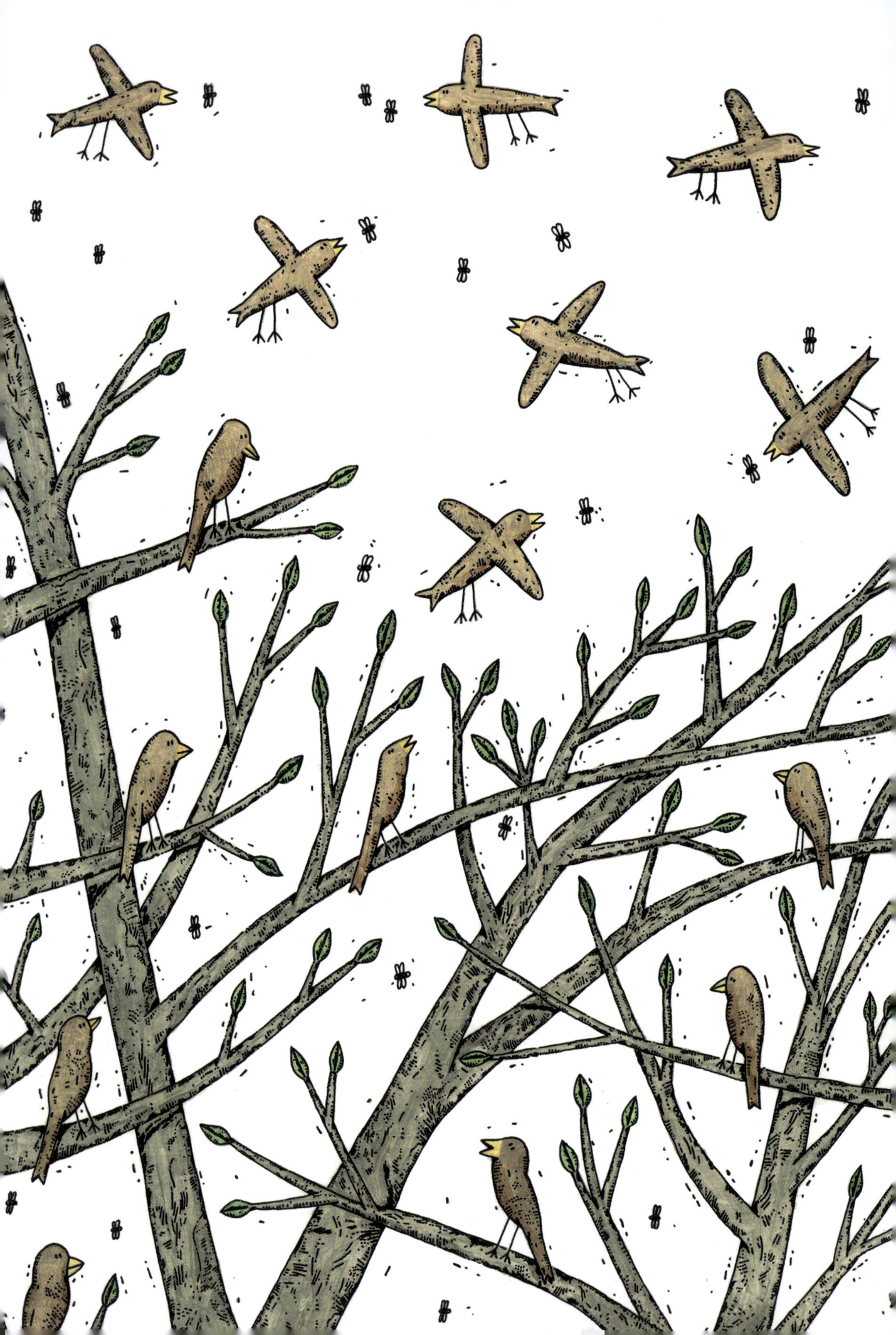

Teamwork

We shall be a single People of brethren.
OATH FROM "WILLIAM TELL," FRIEDRICH SCHILLER

There are jobs you will not want to take on, at least not on your own. And believe it or not, you don't have to. It can be quite expedient to share commissions as long as you know how.
Jobs always come unexpected: The phone rings – "Do you have time?" If the answer is "No," you are at risk of first putting off, then losing a client.
Hence, sharing is one way of avoiding having to turn down work because sharing saves time. Or perhaps a requested commission exceeds your technical or artistic possibilities. Maybe they want the illustration to be animated or produced using some exotic printing technique.
They might request a volume of work that doesn't fit into your time frame or the job is just too humdrum for you. There are plenty of reasons to share and you'll learn that it is often a wonderful solution.
They say, "Share and share alike." But you first have to decide whether it is best to share the work fifty-fifty with your colleague or hire one or a few more or less well-paid subcontractors. Both options have their advantages and disadvantages. If you decide not to share the work equally, but to shoulder a greater share of entrepreneurial risk yourself, it is right and proper that you receive a little more of the profits. It is okay for you to give yourself a margin in return for client communications, acquisition and negotiations. In case the job falls through, deadlines aren't met or payments are delayed, you – as the contractor – still have to compensate your co-workers, so it is more than fair to budget in a little extra for yourself as a fee "just in case." Just keep in mind that if you "overdo it" with the profits, you could damage your relationship with your colleagues.

It's implicit that colleagues should stick together.

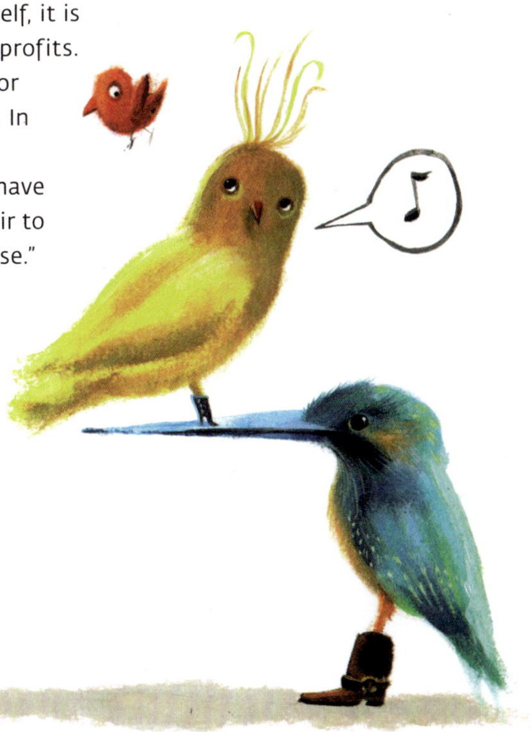

BERND MÖLCK-TASSEL

KATHARINA GROSSMANN-HENSEL

Work is work and particularly if you share a studio it is implied that the actual proceeds have to be shared by all those involved if all those involved perform equal services. Of course, *you* shouldn't be the only one in the office that regularly supplies the others with work. Your co-workers also ought to generate some commissions that can be shared among you. Fairness is not a one-way street.

In practice, I'd recommend that you don't communicate too openly with your client about whether or in what manner you are sharing a job. In the end, they hired *you*. It will cause confusion if you suddenly confront them with more than one contact. (Very large or complicated jobs, like animated film productions, games and similar, are the exception to this. In these cases it may be wiser to present yourselves as a group in order to show the client that you have a team capable of handling the volume of the task.)

When working in a team, make sure that sharing the work does not lower its quality.

Obviously, just because the work is shared doesn't mean that any differences in style or quality can be allowed. Again, how it's done is crucial: You can't share work like slicing up a loaf of bread. It would look odd if you paint one figure in an image and your co-worker another figure. Your teamwork will be less obvious if you divide up the *work phases* for an illustration. For example, one co-worker does the preliminary drawings, another does the inking, and a third does the coloring. A job shared like this not only looks like it was made by one artist, but it takes less time than one completed by one individual.

The advantages of "back and forth" are that it's more entertaining and less nerve-wracking than working alone. United, as they say, you're strong. There's not only more communication, but the decision-making processes are shorter ("What do you think of...?"), and ideally your skills complement one another's.

"Too many cooks spoil the broth," they say, but a glance inside any restaurant kitchen proves them wrong. A greasy spoon is the only place you'll find a single cook nowadays. Restaurants are the domain of teamwork and you can tell how good it is with the first mouthful!

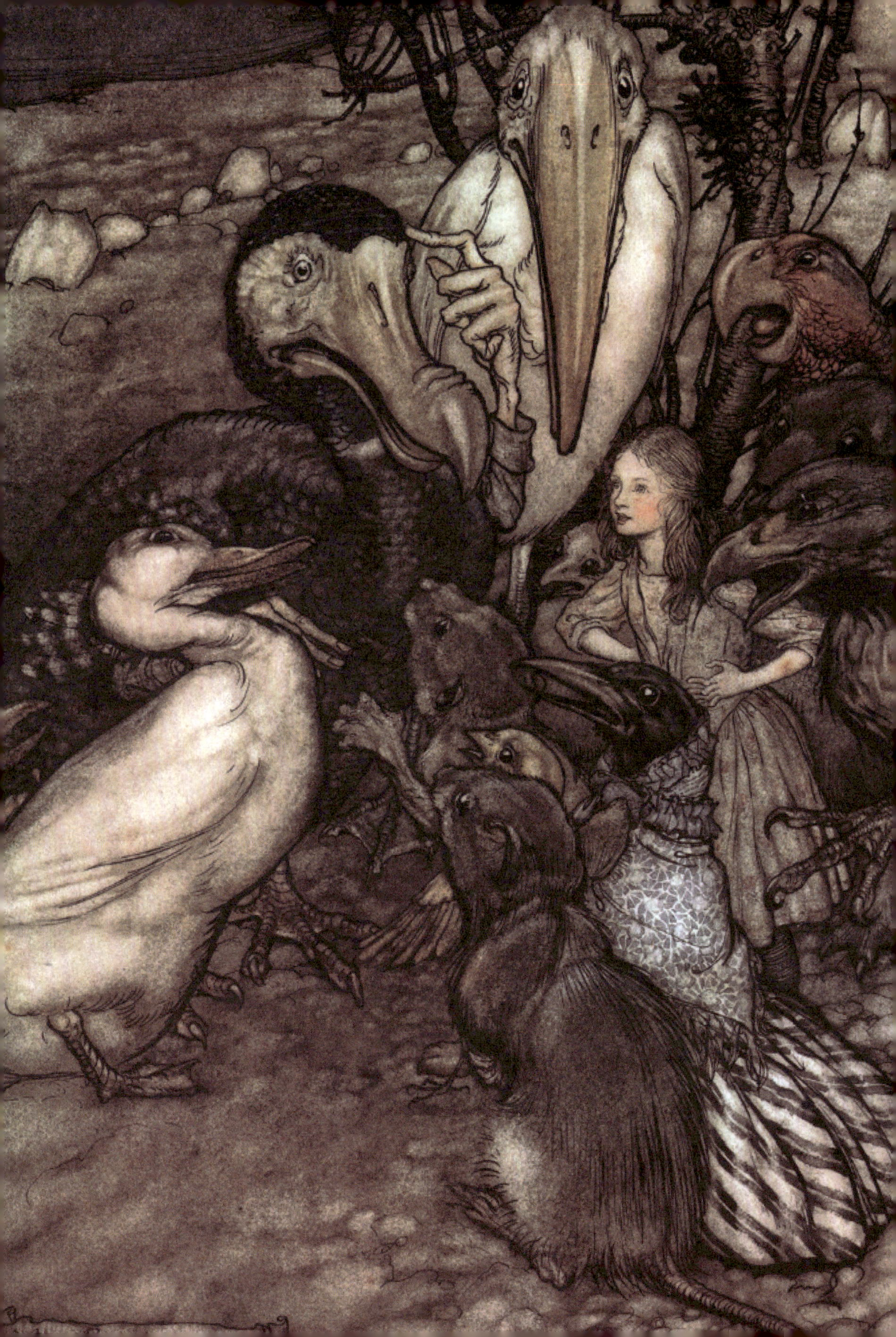

Communicating

> The limits of my language are the limits of my world.
>
> LUDWIG WITTGENSTEIN

Do you understand your client? Does your client understand you? Let's face it: Communication with clients is sometimes really difficult. It begins with not everyone involved speaking the same language. You can describe some things very well in words, but not paint them with brushes. This incomprehension is documented by many instructions given to illustrators in the manner of, "Please don't make the snow so cold and use less white."

It's even graver it seems to me that in complex joint projects all too often a common vision seems to be lacking. And that's not because of a lack of visions. As a rule, everyone involved knows very well what the project should look like in the end.

To explain it using the example of a book: Everyone involved has different priorities. For example, the author wants a meaningful book; the publisher wants a successful one, but the editorial board wants a highly praised book; the seller wants one that sells well, the manufacturer wants a solid book and the illustrator an artistic one. We see that everyone has very clear ideas about the book, but not the same ones.

> As Abraham Lincoln once said, "You can please some of the people all of the time, you can please all of the people some of the time, but you can't please all of the people all of the time."

In addition, all those involved want to scoop the biggest possible piece of fame-and-fortune cake on their plate and everyone wants the division of labor to work for them. This results in any number of construction sites, which means that every successful illustrator also needs to be a successful communicator.

Most communication difficulties can be avoided by clear agreements made in advance. You shouldn't be afraid to ask about the little details. Don't worry about how that might make you look. It really only looks stupid when the project later fails due to things that could have been avoided through good communication. This starts with the technical conditions.

File and image sizes, the scope and timing should be communicated unambiguously. You'd be surprised how much the other side appreciates this kind of clarity. But even the rather unpleasant topics, such as money, deadlines and corrections – that is, everything that typically leads to discrepancies – should be addressed clearly and immediately from the beginning. There's no point in leaving out these things for the sake of peace. Sooner or later, they'll come up anyway, and then it usually only gets more difficult. So it makes sense to strive for a clear language.

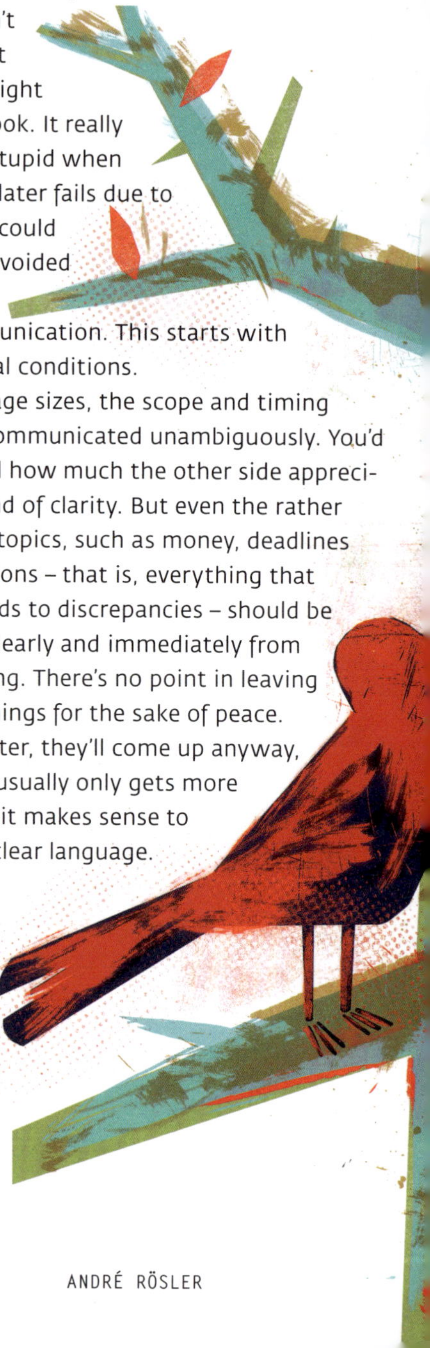

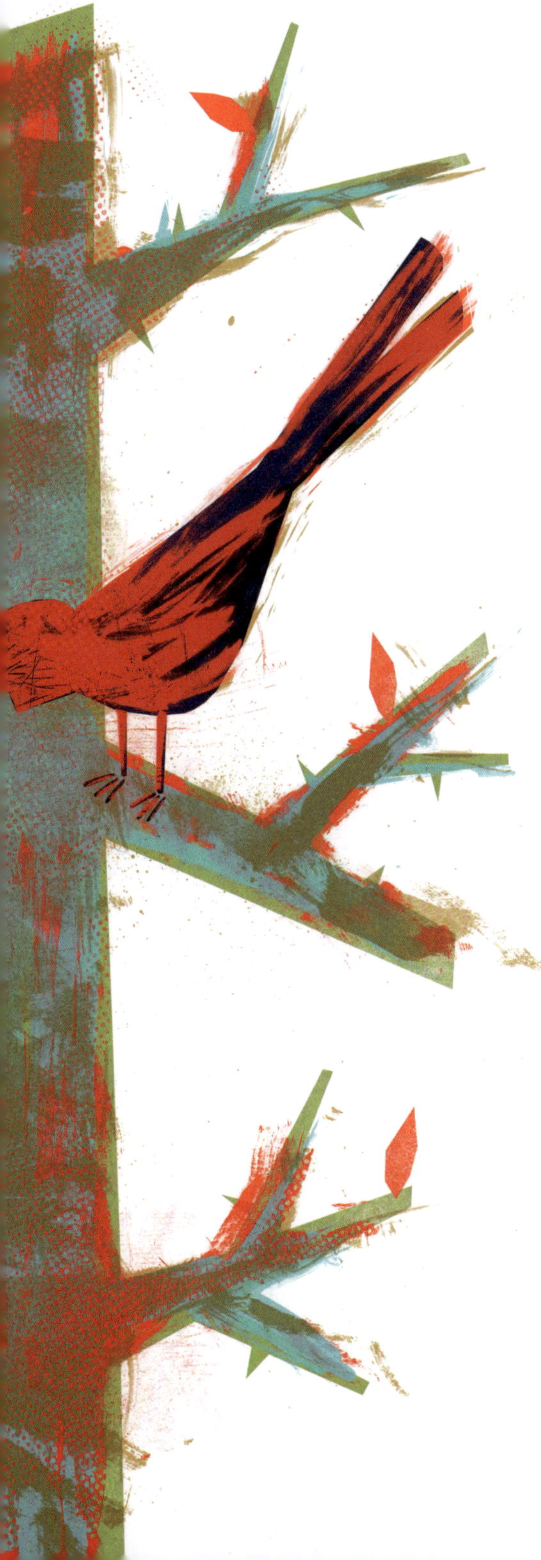

This doesn't mean that we should only talk with each other in legalized technical jargon. On the contrary, good communication requires the right "tone." And a little commitment never hurt anyone.

During the projects themselves, it's wise to communicate from the beginning not only verbally but also visually. Don't forget you're an illustrator! Use your basic skills: Create meaningful sketches from the beginning. When we talk about pictures without seeing them, misunderstandings inevitably creep in. My bird is not your bird, and your client's bird is certainly also another bird. It is therefore essential in practice to safeguard illustrations by making drafts in a layout phase. The advantage is obvious: On the one hand, you get your client involved and give them plannable material in advance. On the other hand, you safeguard yourself, of course. Because when discrepancies arise, corrections in the sketch phase are much less labor intensive (and issues are much easier to clear up) than if you get into disagreement over a folder full of months of work. And after a sketch phase, a client will hardly criticize anything in a final drawing that was already visible in the sketch.

Illustration is pure communication. We relate, describe and entertain with pictures.

Images are a language that we hear with our eyes. Therefore, use communication to make your work as effective as possible so that even a request for "not so cold, less white snow" leads to a satisfactory result for both sides.

Negotiating

I can't get no satisfaction.
THE ROLLING STONES 1965

Say, the phone rings one day and it's a client with a job inquiry. The moment of truth arrives in the first five minutes of conversation: what will the illustration cost? Yes, what does your work cost?

Welcome to the bazaar!

I won't beat around the bush: Negotiating is always a little precarious. You're interested in the job, but you sure don't want to undersell yourself. It's a daily dilemma.

Tip: If your client instantly says, "Great!" your quote was too low.

Basically, you have to get a feeling of what the job is worth to them; after all, you don't want to give away a profit margin. Which brings us to the question of how to assess your own price.

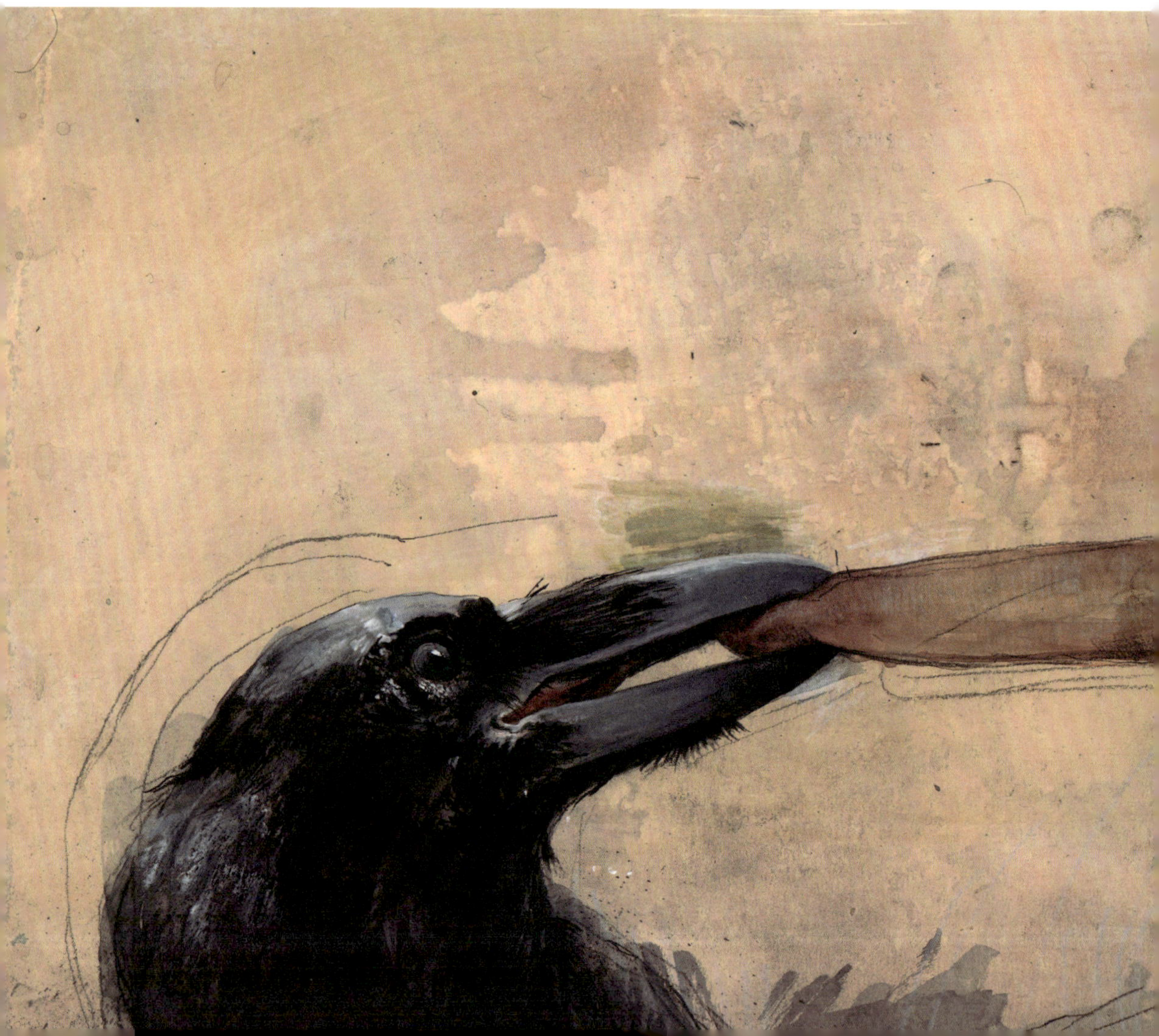

On the one hand, it's a question of personal effort, on the other hand, of the added value your work creates for the client. Both factors involve a few unknown denominators.
So, the first thing you need to do is find out what your own market value is. Did you just begin your career recently, or did you receive the Nobel Prize for Illustration last year?
Of course, your order situation also matters a lot. If your plate is full, it's easier to negotiate (it's also an indicator of your market value). But even if you just graduated from art school, you still have to pay the rent. And it's no good to you or anyone else if you work for free.
In real life, the notion that you can use basement prices to gain a favorable reputation for your career is almost always wishful thinking. "Unpaid internships" do not look very good on your resume. Plus, clients you win over this way will always expect low prices in the future ("Last time it was a lot cheaper"), so in the long run, dumping will get you nowhere.

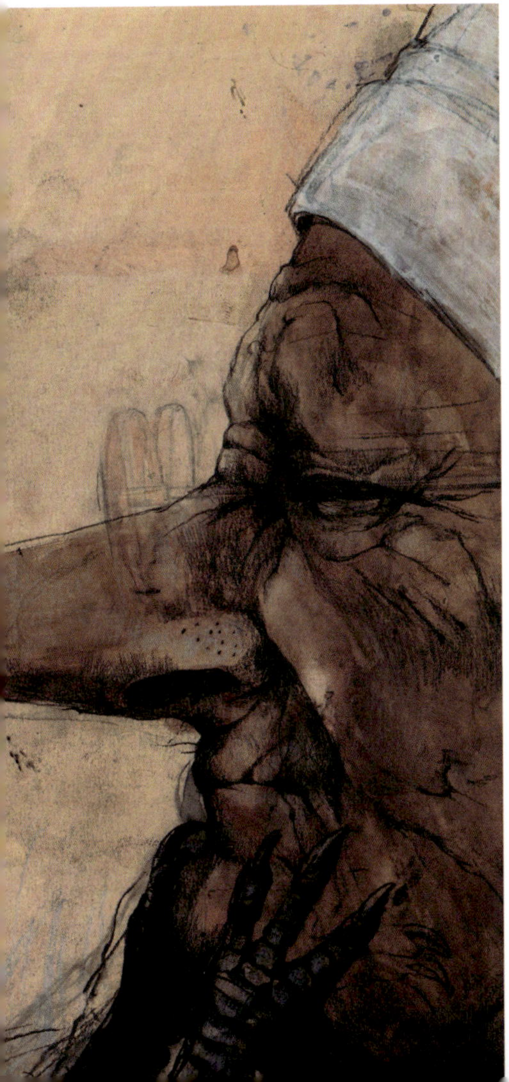

You not only have to assess your own value, but also realistically assess the "opposition." If there's a Saudi prince on the phone, the margin is probably greater than if it's an unknown street musician asking for a CD cover.

All of these factors have to be taken into consideration, so it is wise not to name a price during the initial conversation. It's far wiser to say you have to do some calculations and will get back to them (rest assured, if you name a spontaneous price, you won't be able to take it back later).

Hang up and then take your time to do the math.

If you are a beginner, don't hesitate to ask more experienced illustrators for advice or search the forums for comparable projects.

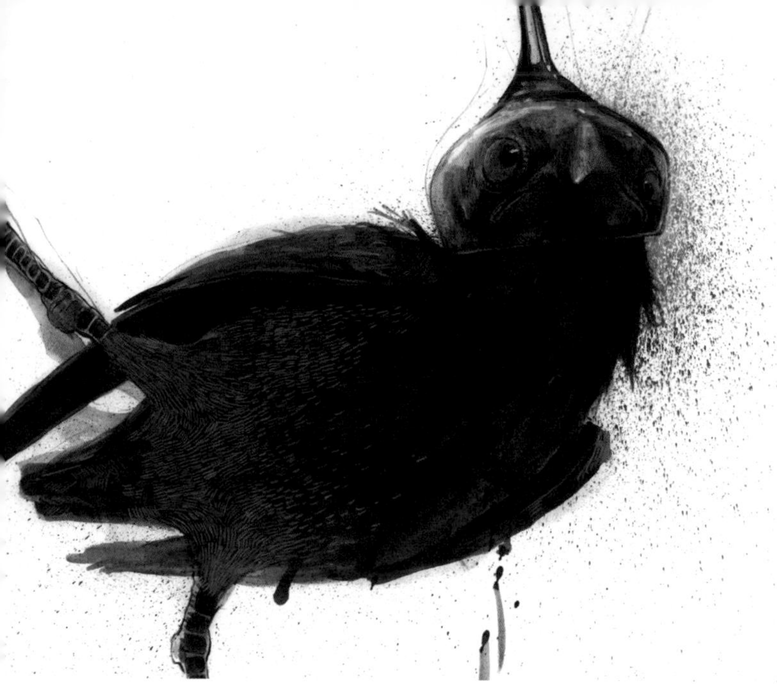

Illustrators' organizations around the world also offer price lists that cite examples (for example, they recommend orienting your price on an hourly rate. That's a very acceptable rate after deducting taxes, operating costs, pension and health insurance). A percentage of sales is also good (e.g. in the book market), if you expect your illustration will be more widely used. Combinations, such as a non-refundable advance, are also conceivable.

If you're afraid of losing a client because they think your price is too high, it always makes sense to word your asking price flexibly. Phrases like "Would the amount of XY be negotiable?" offer a certain amount of leeway and are preferable to phrases like "It's XY or nothing" when it comes to negotiating strategies. In addition, you should always calculate your offers according to the extent of use. For example, you can offer your client the same job for different prices, depending on what scope of use it acquires (for example, a flyer for a children's theater probably doesn't require worldwide use rights). That offers a little leeway.

One helpful model of negotiation is the triad "good – fast – cheap": I usually explain to clients that an illustration can have these three properties, but that as a rule only two of them can be combined. The third property then automatically is eliminated.

Specifically, this means that if an illustration has to be good and fast, it can't be cheap. If, on the other hand, the client needs it fast and cheaply, it won't be very good, and combining good and cheap rules out a fast delivery of the illustration. You can count on your clients to understand that.

Good business relationships are always lasting. The goal should therefore be a win-win situation: You have to be paid appropriately; your client mustn't feel outsmarted. Ideally, everyone involved looks back on the job with satisfaction. Otherwise your client won't come back to you. And that would be just as undesirable in the long term as you turning down any future work from them because they paid too little.

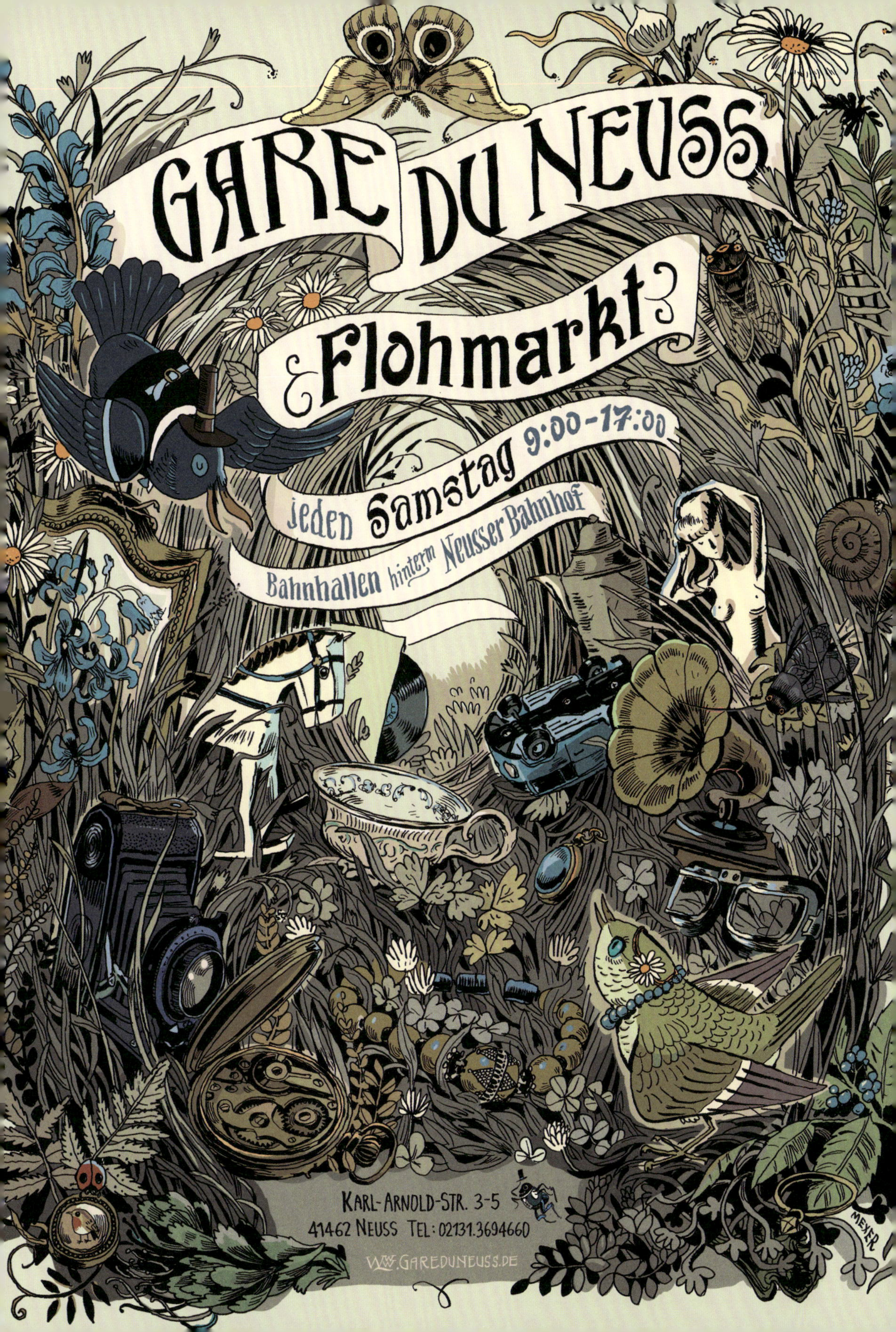

GARE DU NEUSS
Flohmarkt
jeden Samstag 9:00-17:00
Bahnhallen hinterm Neusser Bahnhof
KARL-ARNOLD-STR. 3-5
41462 NEUSS TEL: 02131.3694660
WWW.GAREDUNEUSS.DE
MEYER

Time is Money

And meet the time as it seeks us.
WILLIAM SHAKESPEARE

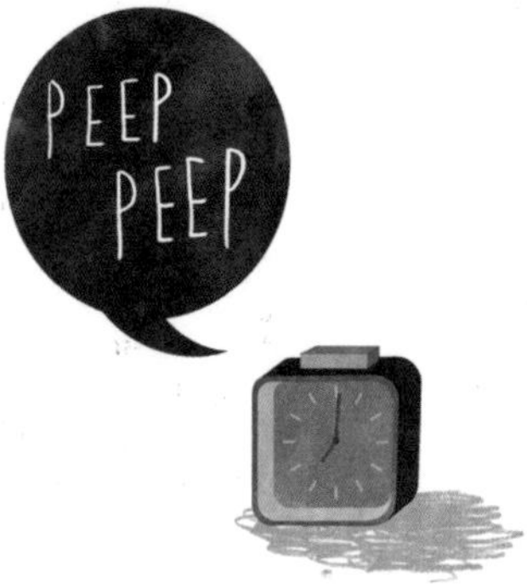

"Time is money," the saying goes. But if you think about it, it's a dumb saying. For, as with many a pithy motto, its logic quickly collapses when you make the effort to think it through.
Time is by no means money. Time is time, and in reality it is far more precious than money. Try to buy youth somewhere or a few years to add to your lifetime. I can assure you, no one would trade with you if your *time* runs out.

The only thing that's a real time-money relationship is *working time*. Basically, this has to do with the relationship between work and money. We could actually leave out the word *time*, if time didn't pass *while* we work. Now that makes the sentence as meaningful as: Sore muscles are money.

Presumably, the statement originally came – as much "human wisdom" does – from an old issue of *Uncle $crooge*. Scrooge McDuck certainly used it occasionally to put off his nephew, Donald, while he was busy with something totally unimportant (like polishing his gold coins), so as not to be distracted by Donald's important matters (like going on vacation with his nephews).
The statement cannot be transferred as such to the real world because the time spent is only *one* factor determining the value of work. And that's also and especially true for such highly specialized work as illustration.

Pictures are not better or of greater value just because they took more time to produce.

You can get carried away for ages on a picture. A failed illustration doesn't get any better with it. By the same token, sometimes the illustrative spark can jump from a quick drawing with an ingenious idea behind it without having spent much time on it at all. According to the classical money-time equation, shouldn't that make that picture cheaper? You'll be surprised that this opinion is quite widespread – bad advice from Scrooge McDuck.

You get what I'm trying to say here (some things have to be said more than once!). Time is only *one* factor that determines the value of a work, but by no means the only one.

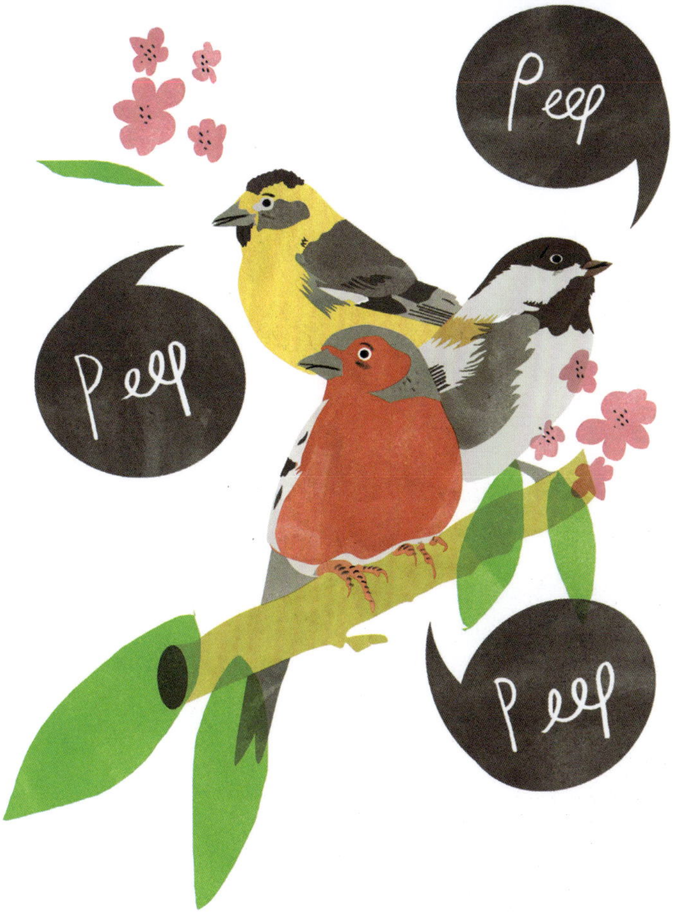

On the contrary, it's better that your client does not pay you for the time you spent on this illustration. Rather, he should pay for some of the time it took you to become so creative and experienced that you were now able to make this illustration. For, as quickly as something seems to have been just thrown on the paper, it sometimes takes time to learn this ease. The best example of this is music. A piece might be played quickly, but mastering the instrument often takes a lifetime.

It is therefore hard to understand why a seemingly "quick" drawing should not be paid for in terms of quality but rather according to how long it took to make.
What applies to dental technicians should also apply to illustrators. We are professionals, and you have to pay for that as well. Experience also takes time, but time that has already passed.
Of course, you still have to consider time in your budget planning. For one thing, we have to live. This means that your working hours are in proportion to your expenses while you are working: rent, insurance, way of life. You also have to calculate how much you would theoretically earn doing another job at the same time (which is especially important if you are doing jobs for the sake of fame or as a favor to a friend). Both are reflected in the triangular price-quality-time relationship.

It is much more important to calculate a job according to how much added value is created by your work. And finally, the quality factor comes into play. What your work will generate later plays a major role.

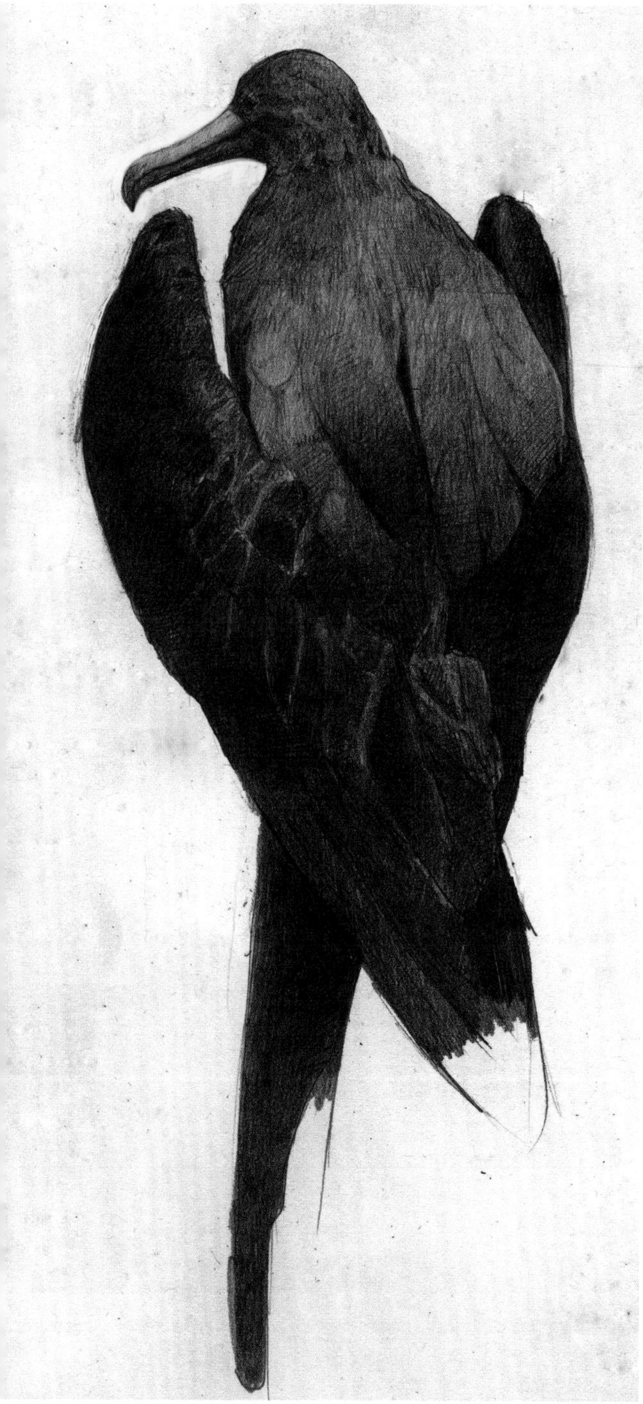

For example, if a character sells a million times simply because your idea is awesome, the hours you worked to come up with the idea cannot be the determining factor. The idea is still decisive. But that's exactly what you can neither usually measure nor predict very well, because we can't see into the future.

The New York graphic designer Milton Glaser once said he came up with the world famous "I ❤ NY" slogan during a cab ride. But I bet he also had a pretty full wastebasket by then.

So it seems reasonable to always set down license agreements and determine kinds-of-use for the future. A percentage share is certainly the wisest way to go with these things. One more thing:

You have to *indulge* yourself a job finished quickly now and then.

Often enough we believe we have to work our fingers to the bone on a job, to fill it up with our time, so to speak – even if you could perhaps have finished much sooner – just to live up to the price we charged. This is simply neurotic and reflects a very twisted apprecia- tion of one's own work. So pull your foot out of the trap: Use the time you gained for yourself. I'm sure you spent so much time and energy acquiring your skills that your "time savings account" still has a big fat balance. Now and then treat yourself to an advance and next time, click on "send" sooner.

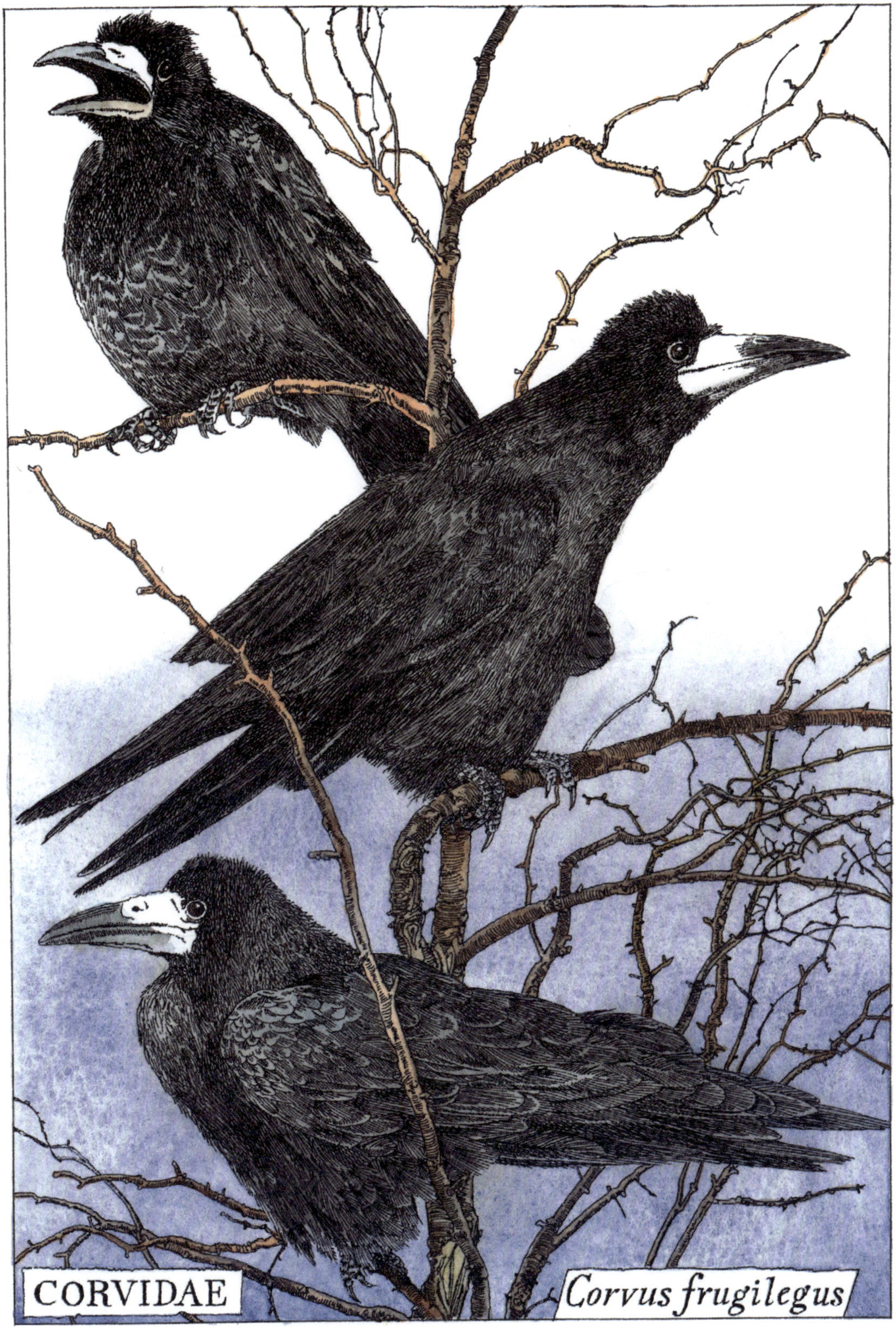

KLAUS ENSIKAT

Your Price

The bare necessities of life will come to you
They'll come to you!
BALOO, THE JUNGLE BOOK, 1967

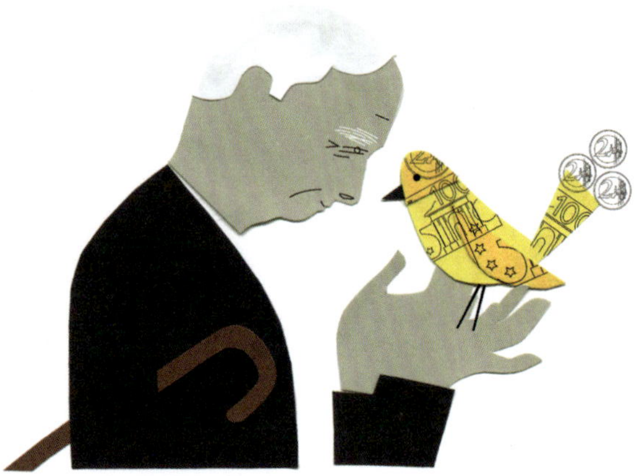

When negotiating with clients, two things are clear from the outset: You want to be paid appropriately for your performance, while the user wants as much performance as possible for their money. Your user may be someone with an MBA. And even if not, he or she is almost certainly more of a businessperson than you, more experienced in these conversations and has less to lose. In short, he or she is the *negotiator*.

As such, they know the famed "good-fast-cheap" paradox. They know that "good" and "fast" cannot be cheap, that "good" and "cheap" cannot be fast, and that "fast" and "cheap" cannot be good – but they'll never admit that to you. On the contrary, their power as a negotiator is to demand the impossible from you ... so that you, if you deliver the *possible*, overspend on at least one side of the paradox.

There are several options for escaping this trap: You can read Sun Tzu's *Art of War* or the Italian strategist Machiavelli to learn to become a better negotiator. It would be even simpler to try not to make it so complicated: Basically, it's enough (and this is true for almost any negotiation) if you know your price, and thus the limit from which you cannot backtrack when haggling.

Successful negotiators always set a point beforehand at which they can stand up and break off talks without regrets.

Incidentally, this is a key element of any negotiation strategy: you must also be able to say NO. An "either – or" is many times more effective than an "either – or ... oh, all right."

As I mentioned before, professional associations for creatives also advocate an hourly rate.

To many, such a fee seems quite high at first because, apart from advertising work, where sometimes between 900 and 2,500 dollars are paid a day, it hardly seems negotiable.
Nevertheless, it's realistic; for example, in Germany, it corresponds exactly to what, according to the Federal Statistical Office, an employee in the manufacturing sector or in the service sector earns on average: 2,300 dollars net per month plus social security contributions plus travel allowances plus food allowance plus training plus continued pay in the event of illness (average of eight days a year) and paid vacation, plus the provision of a workplace and expenses for electricity, heating and consumables.

And why should an illustrator earn less than a skilled technician?

In short, the 65 dollars correspond to the average middle class living in Germany. Because you not only have to pay your taxes from these 65 dollars; you have to pay for your workplace, your material, but also your insurance, pensions, etcetera, etcetera, etcetera, yourself.

Let's say you're asked to deliver 20 simple drawings for 2,225 dollars. If you have to put in *one* hour per drawing (including research, digital post-processing, corrections, etc.), you'll make a good margin. If you have to work *two* hours per drawing, you can already either no longer afford to have children, or no holidays, or no illness or no nights at the movies. If you have to estimate *four* hours per drawing – and now we are (for *simple* drawings) slowly getting realistic – then you have only limited mobility (no car, no rail pass – so no external clients), can neither afford your own home nor an external studio and have to save on food while you're probably a taxi driver on the side or working part-time in geriatric care.

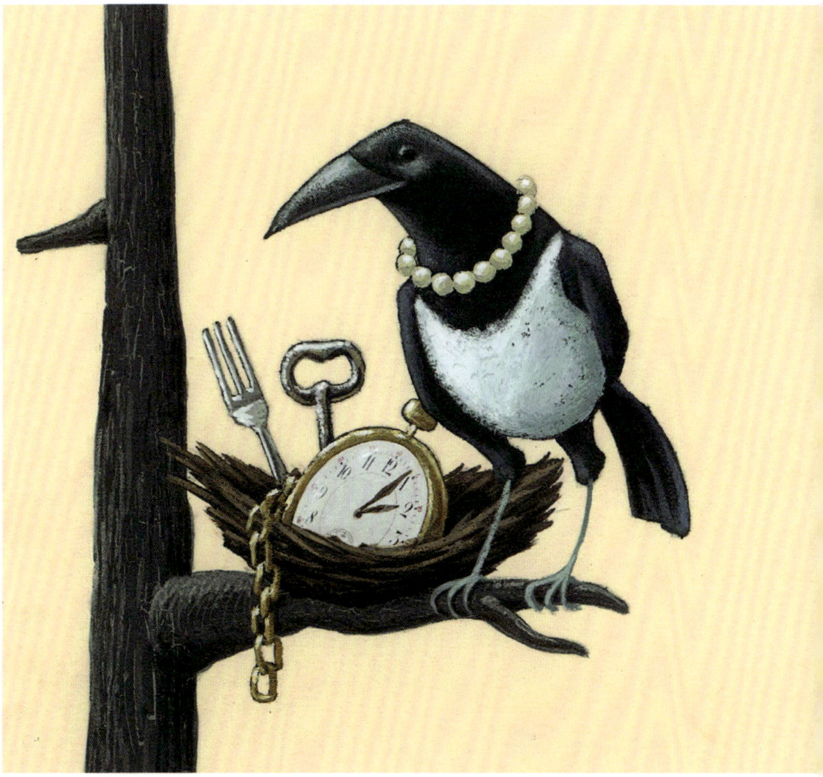

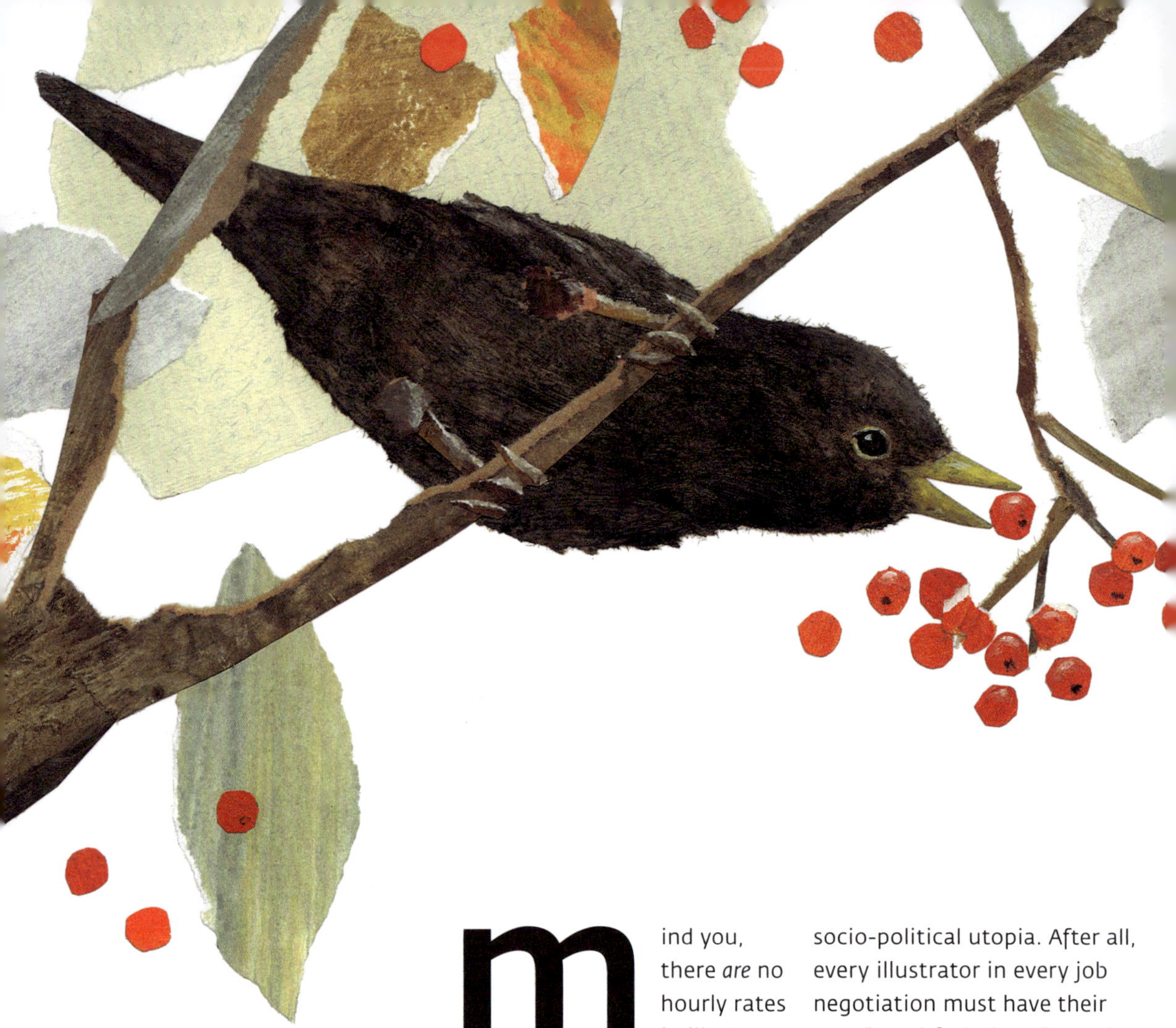

mind you, there *are* no hourly rates in illustration! The recommendation of the professional associations should serve merely as a guideline, which should make it clear to career novices at what point they can live reasonably from their own work. It is the limit described above, from which – if it were universally respected – no illustrator would have to earn money on the side or have to live in precarious conditions.

Nevertheless, "65 dollars per hour" is more than a socio-political utopia. After all, every illustrator in every job negotiation must have their own "good-fast-cheap" paradox in mind.
Less money must either mean to have more time or to sacrifice quality. Both can be calculated. But the basis of any calculation must be a reference: your own price. And why not use exactly the price set as a guideline by the Federal Statistical Office as your reference?

Hence, it more than pays off to correctly set your own price.

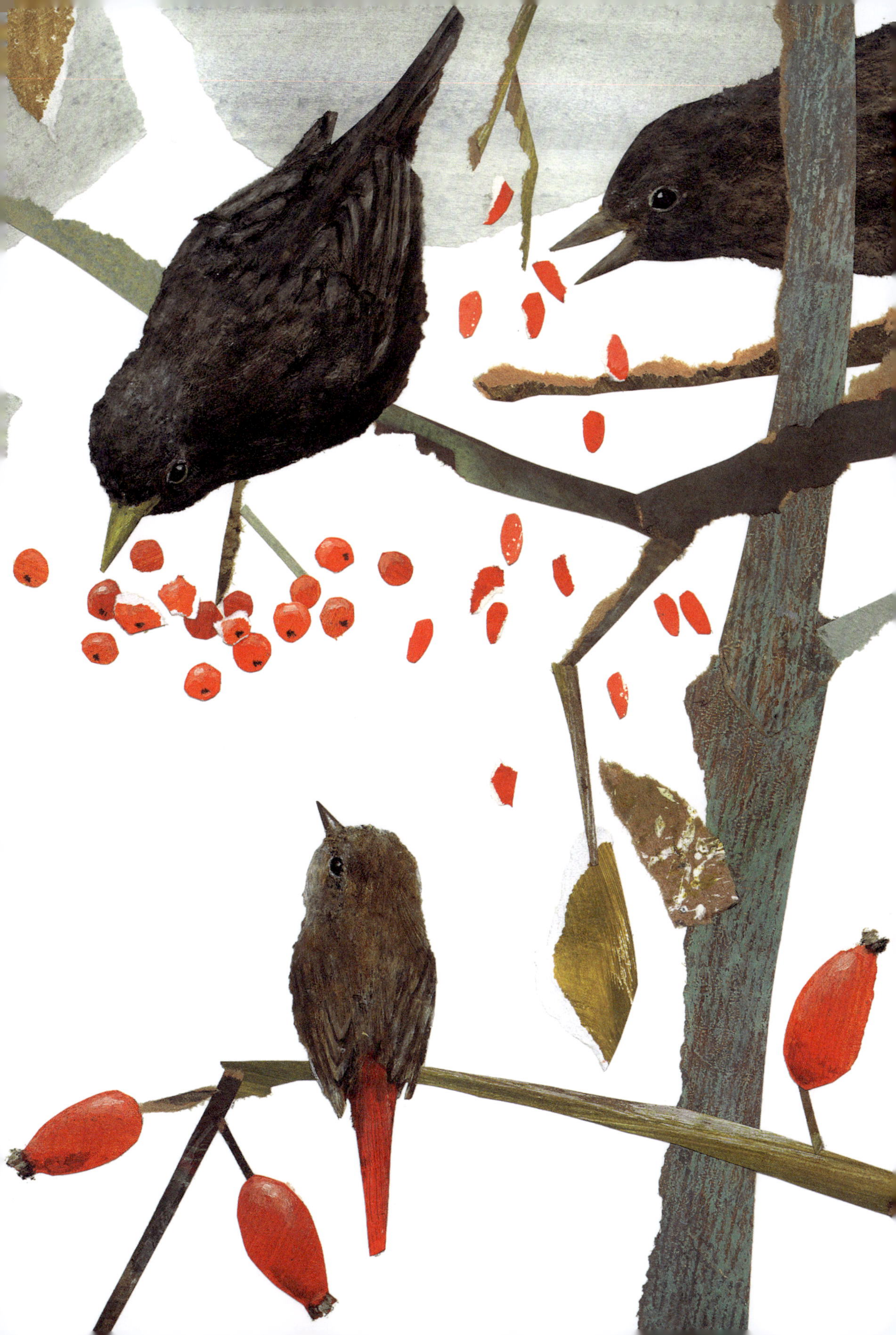

What Does an Illustration Cost?

I can't change the fact that my paintings don't sell. But the time will come when people will recognize that they are worth more than the value of the paints used in the picture. VINCENT VAN GOGH

When asked what an illustration costs, there are many answers, both short and long: the short answer is given below, based on a survey of American illustrators in the winter of 2019. On average, prices vary considerably depending on the country; even in Europe, they vary considerably from country to country.

The slightly longer answer requires a few preliminary comments: Concrete figures can shorten negotiations and save time and nerves. Nevertheless, the numbers mentioned are only average figures. They are not valid for every case, because no job is like another and no illustrator is like another. (That's why one of the previous chapters spoke of "appropriateness" and "your price.")

Vignette, small, b/w, (e.g. layout illustration)	$100 – $300
Freestanding illustration, small	$200 – $400
Freestanding illustration, large	$400 – $700
Animated GIF	$250 – $300
Cover (e.g. book)	$1,000 – $2,000
Cover (e.g. book), all-round	$2,000 – $4,000
Editorial cover	$1,200 – $2,500
Editorial article (e.g., lead picture plus 3 freestanding illustrations)	$1,300 – $2,500
Editorial Comic small	$500 – $750
Poster, low usage (e.g. children's theater)	$800
Poster, national use	$1,000 – $2,000
Cover (e.g. radio play CD)	$1,000 – $3,000
Graphic Novel depending on page count (advance) ca.	$12,000
Illustrated young adult book (advance) ca.	$6,000

The prices listed are a general guide covering "simple" to "complex" illustrations. They are intended to help you assess what is currently considered to be approximately "market standard". The sums given are average values from the USA. Customers from Europe usually pay a little less, and within the USA it depends on whether your customers are located in seaboard areas or inland – usually, in seaboard areas illustrations are better paid than in the Mid-West.
It is important to note that the prices listed in the table refer only to usage rights. This means you can manage how they are used [e.g. a print run]. One thing is clear: you do not "sell" your drawings! As a rule, the originals remain in your possession, any further uses should be remunerated additionally.

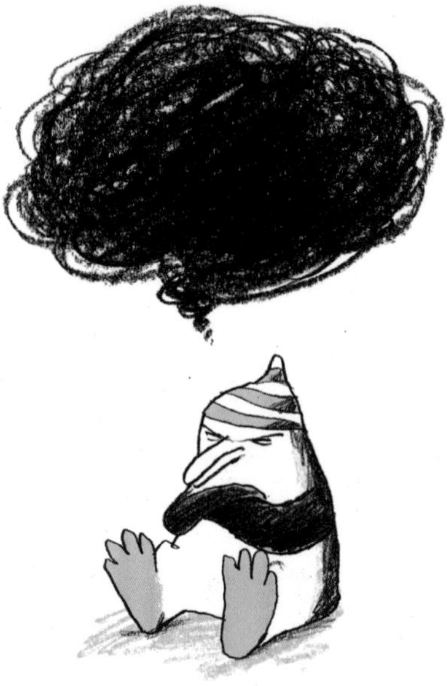

"Beginners" are usually paid a bit less than "seasoned professionals."

However, one can argue that there are actually only two options: Either you do the job as fast and as good as the supposed "seasoned professionals" – then there is no reason to ask for less money for the same job. Or you are more insecure, more inexperienced and slower than the "professional" – then you pay extra anyway, because you need to invest more energy and time in the job. What's decisive is the quality of your work, because that's what your client is paying for.
It's true that anyone who is negotiating with you even though you don't yet have a "big name," obviously doesn't want a "big name" – otherwise they wouldn't negotiate with you. (Experienced professionals are often booked up for years and have no time anyway.) Basically:

It's all a matter of negotiation.

The more you negotiate the better for you. Most clients grant contracts according to their preferences and your reliability anyway and not for a few cents more or less.
The magic word is appropriateness. Your prices should be right for you, and your illustrations should be right for the client.
In fact, good business deals have the quality of leaving only happy business partners.

It's ideal if your client comes back and you're happy to see them again.

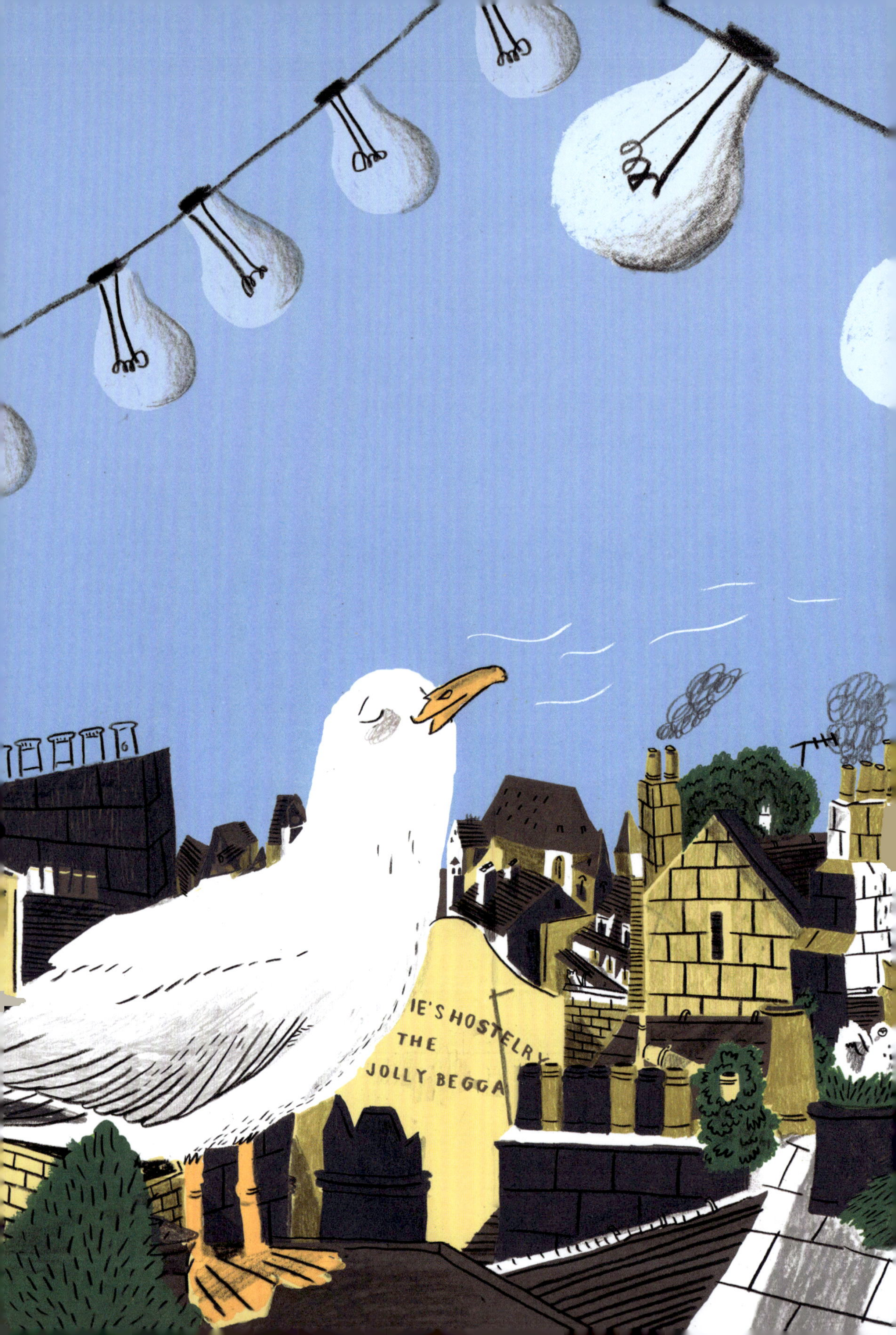
IE'S HOSTELRY
THE
JOLLY BEGGA

Productivity and Time Management

Oh dear! Oh dear! I shall be too late!
WHITE RABBIT, ALICE'S ADVENTURES IN WONDERLAND, LEWIS CARROLL, 1865

Why in the world do some days go by so incredibly unproductively? We crawl along and all we manage to do is a sort of little pile of something. It'll drive you to desperation. Get up, eat breakfast, the dog, the dishes, the mountain of emails. Clean up. First the desktop, then the workplace... Break ... nap. Shopping. A little more work on the picture. Rail at the result, coffee with colleagues, rail again, Facebook. A sudden idea, trial, error, renewed doubt, another mountain of emails.

Thousands of things, all at once and you got nothing done.

Sometimes days are simply inexplicably unproductive and unproductive days become unproductive weeks.
The solution lies in time management. Because it's not just the above-mentioned "fear of the blank page" that hinders our progress sometimes; at times it's the way we organize our work or, more specifically, the way we organize our working hours.

First of all, let me reassure you: If you are familiar with this problem, you are not alone. On the contrary, it happens to so many people that in recent years a lot of research has been done on work efficiency. If you follow a few little rules, you will stand in your own way far less in the future.

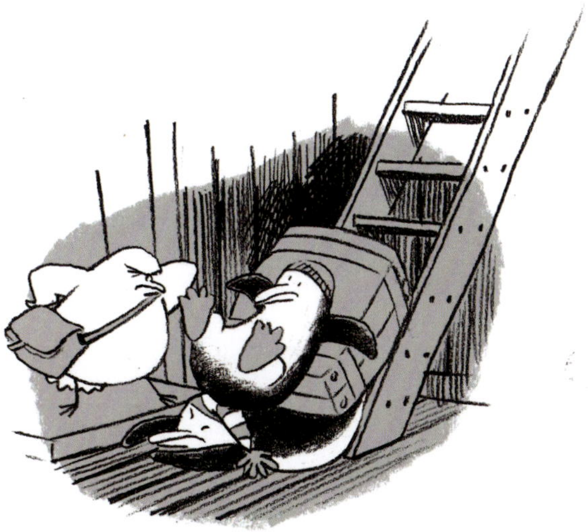

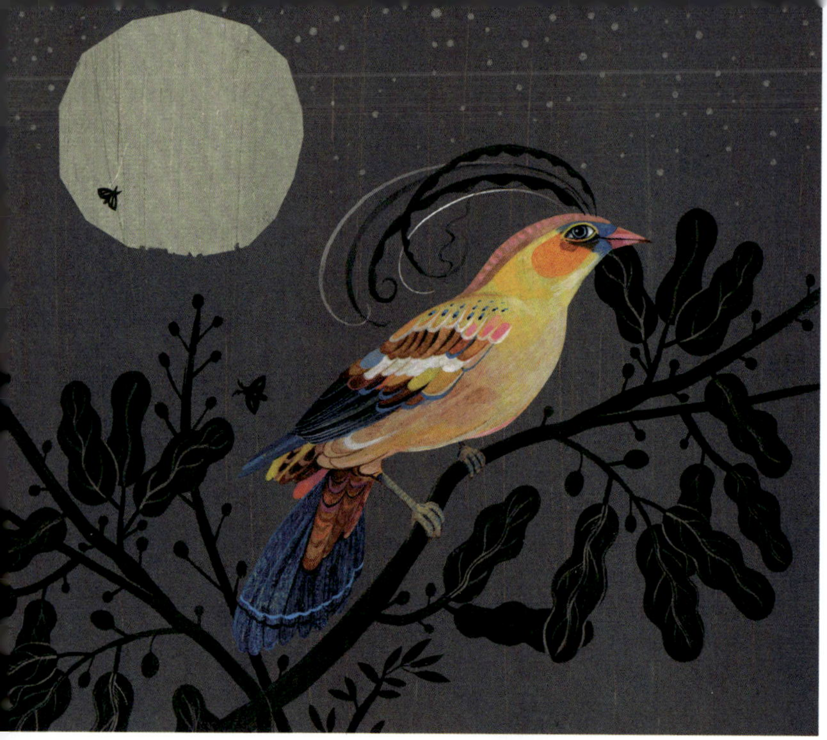

Tip

To divide up your work, it's helpful to use radio plays or longer pieces of music. For example, set a certain number of chapters or songs during which you can do one job productively. Use the music for timing and only take a break when it ends – not when your cell phone beeps.

The first and most important thing is to just start working. Don't waste energy being annoyed that circumstances are not one hundred percent in your favor or that you might not have worked productively enough yesterday or might fail today.
The first and most important thing is to just start. Don't be frightened by the mountain of work. Be persistent in your work and don't do a thousand other things at the same time.

In the fable "The Foolish Old Man Removes the Mountains," the Chinese philosopher Lie Zi describes how stubbornness and steadfastness leads to the goal. Yu Gong starts doing work, even though it seems hopeless. And although there is enough reason for doubt, he does not doubt. On the contrary, he says that he can just start with a small part and not worry about how and when the other parts would be done. In Lie Zi's fable, Yu Gong moves mountains by just beginning to work and continuing on unperturbed.

Basically, this story already shows us the two crucial aspects: first, *to start* and secondly, *to divide up* the work. The second (and equally important) aspect of working productively is to divide the work into bite-sized pieces. Make a schedule and divide the work into manageable items.

It is helpful not to be approximate and vague, but to be very *specific*.
For example, you can use the class schedules they sell for school kids. A daily schedule for any illustration might look something like this: 9:15 - 10:45 sketch, 11:00 - 12:30 preliminary line drawing, 1:00 - 2:30 first coloring, 3:00 - 4:30 details & final varnish, 5:00 - 6:00 scan, edit and send.
As silly as it may sound, such schedules are extremely helpful for working productively.

Scientific studies have also found that we can concentrate really well for about 90 minutes at a time. Make sure that you always plan breaks in between – and that you comply with them. For example, 90 minutes of work, 20 minutes of rest is a good rhythm. This is more effective than slogging away all morning to spend the afternoon napping. And you can easily work your way from the smaller parts to the larger. Draw up primary weekly schedules and primary monthly schedules for them. One advantage of schedules is that they create structure. Each little part is a success, not just the whole thing. This way, you reward yourself with every single step and do so without too many dry spells. Also, schedules are very helpful for setting priorities. You don't let yourself get distracted and work with more concentration. With a realistic schedule, you aren't constantly doing a thousand things at the same time. That alone will help you achieve your goals.

Almost all successful artists work according to rigid daily routines.

What *time* you work, however, plays a lesser role. Schiller is said to have written mostly at night, Thomas Mann in the morning and Ernest Hemingway at noon. Sometimes, by the way, it's just the rough concept that has a structuring effect. For example, the famous Hamburg-based illustrator Horst Jansen worked all his life according to the motto: "A picture every day."

You'll see: Life and work are definitely easier with structure.

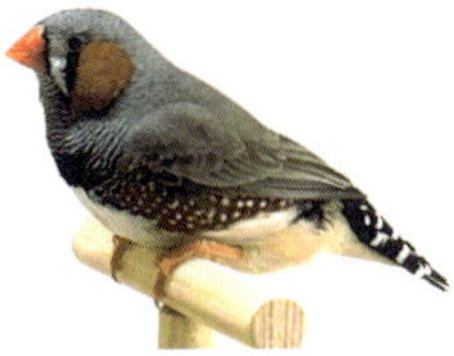

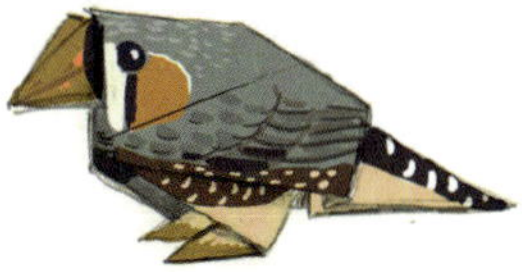

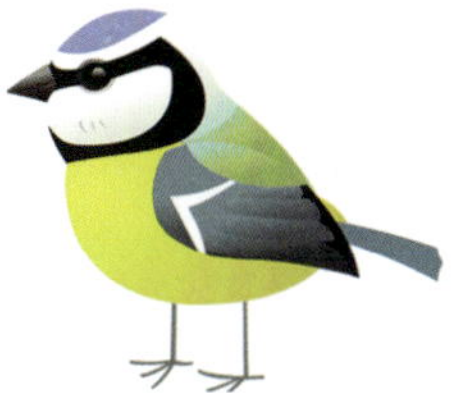

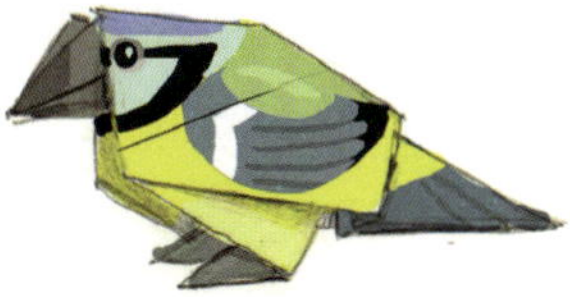

Tip
Turn off your wifi while working and only check your email every couple of hours manually. You'll get twice as much work done.

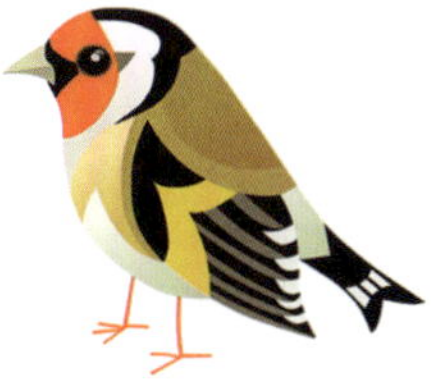

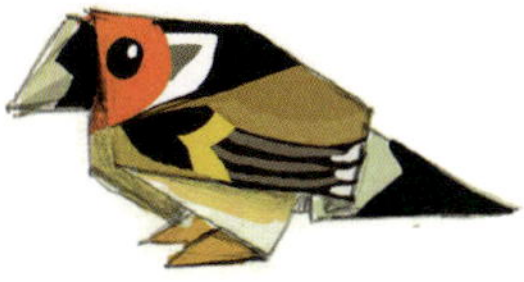

Out of Breath

To achieve great things, two things are needed: a plan and not quite enough time.
LEONARD BERNSTEIN

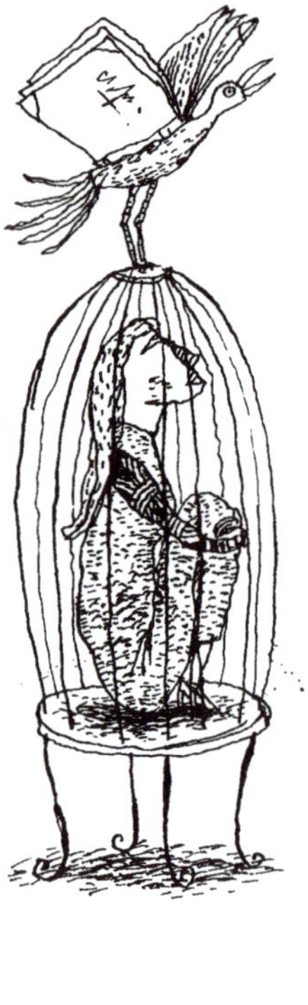

The transition from not enough jobs, which newcomers to the profession often complain about, to "so much work I don't know whether I'm coming or going" can be very brief. Unfortunately, life as a freelancer is all too often like a relay race: you've just barely arrived, hand yourself the baton to immediately sprint to a new destination where you just return to starting position.

This problem is due to the dilemma inherent in almost all self-employed work: job uncertainty. It is impossible to predict whether and how often inquiries will come in. Of course, factors such as the frequency of your acquisition, your style, the overall economic situation or your own market value play a role; but you still can't predict it. Even hard-core professionals seem to be plagued by the unconscious fear that every new assignment might be the last. For these reasons, most of us tend to accept more jobs than we can handle. To make matters worse, we often don't realistically estimate the time a job and follow-up jobs might take. An "I can do it" is said quicker than it does us good and once we get into the situation of having to rework something, we're soon racing from deadline to deadline. It gets really tricky once you begin to fill up your overdrawn time savings account with the time that seems to be most expendable: break time!

It's common for the self-employed to at some point start taking time away from their leisure time, their weekends or vacation time.

This is particularly problematic because spending time away from hobbies, friends or family also means you lose the sources that you normally use to replenish your depleted energy stores. As a result, you increasingly begin to arrange your life around "later," a "later" when everything will be more secure and easier, a "later" that usually, however, never comes. You soon get into a hamster wheel of jobs, jobs and ever-new jobs, which not infrequently ends up in exhaustion.

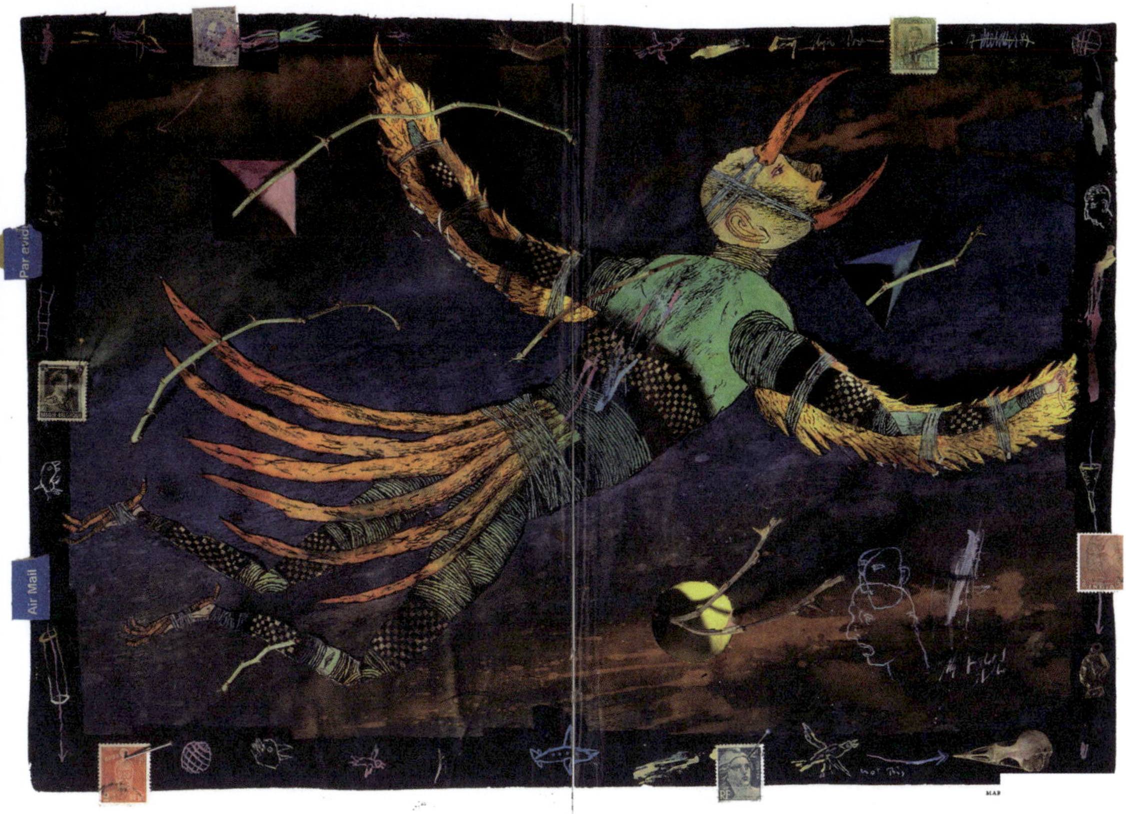

Stress is not so much a symptom of modern life as people think. Some technological developments favor our availability. But it would probably also be stressful if, instead of emails, crowds of mail carriers would besiege your front door every five minutes with proper letters.

As early as 1885, in his short story "How Much Land Does a Man Need?" the Russian author Leo Tolstoy told a story of ambition, stress and self-destructive expansion. The farmer Pahom is driven by the desire to own and manage more and more land. He buys more and more land while becoming more and more harried. One day he is given an offer to buy all the land he can walk around in a single day for a very small price. Pahom runs from sunrise to sunset, and when the evening comes, he falls over and dies. Tolstoy ends his story by answering the title question with the words:
"His servant picked up the spade and dug a grave long enough for Pahom to lie in, and buried him in it. Six feet from his head to his heels was all he needed."

Stress can make you sick and it takes away the security and quality of life that we believe we can attain through more work. But how do you escape the stress trap?

The advice to simply work less is easily said (and may sound reasonable), but in practice it's unrealistic. Low-paid work in particular urges us to work more. And it's true: Illustration is often time-sensitive work with tight deadlines. Especially in the editorial sector, inquiries are often linked to tough deadlines.

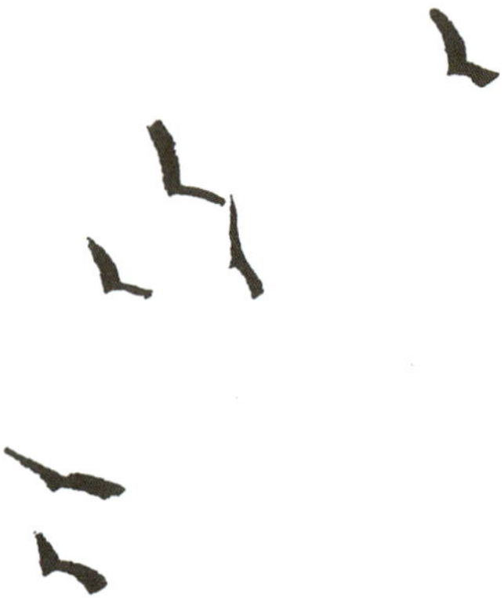

Newspapers and magazines work up to the minute (often on a daily basis) and night or weekend shifts are often expected. Add to this the realistic assessment that you can lose clients permanently if you turn them down too often. (For some advertisers, the tolerance limit is already reached with *one* refusal.)
What to do?
A big part of the answer lies in setting priorities: If you grant all that's expected of you the same priority, it is likely that you'll end up in an impossible predicament.
That's why it's essential in the longer term to decide where it is you want to go.

> One decisive first step is to learn the difference between *urgent* and *important*.

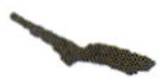

Both are good coordinates for making decisions: *Urgent* must be undertaken in the short term, *important* in the long term. And then there are tasks that are *important and urgent at the same time*. They should have priority. Above all, it is crucial that you be aware of what really needs to be done and in what order you'll approach the tasks assigned to you. Nothing is more stressful than disorderly piles. The unknown has the unpleasant trait of seeming "bigger" because it tends to become a projection screen for our own fears. Usually, piles are nothing more than deferred decisions.
On closer inspection, a lot of what seems necessary to us turns out to be negligible and takes care of itself. Some work can be delegated, other simplified, and some things can be left out altogether because they are simply not that important. So counter your stress with clarity.
Illustration is like a general store. Most of us work in different sectors. So plan to alternate between rigid deadline jobs (editorial and advertising) and more restful jobs (long-term book projects).

And don't forget to put a sufficient time buffer in between. Because when you communicate clear schedules to your clients, both sides can be realistic about it and no one will blame *you*.

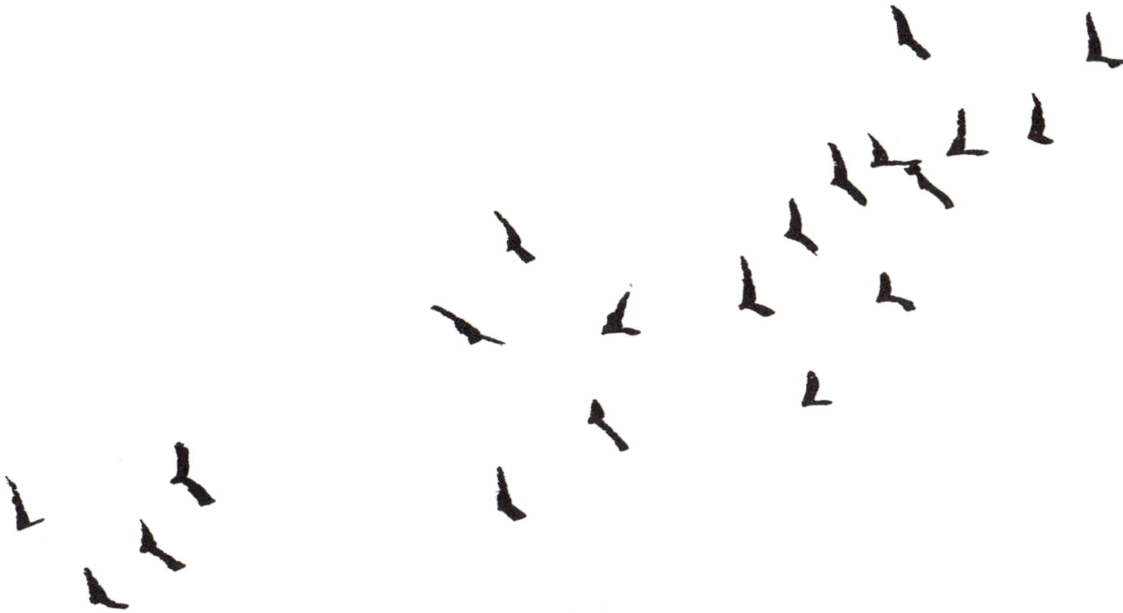

The most important thing is to never forget to refill your drained energy stores.

It sounds banal, but it's still true: Social life, sports and healthy nutrition as compensation have a far greater effect than you'd expect. Pets, hobbies, friends and family are natural allies against burnout. There always has to be time for a game night, cooking with friends or a bike tour. Otherwise your job is going awry and you need to change it before it changes *you*.

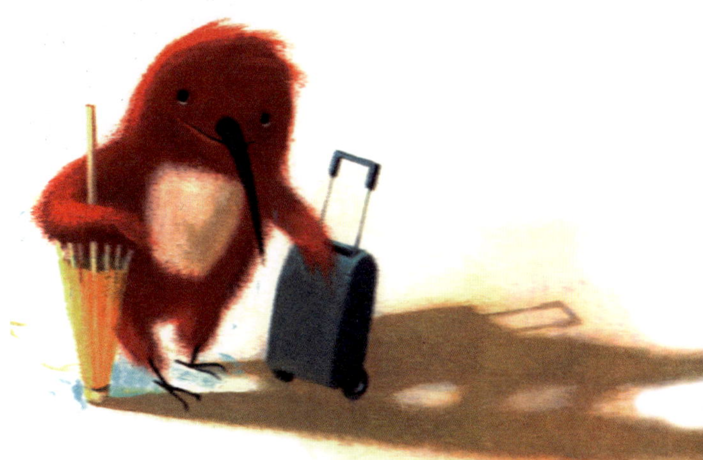

Sideline Settings

What is tragic about every experience is that you make it only after you would have needed it. F. W. NIETZSCHE

As a teenager I made my first attempt to make art a livelihood one summer morning in the pedestrian zone of my hometown. Equipped with a friend and a box of pastel chalks, I sat down in front of the town hall and began to copy the English drunkard and painter Francis Bacon's "Three Studies for Figures at the Base of a Crucifixion" on the pavement. Why we chose a work by the Englishman is, frankly, puzzling. But I suppose it had to do with an exhibition I had just read about as an occasional waiting-room reader of the magazine *Art*. In addition, Bacon's work seemed easy to reproduce. But our outdoor experiment with the copy was, in a word, sobering. It soon became apparent that in the 1980s classical modernism was not yet a fixture in the middle-class consciousness of our hometown.

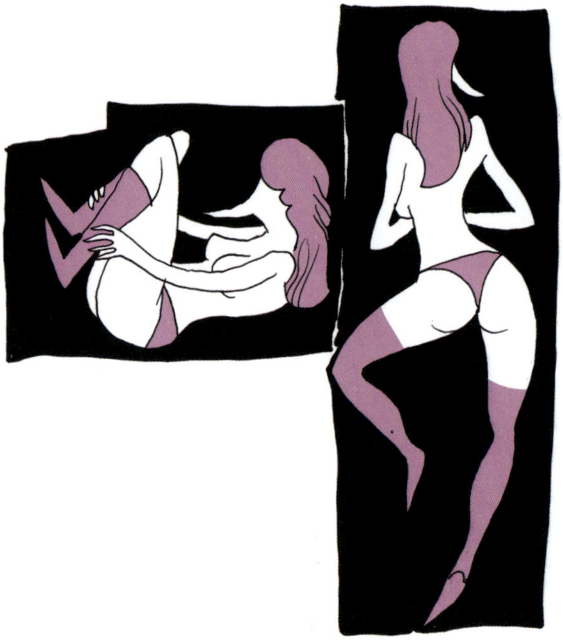

The failure was divided into two phases: During the production phase, the audience was inadequately informed of what we were doing for heaven's sake. "What is that supposed to be ...?" Since Bacon was far less well known than the street painters' usual sunflowers, weeping clowns and Guernicas, the unfinished crucifixion figures evinced scant willingness to make donations. During the second phase, we spent a lot of time sitting in front of the finished picture and explaining why is was art. This did not, however, make our fellow citizens more generous, especially as it turned out that we were not nearly as cute as the little violinist playing twenty yards away. In the course of the undertaking, there was also an unpleasant encounter with a municipal police officer, who interrogated us about trade licenses, permits and similar mysterious papers.

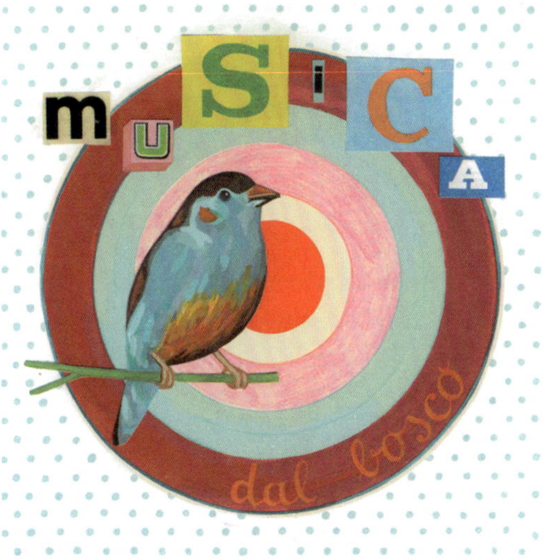

The whole affair did not seem to be on good footing, and when we balanced our earnings with our expenses that evening, the disaster revealed its dramatic proportions.
Art and money, we learned, correspond very inadequately. Presumably, my illustrator career would have ended in this pedestrian zone if I had not discussed the matter with more experienced advisors. As it turned out, we had made several notable mistakes at once. But the matter in itself of "going outside and being active" was by no means wrong.
And not only that: the vision that an illustrator can earn money away from a desk was purposeful.

Actually, sideline settings should not be underestimated and that's why we will take a closer look at them here.

You can make money in illustration beyond its use in print or the web (don't worry; I won't advise you to try street painting – not even sunflowers). In fact, most illustrators make a small but noteworthy share of their income in the "Other" category. It begins with the occasional sale of originals or original graphic products, such as etchings or woodcuts. They can be portrait jobs or murals. They can be event drawings (weddings and corporate events, for instance, are quite lucrative), or the increasingly popular visual recording – the visual documentation of meetings and discussions for large companies. Lectures and teaching also fall under this category in the broadest sense.
In addition, there's the "marketplace," for example, the web shops some illustrators operate in which they sell silkscreen T-shirts, posters, postcards or self-made crafts for children – etc. etc.

If you add graphic services, occasional web pages and similar, it turns out the "Other" field is not that small. But the topic cuts both ways because we should by no means compensate for the results of poor negotiations by adding a sideline. So the – unfortunately quite common – combination "illustrator/wait staff" is not desirable in the long run. But if it's a lucrative, meaningful business idea that organically grows as a sideline from our abilities, there's absolutely nothing wrong with using it.

In reality, the profession of an illustrator is quite similar to the merchandise in a general store.

Although most of us have a main field of work, the offers are fraying in our core business. We may do a lot of books, but posters, CD covers and illustrations for the advertising industry are just as likely. So the move to "Other" is by no means as far as you might think.

In reality, "sidelines" – apart from the additional earnings they offer – are often just a nice change for our daily routine. After all, illustration is a huge field and most of us became illustrators because we didn't want to be geeks working in boring offices, but because we are imaginative and creative. In fact, a little sideline can also be part of the answer to the question of how to make a living from illustration: with the forward slash, as in illustration/visual recording or illustration/teaching.

My advice would therefore be to approach the matter offensively and to occasionally think outside the box of pure illustration.

If you don't overdo your sidelines, but deal creatively with them, they can be an asset not only in the monetary sense. But in my opinion you needn't try street painting.

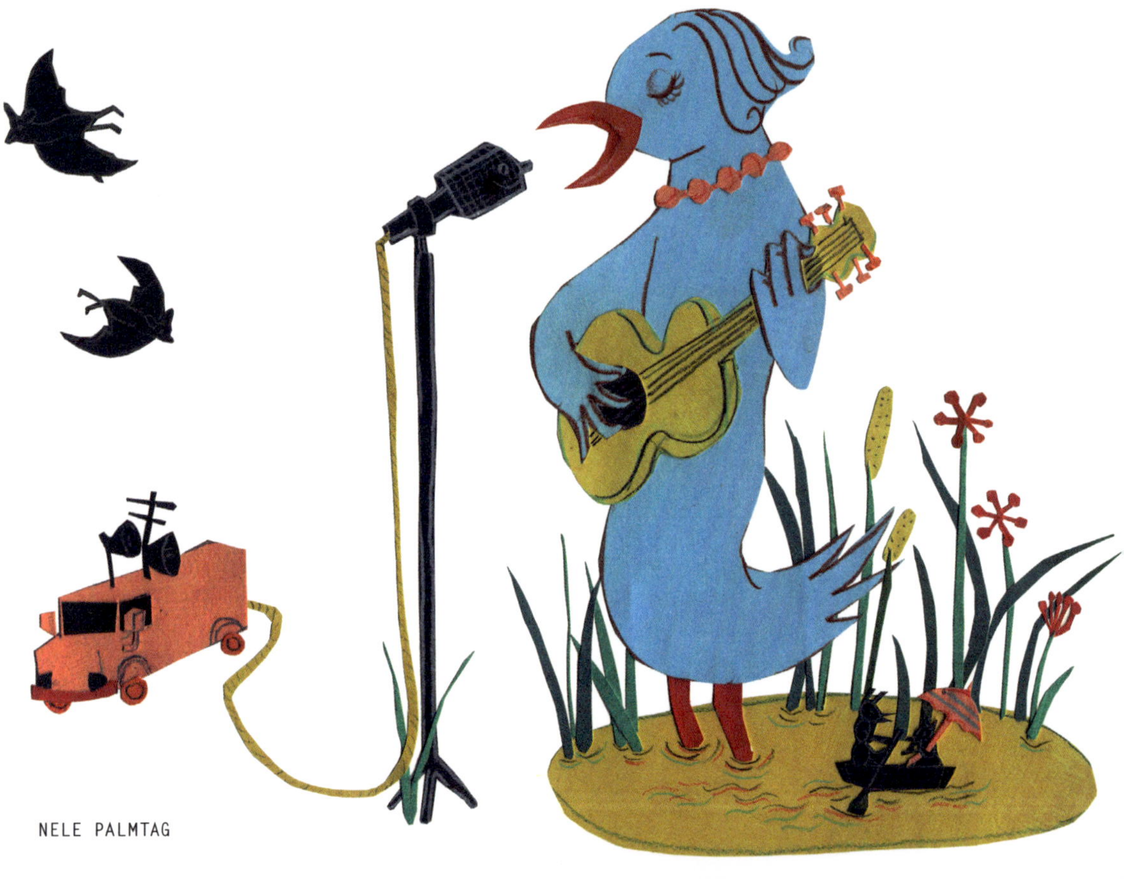

NELE PALMTAG

Correct Acquisition Placement

I took the one less traveled by, and that has made all the difference.
THE ROAD NOT TAKEN, ROBERT FROST, 1916

The most frequently asked question about how to find one's place on the market can be answered most easily by first gaining an overview of the market in order to get your own work to the right address. But where do I find the right address? Now, you're thinking: web search. You're thinking wrong, though. For what you have to offer is crucial to your acquisition and only that can lead to the Where in a second step. So let's get an overview:

Usually, the easiest way is to look right where the market is to find out what it has to offer. For example, there are trade fairs in book illustration where you can do research as well as directly address your clients. Most notably there's the Frankfurt Book Fair, but also the children's book fairs in Paris and Bologna. At trade fairs, you can either join the lines for illustrator appointments (which I recommend) or try to get a personal appointment for a portfolio review beforehand (which I also recommend). If you are interested in the magazine and newspaper segment, you can also start scouting quite simply: In every major city there is, for example, a large bookstore where you can easily see what is currently the rage in the editorial segment. You can search for the addresses and who to contact later on the Internet. (The Association of Children's Book Publishers even publishes an A-Z list in book form every year.)
Leafing through them you can immediately see which print media use illustrations and which don't. In addition, you can find out at a glance which media you like – a not-to-be-underestimated factor – but more on that later.
In the games segment, both trade fairs and Internet research make sense, and you can simply call or visit advertising clients as well as agencies, event, audio or film production companies as they can best be reached by initiating personal contact.

To put it briefly, the problem
is not so much the choice,
but how to go about it.

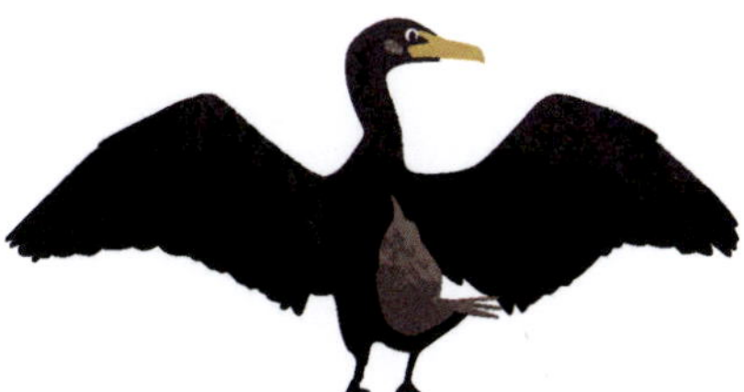

The first question that arises with the majority of potential clients (and there are more than you think) is whether you really need and should contact them *all*. This is not that easy to answer because, in fact, the strategy of simply showing *everyone everything* is just as practicable as targeted application. Above all, I would advise you to learn to assess where cold emailing is promising and where a targeted application makes more sense.

Naturally, mass emails increase the hit ratio, and one can argue that one cannot read the minds of potential clients. Sometimes it truly makes sense to ask fifty people who are not interested in your work if that means you end up reaching two of the right people in the end. Especially in the advertising and editorial fields, a broad distribution can sometimes be recommended.

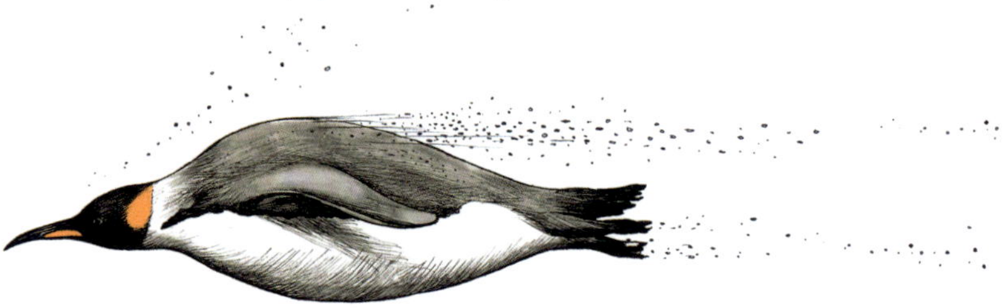

Let's start with the first two options, because both strategies have their advantages. Electronic media in particular entice us to submit a deluge of applications, especially since you can tailor digital portfolios to the needs of clients with a few clicks (and you definitely should: spare women's magazines your technical car illustrations and don't send children's books to science publishers).

However, you shouldn't generalize this because this strategy doesn't suit every client. On the contrary, in many cases such an approach would be pure nonsense. The problem with shooting buckshot is always the collateral damage that you might cause. On the one hand, you have to limit your resources because you don't have unlimited time and energy available for your applications (I suppose from time to time you also want to work). On the other hand, you also run the risk of ending up in spam folders if you overdo it. In fact, especially in sectors that are of a manageable size – like book and game publishers – too broad a spread is not necessarily a good idea. Editors, copywriters and art buyers talk to *one another*, too, and it's not exactly career enhancing in our industry to get a reputation as an unsell-able pain in the ass just because you're constantly sending out the wrong applications.

out how the other side judges you. You just have to feel deep down who it is that *you* like, who *you* would like to spend time with. You'd be surprised: In an unconscious process, sympathy is almost always mutual and liking is recipro-cated. We can feel where it is we – and our art – belong.
In fact, it is very similar to the phenomenon of taste. You could call taste a kind of *visual sympathy*. Again, you usually like each other.

In addition, you need to have a thick skin for such mass applications (and the flood of rejections they will trigger). In general, individuals of the illustrator species will be out of their depth.
Therefore, it is best to find out in advance which publisher, which agency could actually be "right" for you. To decide that, you can trust in one very simple rule:

You'll usually like each other. When you are confronted with a group of strangers, for example, you can easily find

In practice, this means that it is almost always the case that those who make, publish or offer something that you like will often – when it comes to your illustrations – also see eye to eye with you in terms of taste.
By the same token, you'll find that you're unlikely to end up with, for example, publishers whose books you find ugly and visually unappealing.
Taste, like sympathy, is almost always reciprocal. That's why you can trust your own nose.

Simply apply where you find products you like.

You'll see: At least *visual* love is reciprocated more often than you'd think. :-)

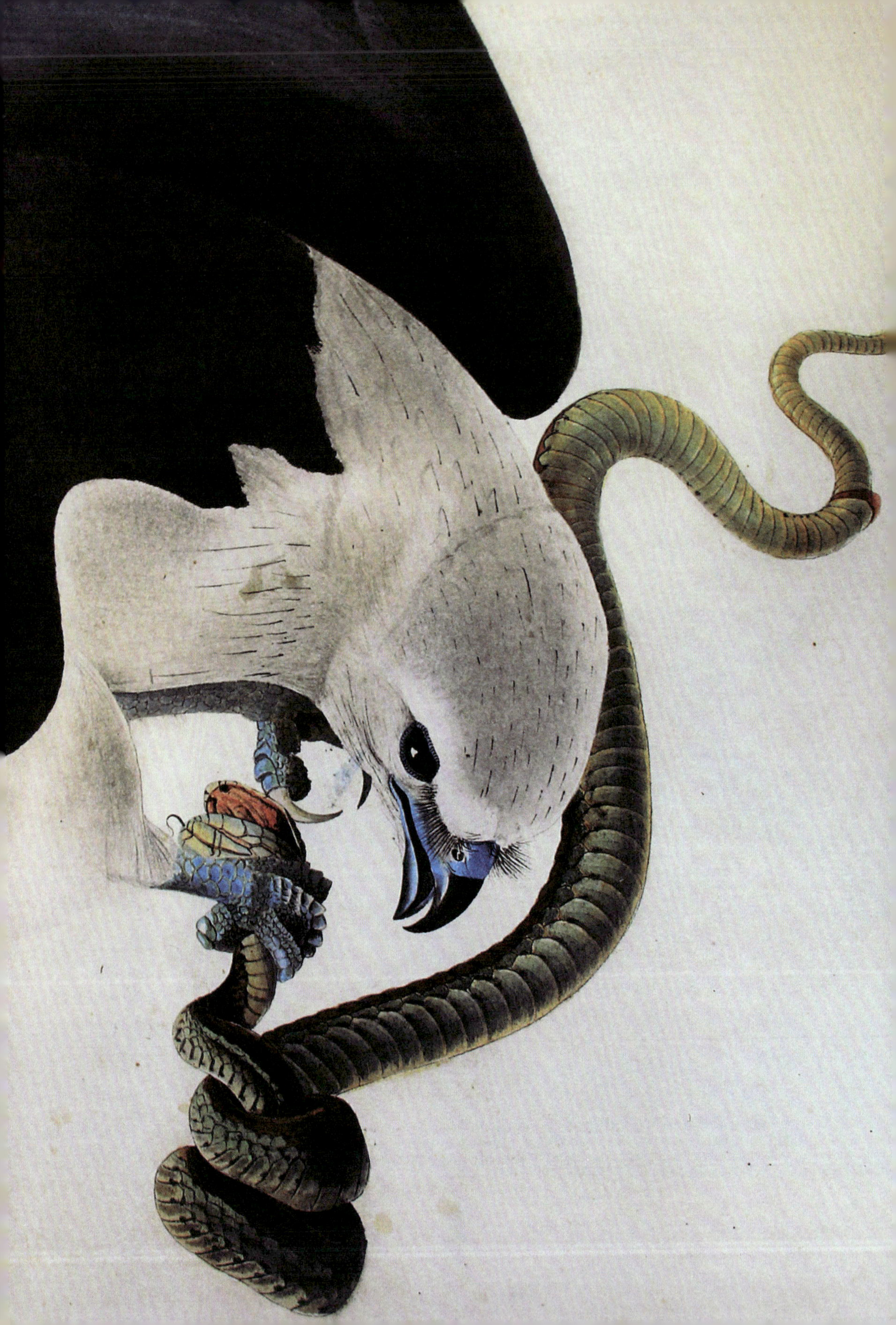

Portfolio Advice

There are four basic human needs; food, sleep, sex and revenge.
BANKSY

The portfolio is the business card of an illustrator. Clients decide whether they want to work with you or not based on your portfolio. So let's take a look at what a *good* portfolio looks like.

We'll start with the exterior. "Size doesn't matter," they say. A typical beginner's mistake is to present a portfolio to your client that you could use to apply for college. Portfolios don't have to be huge. On the contrary, if you take a portfolio with you to the book fair, it is better if it's a handy size. The most proven is a format between A4 and A3. If you break off half the stand with your portfolio when you open it, the editor will certainly remember you, but maybe not positively.

However, it's important that even the handiest portfolio mustn't look shoddy.

If you present your work in old folders and transparent covers, you will hardly be able to convey to why your work should be worth anything to clients if it doesn't seem worth much to you.

So your portfolio is allowed to look impressive. Portfolios can be produced professionally, and you shouldn't be too frugal on this point. For example, bookbinders provide their services in almost all major cities (or on the Internet). You can choose from hundreds of colors, styles and sizes, customize the number of acetate covers and even have your name embossed on the cover.
The price of a personal portfolio depends primarily on the size and features, but is in most cases quite reasonable.

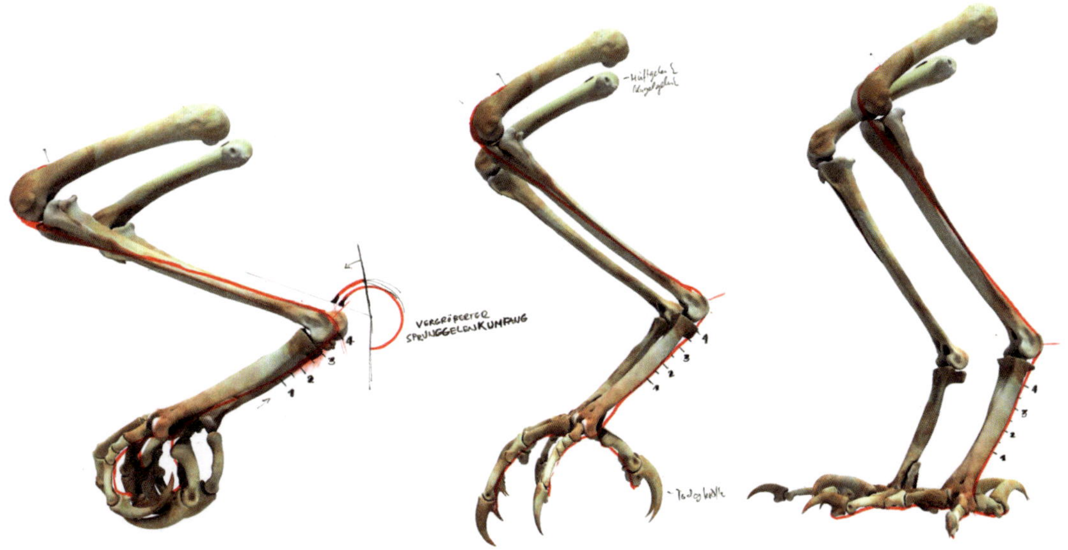

JOHN JAMES AUDUBON

JONAS LAUSTRÖER

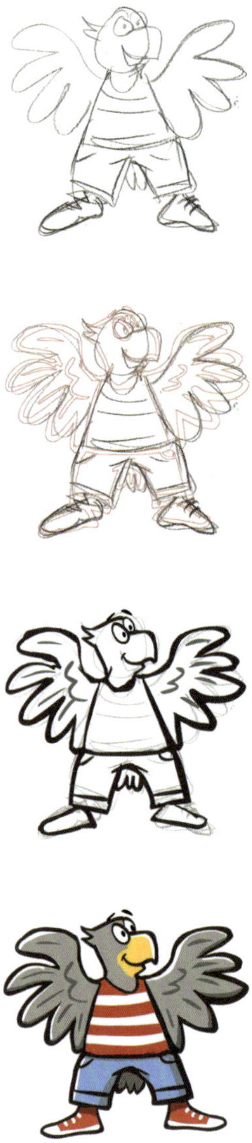

Let's take a look at our portfolio from the inside: Overall, your portfolio shouldn't be too thin or too thick. I think about 20 double pages are enough to describe you and your style. Most of all, you need to be able to stand by your work, so you should choose to put a little less in your portfolio rather than water down a good impression with compromises.

It used to be common to glue pictures to black paper. But I would instead advise that you use white paper, to avoid a "mourning border." Black is simply too depressing. Likewise, I would advise against using colored paper. It will almost inevitably affect your work, and not necessarily positively.

An organizational system or layout is helpful. For example, it doesn't hurt to put the name of the client and/or the project next to the pictures shown (name-dropping always works ;-)). However, the font shouldn't compete with the pictures too much, but be organically integrated into the overall picture. A homogenous and uniform basic grid is highly recommended, so the viewer can quickly "learn" where information is.

It's nice when your portfolio also shows *how* you work.

Some sketches and drafts or intermediate steps here and there explain your approach very well to your clients. In addition, I recommend showing works in their applications. For example, if you take photos of three-dimensional objects, depict an open book or place your pictures in the appropriate context with the copy, you can immediately see what your illustrations look like in use. This can also be fit very well into an overall layout or shown on the portfolio double pages (and you should use your double pages!).

Tip

Never forget to write your address in the front of the portfolio and have extra business cards on hand (which ideally show one of your illustrations alongside your address).

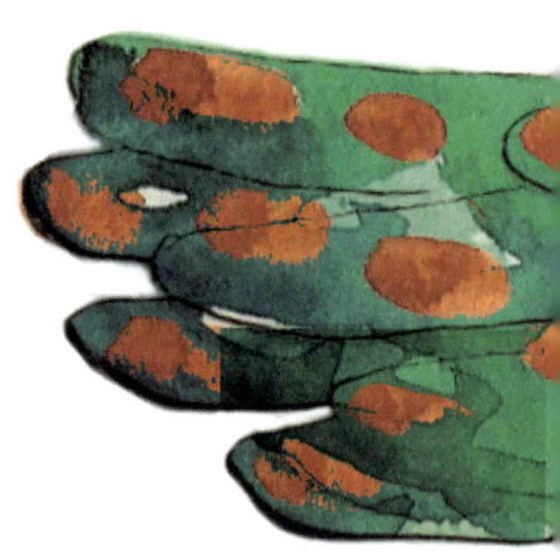

When selecting your own work, the temptation is great to use all your favorite pictures right at the beginning of the portfolio. But don't be wasteful. Of course, your portfolio must begin with a favorite (just to give you a safe feeling at the beginning of the conversation), but the presentation shouldn't fade while leafing through. It is reasonable to show the "best" picture first and to put the second best at the end.

It's best to plan your portfolio as sequential, single sheets. Lay all your work side by side and see how the sequence works. It is particularly good for a conversation when the sequence of pictures is sorted thematically. But don't forget to also present your work in a varied way: After a series of portraits it might be time for an animal again, one or two animals could perhaps be followed by an inanimate object, etc.

Portfolios must also be entertaining.

So much for the framework. We're left with the question of how to fill the portfolio meaningfully: Is it reasonable to have an extra portfolio on hand for each type of client, or should you rather try to serve all kinds of clients with *one* portfolio? The answer is: prioritize.

In fact, it is not helpful to combine as many different styles as possible in a portfolio. Especially at trade fairs the clients just see too many portfolios. The goal of your application is to be remembered; a distinct portfolio makes the most sense here. It's always good if your portfolio is seen as a conscious decision: it must recognizably be your portfolio.

Your portfolio must represent you or the style you intend to use in your jobs. Otherwise, you later face the problem of having to jump through hoops. (In the worst case, this application will tie you down for something you don't like and you'll end up jumping through hoops for all your other jobs, too.) That's why it makes sense to design your portfolio with the work that you really enjoy. Vegetarian chefs shouldn't apply for jobs in steakhouses.

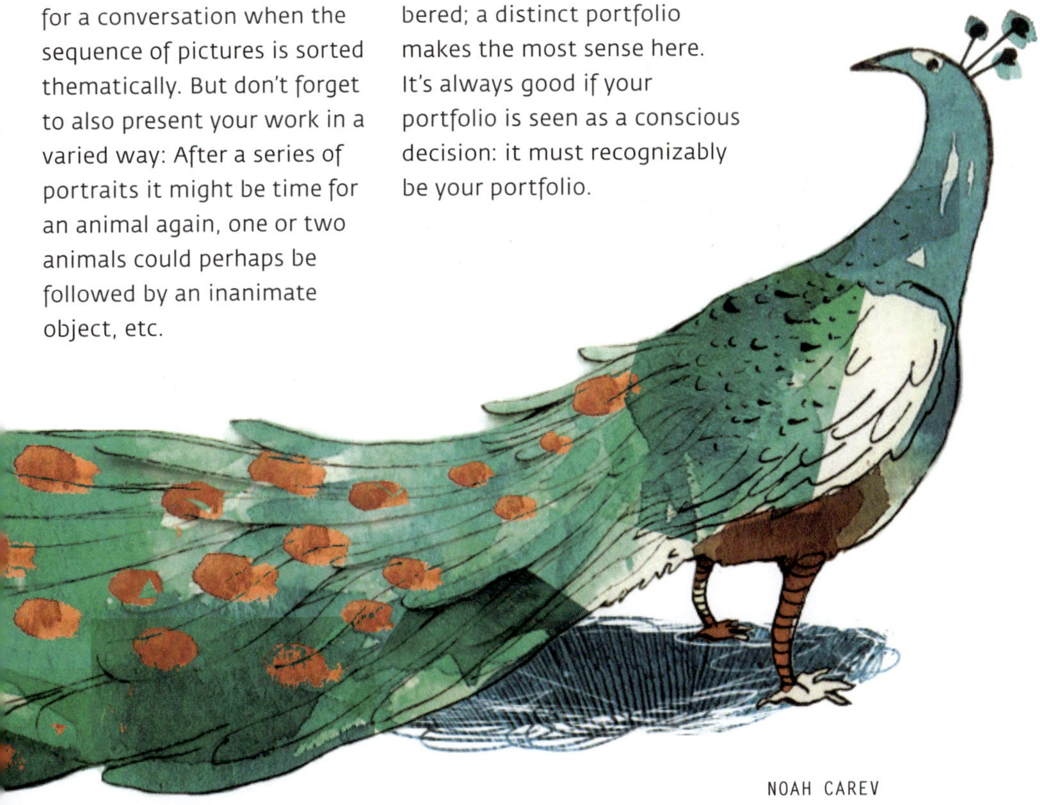

NOAH CAREV

Which brings us to the fact that you should really only look for your potential clients where it makes sense. A portfolio full of adult editorial illustrations probably makes no sense at the Bologna Children's Book Fair, nor does a children's book folder when talking to a science publisher. Take a look at your clients twice beforehand. If you ask the right people on dates, they won't turn you down.

Tip

Originals don't belong in your portfolio. Although the colors sometimes look a little better in manual techniques, that reasoning wouldn't compensate for any loss. Reproductions are sufficient for a job interview.

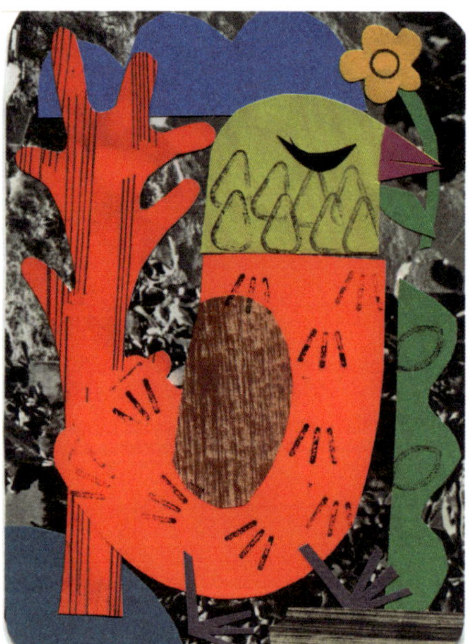

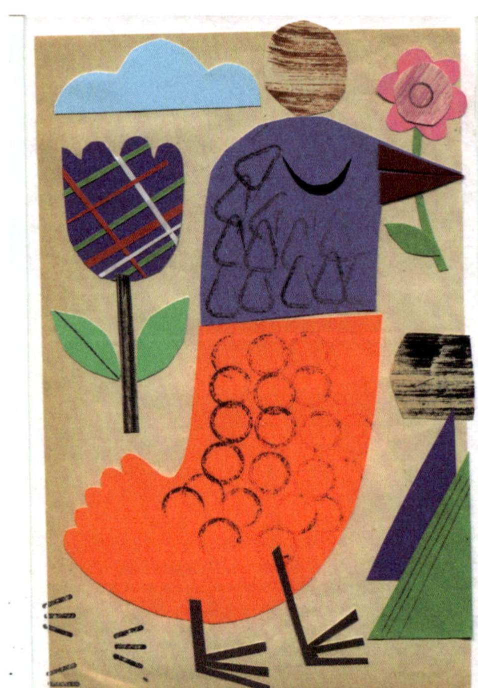

Portfolios

Allah doesn't count the days spent in the chase.
ARABIC SAYING

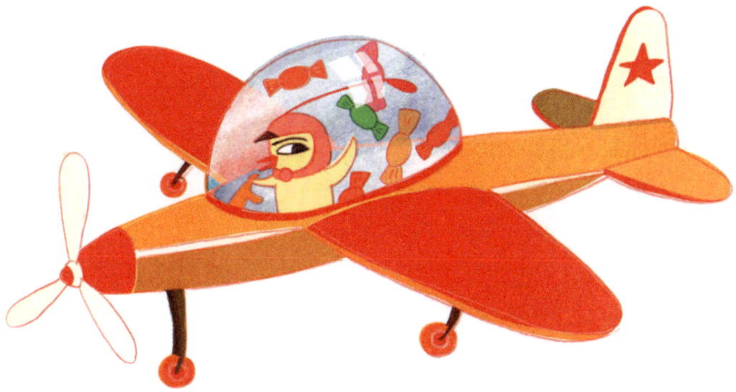

For *digital* portfolios you basically follow the same rules as for a portfolio that you carry around with you. But the main difference is that you can't stand by them to comment while your work is being looked at by the client.
This involves some differences, advantages and disadvantages. Most importantly, though:

Your digital portfolios should be able to speak for themselves.

This starts with a clear label. A guidance system or layout that is easy to understand and facilitates orientation for the client while looking at it is also helpful. This can be done using color or arrangement systems, groupings or a thousand other tricks. What's important is that your layout conveys your concern in a meaningful way, without competing with the actual pictures too much. A simple, informative design grid is certainly the most effective. Since you can't comment on your works, it would also be good if the illustrations are shown not only as pictures, but occasionally in their use in the finished product (photos of magazines, etc.). After all, your client "thinks" in products. In practice, such a photo says more than a thousand words anyway.

When selecting your pictures, trust in yourself and your taste. Portfolios are the same as all other folders and presentations: they are intended to present you and your work, not just attempt to produce things that you think your client wants to see. In reality, you can't read their minds anyway. Therefore, I can only advise you not to fish in the dark, but to put the pictures in your portfolio that you can really stand behind.

And how does your portfolio reach your clients? It makes no sense if your work ends up with the intern. The right people to contact are image editors, art buyers, readers or editors. Some research is needed in advance in order to reach them specifically. It's best to call shortly before and inquire who really is responsible. Incidentally, you can use this opportunity to ask which type of portfolio filing method is favored by the respective client.

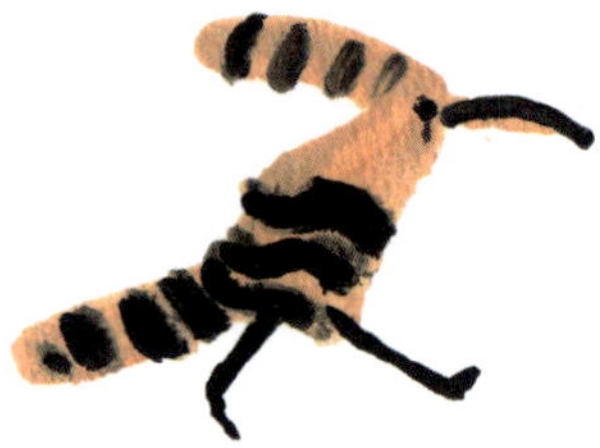

Publishers and agencies use a variety of filing systems, and it's sometimes smart to figure out how they will archive your portfolio. Some want JPGs, others want PDFs, yet another wants prints or sketches along with the final versions. Even clients are only human and thus very different. Just ask them.
A digital portfolio shouldn't be too large. The question of whether it makes sense to send 15 MB as an email attachment can be answered with a clear *no*. Instead of a huge attachment, provide a link to a download. Everything else is like unsolicited direct mail advertising and will certainly produce the opposite impact of what you really want to achieve.
Even with mail portfolios, the size can be slightly smaller. It is best to orientate it to your "proper portfolio" and simply design a slimmed down version (usually 15 pages are enough).

We're left with the question of which is better: digital or analog? The answer is *both*. In most cases it makes sense to also occasionally send something made of paper in addition to your digital portfolios. It could be a handout or a postcard, but usually a small selection of prints is sufficient. The most important thing is that you indicate in the cover letter that the client is welcome to keep the mailing. This way, you make sure that it goes into their files (it's no use to you if they return it. You're already familiar with your work :-)).

For email or mail portfolios – whether electronic formats or "real" printouts – you should make sure that your name and your email address can be found on every page. A small line at the edge of the picture is enough. It may well be that only individual pages of your portfolio are printed and filed, in which case access to your identity should be ensured. Sometimes a postcard with a single beautiful picture is enough to bring you to mind. But even more elaborate handouts are gratefully accepted.

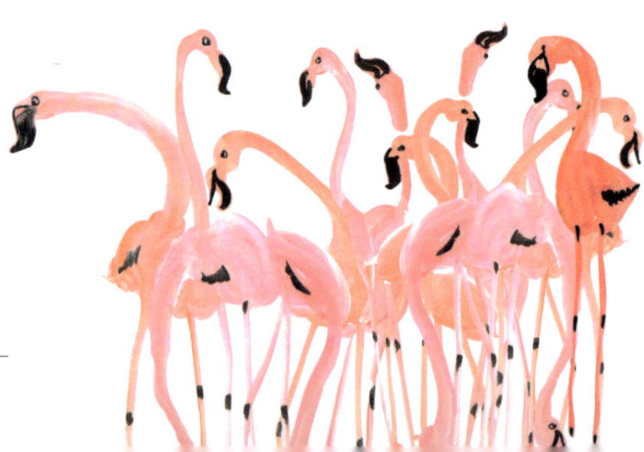

KRISTINA HELDMANN

It makes sense, especially for career novices, to produce your own little book in which to introduce yourself and your illustrations.

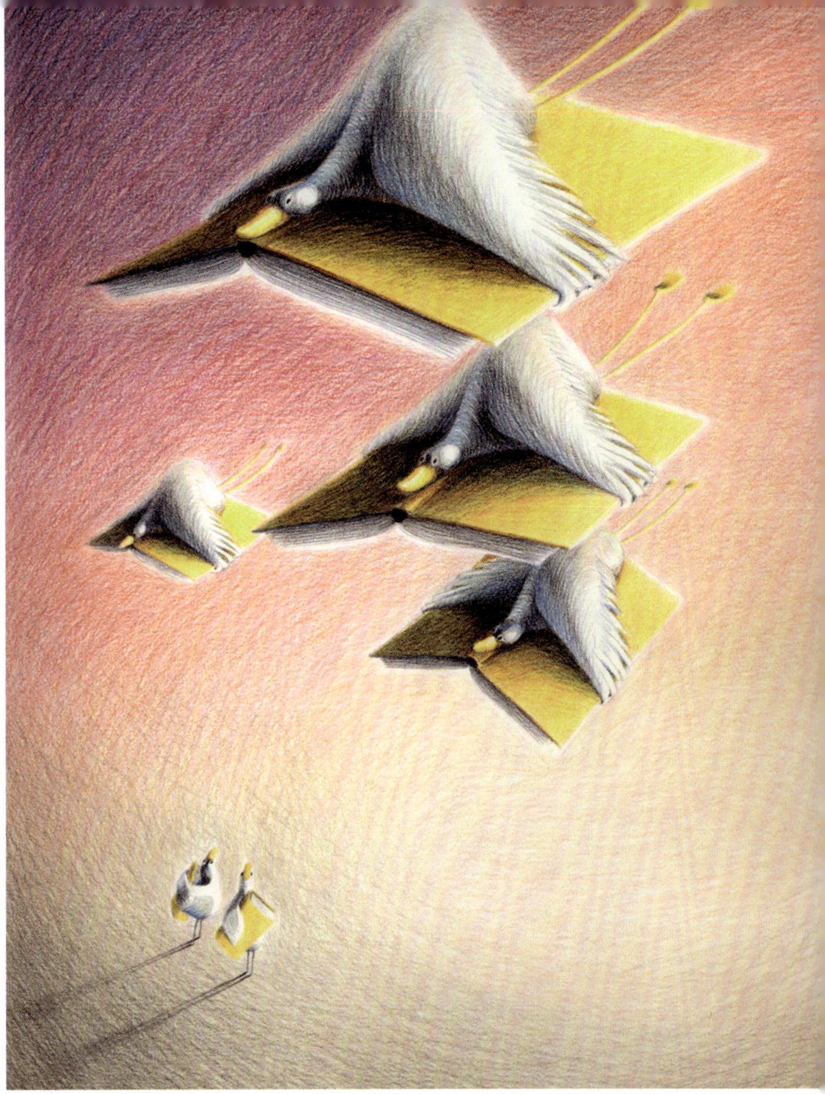

This can be a very simple handout magazine, a fanfold leaflet or a card collection. It doesn't have to be a novel. A few small pages in a handy format are sufficient. Such an investment sent by mail to editorial offices and agencies is usually not more expensive than the registration fee for an illustration archive or an annual, but proves to be many times more effective. Self-invested money is always well invested. What you don't send, you can give away at trade fairs or leave as a business card. You'll be surprised how long people hold on to these products.

Finally, I would like to talk briefly about responses. Many newcomers report that surprisingly little happens, especially after their first mailings. This is unsettling but probably has nothing to do with you. Often it's the result of the slow decision-making processes on the other side. Therefore, I can only urgently advise you to stick with it.
It makes sense, for instance, to call the editor after a while and ask if the portfolio arrived and how they liked it. Don't be shy. Courage pays off.
In the long term I can assure you that it will be easier with time. Once you have had a presence on the market for a while, people will recognize you. And by then, your publications will be your best portfolios.
Somewhere out there are people who might be looking for exactly what you have to offer – people you just don't know yet. The job of a good portfolio is to change that.

Agents and Representation

Take the Money and Run.
ALAN MOORE

The question of whether it's worthwhile to have one's work represented by agents can be confidently answered with: "It all depends."

Alliances and particularly alliances of convenience are entered into to balance one's deficiencies with the strengths of the other. So, first you would have to ask: Do representatives do something for you that you can't do yourself? Does the partner you take on board do such a big share of your job that it justifies the cost? Let's take a closer look at the pros and cons:
In English-speaking countries there are countless illustration agencies. Most of them are companies of one to two people who are mainly involved in the advertising and editorial fields. In recent years, specialized agencies in the children's book sector have also cropped up. Agencies typically acquire illustration jobs by establishing personal contacts with clients and developing these relationships through regular management. In addition, they keep files, are present on the Internet and with additional printed handouts, in some cases even annuals.

The efficiency of agencies is a hotly debated topic in illustrator circles.

Here, too, all agencies are different. The really prestigious agencies represent their clients, I am happy to admit, very well. They coordinate the briefings, communicate problems and provide "their" illustrators with regular and well-paid work. In addition, they are able to review contracts and to collect fees in case of any defaulted payments. In short, they protect and nurture their clients and provide very useful services for the percentage they charge.
However, the "good" agencies by no means will add every illustrator to their portfolio. They prefer illustrators with a distinctive, sellable style. The crux of the matter is that agencies sell sellable goods.
This creates the paradox that agencies often only represent those who, on the basis of their renown and their catchy style, would not have too many difficulties competing in the market anyway. However, it's also understandable that agencies can only manage a limited portfolio and they also need to make a name for themselves. To find a place with a renowned agency pays off especially for newcomers.

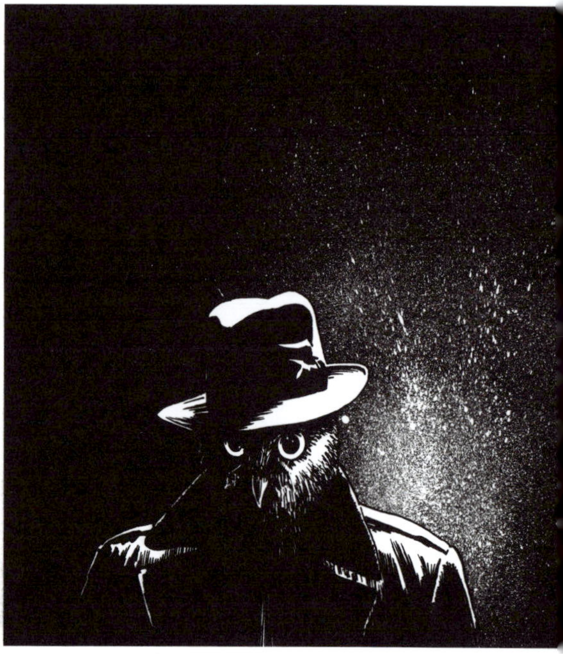

ROBERT NIPPOLT

DIETER JÜDT

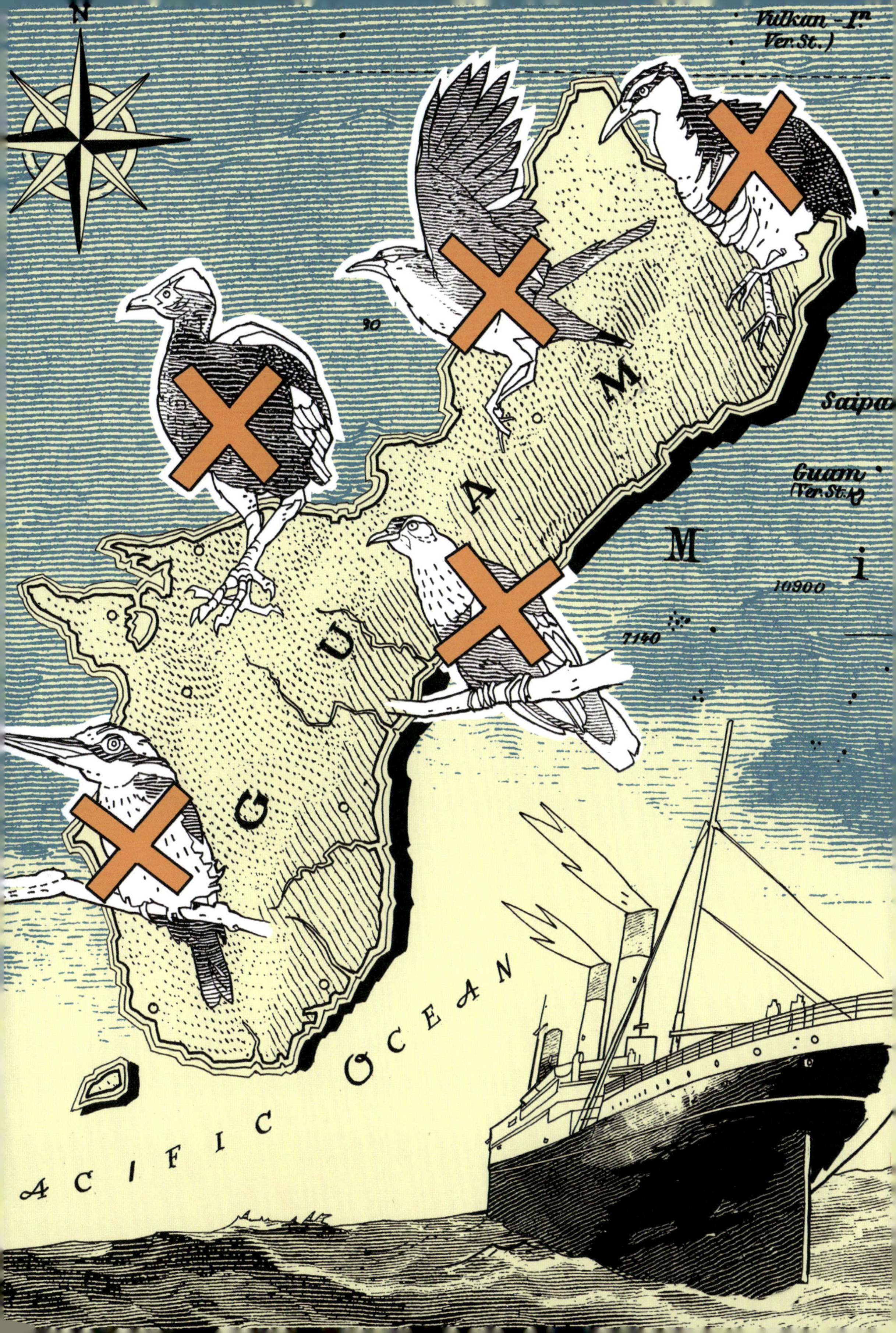

N
Vulkan - Iⁿ
Ver. St.)
90
Saipan
Guam
(Ver. St.)
M
i
10900
7140
GUAM
PACIFIC OCEAN

Most agencies charge a rate of between 15 and 25 percent of jobs they mediate (in some cases even up to a third of the fee). At first this sounds like a lot of money, but you also have to differentiate here: It's not uncommon that at the end of the day your agent only costs you the extra money that they negotiated on your behalf. Especially with advertising jobs, the negotiation margin is often very large, and few illustrators are shrewd enough to really assess the potential of the respective contract.

Often, an agent's skill makes up for the 25 percent that he or she may cost.

In some areas, however, the margin is not that big. Especially in the book and editorial sector the rates are practically fixed. An agent will not be able to get more out of it and you will actually have to deduct their 25 percent stake from your fee.

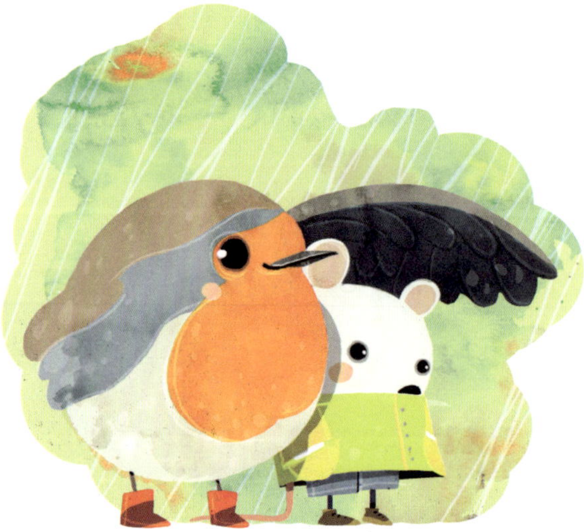

In addition, it should be noted that very many agencies use agreements that illustrators should look at very closely. For example, very long-term, exclusive relationships with the respective agency are common (usually two years and longer), during which the agency wants to secure exclusive rights to represent its clients. The agencies argue that they first need to "build up" the respective illustrators. However, the resulting dependencies often lead to a difficult situation for illustrators.
As long as the agency generates good work, there is little to object to; but if it doesn't, things soon get dodgy. Many agencies also reserve a right to a commission for jobs that they did not actually broker directly, but that are merely follow-up orders from former jobs. My advice would be to contractually restrict this as much as possible in advance. Otherwise working with an agency will soon become a nuisance. Above all an "existing client clause" is advisable here, i.e. a clause in the contract that states that all jobs from clients you had before the contract will be settled in the future without paying a commission to the agency.

Reputable agents only accept a percentage of fees from the jobs they actually acquired themselves.

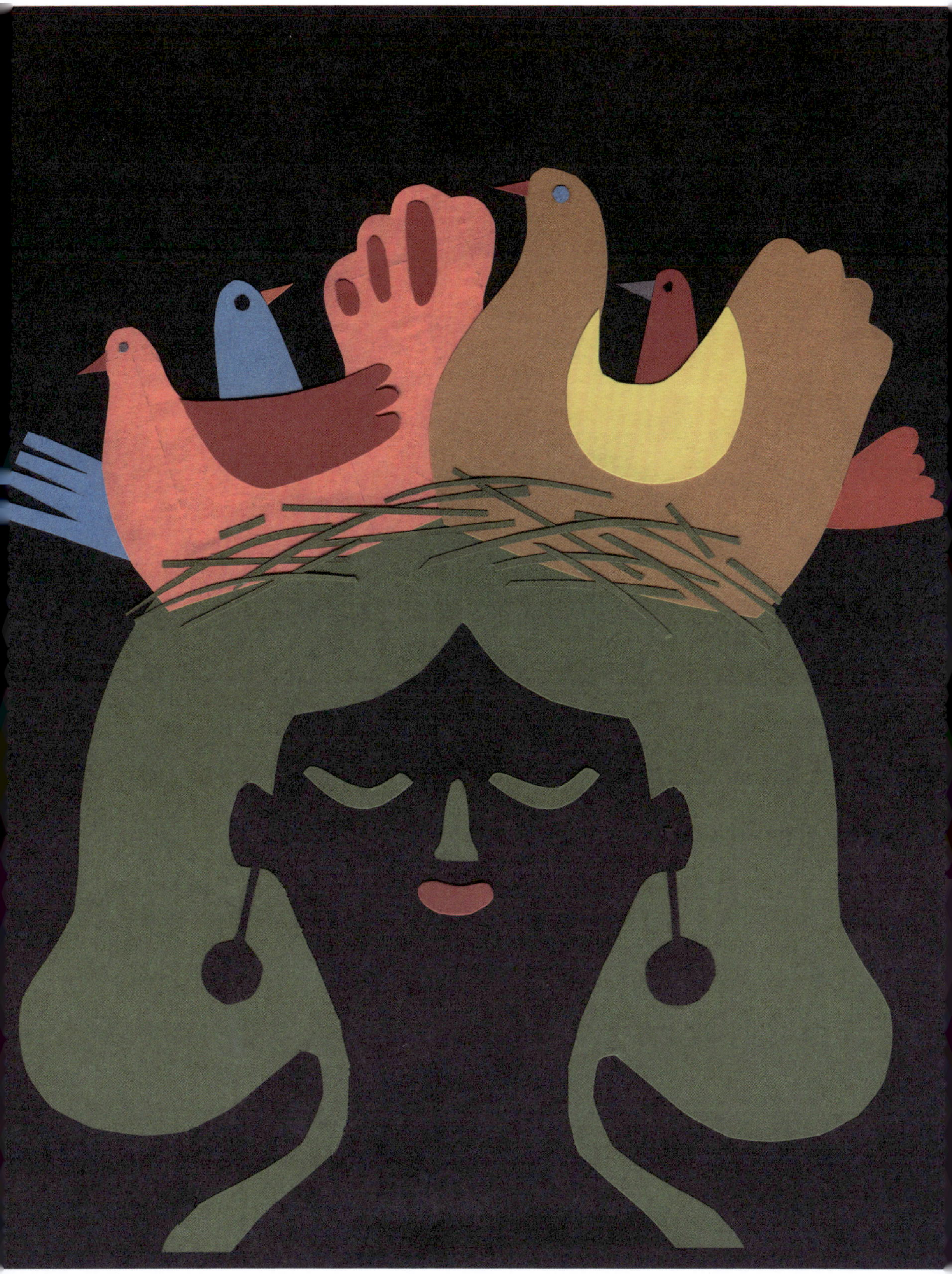

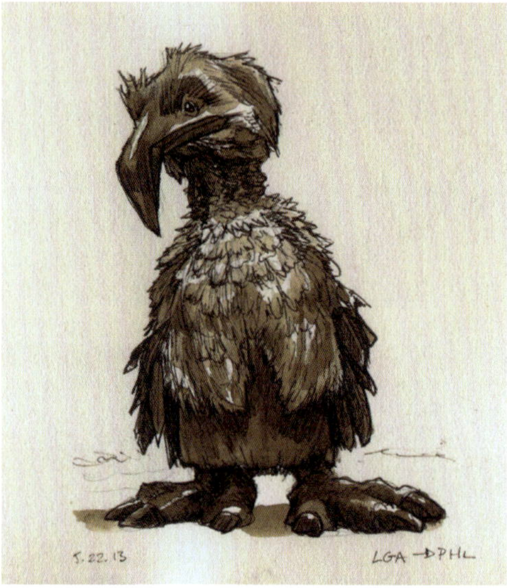

Tip

As with all contracts, agency contracts are nothing more than a transcript of terms and conditions and are thus freely negotiable. So watch out for traps in pre-formulated contracts and make use of your leeway.

◆

It must be said that generally, agencies have lost importance due to the Internet. Annuals have lost much of their impact due to the easy availability of images, so in negotiations with agencies today you can often make better agreements than would have been the case a few years ago.
Pay particular attention to traps in the contracts: Agreements with agents should be terminable with a notice period of three months, they should contain "existing client regulations" and should not charge disproportionate additional costs for annuals, etc.

Of course, you may also need the services of an agency only for a specific area of your business. A representative can be especially useful in cases in which it is more difficult for potential clients to contact you. The UK and US markets are a good example of this, where agencies are the common model; therefore it makes perfect sense to be represented here for these regions. Even staked off parts of your work could prove to be reasonably "representable." For instance, you may know half the people in the book scene, but from time to time would also like jobs in advertising. In this case, collaborating with an agency would certainly be desirable.

So it may be wise to use agencies only as needed.

However, as soon as your representative exhibits little self-initiative and you have to predominantly do your own self-promotion, you can confidently give up that agency and sell your work just as well via Internet portfolios on your own. Overall, I stand by my initial assessment that "it all depends." We are all different, and our needs and possibilities are just as different.

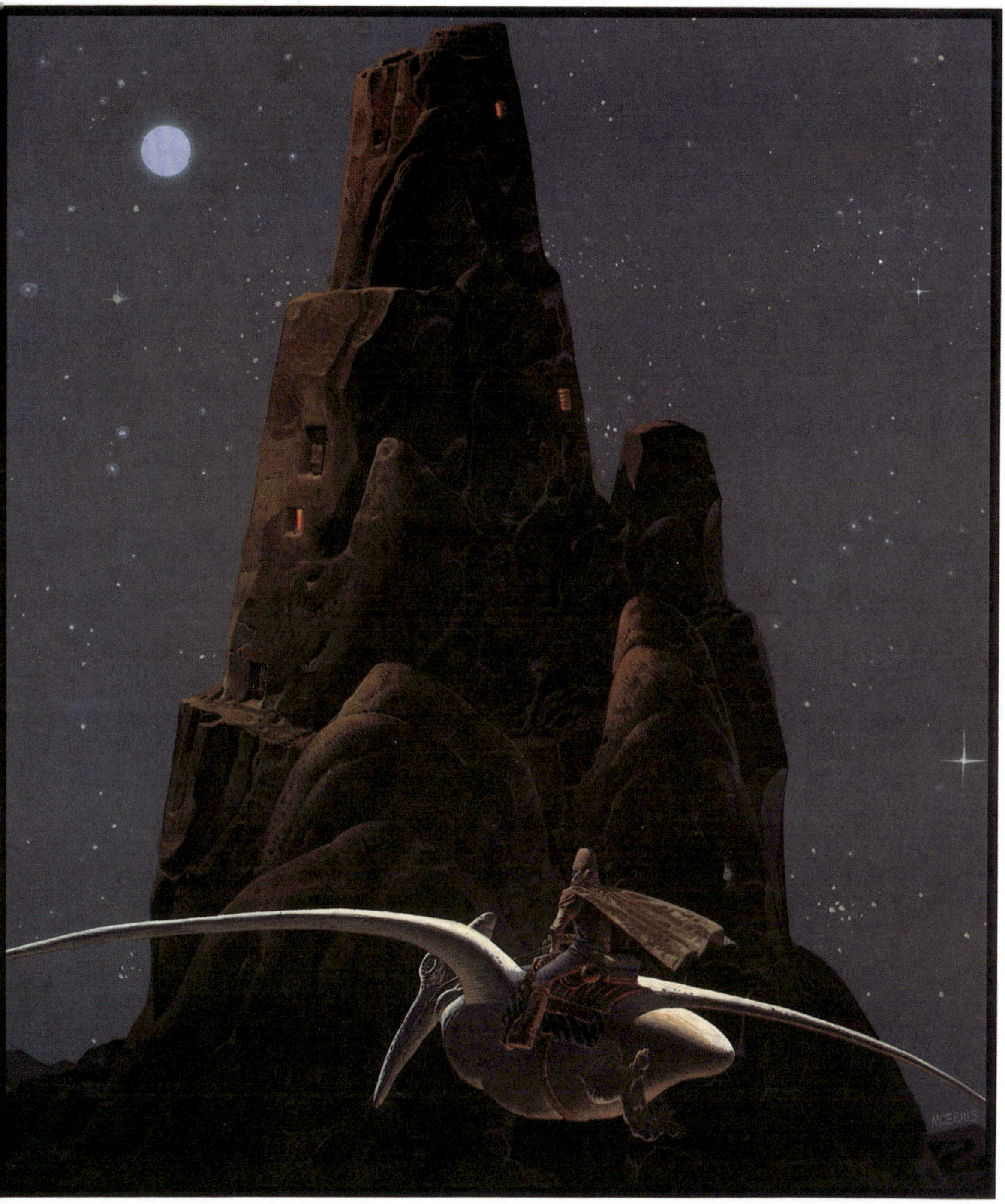
MŒBIUS

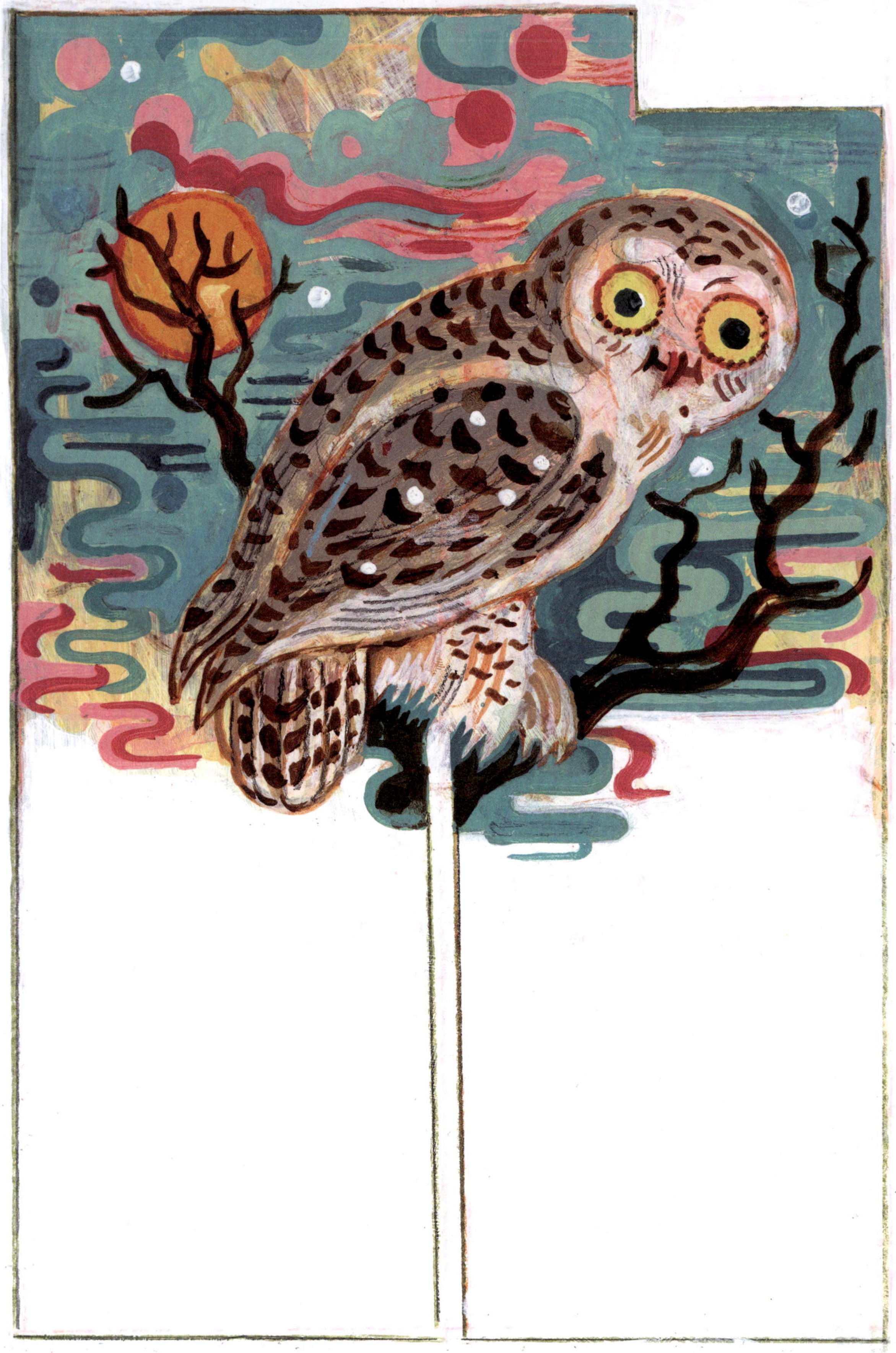

Illustration Archives

Mama's gonna keep you right here under her wing, she won't let you fly but she might let you sing. "MOTHER," PINK FLOYD, 1979

In addition to agents who actively look for clients for you, there is another type of service provider in the illustration market that promises to provide jobs. Illustration archives and annuals entice you with offers to make your annoying acquisition easier. Usually, this is because the archives present your pictures in places with high client frequency (e.g. at trade fairs) or that they send your illustrations to potential clients in the form of an annual.

On closer inspection, what sounds good has a couple of catches. It begins with the fact that this type of presentation usually involves a painfully expensive fee. Money that, in contrast to agencies, is due no matter what and not only when your agent has landed a real job for you through active mediation. It's not for nothing that illustrator circles are puzzled over the benefits of archives, especially since these archives are in no way interested in subjecting the efficiency of their services to a neutral investigation. Their very existence proves that the business model works for them at least. (Don't get any ideas: you probably don't want to open another archive, but instead learn whether participation is worthwhile for you as an illustrator ...)

In order to shed some light on the matter, it's worth taking a look at the forums and blogs where illustrators discuss their experiences.

In fact, assessments are divided here: Although there are actually illustrators who occasionally generate orders from archives, one must also say that the response is overwhelmingly negative.

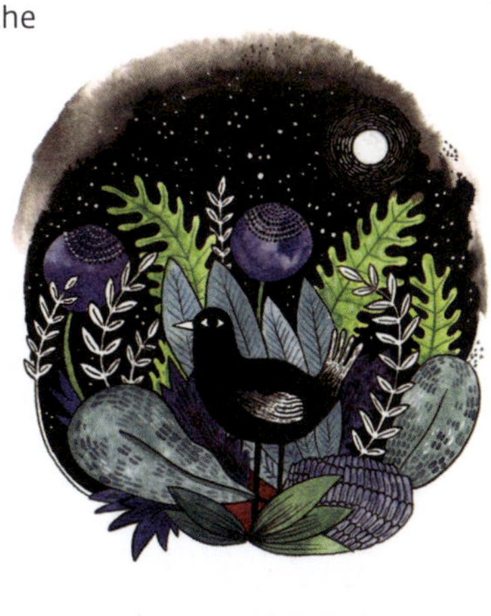

This is due to the nature of most of the jobs generated by archives. Illustrators frequently report that they are mostly low-paid jobs that simply take the detour through the archives because they are considered difficult to sell on the "first illustration job market." In addition, the structure of the business model is criticized: Archives collect no matter if they are successful in placing their illustrators or not. That's why they're not interested in quality assurance, but instead in having the largest possible number of participants. In fact, the selection in the popular illustration archives is of Babylonian proportions. Many illustrators report that the first letter of their last name has a greater impact on the frequency of inquiries than the work presented. Thus, participants with last names beginning with A receive significantly more requests than XYZ surnames.

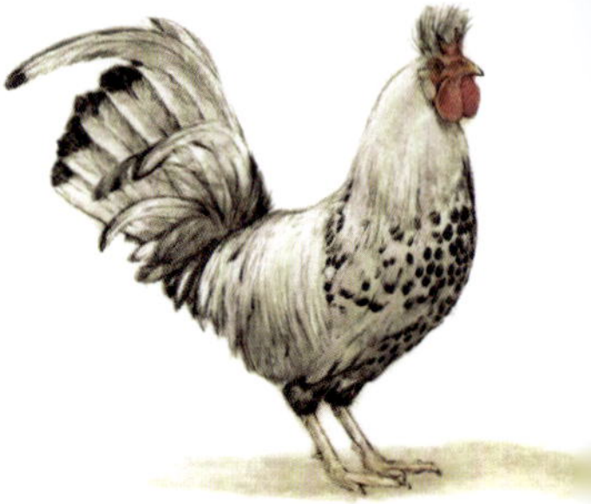

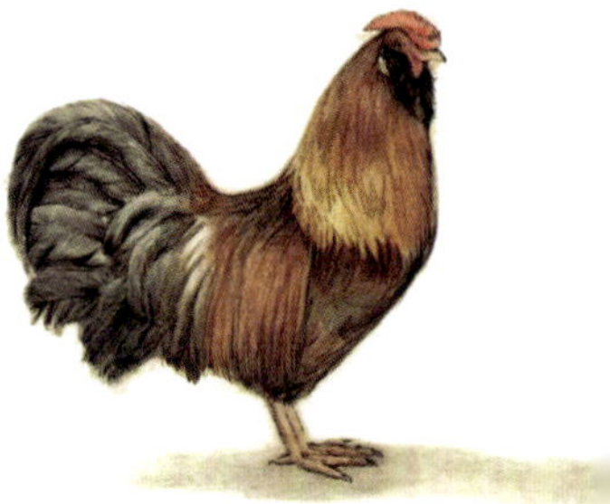

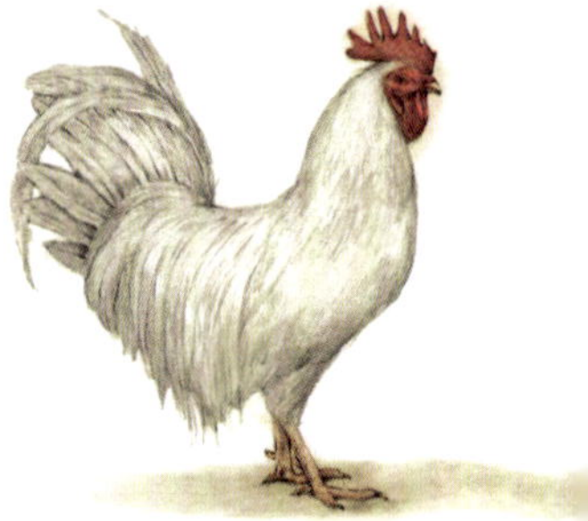

"Quantity over quality" is the motto of the vast majority of archives.

In general, you may tend to assume that you would shine as a participant in an exhibition if you were "the best." The idea of having a better chance of being "discovered" when surrounded by weaker competitors soon arises. But on the contrary, experience shows that it's by no means helpful to be king of the hill. The neighborhood rubs off on you. If you present your pictures among weaker ones at an exhibition, your work also seems less good; conversely, good neighbors heighten your impact.

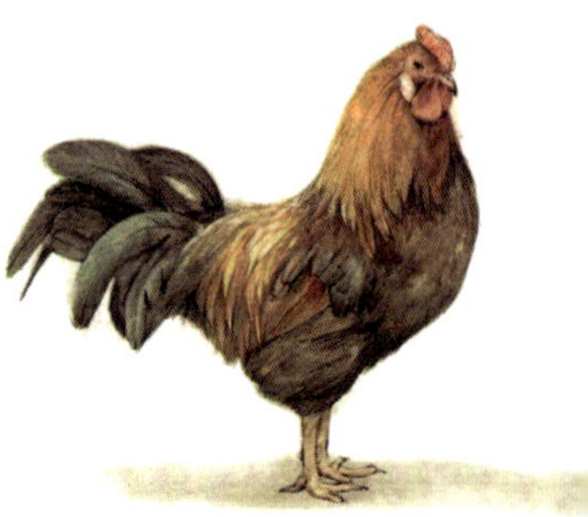

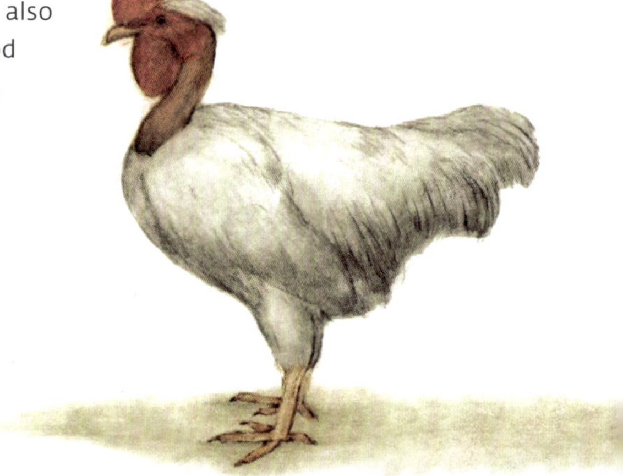

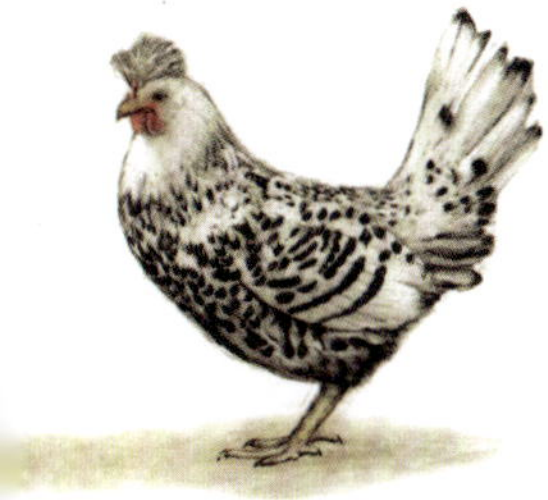
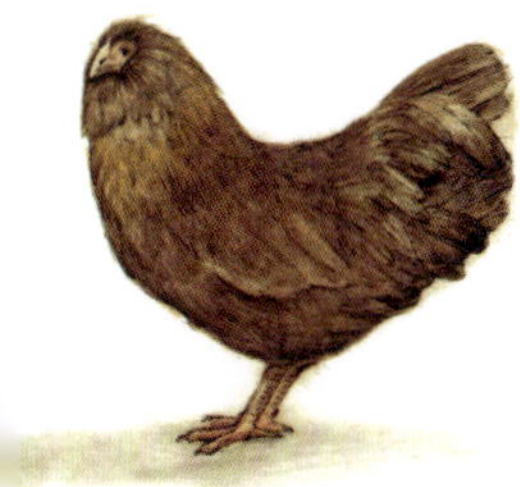
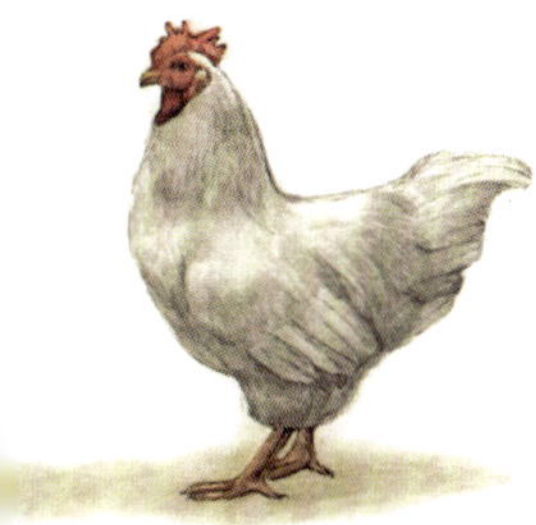
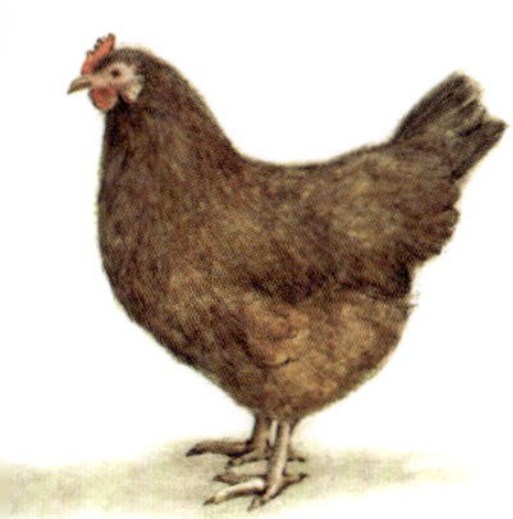

And this is certainly not just an optical or aesthetic phenomenon. You're likely to receive less attention at a weak event simply because bad exhibitions are less frequented than good ones. Exactly this phenomenon also applies to annuals and archives. Archives in particular like to root out the more inexperienced, semi-professional illustrators from a target group.

In the worst case, then, you're spending money to disappear amidst a host of weak illustrations.

The archive itself understandably has no problem because its source of income is presentation, not mediation.
The reason why archives nevertheless are accepted – for example among children's book publishers – is less the quality than the convenience.
Since they can be leafed through quickly, archives help potential clients to separate the ostensible chaff from the wheat. They save the client side (e.g. the children's book editors) from having to tell the illustrators to their faces that they are not interested in them for their project. This is convenient for the clients; they can choose but do not have to spend time with the illustrators. In extreme cases this leads to the almost obscene phenomenon that the illustrators who are at the beginning of their careers pay the archives for not receiving *any* feedback on their quality.

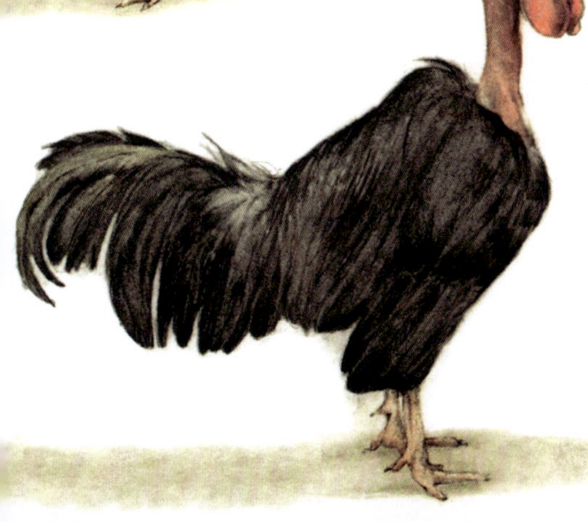

To put it briefly, archives mainly benefit the client side – but they are subsidized by the illustrators. For this reason, one must treat archives with caution, however present they may appear at the trade fairs.

With illustration annuals and yearbooks, it's often the same, but not always. Reason enough to look at them more closely, too:

In fact, it very much depends on which catalogues we're talking about. That's because many annuals, unlike most of the illustration archives, pay close attention to who they're putting into their portfolio: annuals are usually judged. This is partly due to the printing and shipping costs, but in large part to the reputation that many annuals would lose if they only relied on quantity. So some annuals, especially in the Anglo-Saxon market, turn out to be really useful. In fact, quite a few international careers were launched in magazines like *3x3*. It's also obvious why annuals are particularly useful abroad: Most of the illustration archives that present your work, for example, at a German trade fair, usually reach only those people who could have addressed you with little effort on their own. Whether you would reach a magazine on the East Coast of the U.S. with similar ease is doubtful. This makes annuals really helpful allies as far as self-marketing is concerned, especially as the costs, particularly for reputable catalogues, are within reasonable limits. Basically, the same applies to archives and annuals as to agents:

If an archive is able to generate clients that you do not know yet or that you can't reach, participation may prove useful.

If not, you would better invest your money differently, for example, in postage stamps for a customized application or in membership in a professional association. Because these too usually have archives or publish annuals. And with them, you can be sure that your membership fee will be used for additional services that actually benefit you (such as legal expense insurance) instead of disappearing into the pockets of private companies.

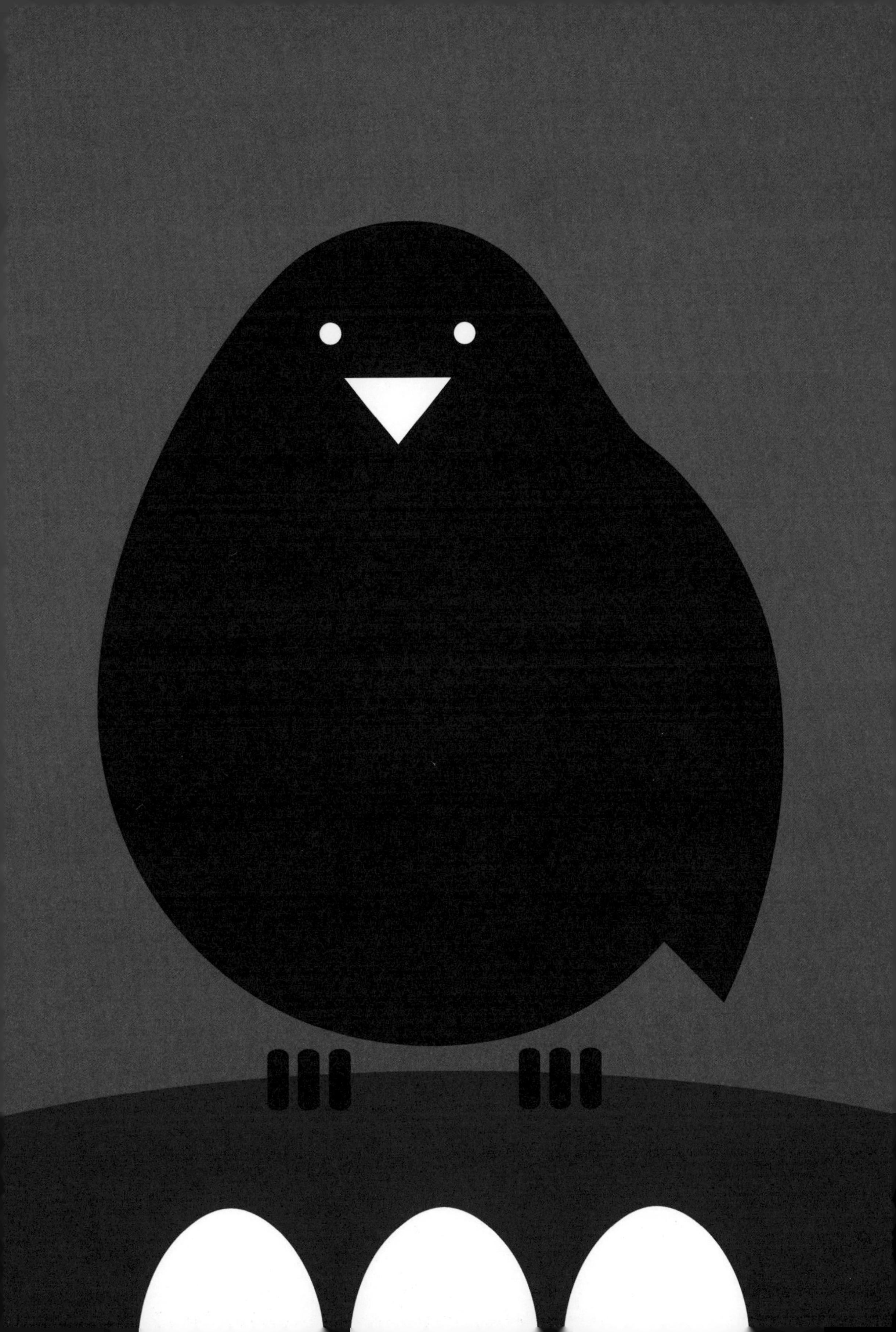

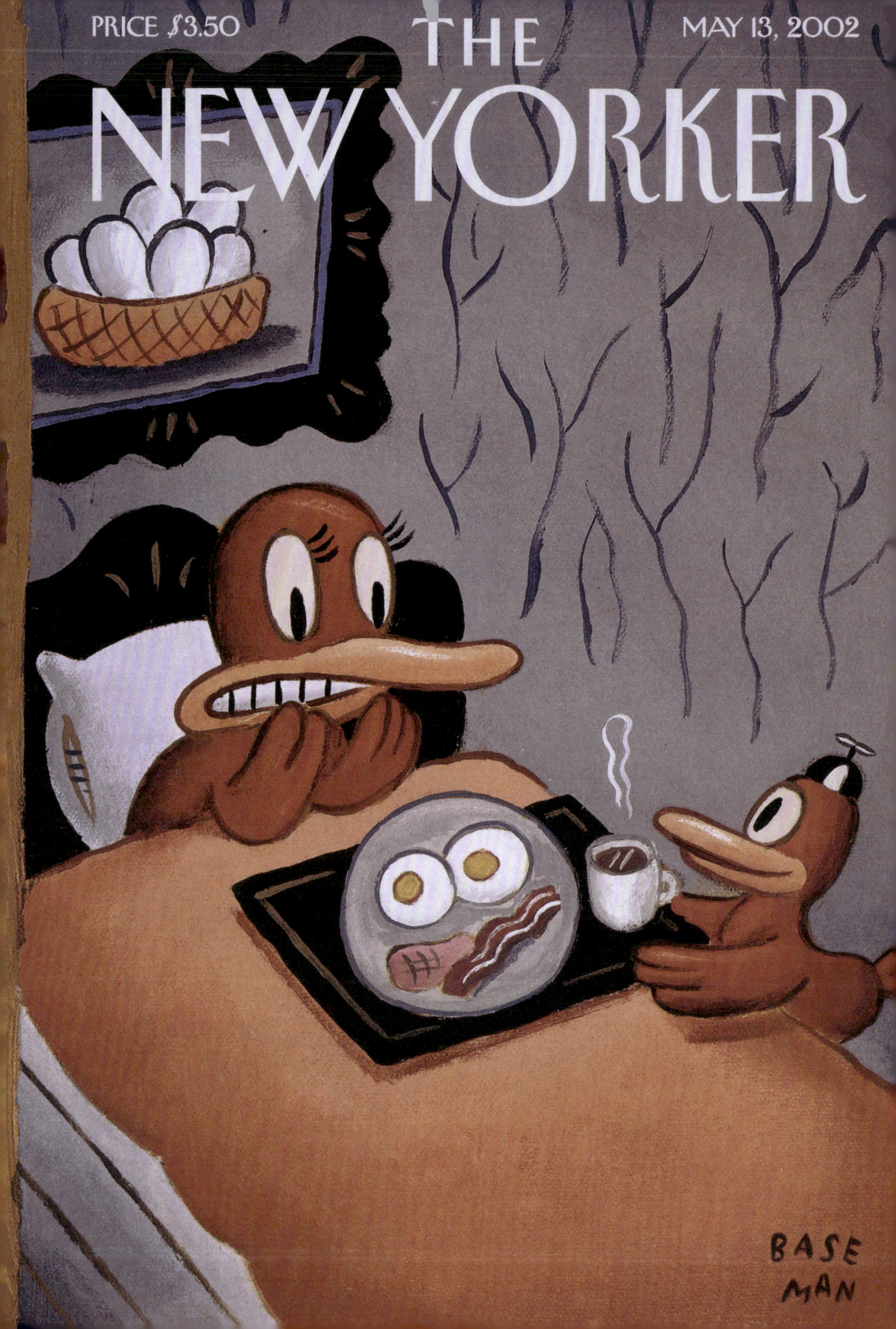
PRICE $3.50
THE NEW YORKER
MAY 13, 2002
BASE
MAN

Your Own Projects

Then you better start swimmin' or you'll sink like a stone,
for the times they are a-changin'.
"THE TIMES THEY ARE A-CHANGIN'" BOB DYLAN 1964

Everything in art speaks for self-initiative! It doesn't matter if you are writing a comic or a cookbook, constructing pop-ups, creating games or filling a travel guide with on-location sketches – combining your illustrative talents and your *other* interests almost always pays off! Look at it this way: every new job makes us ask ourselves whether we are really interested in the subject matter (and we almost always make huge compromises). By contrast, *our own projects* always suit us perfectly. We don't dream up things that don't interest us.

It's no coincidence that illustrators who push their own projects are often the most successful.

It starts by combining images and copy: Many renowned illustrators are also famed authors. Those who write their own books (for example, children's books) often deliver the most persuasive results.

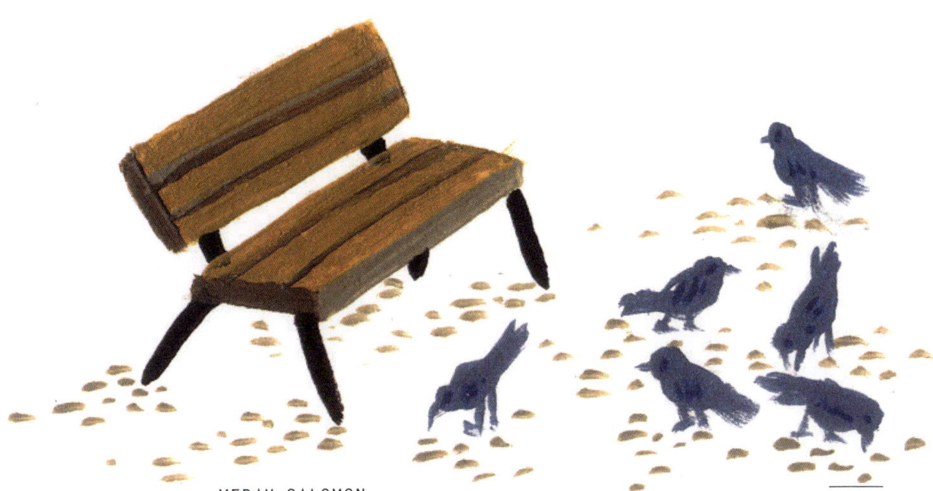

GARY BASEMAN

MERAV SALOMON

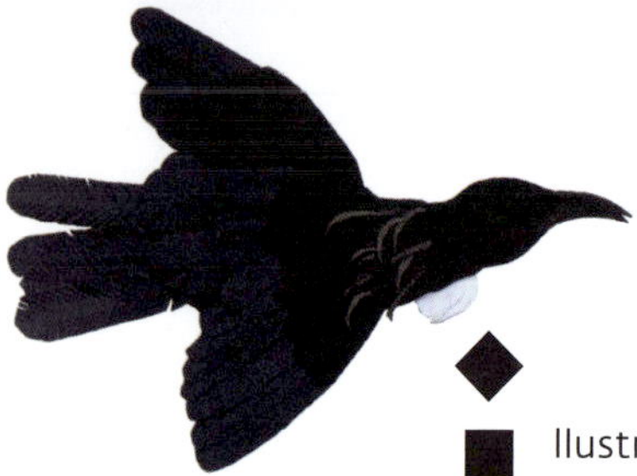

Illustration is basically the pleasure of telling stories with pictures and therefore most of us – often unbeknownst to us – possess narrative talent.
It is only one short step from a picture to a story because the two arts are related. Indeed many writers have training in the visual arts (for example, *Inkheart* creator Cornelia Funke studied illustration in Hamburg.)

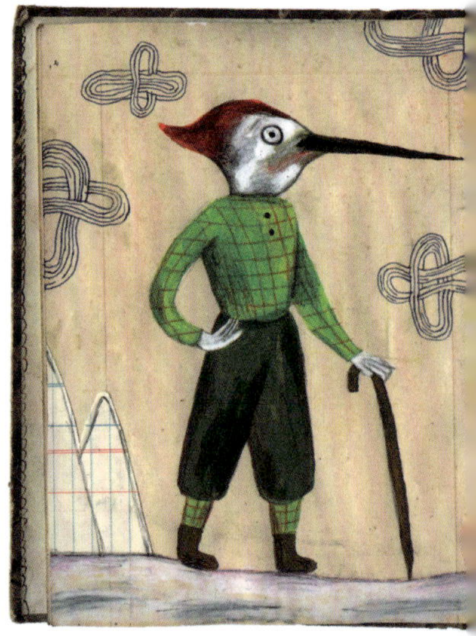

And just as it is only a small step from picture to words, it is a mere stone's throw from an idea to a project. Animations, pop-ups, games and countless illustrative devices offer a rich sphere of activity for explorers.
This is worth our while for many reasons. For one, we naturally have a very different standing when we are no longer acting as a contract artist following instructions. It is also obvious that we put more of our heart's blood into "our own" subject matter, which will be noticeable in the quality of our work. How much love or tedium went into a project is self-evident.

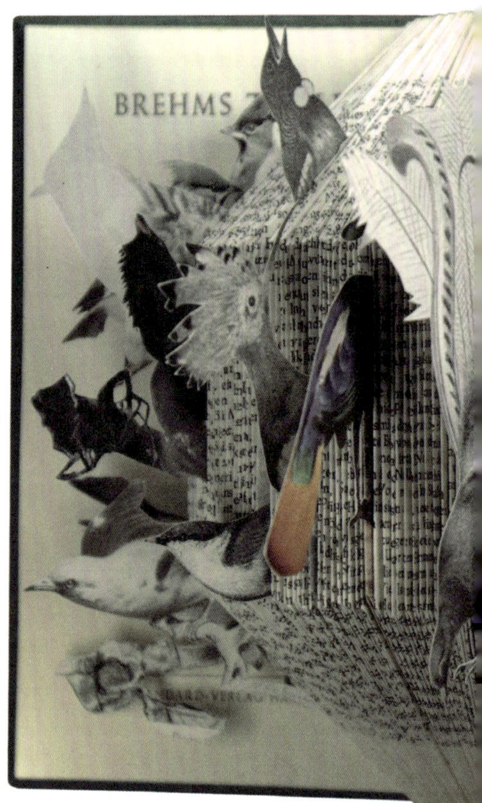

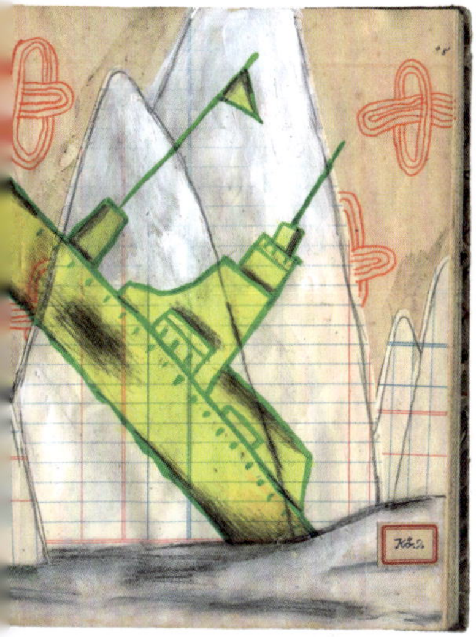

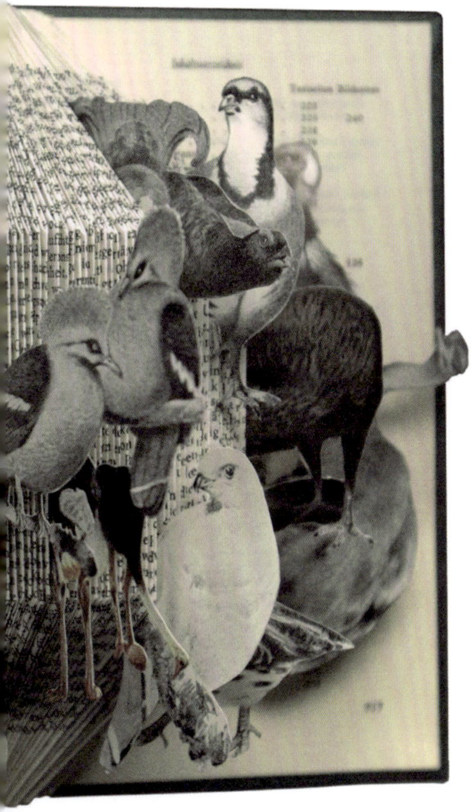

Our own projects are usually good just because they are important to us.

Additionally we can't ignore the fact that if our own projects are published, they pay far better. In the book industry, for example, it means double the fees.
It's a well-known fact that children's book publishers are quite grateful when they are offered illustrations along with a story, but magazines, game publishers, juvenile, comic and gift book producers are also quite open to this. Moreover, it never fails. Even if we may not have produced a "blockbuster" business-wise, we have created something that really interests us. How often do we as illustrators create beautiful images for other people's dreams without much to show for it in monetary terms?

With your own projects you are doing something for yourself, first and foremost. In the end, that may be the greatest benefit.

ABOVE:
NORA KRUG

BELOW:
ASTRID HAAS

Bread-and-Butter Jobs and Ersatz Identities

Now once I used to think it might be worthy to be
a brave and sacrificing person.
I soon found out it wasn't reimbursin';
decided to continue being earthy.
MACHEATH IN *THE THREE-PENNY OPERA*, BERTOLT BRECHT, 1928

kitschy bright pink for a commercial book? A mascot for a kitchen studio? A house view for an architect? Wooley the wool sheep takes a trip around the world? Welcome to illustrative reality. The question is: How do you deal with commissions that don't make you artistically happy? Bring 'em on? Or only with stomachaches?

It's not for nothing that most of us have reservations about what we laconically call "bread-and-butter jobs." We wanted to be a little bit of an artist. After all, we started out with aspirations for art and creativity. Nothing against earning money – but with stuff that's not at all sexy? Let's face it: Bread-and-butter jobs scratch at the façade of our honor. You soon feel degraded as the proxy-bound made-to-order painter. – On the other hand, why in the world shouldn't you accept any bread-and-butter jobs? For as easy as it is to argue that one should be true to oneself and that one should not sell his soul to the first demon that comes along, it's just as hard to see why you should be condemned to being a starving artist if you choose to become an illustrator. Very few of us have only hip clients with hip assignments, and only very few illustrators are blessed with rich patron aunts from the Hamptons.

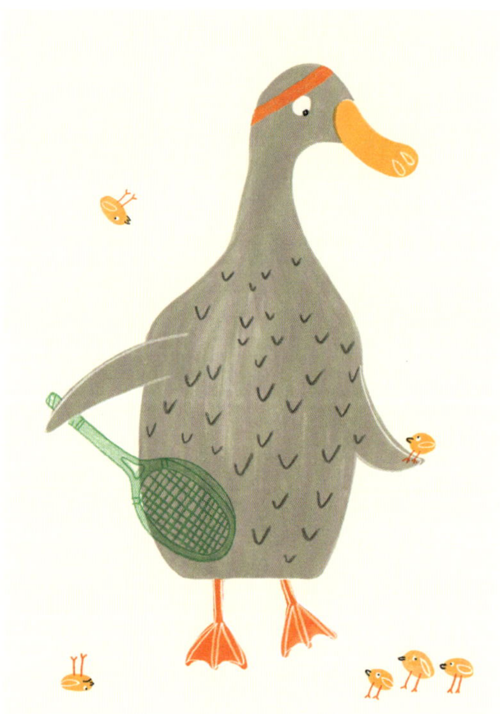

The solution is somewhere in the middle. There's nothing wrong with creating a nice mascot for the kitchen studio. Or to live for a while on pink unicorns (after all, we're at least still artists and don't work in the arms industry ...). Especially when starting out, compromises are part of the job.

What's important is not to spend your whole life making compromises.

Earning a living should actually serve only the purpose of putting bread on the table. Imagine a triangular model here:

A job can bring you glory and honor, make good money, be fun.

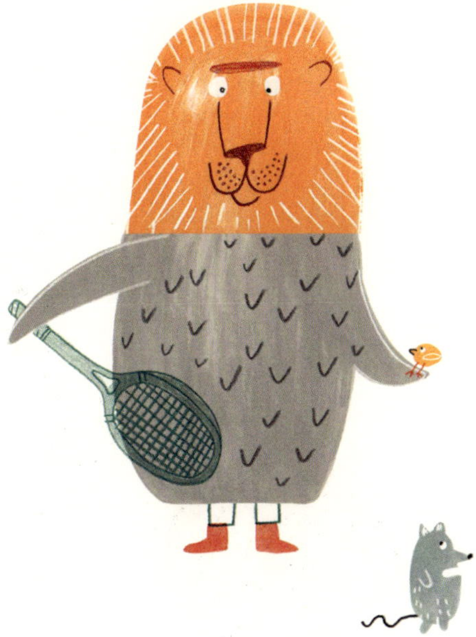

Admittedly, it isn't too often that all three factors are met. In most cases, one of the three will prevail and the other two will fare worse. So we take into account that a job that will bring us fame (a comic project of your own or something similar) won't pay as well. By the same token, we may accept that a job that really brings in some money has a lesser fun factor, or that a really interesting job involves a lot more work.

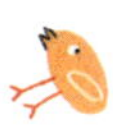

In short, we are naturally willing to compromise when at least one of the three factors is met. What's important is that these factors actually influence each other. If they're all negative, something's wrong with the job. And we therefore have our answer to the question of whether to take on bread-and-butter jobs: They should pay appropriately. The reason for this is our general job motivation.

As a rule, the more self-responsibility there is in a job, the more curiosity, fun, own ideas that go into a job, the more you'll enjoy it. If you take pleasure in the work, when you approach it playfully and passionately, then you can do *anything*. But if you're neither interested nor enjoy it, you'll find it hard. Motivation is the alpha and omega. And precisely this is what you'll find with the least bread-and-butter jobs. Your only motivation is the money.

You should therefore always negotiate bread-and-butter jobs so that you don't waste your time with them. The reckoning "I'll work while I'm eating for as much as I consume" leads directly into slavery. Ideally, with a bread-and-butter job you should earn so much more that the added value you gain gives you the capacity to implement the creative ideas that lay dormant during the bread-and-butter job.

My advice is: Do it. Not at the expense of other more creative jobs, but to *their benefit*. Take the bread-and-butter job to finish your great comic project.

Tip

Use a pseudonym for bread-and-butter jobs. If you want to produce bright pink kitsch, go ahead. But a pseudonym will protect you from the kitsch ruining your reputation in the long term.

Ready or Not, Here I Come!

I don't care to belong to any club that will have me as a member.
GROUCHO MARX

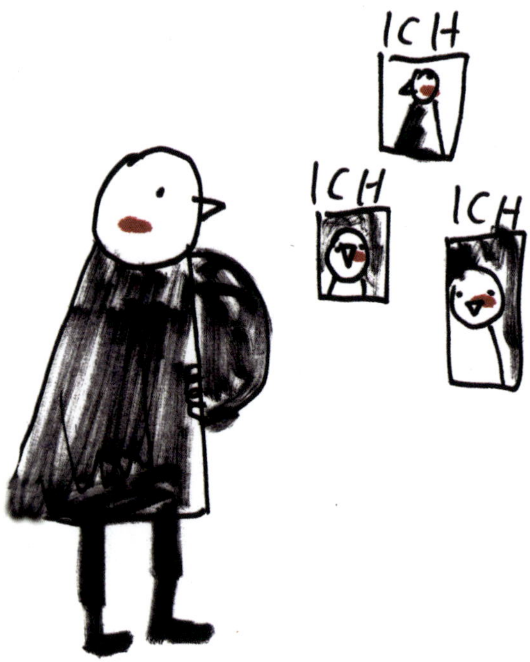

I got an early lesson in self-esteem during a class trip in the late 1970s. It was on a bus full of sixth graders. A return trip from the Edersee Dam, an excursion to the countryside followed by a visit to the inner-German border. Noisy children, 4:30 pm.
We're in the back of the bus, huddled around the child hero of our class, a self-confident spokesman, beaming, good-humored and curly-haired – the undisputed epicenter of the gathering.
I, not very self-confident and a member of the "B-team" of the class hierarchy, was proud to be allowed to sit there and have a say. We joked, chatted and laughed. The hero held court and everyone clung to his words – one joke after another. Having become cocky due to this unfamiliar proximity to power, during a pause, I tried my luck: I told a joke, which, I thought, would certainly gain me respect and recognition. I dared, I failed. – Nobody laughed. Uncomprehending silence in the auditorium. Did I tell my joke too softly?
But then something remarkable happened: The hero *stole* my joke. He repeated it as if he had just invented it – and to my astonishment they all laughed.

"... For there's some who are in darkness, and there's others in the light; but you see the ones in brightness, while the others drop from sight," is a line from the Three-Penny Opera.

Self-confidence, recognition and affirmation are rather difficult topics for many artists. That's not only true when we discuss payments – or the monetary recognition. It's the topic in general. Recognition (or the struggle for it) is one of the main drivers of our work even though we are often not aware of it. What we call ambition is often just the desire to be seen and noticed. At the same time, recognition is the nose-ring that we let ourselves be tugged around on in business. Because the pursuit of recognition is often shaped by the unconscious desire to use art to patch over all the humiliations, both small and large, that have damaged our biographies. This is often why we sometimes very readily accept obviously dubious fees.

The attitude that we must win attention and recognition at all costs opens us to blackmail.

The phenomenon isn't new: Artists typically take on so-called outsider roles (perhaps because they simply shy away from the competition of the alpha types who like to – let's say – be pilots :-)), to then stake out their claim from there. However, there is now an entire industry that lives from these same people: Portals like Tumblr generate their income exclusively from people's desire for attention and recognition.

The Internet is full of artists – lonely artists. This is remarkable in that it's almost a social phenomenon. It starts with young people in casting shows allowing themselves to be bawled out by people whose opinion or acquaintance no one would value under normal circumstances.

If that's not enough, in our industry in particular people are often enslaved by being told that they could someday – if they hold out long enough – have a place at the tiller (hosts of unpaid trainees in the design industry can tell you a thing or two about it). Some clients seem positively convinced that they are doing us a favor by letting us work for them. And the deficits described are increasingly being used to keep prices and payments low.

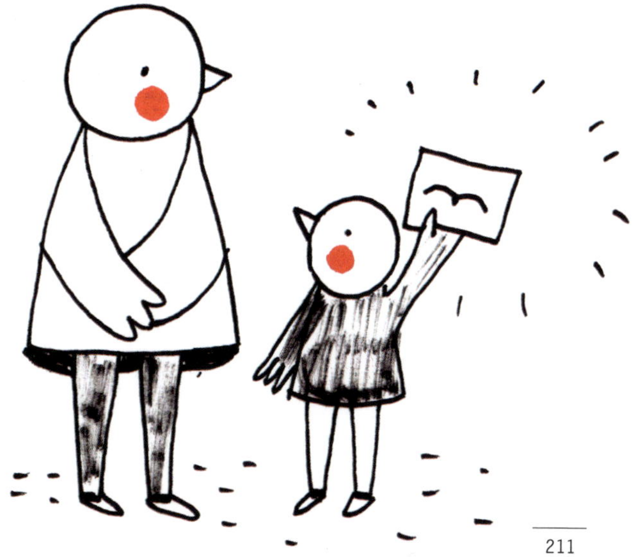

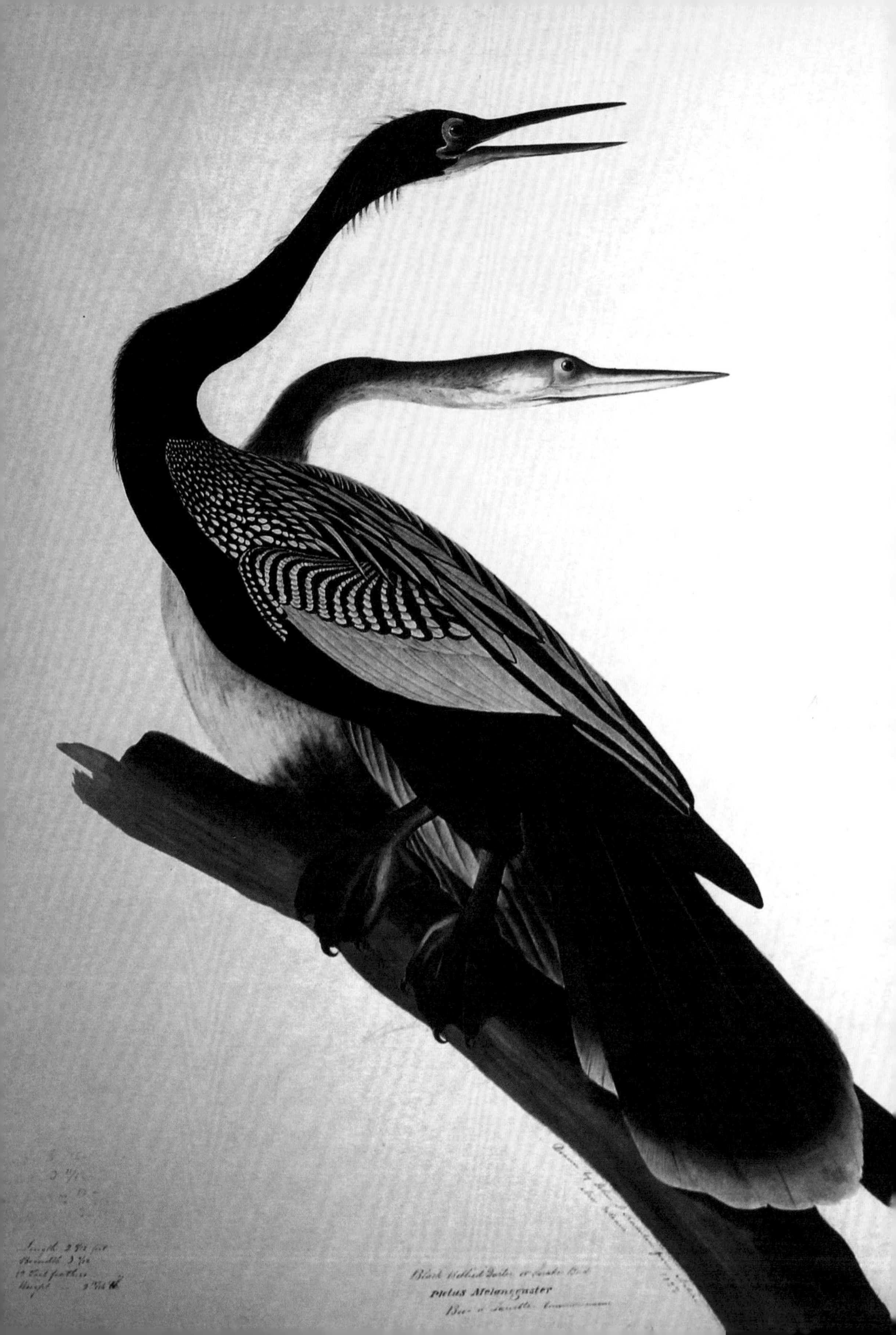
Plotus Melanogaster

That wouldn't be so bad if we all, the whole industry, were one big community of solidarity. But sadly, we often are very alone with our willingness to sacrifice. Because everyone else who otherwise deals with the products we make actually earns money!
No editor, no paper manufacturer and no printer and no salesperson works for free. There's no reason to, because money is made with these manufactured products.

You either have self-esteem or you don't – or better said, it wasn't taught to you. And that is a part of the problem:
If you give in to the temptation to compensate for attention deficits through art with accumulated attention (according to the motto: mommy didn't love me enough, so now the whole world has to love me to make up for it), then you're either really going to have to become a rock star or become desperate. Sadly, most only attain the latter.
In fact, that – not being self-assured about yourself and your work – is one of the (maybe even *the*) chief flaws that many artists struggle with. At the same time, the desperate desire to "make it" blocks your view of a realistic way out of the dilemma. What to do?

Most important, certainly, is to learn more about yourself. Face your demons. What is important to me, and where can I achieve happiness and satisfaction without getting taken advantage of? (You can always get professional counseling – it's nothing to be ashamed of, but very useful, especially if you repeatedly reach the same limits). In addition, it seems expedient to me to simply consider the profession with a little more pragmatism.

It's natural to want praise, but we can't live from praise and recognition alone.

For example, I personally always think it's helpful to imagine how other professions deal with achievement, recognition and transactions. For instance, I'm pretty sure that the butcher around the corner would be outraged if you suggest that you merely give him recognition rather than cash for his products, for example, by promising, "If I eat the sausage in front of your shop, you'll become *better known*. Everyone would see that I enjoyed your sausage and then you could ask for money from the next customer..."
Nor would your landlord be inclined to let you live in his building for free just so that other tenants can see what a splendid place it is to live. Or what if you were to order five sample dishes next time you're at a restaurant so you can choose – and pay for – just one?
See? It's sometimes helpful to imagine how "regular" occupations would deal with offers that we sometimes readily accept. (By the way, from the imagined reactions, you can learn how you ought to react to such requests...). In the next step, we should start to change our own behavior in such situations.

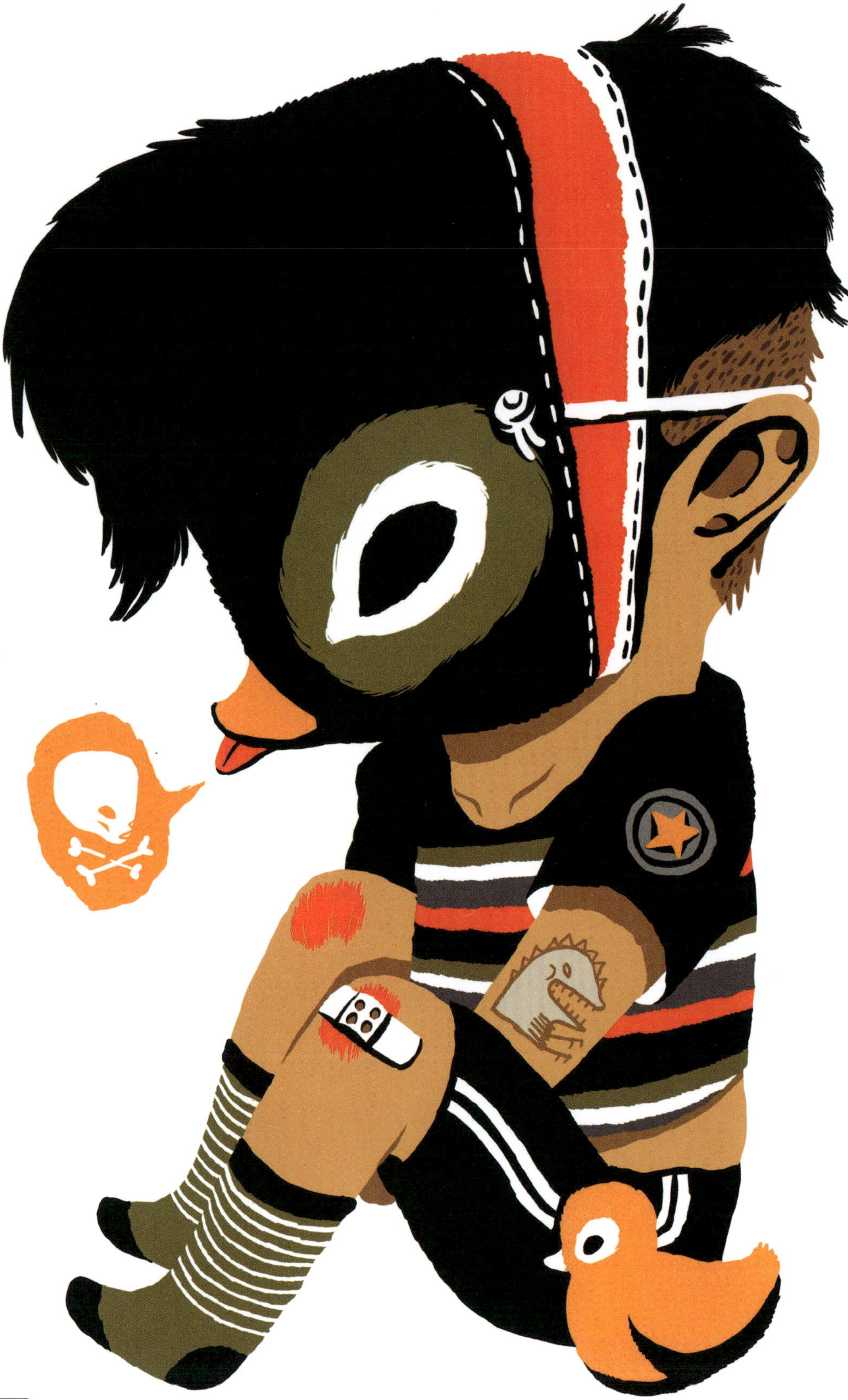

Ever Wish You'd Gone into Banking?

...Each day is numbered, no good when slumbered, with only one life to live...
ONE LIFE TO LIVE, KURT WEILL, 1941

Do you sometimes wish you'd studied banking? Oh, my! Of course, life as an artist isn't always easy. But the truth is: You only have this one life. And every moment goes by as it's experienced and goes for good to wherever the dinosaurs are waiting.
That's why we create art. It enables us to slow down the time slipping through our fingers for a moment. While creating, we recharge it with the moment of making. We create a bit of permanence; allow our view of the world to endure while around us time is slipping away. Every second that passes is either a win or a loss. Don't waste your lifetime. The work we do may be tough, tedious and poorly paid. But it is beautiful.

So please don't ever regret not having gone into banking.

At worst, you would wake up one day to realize that you've created nothing but money.
While we create something new, add something to the world instead of consuming something from the world. We make the world more beautiful and meaningful.

Illustration means enlighten. Let it shine!

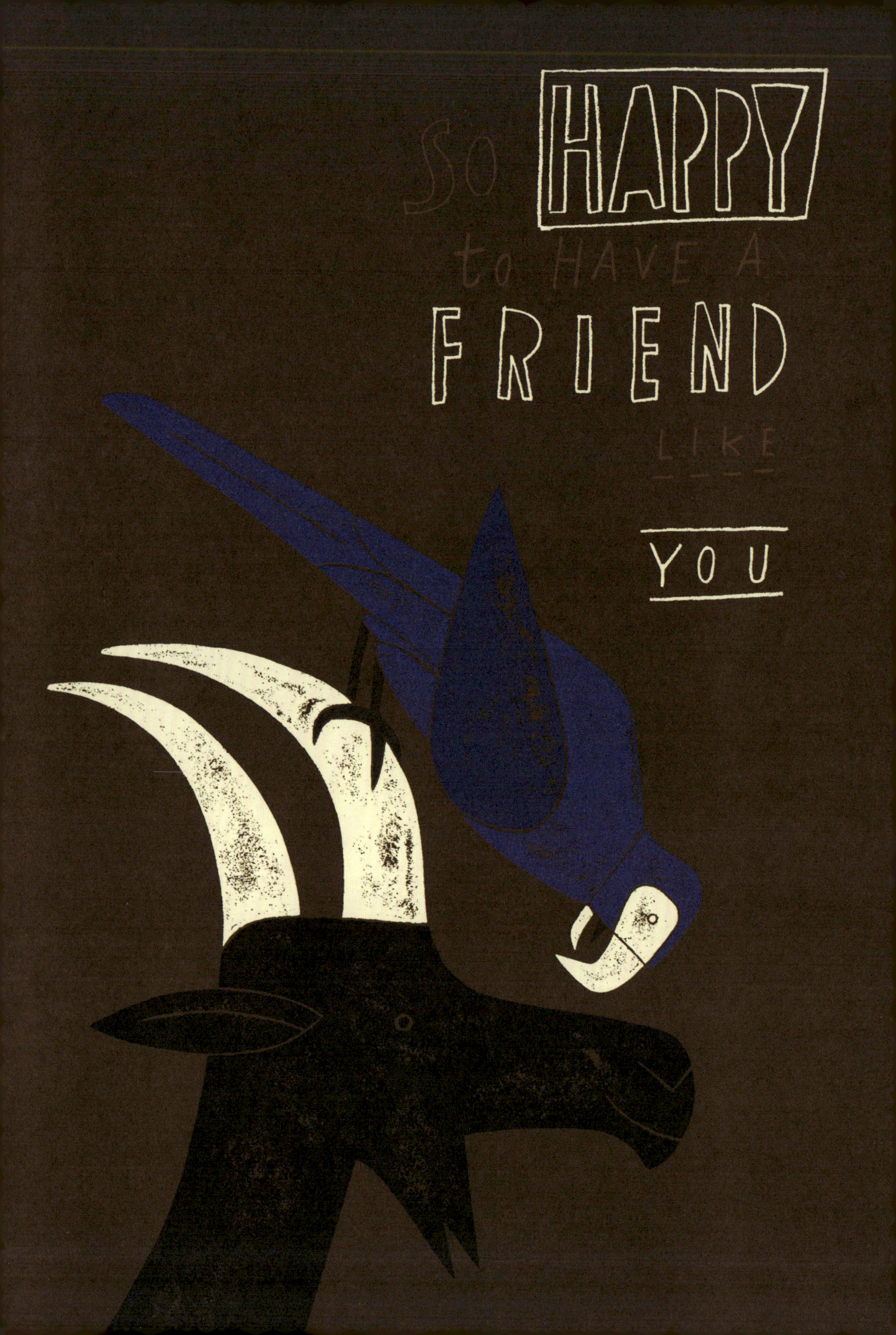
So HAPPY
to HAVE A
FRIEND
LIKE
YOU

Grand Merci!

The cover of a book shows the name of the author, but that line should also belong to all those without whom the book would not have been possible. I would therefore like to take this opportunity to thank all those who have supported me with a great deal of help in *words and deeds*, but also with their patience, with cups of tea and with many a dinner and without whom this book would have been nothing, never finished or even sillier.

First and foremost, I would like to thank all my colleagues who without hesitation provided me with their illustrations and sent all the birds that now populate the book. Without you it would have been a gray wasteland; your art gives it all meaning! Thank you! Furthermore, I would like to thank my students from the FH Münster, because they also contributed birds. Then there are my friends who kept putting me on the right track with their patience, but also with their open eyes. Here I should mention Aljoscha Blau, Andreas Bornemann, Johannes Frank, Marcus Herrenberger, Dieter Jüdt, Nora Marleen, Wiebke Lang, Rüdiger Quass von Deyen, Andreas Rauth, Meike Staats and Thomas Winckler.
My thanks to the Illustrators' Organization (IO), which supported me again and again, and to the board of the IO, especially Juliane Wenzl and Tim Weiffenbach, who provided me with tips and suggestions and who I hope forgive me for getting on their nerves with all my questions.
I would particularly like to take this opportunity to thank the Vice President of the Illustrators' Organization, Jens R. Nielsen. Jens repeatedly provided me with his expertise and academic advice for many months (especially when writing about "tricky" legal issues) and I can quite rightly say that he played an essential role in this book.
From my heart, I thank Christiane Steen, who read nearly every chapter one by one, removed the spelling mistakes and my gibberish and who hosted me in her Hamburg kitchen with Riesling, delicious food and wonderfully entertaining evenings.
I would also like to thank my publishers Karin and Bertram Schmidt-Friderichs, for their clever ideas and their friendship, but also for showing so much love and commitment to illustration. Then there's the team at Verlag Hermann Schmidt and the interns Katja Gendikova and Pia Neumann, who also made great contributions to the success of this project. Thanks also go to Karoline Deißner for her meticulous proofreading and to Sandra Mandl, Sabine Romanowsky and Jule Schlegel for making everything even better in the final stretch.
Finally, I would like to thank my family and friends for their patience and all the others that I didn't list here, but who were nevertheless important.

In reality, it's your book and my part in it is small. All I did was write it down.

A thousand thanks for your help, *grand merci!*

Participating Illustrators

Copyright Credits

PAGES 105 AND 198
Atak, Twain, Mark, *Der geheimnivolle Fremde*, Carlsen, Hamburg, 2012.

PAGE 116
Kono Bairei, Seiho, *Takeuchi, One Hundred Birds*, Thomas Müth collection.

PAGE 204
Gary Baseman, "To My Mon", *The New Yorker*, New York, 2002.

PAGES 27 AND 29
Louch Beach www.loubeach.com.

PAGE 37
Orit Bergman: promotional image.

PAGE 138
Orit Bergman, *Molly Mollo*, Edition du Rouergue, Arlés, 2013.

PAGES 208 AND 209
Claudia Boldt, picture book, NordSüd Verlag, Zurich, 2014.

PAGE 223
Els Cools & Oliver Streich, Schami, Rafik, *Der Schnabelstehe*, new edition, 2013 © 1995 NordSüd Verlag AG, Zurich.

PAGES 174 AND 175
Henrik Drescher www.hdrescher.com.

PAGE 19
Tom Eigenhufe www.eigenhufe.de.

PAGES 72 AND 73
Anke Feuchtenberger, *weh.weh.superträne. Die Hure H. wirft den Handschuh.*

PAGES 28, 36, 54, 55, 159, 173 AND 178
Max Fiedler www.mexer.pigsell.com.

PAGES 38 AND 39
Katja Gehrmann, *Piraten und andere Grünschnäbel*, Carlsen, Hamburg, 2004.

PAGES 151 AND 177
Katharina Grossman-Hensel, *Mukulele*, Sauerländer Verlag, Frankfurt.

PAGES 206 AND 207
Astrid Haas, *Brehms Tierleben: Die Vogel*, own edition, 2011.

PAGES 36 AND 203
Katharina J. Haines www.haines.de.

PAGES 35, 138 AND 139
Olaf Hajek www.olafhajek.com.

PAGE 16
Stefanie Harjes, *Vogeldame schönfärbend*, 2013.

PAGE 36
Herbert Holzing, *Krabat*, picture book, large format, Thienemann, Stuttgart, 2005, there is a standard edition too.

PAGES 32 AND 33
Dorothea Huber www.dorohuber.de.

PAGE 99
Omar Jaramillo: omar.paint@gmail.com.

PAGES 5, 108 AND 109
Hendrik Jonas www.hendrikjonas.de.

PAGES 7 AND 18
Alexandra Junge, *Vom Fischer, der ein Künstler war*, Mixtvision, Munich, 2011.

PAGE 18
Sebastian Koch www.sebkoch.de.

PAGE 165
Tobias Krejtschi, *Wipfelwärts + Wurzelwärts*, Peter Hammer Verlag, Wuppertal, 2012.

PAGES 52 AND 53
Silke Luise Langner www.BirdsAndinsects.wordpress.com.

PAGE 18
Max Ley illu@max-ley.de.

PAGE 148
Carolin Löbbert www.carolinloebbert.de.

PAGES 8 AND 9
Il mistero dell antiche creature © Lorenzo Mattotti.

PAGE 197
Arzach, Moebius © 1976 Humanoids, Inc., Los Angeles

PAGES 166 AND 167
Anne Möller, *Rotschwänzchen – was machst du hier im Schnee.* Atlantis, Zurich, 2003.

PAGES 149, 169 AND 171
Jörg Mühle, *An der Arche um Acht*, Sauerländer Verlag, Frankfurt.

PAGE 94
Jens R. Nielsen www.illustratorenorganisation.de.

PAGE 192
Robert Nippolt www.nippoldt.de.

PAGE 121
Andrea Offermann, sketches for *Thiucery* by J. A. White, Harper Collins Publisher, New York.

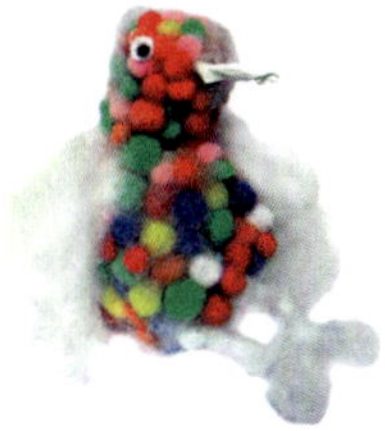

PAGES 110 AND 111

Sarah Palisi, *Die Angst vor dem weißen Blatt*.

PAGE 199

Geffen Refaeli www.geffenrefaeli.com.

PAGES 154 AND 155

André Rösler www.der-roesler.de.

PAGE 106

Christian Schlierkamp, Eagle from Rudolph Pauels falconry, life-size.

PAGE 142

Nina Spranger www.ninaspranger.de.

PAGES 44 AND 45

Dodo, de Ralph Steadman © 2012. Ralph Steadman.

PAGE 65

Einar Turkowski, *Als die Häuser heimwärts schwebten*, Mixtvision, Munich, 2012.

PAGE 78

Tomi Ungerer, Sans titre. Pour le 50ième anniversaire de L'America Institute of Graphic Arts, 1966, Lavis d'encre de Chine et d'encres de couleurs sur papier cartonné 70.7 x 54.7 cm © Diogenes Verlag AG, Zurich, *Tomi Ungerer. Eine Retrospektive*. Photography: Musée de la ville de Strasbourg, Martin Bernhart.

PAGE 76

Sabine Wilharm, *Trichtervogel*, own edition, 2009.

PAGE 97

Lisbeth Zwerger, *Die sieben Raben* by Brothers Grimm © 1981 Verlag Neugebauer Press, Salzburg/ Munich, new edition, 2008, NordSüd Verlag AG, Zurich.

About the Author

Felix Scheinberger was born on 14 October 1969 in Frankfurt am Main (Germany). Drums were more important to him than schooling. Instead of finishing high school, he played in punk bands until he was 22 years old. The entrance exam for the FH für Gestaltung, Hamburg (University of Applied Sciences, Hamburg, Germany) would be his ticket to an education. There he studied illustration, which then seamlessly resulted in self-employment. In the past ten years, he has illustrated more than fifty books, worked for prestigious newspapers and collected various prizes and awards. He has also taught in Mainz, Hamburg, Münster (Germany) and Jerusalem (Israel). His previous publications have influenced design agencies to rediscover hand-rendered drawing as well as pencil and watercolours. Felix Scheinberger now lives in Berlin and is a professor of illustration at the FH Münster (University of Applied Arts, Münster, Germany).

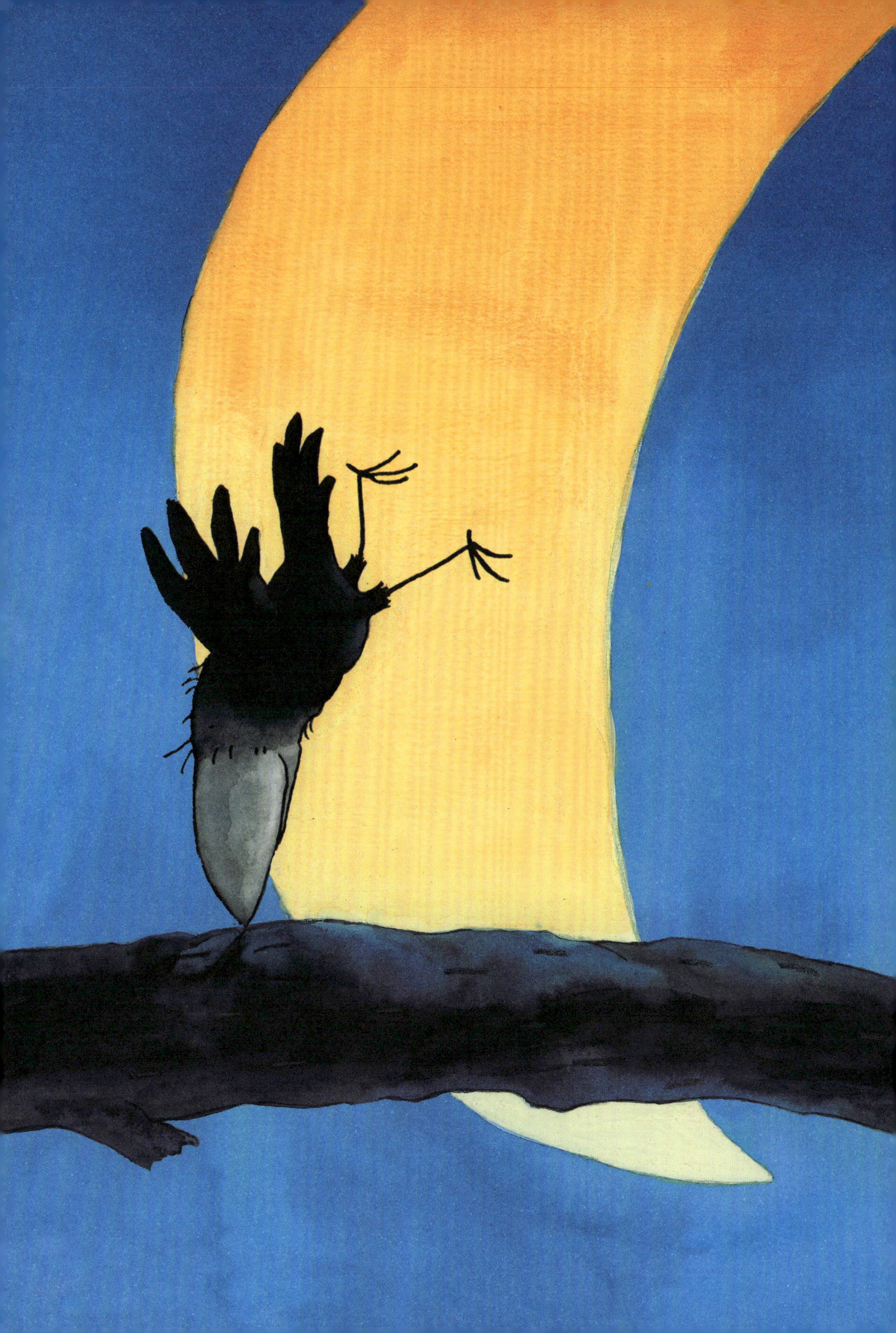

HOAKI

Hoaki Books, S. L.
C/ Ausiàs March, 128
08013 Barcelona, Spain
T. 0034 935 952 283
F. 0034 932 654 883
info@hoaki.com
www.hoaki.com

hoakibooks

Becoming an Illustrator
100 Ways to Draw a Bird and Turn Art into a Living

ISBN: 978-84-1065-089-3

Second edition

Author: Felix Scheinberger
Faith Gibson, Gibson Translations, Philadelphia

DL: B 1556-2026

Printed in China

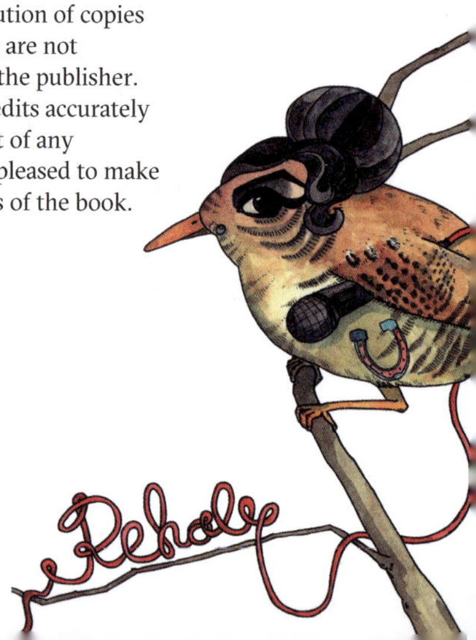

PIA NEUMANN